Urbanizing Suburbia

Hyper-Gentrification, the Financialization of Housing, and the Remaking of the Outer European City

Tahl Kaminer /
Leonard Ma /
Helen Runting (eds.)

jovis

CONDITIONS AND PROCESSES

06 Suburbia Transfigured *The Editors*
24 On the Edge: Suburbia, Disturbia, Futurbia *Jennifer S. Mack*
46 Fifth-Wave Gentrification and the Financialization of Housing *An Interview with Manuel B. Aalbers*

I. AMSTERDAM

eds. Tahl Kaminer and Timothy Moore

64 "Creative" Regeneration and the Dissipation of Amsterdam's Suburbs *Tahl Kaminer*
81 The View from the City: Amsterdam Noord, Self-Build, and Broedplaats *An Interview with Paco Bunnik*
89 The View from the City: Vision 2050 and the Nieuw-West *An Interview with Flora Nycolaas*
96 Rolling Out the Center: The Temporary Use of Tolhuistuin in Longer-Term Urban Development in Amsterdam Noord *Timothy Moore*

II. BERLIN

eds. Maroš Krivý and Leonard Ma

114 Culture in the Trenches: Housing and Resistance in Berlin *Maroš Krivý and Leonard Ma*
134 Hufeisensiedlung as Financialized World Heritage *Anne Kockelkorn*
141 Theorizing Gentrification from Berlin *An Interview with Matthias Bernt*
155 The Question Is No Longer Whether to Expropriate, but Why It Hasn't Happened Yet *An Interview with Katalin Gennburg*
164 Playing Our Match to Win Battles All Over the World *An Interview with Berta Del Ben and Jenny Stupka*

III. LONDON
ed. Tahl Kaminer

174 The Transformation of London's Outer City *Tahl Kaminer*
190 Housing and Social Change in Outer London *Paul Watt*
212 From Inclusive Legacy Promises to Exclusive Realities: Planning, Design, and Displacement in Post-Olympic East London *Juliet Davis and Penny Bernstock*
235 The Normalization of Thamesmead: Part A *Tahl Kaminer*

IV. STOCKHOLM
ed. Helen Runting

244 Welcome to New Stockholm: Soft Tactics and Hard Change in the Outer City *Secretary*
270 Postage-Stamp Planning *An Interview with Sara Vall*
280 Neon Lights *SIFAV*
288 South of the South in Venice of the North: Theorizing Change in Hökarängen *Secretary*

MAPPINGS

304 Integrating Amsterdam Noord
312 Cultural Assets in Schöneweide
320 The Normalization of Thamesmead: Part B
328 South of the South in Venice of the North: Mapping Change in Hökarängen

336 Other Narratives: Reading Sub/Urban Theory Differently *Postscript by Ross Exo Adams*

348 Contributing Authors
351 Acknowledgements

CONDITIONS AND PROCESSES

Suburbia Transfigured

The Editors

You may find yourself opening this book in a café, public library, park, coworking space, or studio apartment in an area that no one would dare to call "inner-city" but that doesn't conform to established images of "suburbia" either. Amidst fields of detached houses, scattered across landscapes like tiny sugar cubes packaged in picket fences, higher-density apartment buildings are being built or renovated, making their surroundings denser, more heterogeneous, and in many cases less affordable. While creative directors love attaching the "urban" moniker to virtually anything that crosses their desks—be it a new coffee chain, electric bike-share service, or neighborhood—the "suburban" occupies an increasingly ambiguous (if not openly contested) space in European imaginaries. The promises of home ownership or regulated rents, green and leafy surrounds, the separation of life and work, and indeed the separation of people from each other based on class or regimes of (often racialized) "belonging" are becoming increasingly unstable. And yet, as these foundations crumble, in key global cities at the nexus of global financial speculation the suburbs of the outer city continue to provide the physical armature for new urban dreams.

As the inner city faces acute housing affordability issues, the outer city offers housing options for struggling prospective homeowners, a growing working-class housing precariat, a speculatory middle class, and for global financial capital, which has found in the high-rise suburbs of modernism and the non-place of bungalowland a space for accumulation through en-bloc purchases of housing stock; renovation, renoviction, and resale; and densifying infill. The patchwork of "chubby" apartment buildings; clubs, art halls and makers' spaces; transport nodes; luxury housing developments; and foodbanks and crisis accommodation that punctuate this new suburban landscape—all developments addressed in this book—attest to the fact that suburbia *ain't what it used to be*. It's not only how suburbs look and feel that has changed, but the role that they play in the city at large, the economy, and our lives as city dwellers. Across Europe, the context that unites the case studies of this book, outer cities have, to put it simply, become increasingly *urbanized*.

Not that long ago, around 2007, much was being made of the world's population "becoming urban"—the proclamation that "for the first time in history 50% of people on Earth are living in cities" graced not only the covers of the UN's State of the World Population report (subtitled "Unleashing the Potential of Urban Growth") but also of Deutsche Bank-sponsored coffee-table books and the Turbine Hall of the Tate Modern.[1] A historic and symbolic threshold had apparently been crossed. "Planetary urbanization" has been one of the many terms used by urbanists in the last decade to capture the sheer magnitude of changes underway in very different contexts worldwide;[2] but given the concentration of growth in the peripheries of the world's central cities, "planetary suburbanization" may in fact be more accurate.[3] If such a "process" can indeed be identified at this scale—a questionable endeavor, at a moment characterized by a critique of the colonial violence of modernism's universalizing tendencies—*the urbanization of suburbia* must be explained and theorized in a situated, contextualized manner that acknowledges its spatial and temporal specificities. It must be addressed at the scale of the cities that it affects.

Taking on this challenge, *Urbanizing Suburbia* addresses four major European cities: Amsterdam, Berlin, London, and Stockholm, documenting the remaking of suburban belts through investment, densification, population growth, demographic changes, and the realization of morphologies and typologies more typical of the inner city. Proceeding by way of densification and in-fill, rather than the spatial expansion that typifies "sprawl," the modes of urbanization that are documented here challenge existing relations between core and periphery. As urbanist Roger Keil writes, "[t]oday, we are facing new realities of globalized urbanization, where central city and fringe are remixed."[4] Again: this is not a process which is smooth or uniform in its unfolding. Still in its infancy, the urbanization of suburbia at present can be identified in many cities that have, for diverse reasons, experienced extreme housing price hikes in their inner cities. In some cities, transnational investments have led to untenable housing costs in the inner city and to the processes we call "hyper-gentrification" (more on this later), pushing development to the suburbs; in others, dominant heritage discourses and municipal or regional decentralization strategies have ensured that inner cities are suspended in a state of polished *fin de siècle* stasis, free of contemporary influences and demographic diversity, pushing residents to seek out housing outside of this *cordon sanitaire*. In both cases, the middle class, working class, and urban poor are displaced to the suburban belts. The construction of new, higher-density housing in previously lower-density areas (either situations of sprawl or modernist housing estates) thus satisfies a vast array of interests: municipalities, existing homeowners, banks, displaced residents from the inner city, pension funds, financiers, and developers—some of whom stand to make considerable profits if they play their cards right. As the authors assembled in this book show, there are winners and losers and these developments also contain within them a darkness which points towards increasing segregation, displacement, and precarity, as well as the erosion of living environments and the status of the human right to housing.

The urbanization of suburbia has taken place in the context of a valorized ideal of inner-city living, championed over the past half-century not only within popular culture but also by the field of urban studies and professional doctrines within urban planning and design. The latter extend from culturally conservative imaginaries of an "urban renaissance," advocated by proponents of New Urbanism (including the current King of England), to the sustainable "regenerations" of the compact city and landscape urbanism movements. These densification doctrines argue that population growth can be achieved without spatial expansion; greenbelt protections, legal constraints, transportation investment, and planning policy ensure that suburban densification can be achieved through the gradual replacement of low-density outer-city neighborhoods (including residual brownfield and greenfield sites). Reshaping the structure of the city and its region, in densification without growth we witness the end of the concentric model of gradual diffusion from center to periphery. This is a radical shift. Throughout much of the nineteenth and twentieth centuries, urbanization did the job of linking population growth to spatial growth on the metropolitan periphery—cities grew by means of a process of urbanization by suburban expansion.[5] As a metropolitan area grows outwards, older, inner-ring suburbs densify and become more urban. In the majority of the cases addressed here, the urbanization of suburbia offers alternatives to (and many times occurs in the total absence of) spatial expansion. It is this particular condition of *densification*, by way of *in situ* development and *in situ* population growth, that sets the process discussed here apart from earlier forms of urbanization. There are many possible outcomes: a return to a pre-modern city/country divide, with its clear urban edges; the disruption of relations between center and periphery and between the city and its commuter towns; a much-longed-for reversal in sprawl dynamics in the face of anthropocentric climate change; or perhaps even the complete elimination of suburban characteristics in the outer city. For better or worse.

"The end of the suburb"—just like the "death of the city" before it—has been declared by many commentators already, whether in reaction to rising fuel prices or the demands of sustainable living.[6] But what we are witnessing today is far more complex than a simple termination. *Urbanizing Suburbia* is not a book about suburbanization. Quite the opposite. This edited volume addresses the *transfiguration of suburbia* through its dissipation, densification, hybridization, and urbanization in the outer city. This is a "de-suburbanization" that accelerates our passage through what might be termed a "post-suburban" condition.[7] This shift is in its infancy; centered around global cities and playing out through a patchwork of seemingly unrelated projects (the "postage-stamp planning" in Stockholm's suburbs or the temporary situations created by Amsterdam's creative-led regeneration strategies) or through plays so large that they barely register (the en-bloc purchases of housing stock seen in Berlin), this urbanization is easily dismissed as the work of an "invisible hand"—a byproduct or emergent condition, rather than a strategy and goal in its own right. Even in cases in which clear municipal policies are the main driving force, there is never an articulation of the long-term form of the trajectory and its impact—and nowhere is the end of suburbia flagged as a destination. As editors of this book, we aim to assemble a series of spatially and temporally situated North European case studies that together might encourage policymakers, researchers, built environment professionals, and residents to avoid passive acceptance of the current trajectory: instead, we suggest, they might adopt a critical stance vis-à-vis these processes, thereby taking control over and shaping them for the benefit of the city and its residents.

The Idealization of Suburbia

In popular culture and for a range of generations (from those born in the midst of the baby boom of the 1940s and 1950s through to the teenagers of 1990s and early 2000s raised on "mall" culture), the word "suburb" conjures the image of tidy lawns, neat detached homes, cars, middle-class nuclear families built around troubling norms of whiteness, compulsory heterosexuality, and gendered divisions of labor, as well as a conservative civility often described in vague terms of "neighborliness." Despite the allure and reach of this image of "the American dream," and as Jennifer Mack demonstrates in her chapter, the reality of suburbia is more complex, messy, and difficult to pin down.

The emergence of the modern suburb has roots which trifurcate along three lines: one that is usually identified with late-eighteenth-century urban extensions in cities such as London, to which affluent traders relocated to escape the productive and polluted inner city and to vaunt their social status through their opulent homes; a second, which came to prominence after World War II, whereby the American ideal of the single-family home was embraced as an alternative to the "socialistic" housing programs of Europe and supported by the low-cost mortgages made available by the 1944 G.I. Bill;[8] and a third trajectory, wherein modernist neighborhoods were built to house working-class and middle-classes families in prefabricated multi-unit towers and slabs set amidst landscapes of parks and community facilities. The European neighborhoods that are addressed as "suburbs" in *Urbanizing Suburbia* indeed include the leafy neighborhoods of the wealthy and their villas, middle-class areas of semi-detached and terraced housing, and working-class areas of high-rise postwar social housing estates, a schema that not only confirms a common lineage but also the modern project's tendency to segregate through typology and morphology.[9]

"[M]odern suburbanization has three major defining characteristics," suggested the urbanist Richard A. Walker: "spatial differentiation, decentralization, and identification with the waves of urban landscape laid down since the Second World War."[10] It was not just social classes and genders that were differentiated through this technology; it was also the city from its hinterland. "[T]he modern suburb," wrote the historian Robert Fishman of the structural impact of suburbs on cities,

> involved discarding the old preference for center over periphery; radically disassociating home and work environments; creating neighborhoods both on the idea of a single class and that of a single (domestic) function; and, finally, creating a new kind of landscape in which the clear line ... between city and country becomes thoroughly blurred in an environment that combines the two.[11]

Located in the outer city, the areas addressed within these pages—from Berlin's Schöneweide to Hökarängen in Stockholm to London's Thamesmead and Amsterdam Noord—are all found at a relative distance from the city center and in relative proximity to the urban boundary; their densification indeed suggests a sharpening rather than a blurring of this edge.

The densification traced in these areas tends to demand as a basic precondition an initially lower density than might be found in the inner city—this was either delivered by virtue of the generous landscaped settings that surround slabs and towers, or the back and front yards that bracket their single-household homes. Finally, these "suburbs" also tend to be dominated by a particular tenure type (majority home ownership in "leafy" suburbia and a high proportion of public rentals in the modernist estates). These characteristics are all relative: failing to account for *all* forms of suburbia, they nonetheless provide useful contours for the research presented in this book.[12] As the urbanists Roger Keil and Jean-Paul Addie remind us, suburbs "are locally contingent, contradictory and contested socio-spatial landscapes,"[13] despite their supposedly common relation to a universal, modern imaginary.

Suburbs are neither ahistorical nor static. The process of *suburbanization* cannot be in any case thought outside of its relation to the dynamics of capital and the real estate market's ever-changing attempts to extract the highest rents possible from land. As David Harvey has argued, "investment increasingly takes the form of a negotiation between international finance capital and local powers doing the best they can to maximize the attractiveness of the local site as a lure for capitalist development."[14] Suburbs establish spatial relations that reproduce the economic and social structures and logics of society at a given time, determining where key economic sectors are located and their products produced; where the workers employed in these sectors reside; and so on.[15] Such relations are deeply historical, situated, political, and subject to radical transformations.

Hyper-Gentrification and the Periphery

The urbanization of suburbia, however, should not be perceived as a reversal of the inner city revivals of the last decades. In his influential critique of the "back to the city" movement in 1979, Neil Smith argued that gentrification was a structural product of capitalist land and housing markets, rather than based on changing consumer tastes, noting simply that "capital flows where the rate of return is highest."[16] Smith argued that the fixity of land investment and the depreciation of inner city capital produced a "rent gap" that drove the movement of capital from the suburbs into the inner city. The process we describe in this book, the urbanization of suburbia, acts as an addendum to the "back to the city" process, and our arguments extend rather than question Smith's theory. Since the financial crisis, property prices and rents have skyrocketed, particularly in inner cities, and suburban sites have in turn become increasingly viable for capital investment. Instead of sprawl, this generates yet more of the dense urbanity that characterizes the inner city, as the outer city transforms into neighborhoods that resemble the gentrified inner city ideal. Learning from Smith, therefore, the urbanization of suburbia is not a process driven by consumer tastes; rather, it provides evidence of the shifting dynamics of investment and development strategies particularly with the financialization of the economy.

In her pioneering study of gentrification in Brooklyn Heights during the mid-1990s, Loretta Lees identified a process of "super-gentrification," driven by a new cohort of super-rich "Wall Street types" employed within international finance.[17] This process saw already gentrified neighborhoods subject to further gentrification by highly paid executives and managers who displaced the previous generation of gentrifiers, opening the gates for contemporary "financializations" of the built environment. With the growing sophistication of financial instruments, global financial capital has increasingly been able to move across political borders and regimes, fueling a further process, which Loretta Lees, Hyun Bang Shin, and Ernesto López-Morales describe as "hyper-gentrification."[18] For financial players such as private equity funds, real estate investment trusts, and publicly-listed housing companies, real estate has emerged as an asset class to be prized not just in terms of its income (rent) but also its relative security (treated as "safety deposit boxes"). Tapped into a global flow of finance, hyper-gentrification is a process that sees distorted local dynamics between property values, rents, and salaries.

The urban geographer Manuel B. Aalbers—interviewed in this book—uses the term "fifth-wave gentrification" to describe the "urban materialization of financialized or finance-led capitalism."[19] Building upon an earlier periodization of gentrification by Jason Hackworth and Neil Smith, and the "fourth wave" introduced in 2008 by Loretta Lees, Tom Slater, and Elvin Wyly,[20] in the fifth wave, the state continues to play a leading role in gentrification but is now supplemented by finance.[21] Throughout our book, "hyper-gentrification" will be used to refer to the forms of gentrification that fall within Aalbers' "fifth wave." The purpose of the deployment of the term "hyper-gentrification" here is twofold: first, to underline the argument that fifth-wave gentrification engenders a process that is qualitatively and radically different from earlier forms of gentrification, and, second, to refer to and yet go beyond the more familiar term "super-gentrification."

There is a growing body of research on the role of finance in housing.[22] The ease with which capital now moves across borders in its search for assets (real estate) to acquire can be linked to the emergence of a "planetary rent gap," as cities increasingly compete for investments, allowing prices to be compared despite radically different contexts.[23] After the financial crises of 2008, the growing demands placed on pension funds is fueling further investments into real estate, which is treated as a form of capital switching to direct capital from other markets into the built environment. The growing role of institutional investors and private equity in the search for alternative asset classes suggests the presence of a "financialized rent gap," which would account for phenomena such as the investments made into housing in Berlin since the 1990s despite low wages and high unemployment.[24] Finance-led capitalism and the hyper-gentrification it causes are having a very real effect on cities, detaching housing prices from local salaries, destabilizing previously secure tenures, and instigating evictions and displacement. Research on these processes has largely focused on the inner city, where prices are the most extreme, but hyper-gentrification's pressures on the inner city indirectly effect also the urban periphery. Beyond the negative externalities of high prices and displacement, there is an underlying tension within finance-led capitalism, as residents are priced out not just by speculative investors but also by their own pension funds, and by a governing apparatus that must compete for global financial capital.

The Financialization of Suburbia

Aalbers identifies four key fields of housing financialization: mortgage debt, mortgage securitization, rental housing, and housing companies.[25] Mortgages played a key role in earlier waves of gentrification, first by facilitating home ownership through bank loans, allowing a home purchase to be paid off with recurring payments much like rent. With rising prices and fluctuating inflation and interest rates, mortgage securitization was introduced to further expand the pool of capital available to service mortgages, by grouping mortgages into packages that could then be sold on the stock market. Mortgage-backed securities were particularly attractive investments for pension funds, he notes, as they offered an underlying asset that could be foreclosed in the event of a default, making them safe as long-term investments. Further innovations such as collateralized debt obligations and credit default swaps allowed speculation in mortgage-backed securities as a form of insurance, spurring the real estate bubble that burst in the 2008 subprime mortgage crisis.

After a brief interlude,[26] real estate values quickly recovered from their losses after 2008, despite a limping economy. Taking advantage of the low prices, institutional investors mobilized their deep capital reserves and the seemingly endless supply of credit and low interest rates to capitalize on foreclosed and depreciated real estate assets. This process, entailing the movement of finance from secondary investment in mortgage-backed securities to the securitization of rental housing, is the main driver of fifth-wave gentrification.[27] Categorized as an "alternative asset class," rental housing became an extremely attractive investment in the low interest rate and risk-averse economic environment after the financial crisis. This "new wave" of financialization, Raquel Rolnik notes, includes the consolidation of rental housing under large corporate entities, which affords the latter significant control of rental markets as well as influence over political decision-making.[28]

The context through which housing has become financialized should be viewed within a worldwide restructuring of the economy along the lines of finance, which Greta Krippner describes as a "pattern of accumulation in which profits accrue primarily through financial channels rather than through trade and commodity production."[29] The shift from housing as a commodity to housing as a financial asset is perfectly reflected in the contrast between the sprawling suburban landscapes of the postwar outer city and the process of outer-city urbanization.

As Sara Stevens notes, the early innovation of suburban developers was the "construction of certainty ... to create the assurance that a financial investment such as a house or a piece of land would be stable."[30] The suburban single-family home, therefore, was founded on the principle of commodification and price stability, not assets and appreciation. There are inevitable limitations to the securitization of single-family homes—property management and maintenance become more complex, transaction costs are compounded, and larger properties demand higher rents that could otherwise be turned into mortgages. Large institutional investors such as Blackstone, who entered the rental market for single-family homes after the financial crisis, have already halted further investments in the market.[31] Multi-family dwellings on the other hand, allow for an ease of management and transaction that produce a much more fungible product for financial portfolios. In Europe, municipal housing has proven to be a particularly attractive target for private equity investments, allowing them to engage in en-bloc purchasing and to apply cohesive strategies for rent extraction such as those documented in the Berlin section of this book. The urbanization of the outer city cannot be addressed without understanding these dynamics, whereby changing ownership structures might not "transfer" housing to another tenure category but rather radically affect what a given tenure category does or means (it is a very different proposition to rent from a municipal housing company or cooperative in Berlin, Stockholm, London, and Amsterdam than to rent from a private actor). Financialization "reprograms" and "internally re-organizes" governmentalities, echoing and amplifying the transformative tendencies of neoliberalism.[32]

Asset-Based Suburbia

Access to housing, once a foundational principle of the European social democratic project, has dramatically transformed over the last decades. Housing equity is now promoted by neoliberal governments as a safety net for households, whereas citizens in many cities engage in entrenched battles in order to retain control over aging social and universal rental housing systems. As Marja Elsinga and Janneke Toussaint note, homeownership forms the bedrock of an "asset-based welfare," an alternative to "means-tested welfare"—and, we might add, casting an eye to the late welfare states of Scandinavia, "universal welfare." Encouraging citizens to take mortgages and accumulate assets becomes a means for European governments to "reduce their expenditure on welfare. Encouraging homeownership seems a straightforward solution."[33]

Lisa Adkins, Melinda Cooper, and Martijn Konings suggest that the dynamics of class are fundamentally altered by homeownership and asset-owning societies.[34] Traditional definitions of class that tend to focus on employment-based categories such as occupation or wages are now instead stratified along typically generational lines of asset ownership. The spread of property investment through homeownership policies since the early 1970s has allowed a section of the population to gain significant wealth and encourages a vested interest in the continued inflation of housing prices.

"[F]ar from only concerning the very rich or a rentier class," wrote Adkins, Cooper, and Konings, "this structural reconfiguration is thoroughgoing, such that it is the relationship to assets rather than employment that operates as the key decider and distributor of life chances."[35]

The class dynamics of hyper-gentrification and financialization in the asset economy are key to understanding the changes currently being witnessed in the outer city, as residents displaced from the inner city, pushed out by evictions, rising rents, and spiking property prices, are accompanied by middle-class residents in pursuit of opportunities to purchase real estate assets, whether as a home for themselves or a Buy-to-Let investment. Even in countries with strong tenant rights and social housing, the ability to participate in real estate appreciation has a significant impact on household planning.[36] The movement of capital to the periphery in global cities, tapped into the circuits of international finance, has not brought with it a corresponding depreciation in the inner city as a site for "capital switching." Rather, the financialization of housing combined with homeownership stimulates demand, producing a "win-win" scenario for capital as it expands its sights to the 'burbs.

Reshaping Suburbia

The relocation of residents from the inner to the outer city and the growing investments in the suburban belt by developers, Buy-to-Let landlords, and, in some cases, corporate investors, is taking place in a context in which inner-city living is valorized and the social norms of postwar suburban life, while not fully rejected, are being challenged and fundamentally modified. This can explain why the process entails not only redevelopment and higher densities, which would suffice to maximize returns, but also aims at creating other inner-city conditions in the outer city, including urban morphologies and typologies, and a higher live/work ratio. In this sense, displaced inner-city residents and developers experienced in inner-city redevelopment share, to a degree, an ideal of inner-city living with policymakers who have internalized compact city ideas.

Consequently, recent suburban redevelopments have contributed to the burgeoning of the symbols of inner-city lifestyle in the outer city such as cycling lanes, hipster cafes, "urban beaches," makers' spaces, and boutique hotels.

However, much like Smith's critique of the "back to the city" movement, the urbanization of suburbia is not just an instance of consumer-based demand, but one driven by the interests of capital. More precisely, it is the result of an intersection of capital's desire to maximize profits (for instance, developers, municipal housing companies, and home-purchasers leveraging local rent gaps), policy aims (sustainable development; alleviating housing crises; supporting the property market; increasing home ownership; protection of historical inner-city neighborhoods); and current conditions (an asset-based economy; high inner-city housing prices; a local rent gap in the suburban belt; dependence on market-led development; weak protection of tenures).

With the acute challenges of anthropogenic climate change voiding sprawl and with no way back into the inner city, it is easy to imagine the urbanization of suburbia as the inevitable destination of the contemporary city. The themes we have outlined in this introduction—de-suburbanization, hyper-gentrification, and the financialization of the economy—help to denaturalize the urbanization of suburbia, as we go on to explore it in Amsterdam, Berlin, London, and Stockholm. While the developments traced in those places may resemble familiar patterns of "urbanization," "gentrification," and "densification," the familiar returns to us transfigured. Not quite city and not quite suburb, the urbanized suburbia of the outer city is uncanny; it promises an "internal reorganization" of urban life, the edges of which are yet to be fully determined.

Structure

Urbanizing Suburbia opens with three introductory chapters. This general introduction is followed by Jennifer Mack's discussion of European suburbs, in which she addresses the "chaotic" idea of the suburb and the contradictory reality of multiple suburban types—a variegated suburbia—by comparison to the American suburb. An extensive interview with Manuel B. Aalbers follows, which is focused on unpacking the process of housing financialization and his conception of fifth-wave gentrification, which we here address as "hyper-gentrification." It raises questions regarding key definitions of gentrification and the evolution of the process.

These chapters are followed by four sections, each dedicated to a different city: Amsterdam, Berlin, London, and Stockholm. Each section accentuates a different aspect of the processes in question, comprising of an introductory chapter discussing housing, redevelopment, regeneration, and gentrification in the relevant cities, as well as chapters presenting narrower discussions of particular issues. A fifth section includes studies of particular neighborhoods in each of the cities through extensive use of mappings and photographs. Each case demonstrates how local contexts and path dependencies determine a different urbanization of suburbia. London provides the opportunity to study the process of urbanizing the outer city in a context characterized by a strong free market and a weak planning system. Berlin enables the study of forms of resistance to global capital, both by the municipality and by anti-gentrification and housing activists. Amsterdam provides a means of critically examining "creative-led" regeneration, now applied not to the inner city but to the suburbs, whereas Stockholm allows a study of upping housing densities by means of symbolic interventions, in city-wide programs of densification driven not only by the municipality and its semi-autonomous municipal housing companies, but also by residents caught in a vicious, neoliberal bind of total precarity and exploitative entrepreneurialism. To end this volume, Ross Exo Adams provides critical reflections in a postscript chapter.

Urbanizing Suburbia is a jigsaw puzzle formulated by an amalgam of different pieces, reflecting the patchwork development and "postage-stamp planning" that characterizes its subject matter. Together, these pieces form a first extensive critical interrogation of a process which is radically remaking the suburbs of European cities, studying the actual changes underway and the forces and processes driving these changes. As stated above, the ambition of the book is to place the withering and transformation of the suburban belt "on the table" as a means of generating discussion and critique of a major process underway in certain cities, a process that has taken place until now under the radar yet requires meaningful debate and consideration.

1 We refer here to the United Nations Population Fund (UNPF) "State of World Population 2007: Unleashing the Potential of Urban Growth" (Jan 1, 2007); Ricky Burdett and Deyan Sudjic's *The Endless City* (London: Phaidon, 2007); and the accompanying exhibition "Global Cities" (2007), which partially built upon "Cities, Architecture, and Society" from the preceding year's International Architecture Biennale in Venice, and was shown in the Turbine Hall at the Tate Modern in London, June 6–August 27, 2007.

2 Neil Brenner, ed., *Implosions/explosions: Towards a Study of Planetary Urbanization* (Berlin: JOVIS, 2014).

3 Roger Keil, *Suburban Planet: Making the World Urban from the Outside In* (Cambridge; Medford, MA: Polity, 2018).

4 Keil, *Suburban Planet*, 42.

5 As a metropolitan area grows outwards through such suburban expansion, older, now inner-ring suburbs densify and become more urban. Jean Gottmann, *Megalopolis: the Urbanized Northeastern Seaboard of the United States* (Cambridge, Mass.: MIT Press, 1964).

6 Rachel Heiman, "The Last Days of Low-Density Living: Suburbs and the End of Oil," *Built Environment* 33, no. 2, (2007): 213–26.

7 Nicholas A. Phelps, Nick Parsons, Dimitris Ballas, and Andrew Dowling use the term "post-suburbia" in order to capture the diversity and hybridity of today's outer cities across the globe, including areas as disparate as "edge cities," sprawl, industrial estates, business parks, postwar housing estates, town centers, shopping malls, and infrastructure. But the relevance of this term is limited in the context of the book's focus: "post-suburban" describes a condition, while *Urbanizing Suburbia* studies a process, and, more specifically, a process that renders the post-suburban condition a transitory condition as the outer city areas increasingly shed any veneer of suburbanism. Nicholas A. Phelps, Nick Parsons, Dimitris Ballas, and Andrew Dowling, *Post-Suburban Europe: Planning and Politics at the Margins of Europe's Capital Cities* (Basingstoke; New York: Palgrave Macmillan, 2006); Keil, *Suburban Planet*; Nicholas A. Phelps and Fulong Wu, eds., *International Perspectives on Suburbanization: A Post-Suburban World?* (New York: Palgrave Macmillan, 2011).

8 This model of homeownership and mortgage issuance would come to serve as the bedrock to the rhetoric of free-market rights, which proliferated around the world in the form of US housing aid. Nancy H. Kwak, *A World of Home Owners: American Power and the Politics of Housing Aid* (Chicago: University of Chicago Press, 2015).

9 As urban theorists Karin Grundström and Irene Molina note, "segregation" (the spatial separation of various social categories, affecting where people live) is intimately connected to "segmentation" (what types of dwellings people inhabit, including tenancy form). Karin Grundström and Irene Molina, "From Folkhem to Lifestyle Housing in Sweden: Segregation and Urban Form, 1930s–2010s," *International Journal of Housing Policy* 16, no. 3 (2016): 316–36, DOI: 10.1080/14616718.2015.1122695.

10 Richard A. Walker, "A Theory of Suburbanization: Capitalism and the Construction of Urban Space in the United States," in *Urbanization and Urban Planning in Capitalist Society,* eds. Michael Dear and Allen J. Scott (London; New York: Methuen, 1981), 383.

11 Robert Fishman, "Bourgeois Utopias: The Rise and Fall of Suburbia," in *The Suburb Reader*, eds., Becky M. Nicholaides and Andrew Wiese (New York; London: Routledge, 2006), 34.

12 Suburban studies have expanded the definition of suburbs beyond these considerations as a means of accounting for non-Western suburbs. Urban extensions in Eastern Bloc cities in the 1960s and 1970s, for example, would be completely excluded from any definition of suburbs that relies on tenures such as owner-occupier or on capital investments. Nevertheless, for the specific context of European suburbs today, these somewhat conventional and in some senses problematic criteria suffice. See an overview of the discussions in Keil, *Suburban Planet.*

13 Roger Keil and Jean-Paul D. Addie, "'It's Not Going to be Suburban, It's Going to be All Urban': Assembling Post-Suburbia in the Toronto and Chicago Regions," *International Journal of Urban and Regional Research* 39, no. 5 (2015): 893.

14 David Harvey, "From Managerialism to Entrepreneurialism: The Transformation in Urban Governance in Late Capitalism," *Geografiska Annaler: Series B, Human Geography* 71, no. 1 (April 1989): 5, DOI: 10.1080/04353684.1989.11879583.

15 Walker, "A Theory of Suburbanization"; Richard Walker and Robert D. Lewis, "Beyond the Crabgrass Frontier: Industry and the Spread of North American Cities, 1850–1950," *Journal of Historical Geography* 27, no. 1 (2001): 3–19.

16 Neil Smith, "Toward a Theory of Gentrification A Back to the City Movement by Capital, Not People," *Journal of the American Planning Association* 45, no. 4 (October 1, 1979): 546, DOI: 10.1080/01944367908977002.

17 Loreta Lees, "Super-Gentrification: The Case of Brooklyn Heights, New York City," *Urban Studies* 40, no. 12 (2003): 2487–509.

18 Loretta Lees, Hyun Bang Shin, and Ernesto López-Morales, *Planetary Gentrification* (Cambridge: Polity, 2016).

19 Manuel B. Aalbers, "Introduction To The Forum: From Third To Fifth-Wave Gentrification," *Tijdschrift Voor Economische En Sociale Geografie* 110, no. 1 (2019): 2, DOI: 10.1111/tesg.12332.

20 Loretta Lees, Tom Slater, and Elvin Wyly, *Gentrification* (New York; London: Routledge, 2008).

21 Aalbers, "Introduction To The Forum": 6.

22 See, for example: Michelle Buckley and Adam Hanieh, "Diversification by Urbanization: Tracing the Property-Finance Nexus in Dubai and the Gulf," *International Journal of Urban and Regional Research* 38, no. 1 (2014): 155–75; Beng Huat Chua, "Financializing Public Housing as an Asset for Retirement in Singapore," *International Journal of Housing Policy* 15, no. 1 (2015), 27–42; Dorothee Bohle, "Post-Socialist Housing Meets Transnational Finance: Foreign Banks, Mortgage Lending, and the Privatization of Welfare in Hungary and Estonia," *Review of International Political Economy* 21, no. 4 (2014): 913–948.

23 Tom Slater, "Planetary Rent Gaps," *Antipode* 49, no. 1 (2017): 114–37, DOI: 10.1111/anti.12185.

24 Laura Calbet i Elias, "Financialised Rent Gaps and the Public Interest in Berlin's Housing Crisis: Reflections on N. Smith's 'Generalised Gentrification'", in *Gentrification as a Global Strategy: Neil Smith and Beyond,* eds. Abel Albet and Núria Benach (London: Routledge, 2017).

25 Manuel B. Aalbers, "Financial Geography II."

26 Housing prices in inner cities of global cities were only modestly affected by the crisis—if anything, the more burgeoning inner cities proved their market prowess. In the New York region, for example, most foreclosures took place outside Manhattan, in New Jersey, east Queens and so on. While in Northern English cities housing prices collapsed, in London they merely dipped.

27 Manuel B Aalbers, "Introduction To The Forum."

28 Raquel Rolnik, *Urban Warfare: Housing Under the Empire of Finance* (London; NYC: Verso, 2019).

29 Greta Krippner, "The Financialization of the American Economy," *Socio-Economic Review* 3, no. 2 (May 1, 2005): 174, DOI: 10.1093/SER/mwi008.
30 Sara Stevens, *Developing Expertise: Architecture and Real Estate in Metropolitan America* (New Haven, Conn.: Yale University Press, 2016), 64.
31 Candyd Mendoza, "Home Partners to Halt Single-Family Home Buying in 38 Markets," *MPA*, 29 August 2022, accessed December 6, 2022, at: https://www.mpamag.com/us/news/general/home-partners-to-halt-single-family-home-buying-in-38-markets/418483.
32 Michel Foucault, *The Birth of Biopolitics: Lectures at the Collège de France 1978-1979* (New York: Picador, 2004), 116.
33 Janneke Toussaint and Marja Elsinga, "Exploring 'Housing Asset-Based Welfare': Can the UK Be Held Up as an Example for Europe?" *Housing Studies* 24, no. 5 (2009): 669–92, DOI: 10.1080/02673030903083326.
34 Lisa Adkins, Melinda Cooper, and Martijn Konings, *The Asset Economy* (Cambridge, UK; Medford, MA: Polity, 2020).
35 Lisa Adkins, Melinda Cooper, and Martijn Konings, "Class in the 21st Century: Asset Inflation and the New Logic of Inequality," *Environment and Planning A* 53, no. 3 (2021): 567.
36 John Doling and Marja Elsinga, "Homeownership as a Pension," *Demographic Change and Housing Wealth*, 2013: 101–17, DOI: 10.1007/978-94-007-4384-7_5.

On the Edge: Suburbia, Disturbia, Futurbia

Jennifer S. Mack

In comments on the radio in 2002, then-President George W. Bush proclaimed that "owning a home lies at the heart of the American Dream."[1] New American legal measures to increase private ownership would be taken to support the purchase of single-family homes, including the "American Dream Tax Relief Act" and the "American Dream Downpayment Act," both of 2003. These measures echoed the sentiments of the post-World War II period, when returning GIs were offered favorable loans for single-family homes, spawning a suburban revolution. Bush's ostensible objectives centered, however, on reducing "barriers to minority homeownership" and thus distributing suburban homeownership more equally.[2]

As the suburban historian John Archer points out, "[t]he American dream, in the form of the dream house, is central not only to how we design our physical world and orchestrate our lives but also to public and fiscal policy."[3] But was this dream mere fiction? For many people, two-story homes with white picket fences and middle-class, white nuclear families *are* the suburbs, and, since the 1950s, a typology deeply linked to the American landscape and its capitalist society favoring and bolstering private ownership. From that time, writes historian Dolores Hayden, the suburban house has signified "a private life without urban problems such as unemployment, poverty, hunger, racial prejudice, pollution, and violent crime."[4] Notably, then, this dream's potency has relied not on individualism and unique architecture but on protection from social ills: a familial haven. Its power is symbolic, narrative, and often not quite real.

In Europe, another suburban landscape emerged in parallel in this same period. While these largely suburbs comprised high- and mid-rise blocks of multi-family housing, the stories meant to take place there—whether in *Siedlungen* in Germany, *banlieues* in France, or *förorter* in Sweden—were not very different from their North American counterparts.[5] These suburbs would create better housing for modern families and, in the process, a better society.

But were the conditions of these two postwar suburban dreams so different? In North America, a mass-produced house of the 1950s generated individual stories within limited architectural designs—perhaps Tudor, Cotswold, or Ranch? There, "unique design features" could be an unusual color for aluminum siding or a unique species of tree chosen on the lawn outside. In postwar Europe, suburbs made from standardized designs using new building and construction technologies and materials such as concrete panels would bring modern living to welfare-state citizens.[6] Building standards met new ideas of streamlined housework and, in places like Sweden, new initiatives produced collaborations between public and private sectors in neighborhood and housing design, creating a new class of "rational" citizens who would buy new consumer goods.[7] In both the US and Europe, in other words, visions of suburbia aimed to distribute new urban forms and norms to the populace in the broadest possible sense, and the place chosen for this was in the leafy green areas outside of city centers.

This suburbia—whether in mass or single-family housing—lay far from the noise and dirt of the inner city, and for this reason it was a place where, for instance, "appropriate" childrearing activities could take place. Boosters of the mid-twentieth century (both American and European) promoted conformism to both form (as architecture and suburban design) and norms (of social mores and the ideal of the nuclear family) as comforting antidotes to the problems of the central city. Suburbs would offer modern conveniences, including supermarket shopping and the latest appliances and homemaking tools. Suburbs would be spaces for homemaking: peripheral to the centers of economic and political power (where only the men travel) and generators of a social conformity that was also regarded as supporting feelings of belonging in the modern nation-state. The designs of suburbs on both continents were predicated on ideas about their standardized designs, which offered forms of comfort and control to their occupants, not unlike those praised by Reyner Bahnam in his assessment of Frank Lloyd Wright's oeuvre as inspiration for international hotel designs: where the ideal is "visually undemanding, acoustically quiet, [and] thermally comfortable."[8]

Despite these common starting points, popular representations and analyses of American and European suburbs diverge drastically today. In film and television, depictions of North American suburbia often suggest that the postwar period of the 1950s and 1960s never ended: a wage-earning man is still coming home from the city in a car, and driving into a garage and then walking onward to a housewife who has been homemaking and taking care of children all day, and dinner is still waiting on the table. Twenty-first century US suburbia still has its resident Don and Betty Drapers, apparently. Furthermore, all the neighbors are white, heterosexual, and middle-class. Front and back yards are fenced off from the neighbors' identical ones, the family room has a prominently positioned TV, and the kitchen offers the latest appliances. When "suburbs" are discussed around the world, then, it is often this North American suburbia—and the "exurban" landscapes of office parks, or "edge cities"[9]—that come to mind. Recent scholarship, however, has emphasized how erroneous these predominant views of suburbia as socially, economically, and formally monolithic are; the work of scholars like Jennifer Fang, Sarah Lopez, Tim Retzloff, and Andrew Weise have narrated the heretofore mostly invisible histories of suburbs established by minority groups, gay suburbanites, heritage practices among suburban immigrants, and suburbs afforded through transnational remittances, among others.[10]

Meanwhile, in Europe, the word "suburb"—the French *banlieue*, Swedish *förort*, or even the satellite town—has another connotation altogether. European suburbs typically comprise of modernist high- and mid-rise buildings for multi-family living built by welfare states during the mid-twentieth century. Rather than the American Dream, however, these neighborhoods are often presented, especially in the media, as nightmarish dystopias of crime, unemployment, segregation, and violence. When maintenance goes missing and social conditions produce narratives of economic and cultural exclusion about residents, these suburbs become stigmatized and treated as failed experiments.[11] This perspective persists, despite increasing attention to residents' actual experiences of the places, or what I have elsewhere called "impossible nostalgia."[12]

From the prototypical Levittowns to the "ABC City" Vällingby in Sweden to the "monster houses" of Vancouver or Fremont to the "social project" of the French *banlieues*,[13] suburbs on both sides of the Atlantic occupy a new "Middle Landscape."[14] How should one approach these suburbs, both as remnants of mid-twentieth-century thinking and as evolved, living spaces of the twenty-first century? In this essay, I investigate "the suburbs" as parallel phenomena in North America and Europe across three thematic axes: sprawl, Blackness, and gender. I investigate how they were envisioned, how they have evolved, and how we might begin to approach them today. Leo Marx's definition of the suburb is as "a new distinctively American, post-romantic, industrial version of the pastoral design"; today, however, the pastoral is increasingly hard to come by, and—as noted—suburbs are far from a "distinctively American" phenomenon.[15] Are they still a place between the country and the city? Do they still reinforce conformism? Who are their residents? And what is the future of suburbia? Here, I offer some reflections and provocations on a short trip to suburbia, disturbia, and futurbia.

Suburbia Takes Over

Both North American and European suburbs represent utopian reactions to the industrialized cities of the nineteenth century and their poverty, overcrowding, and pollution. Boosters therefore understood location in protected, greener spaces as a key tenet of their construction, yet such spaces would not be rural either. Leo Marx writes that the suburb occupies a space between the "chaos, garbage, and immigrant-dense metropolis" and the "uncivilized, provincial, and poor countryside."[16] I will turn to their whiteness in the next section, but here investigate how suburbs intended to model newness, hygiene, and modernity necessitated new, geographically expansive planning models. The squalor of London, for instance, generated one of the world's most famous models for development beyond urban centers, Ebenezer Howard's Garden City, a "compact urban entity with a hierarchical order of functions and services."[17] Yet, these compact entities were nonetheless peripheral, and, eventually (and to the dismay of many Garden City boosters), they became not autonomous towns but "suburbs" that were unquestionably dependent on central cities, both economically and socially. In Howard's 1902 book *Garden Cities of To-Morrow*, the diagram "Three Magnets" explains the benefits and problems of both "Town" and "Country" before turning to his invention, the "Town-Country," which Robert Fishman has described as a form of "moderate decentralization."[18] In this world between the rural and the urban, residents would attain the best of both worlds, a utopia.

In the United States during the 1930s, Frank Lloyd Wright proposed an even more radical decentralization to solve some of the same urban problems found in Howard's London, with his commuters traveling by private helicopter: Broadacre City. As Fishman writes, "Wright's essential insight was that decentralization, if taken to its logical extreme, could create the material conditions for a nation of independent farmers and proprietors. If properly planned, cities could spread over the countryside and still not lose their cohesion or efficiency. The diffusion of population would create conditions for the universal ownership of land."[19] Wright wrote in 1932 that "[t]o look at the plan of a great city is to look at the cross-section of some fibrous tumor;" Broadacre City would alleviate this medical condition.[20] Here, what came to be known later as "sprawl" is cast as fundamentally positive, permitting both personal freedom and social harmony and accounting for a vision of American land as vast and limitless.

In Europe, however, suburban sprawl eventually took on a different character. The garden cities of the early-twentieth-century United Kingdom gave way to urbanization around cities and into rural spaces, both with much longer histories than their American counterparts. This produced a "strange urban-rural landscape as a new form of city" that German urban theorist Thomas Sieverts—using the region of the Ruhr Valley as inspiration—defines as the *Zwischenstadt* (the title translated into English as *Cities without Cities*).[21] This is a place where landscape and city are so deeply intermingled that they become indistinguishable, a city "in an 'in-between' state."[22] Sieverts writes that the *Zwischenstadt* "is a field of living which, depending on one's interest and perspective, can be interpreted either as city or as country," a place that explicitly contradicts Howard's vision of distinct suburban homesteads and recalls, perhaps, the interdependency of the urban and rural in William Cronon's analysis of Chicago in its regional context.[23]

Thus, while the image of suburban "sprawl" is often presented as typically American, the sheer density of European countries vis-à-vis their counterparts across the Atlantic has produced forms of settlement that certainly fulfil the definitions. Scholar of sprawl Robert Bruegmann writes that this once-obscure term is now a part of "everyday speech," signifying "unplanned, scattered, low-density, automobile-dependent development at the urban periphery"; he also notes the negative symbolic space of sprawl, which "threatens to destroy open space, consume agricultural land, drive up utility costs, undermine urban social life, heighten inequalities, deplete natural resources, and damage the environment. And, by the way, it is ugly."[24] This view was of course radically opposed by Reyner Banham, in his assessment of the "autopia" he found around Los Angeles.[25]

In both the United States and Europe, sprawl has also been connected to processes of gentrification. In the former, center-city gentrification encouraged people without the means to remain to move farther out of the urban center to suburbs they could afford,[26] a process exacerbated by the "white flight" of the postwar period and inverted in more recent "back to the city" movements. European sprawl and gentrification intersect in a different way: the stigmatization of modernist-era suburbs around cities in France, Germany, or Sweden has created a condition described by urban historian Florian Urban as "the concrete cordon around Paris."[27] Here, the extensive rings of neighborhoods around urban centers may signify social barriers toward the inner city for suburban occupants, a place where the utopian origins of these projects have given way to dystopian visions of the same spaces.

Indeed, regardless of their origins in distributive capitalist policies or welfare-state megaprojects, the utopias produced have become increasingly off-limits for large segments of the American and European populations and their sprawl is now analyzed as environmentally and socially destructive. US suburbs and exurbs are spatially wasteful and encourage gasoline consumption, while European suburbs are criticized for their social exclusion and architectural failures. For many in Europe, in fact, the utopias of the past are now portrayed as the dystopias of the present, as Celeste Olalquiaga has described: "In the same way that the ruins of the world's fairs, which once grandiosely represented this belief, have aged, so too has modernism, leaving only the dusty shells of its dreams behind."[28] This portrait of suburbs in ruin often exemplifies the *banlieues* or *förorter*, where one-dimensional accounts of living neighborhoods convey the sense that they are "no-go zones," as the police in several countries have labeled them. But for whom does this image resonate? These questions become quickly racialized, as I will now explore.

Suburban While Black

In the late nineteenth century, W. E. B. Dubois conducted a study of the Seventh Ward of Philadelphia to determine why there was so little upward mobility in this "ghetto" and to analyze connections between race and social problems. From this work, he later published *The Philadelphia Negro* in 1899, outlining the wide diversity of Black socioeconomic classes in the area and debunking biological racism as "causing" crime or violence.[29] Dubois also identified structural reasons for European immigrants' greater "success" in American society, concluding that whiteness facilitated their search for housing and employment, even as they were seemingly unaware of their advantages. As he wrote, most "regard color prejudice as the easily explicable feeling that intimate social intercourse with a lower race is not only undesirable but impractical… they cannot see how such a feeling has much influence on the real situation or alters the social condition of the mass of Negroes."[30]

Numerous refugees and their descendants have found new homes in suburban Europe, especially since the 1970s. European suburbs are increasingly "racialized" and thus cast as dangerous and ugly; in the process, their "segregation" has gripped policymakers, planners, and scholars across the continent, where the nuanced perspectives of Dubois are often sorely lacking. The stigmatization of the suburbs where they live has produced a host of new dystopian tropes and terms: "zones," "alienation areas," "vulnerable areas," "parallel societies," "ghettos," and more.

George Lipsitz has analyzed "the possessive investment in whiteness" as the means by which Blacks are systematically discriminated against; whiteness is not merely privileged but economically supported through what he terms a "whiteness subsidy:" whites acquire loans more easily, pay comparatively less for similar housing, and enjoy tax breaks.[31] This is the case, Lipsitz argues, even as many whites believe that their advantages stem from a "lack of willpower" among Blacks.[32] These discourses also saturate discussions of European suburbs, where populist politicians have increasingly blamed ethnic minorities for the social problems faced by those communities. This development also neatly dovetails with neoliberalism's doctrines of personal choice: a field of options for individuals who are said to enjoy "freedom" but who are actually judged for their own ability to avoid catastrophe—or, as Wendy Brown describes it, for leading a "mismanaged life."[33] Likewise, in their theorization of the "indebted woman," Helen Runting and Hélène Frichot describe a society where personal ruin "represents a biographical rather than a structural failure."[34] When individuals are blamed for their own suffering, populist proposals link up with perceptions about rampant crime and violence in neighborhoods to cure the "chaos" that residents have "caused," facilitating all manner of interventions.

When American Blacks have demonstrated "willpower," however, the inhospitable conditions for such suburban residents and would-be residents have come to the surface. The 1957 film *Crisis in Levittown* captures the social unrest that emerges after the first Black family moves into one of the famous Levittown suburbs.[35] In tract housing estates like this, being suburban while Black was a dangerous proposition, as many other ethnic minority groups experienced over time. Sometimes, racially segregated suburbs became a means toward Black suburbanization, as Andrew Wiese describes in his study of Chagrin Falls Park, Ohio, an unincorporated Black suburb originating from the 1920s.[36] While outsiders understood Chagrin Falls Park as a place lacking basic services (or ignored the suburb entirely), its residents—mostly migrants from the South—understood it as a robust site of community-building and collective living where "[i]t's better to live in a 'shack' that's your own than to abide in a palace that belongs to another."[37] In one of several Black suburbs of this era, lots were advertised in newspapers and appealed to the desires of Southerners hoping to cultivate land and raise animals near their homes.[38] Even so, Chagrin Falls Park was presented as a "shantytown" in the *Cleveland Plain Dealer* in 1959.[39]

Suburban while Black is not antimony in Europe, as noted. Quite the contrary. Here, a converse condition exists in which the social and economic circumstances of European suburbs—particularly those built during the mid- to late twentieth century—are equally the result of a "possessive investment in whiteness" elsewhere, especially the central city. The Blackness of European suburbs is, in fact, a defining feature, used to separate and segregate both people and spaces. Such a perspective has also led to uncanny erasures of large swaths of metropolitan space from many a European "social imaginary": an imaginary of European cities that fails to include their suburbs.[40] Regarding Paris, for instance, Florian Urban describes the *banlieues* as having "appeared as an eerie flipside that the City of Love for a long time has managed to bar from both its municipal boundaries and public image."[41] For many white Europeans, these suburbs do not exist.

This bond between European suburbs and Blackness was not always so unassailable, however. In his influential *Badlands of the Republic*, Geographer Mustafa Dikeç describes a shift in signification as the suburbs of France were increasingly linked to migrants from the 1970s to the 1990s.[42] The white "hooligans and hoodlums" depicted on the cover of the major French magazine *L'Express* in the 1970s had become Black hooligans on the cover of the same magazine in the 1990s, a transformation, he argues, that "best exemplifies the changing color of fear of '*the banlieue*'" during this period.[43] These *banlieues* have, in parallel, become the nation's "badlands,"[44] with similar conditions now seen in Amsterdam, Stockholm, Copenhagen, and, to a degree, London. Indeed, these are not, following geographer Wei Li, "ethnoburbs," or commercial and social concentrations of ethnic minorities in suburbs that sometimes partially replace a more centrally located Chinatown.[45]

In Sweden, neighborhoods with qualities like those of Dubois's Seventh Ward or Chagrin Falls Park—comprising mainly nonwhite residents and presented externally as undesirable—have been the focus of recent political campaigns and media discourse. In 2018, the Swedish Police initiated a series of actions, described in the evaluation report *Right Action in the Right Place*, in order to target certain neighborhoods for additional police and police resources.[46] Found across Sweden but characterized by modernist suburbs built during the so-called "Million Program" of 1965 to 1974 (when Sweden built one million dwelling units), the police list identified specific suburbs as "vulnerable" (*utsatta*) or "especially vulnerable" (*särskilt utsatta*) areas. Under earlier Swedish governments, they were known as "alienation areas" (*utanförskapsområden*).

In Denmark, the "Parallel Society Plan" of 2018, developed by the national government, presented several statistical factors that facilitated the labeling of some Danish neighborhoods as "ghettos," with the percentage of residents with a "non-Western" background being one of the determining factors.[47] This list has since been used to justify extreme physical and social interventions into the identified areas, such as building demolitions and privatization projects intended to enforce a rule that no more than 40% of the dwelling units be family social housing.[48]

So how can we understand the qualitative differences between racialized suburbs in Europe and the United States, beyond their opposition as spaces of Blackness and whiteness, respectively? Sociologist Loïc Wacquant notes that planners and politicians intervening in European suburbs have imported the term "ghetto" into their lexicon even as, he contends, there are vast structural differences between these and the French *banlieues*, for example.[49] While he accedes that both are sites of "urban exile," Wacquant cautions against imported concepts, not least because of their stark geographic differences: the *banlieues* are located on the urban periphery, unlike the US neighborhoods he investigates (mainly in inner city Chicago).[50]

More perilous from my perspective, however, is European politicians' and planners' uncritical use of "ghetto" as descriptor. This new context for its use does not obliterate or neutralize its history as a racialized concept producing profound tragedies of power and loss for earlier minoritarian communities, including European Jews. For actors pushing demolitions and large-scale renovations, these suburbs are apparently irredeemably lost. Instead, they hope to create new spaces of whiteness in the mold of their ideal: the historical, central European city.

Intriguingly, these images of whiteness and the spaces in which it dwells contrast profoundly those idealized in suburb settings in the United States, not just with respect to their location in the regional geography. These differences are also formal and symbolic. Architectural historian Dianne Harris has described how whiteness pervaded architectural renderings of US suburbs. As she writes, "[t]he appearance of the drawings is remarkably homogeneous: clean, tidy, orderly, shiny, and bright, they broadcast the symbolism of sameness, safety, and assimilation."[51]

Notably, the "sameness" and orderliness that Harris locates in advertisements for American suburbs were the very spatial and social promises that underscored the construction of modernist housing in European suburbs. Today, journalists and popular cultural references present these same spaces as containing a threatening lack of whiteness, a counterpoint to the "safety" of historical city centers with their medieval street networks and older buildings. Steeping buildings in discourses of European nationalism, populist politicians then refer to preindustrial forms of architecture as heritage sites and hint at their being unsullied by unwanted newcomers. For instance, in the 2022 Swedish elections, a poster advertising the platform of the far-right, white nationalist Sweden Democrats promised "beautiful architecture" alongside "safety for real" during a campaign otherwise defined by parties vying to fight "gang criminality" and crime. Such dog whistles position suburbs as sites like Dubois's Seventh Ward: socioeconomically monolithic and defined by blame.

In her theory of dirt as "matter out of place," anthropologist Mary Douglas argues that social constructions of order and cleanliness determine their opposites, a position that Sweden Democrats imply in posters with photographs of wooden countryside cottages (paired with the words "Harder Punishments," written in pink cursive). In *Even in Sweden*, geographer Allan Pred describes how residing in certain Swedish neighborhoods presents difficulties for potential employees on the job market, when their addresses (and often names) are treated with suspicion, a condition that has only increased since he published the book in 2000.[52] In this sense, the "possessive investment in whiteness" in Europe—defined as the opposite of the *banlieue*—has economic, legal, social, and cultural ramifications. I now turn to another critique of suburbia: that it is a place that is suffocatingly conformist, especially for women.

Disturbia, A Woman's Life

The homogeneity that Dianne Harris identified as commercially attractive for white residents also buttressed a major critique of US suburbs, where strict social codes were said to define a highly gendered and spatialized division of labor. While women's responsibilities for the family and housework predated suburbs like Levittown, the movement of men into the inner city during the daytime and the concomitant domination of the suburban neighborhood by women produced a greater hegemony for these gendered ideologies. Yet conformism itself simultaneously worked against other American philosophical orientations. Herbert Gans notes that "homogeneity violates the American Dream of a 'balanced' community where people of diverse age, class, race, and religion live together. Allegedly, it creates dullness through sameness."[53]

Lives in these "safe" and "clean" suburban neighborhoods produced a sense of a loss of meaning in the lives of many women, who were largely confined to their homes and socially assigned repetitive, unpaid work as "housewives" and "homemakers." As the suburbs became more common living environments, a binary division between urban and suburban space emerged that categorized them as male and female, respectively, a division that became pronounced in interventions at the scale of architecture, such as the kitchen. In views of these purportedly ideal home environments, as Mark Clapson writes in his 2003 book *Suburban Century*, "Women and 'the suburbs' have thus been conjoined in a depressing and gendered myth of passivity and pointlessness . . . women in the suburbs have been seen as living passive and trivial lives, cooped up at home all day in comfortable coffins for living."[54] Men who sleep in these same suburbs are, by contrast, portrayed as active, with intellectual and productive lives taking place in the central urban areas that they visit on a daily basis.

The early years of European suburbanization—where modernist architecture and planning defined new urban designs—were also defined by new ideals of women's homemaking that also centered on new architectural ideals for interior spaces. Architects and planners produced ideal standards for European housing, drawing on research to produce more efficient kitchens and domesticity for a new corps of suburban women settling in new *Siedlungen*, Garden Cities, and New Towns in countries like Austria, Germany, Sweden, and others. While these interior interventions were meant to be universal in the new modernist city of the early and mid-twentieth century, new architectural models for women's spaces ultimately became a mostly suburban phenomenon.

For example, Margarete Schütte-Lihotzky sought to optimize women's workspaces, beginning with a Viennese kitchen design that would also accommodate cooking with post-World War I food shortages.[55] She later adapted this model into the more technologically streamlined and better-known "Frankfurt Kitchen," used by architect Ernst May in many designs for new German housing in the 1920s. Incorporating a "stove complex" and a "wet complex," she drew on evidence from time-motion diagrams to answer the question: "How can we translate to housework the principles of labour-saving, economical business management, whose implementation has led to unexpected increase and productivity?"[56]

In Sweden, Alva Myrdal and Sven Markelius collaborated on the Collective House of 1935, with its designs meant to reduce women's share of labor through the inclusion of a collective kitchen and daycare.[57] During the 1940s, the "Home Research Institute" (*Hemmens Forskningsinstitut*) observed women performing housework in laboratory studies involving breathing and motion measurements. The standardized housing produced during the Swedish Million Program incorporated the new "Swedish Kitchen" developed out of these studies.[58] Across Europe, suburbs of mass housing and modernism were meant as "her" space, especially when the men left for work in the city, a place that Heidi Svenningsen Kajita and I have elsewhere described as "hertopia."[59]

US and European politicians even sparred over how much better women would have it in their preferred forms of suburbia. In 1959, the exhibition of a new model kitchen of the "typical American house" in Moscow also became the site of a televised debate between Richard Nixon and Nikita Khrushchev. During the conversation, Nixon said, "This is our newest model. This is the kind which is built in thousands of units for direct installations in the houses. In America, we like to make life easier for women ..." to which Khrushchev replied, "Your capitalistic attitude toward women does not occur under Communism." Nixon retorted, "I think that this attitude towards women is universal. What we want to do, is make life more easy [sic] for our housewives."[60] This debate accentuated the ideological underpinnings of suburbia for two diametrically opposed politicians, with Richard Nixon and Nikita Kruschev highlighting how ideas of communal living in the Soviet Union (and others like them across the continent) were situated as conceptually opposite the technological innovations in electric appliances—available through capitalist consumerism—that the Americans accentuated.

Despite these apparently benevolent aims to improve women's everyday lives through new suburban designs in both Europe and the United States, it was malaise that came to represent women's suburban lived experience instead. In Europe, headlines explained that housewives had turned to alcoholism to contend with their suburban melancholy, with modernist built environments blamed for addictive behaviors. In the United States, on the other hand, advertisements marketed sedatives and alcohol to unhappy suburban housewives. For instance, advertising copy claimed that Blatz Beer could be a pick-me-up for young mothers while also providing nutritional benefits for a nursing baby. European exposés about everyday life in neighborhoods of mass housing, such as the Swedish suburban life described in *Kvinnoliv Förortsliv* (*Women's Life, Suburban Life*), explained how a lack of services promised (such as daycare) had made the dream of the suburb into a prison instead, conveying the sense that women were living on the edge: psychologically, economically, and even culturally. Women's life in the suburbs may have been well-designed, but it sure was unpleasant.

These portrayals also pervaded fictional accounts. Famously, the 1975 film *The Stepford Wives* depicted suburban women in the United States as so devoid of personality that they could be killed and replaced by robots without notice. Likewise, the "boredom" of *banlieue* housewives—along with its only apparent antidote in consumerism—produced the suburban housewives' prostitution ring of Jean-Luc Godard's 1967 film, *Two or Three Things I Know about Her*. Or the Swedish film *The Stone Face*, about a youth gang hired for contract killings of those responsible for the design of the suburb Skärholmen; the man doing the hiring is dating a divorced single mother whose life is depicted as one of overwork, desperation for a father figure for her son, and discontent in an already dystopian world.

Conformism was itself a suffocating force for women, as suggested by the phrase "keeping up with the Joneses," from an early-twentieth-century comic strip by the same name. Housewives observed one another through their kitchen windows, claimed Herbert Gans in *The Levittowners*. The women of the US suburbs were not only said to be boring and passive, but they were soon pathologized with terms like "new town blues" or "suburban neurosis," which were both psychological afflictions that connected suburban living to problems like "backache, weight loss, loss of breath, and insomnia."[61] Meanwhile, non-heterosexual residents of the suburbs were portrayed as non-existent, despite extensive evidence to the contrary.[62]

Notably, women in the suburbs of Europe and the United States had typically migrated from the city centers to these new areas, leaving behind extended family in the process. Most did not work, making them completely dependent on their husbands and the entertainment offerings of the local area. As Mark Clapson writes:

> the isolation and loneliness caused by the apparent absence of community and kin . . . [were met with new] "false values": women were presented as victims of the advertisers of labour-saving devices such as Hoovers, electrical and gas goods, and ready-made clothes. These items left women with too much time on their hands . . . and engendered a sense of worthlessness which undermined well-being.[63]

Likewise, Helena Mattsson has described how new settlements like the suburb of Skärholmen, Sweden, which opened in 1968, encouraged consumerism and residents who understood shopping as a key tenet of their societal responsibilities.[64]

For women, then, these suburban settings were a far cry from the "hertopias" promised. In her 1963 essay *The Feminine Mystique*, Betty Friedan writes, "[e]ach suburban wife struggled with it alone. As she made the beds, shopped for groceries, matched slipcover material, ate peanut butter sandwiches with her children, chauffeured Cub Scouts and Brownies, lay beside her husband at night—she was afraid to ask even of herself the silent question—'Is this all?'"[65] In suburbs, new mental health crises, a unique social world of young and female daytime residents, and a lack of consideration about the consequences of these developments had made suburbia into a new dystopia that Richard E. Gordon, Katherine K. Gordon, and Max Gunther defined as "disturbia" in their 1961 book, *The Split-Level Trap* (a book later critiqued by Herbert Gans for its evidential "cherry picking").[66] Disturbia, they contended, was a place of neurotic women with ulcers and men on the verge of heart attack.[67]

Even so, many women ultimately took matters into their own hands, became activists for missing services or politically active. Amy Bix describes how women of some mid-twentieth century moments were actually "chicks who fix" and encouraged to operate their own power tools by magazine ads proclaiming, "[i]f you can ice a cake, you can lay bricks!"[68] These expectations for roles changed over time, however.

Even so, women succeeded, for example, in getting media attention paid to their cause through exposés, and American suburban women are now considered one of the most important voting blocs in the political landscape. As Alice Friedman analyzes in her book on women clients for new houses and new domestic interiors in privately commissioned modernist homes, women of the suburbs slowly altered the built environments and social conditions of their performed domesticities.[69] As women's roles in the economy turned women suburbanites into commuters and wage-earners as well, this further changed conditions.

A Futurbia on the Edges of Europe

This tour along the outer belts of cities on two continents unites two types of suburbs built from the 1950s to the 1970s; these worlds share utopian aspirations, peripheral urban geographies, and social dilemmas. Even so, their forms, their histories, and their socioeconomic and political worlds lead us to very different off-ramps. Monolithic, traditional portrayals of American suburbia glossed over housewives suffering from depression and African-American suburbanization and exclusion. European suburbs—often built at the height of their respective welfare states—sought to offer modern living in modernist housing and greater equality for citizens,[70] yet these suburbs are now represented as "achieving" the opposite as spaces of inequality stuck in a future that never arrived.

Today, the story is even more complicated, with the foreclosure of 6 million homes throughout US suburbs between 2006 and 2013, a result of the unpaid mortgages of the 2008 financial crisis and forcing households to relocate on a scale unseen since the Great Depression.[71] The virus of "foreclosure landscapes" became endemic in places like California, Arizona, and Nevada, notably also places with large Latino populations.[72] In parallel, European suburbs have been, over the past few decades, heavily exploited by international risk capitalists who buy and sell mass housing with a chilling disregard for the ability of residents to remain in their homes, as notoriously chronicled in the 2019 documentary film *Push* by Swedish director Fredrik Gertten.[73] What is the future of suburbia, then, as we contemplate this "post-suburban" world?

And how do we understand the suburbs ideologically in our post-postmodern, post-global times, with populist politics on the rise and a climate catastrophe on the horizon? Together, Senator Joseph McCarthy and William Levitt promoted single-family houses to support the burgeoning American capitalist society, even as other politicians imagined standardized suburbs as potential socialist threat on the grounds that it encouraged residents to relinquish forms of distinction. European politicians of the mid-twentieth century envisioned new suburbs as key components of the expanded welfare state they were bringing to their citizens. Will the suburbias and disturbias of the past and present give way to a new futurbia for contemporary living with new notions of solidarity and society?

In his book, *The Country and the City*, Raymond Williams examines British literature from the late Middle Ages to the twentieth century in order to trace the relationships and evolving social understandings of "the country and the city" as two potent and interconnected symbols.[74] Defining particular "structures of feeling," Williams demonstrates the various ways in which the peasantry and, later, the working classes were exploited along the lines of land seizure, agrarian capitalism, and blindness to the reality of their role in the economy.[75] More potently, his work illustrates that the idealized image of the country—as a contrast to the symbolic corruption of the city—was used to support certain ideologies and class structures.

While the "pure" countryside has often been pitted against the "evil" city, Williams highlights their continuous tension in descriptions of them: a dialectic never fully resolved. Or, as Rem Koolhaas argued in 2020 (based on a lecture from 2012), the undue emphasis on cities has turned today's countryside into a "terra incognita," a place to which narratives can be ascribed but where there "are too few people in the countryside to verify these narratives."[76] The spread of "US-style" suburbs around what was the European countryside buttresses this postulation. Today, it is the suburbs—not the city center—that are demonized in narratives, much like the urban centers of the past.

If suburban landscapes are not quite "cities without cities," some authors, such as Nicholas A. Phelps, argue for the existence of a "post-suburban era," where the categories of urban, suburban, and rural no longer apply.[77] Recent journalism on climate change casts the suburb as the site of waste and an illogical calculus about resource distribution, such as an exposé about an Arizona suburb where legal shenanigans evaded rules on water supply, leading to shortages.[78] The city, in contrast, is presented as "authentic" and "lively," even if this is—in the late capitalist era—perhaps another fiction.

In Europe, the widespread disparagement of modernist architecture caused political handwringing as the buildings were being constructed, whereas populists have made suburbs the targets of their political platforms in the contemporary period. The suburb as a homogeneous built and social environment or a controllable utopia now appears to be a fiction. It seems it always was. In a time when the environmental and social effects of sprawl are readily apparent, and when questions of race, ethnicity, and gender require new, twenty-first-century responses, where will futurbia take us?

1 HUD (Department of Housing and Urban Development), "President Bush's Radio Address to the Nation: Barriers to Minority Homeownership" (June 15, 2002) https://archives.hud.gov/news/2002/homeownradioaddress.cfm.
2 Ibid.
3 John Archer, *Architecture and Suburbia: From English Villa to American Dream House, 1690-2000* (Minneapolis: University of Minnesota Press, 2005), 261.
4 Hayden is quoted in Archer, *Architecture and Suburbia*, 292.
5 A focus in the essay on Swedish (and, to a degree, Danish) cases emerges from my own extensive research into the housing and urban design in those countries and contexts.
6 See Pedro Ignacio Alonso and Hugo Palmarola, *Flying Panels: How Concrete Panels Changed the World* (Berlin: DOM, 2020).
7 Helena Mattsson, "Where the Motorways Meet: Architecture and Corporatism in Sweden," in *Architecture of the Welfare State,* eds. Mark Swenarton, Tom Avermaete, and Dirk van den Heuvel (London: Routledge, 2014), 154–75; Jennifer Mack, "Hello, Consumer! Skärholmen Centre from the Million Program to the Mall," in *Shopping Towns Europe: Commercial Collectivity and the Architecture of the Shopping Centre, 1945-1975,* eds. Tom Avermaete and Janina Gosseye (London: Bloomsbury, 2017), 122–37.
8 Reyner Banham, *The Architecture of the Well-Tempered Environment* (London: The Architectural Press, 1969), 94. Helen Runting explores these accolades from one "(cis, Anglo-American)" man to another in her own experience of a quarantine hotel in Australia; see Helen Runting, "Quarantine Dreams 2: No-Set Sci-Fi," *Site Zones* (June 30, 2021), https://www.sitezones.net/articles/quarantine-dreams-2-no-set-sci-fi.
9 Joel Garreau, *Edge City: Life on the New Frontier* (New York: Anchor Books, 1991).
10 See, for example, Jennifer Y. Fang, "'To Cultivate Our Children to Be of East and West': Contesting Ethnic Heritage Language in Suburban Chinese Schools," *Journal of American Ethnic History* 34, no. 2 (Winter 2015): 54–82; Sarah Lopez, *The Remittance Landscape: Spaces of Migration in Mexico and Urban USA* (Chicago: University of Chicago Press, 2015); Tim Retzloff, "The Association of (Gay) Suburban People," *Places Journal* (April 2015), https://placesjournal.org/article/the-association-of-gay-suburban-people/?cn-reloaded=1; Andrew Wiese, *Places of Their Own: African American Suburbanization in the Twentieth Century* (Chicago: University of Chicago Press, 2004).
11 Ola Andersson, *Vykort från utopia* (Stockholm: Dokument Press, 2012); Alice Coleman, *Utopia on Trial: Vision and Reality in Planned Housing* (London: Hilary Shipman, 1985).
12 Jennifer Mack, "Impossible Nostalgia: Green Affect in the Landscapes of the Swedish Million Programme," *Landscape Research* 45, no. 4 (2021): 558–73.
13 David Ley, "Between Europe and Asia: The Case of the Missing Sequoias," *Ecumene* 2, no. 2 (1995): 185–210; Willow Lung Aman, "That 'Monster House' Is My Home: The Social and Cultural Politics of Design Reviews and Regulations," *Journal of Urban Design* 18, no. 2 (2013): 220–41; Kenny Cupers, *The Social Project: Housing Postwar France* (Minneapolis: University of Minnesota Press, 2014).
14 Peter G. Rowe, *Making a Middle Landscape* (Cambridge, Mass.: MIT Press, 1991); Leo Marx, *The Machine in the Garden: Technology and the Pastoral Ideal in America*, 35th edition (Oxford University Press, New York, 2000 [1964]).
15 Marx, *The Machine in the Garden*, 32.
16 Ibid., 280.
17 Thomas Sieverts, *Cities Without Cities: An Interpretation of the Zwischenstadt*, English language ed. (London: Spon Press, 2003), viii.
18 Ebenezer Howard, *Garden Cities of To-Morrow* (London: Faber and Faber, 1965 [1902]); Robert Fishman, *Urban Utopias in the Twentieth Century* (Cambridge, MA: MIT Press, 1982).
19 Fishman, *Urban Utopias*, 123.

20 Frank Lloyd Wright, *The Disappearing City* (New York: William Farquhar Payson, 1932), 26.
21 Sieverts, *Cities Without Cities*, ix.
22 Ibid., x.
23 Ibid., 3; William Cronon, *Nature's Metropolis: Chicago and the Great West*, 1. ed. (New York: W.W. Norton, 1991).
24 Robert Bruegmann, *Sprawl: A Compact History* (Chicago: University of Chicago Press, 2005), 2.
25 Reyner Banham, *Los Angeles: The Architecture of Four Ecologies* (New York: Harper and Row, 1971).
26 Bruegmann, *Sprawl*, 4.
27 Florian Urban, *Tower and Slab: Histories of Global Mass Housing* (London: Routledge, 2012), 37.
28 Celeste Olalquiaga, *Megalopolis: Contemporary Cultural Sensibilities* (Minneapolis: University of Minnesota Press, 1992), xx.
29 In 1909, Dubois became one of the founders of the NAACP, devoted to improving the status of African Americans in cities. W. E. B. Dubois, *The Philadelphia Negro* (Philadelphia: 1899).
30 Ibid., 58.
31 George Lipsitz, *The Possessive Investment in Whiteness: How White People Profit from Identity Politics* (Philadelphia: Temple University Press, 1998), 385.
32 Ibid.
33 Wendy Brown, "Neoliberalism and the End of Liberal Democracy," *Edgework: Critical Essays on Knowledge and Politics* (Princeton: Princeton University Press, 2005); Wendy Brown, *Undoing the Demos: Neoliberalism's Stealth Revolution* (New York: Zone Books, 2015).
34 Hélène Frichot and Helen Runting, "The Promise of a Lack: Responding to (Her) Real Estate Career," in *The Avery Review* 8 (May 2015): 4, http://averyreview.com/issues/2/the-promise-of-a-lack.
35 *Crisis in Levittown*, directed by Lee Bobker and Lester Becker (Dynamic Films, 1957), 0:32:00. https://archive.org/details/crisis_in_levittown_1957.
36 Wiese, *Places of Their Own*.
37 Ibid., 67.
38 Ibid., 72.
39 Ibid., 67.
40 Charles Taylor, "Modern Social Imaginaries," *Public Culture* 14, no. 1 (Winter 2002): 91–124.
41 Urban, *Tower and Slab*, 37.
42 Mustafa Dikeç, *Badlands of the Republic: Space, Politics, and Urban Policy* (Oxford: Blackwell, 2007).
43 Ibid., 8.
44 Ibid., 7.
45 Wei Li, "Ethnoburb versus Chinatown: Two Types of Urban Ethnic Communities in Los Angeles," *Cybergeo* (1998), DOI: 10.4000/cybergeo.1018. See also Erica Allen-Kim, "Exile on the Commercial Strip: Vietnam War Memorials in Little Saigon and the Politics of Commemoration," *Buildings and Landscapes: Journal of the Vernacular Architecture Forum* 21, no. 2 (2014): 31–56; Lung Aman, "That 'Monster House' Is My Home."
46 *Riksrevisionen, Rätt insats på rätt plats—polisens arbete i utsatta områden* ["Right Action in the Right Place], RIR 2020:20 (Uppsala: Riskrevisionen, 2020), https://www.riksrevisionen.se/download/18.7546977617592429b913d517/1604927340756/RiR%202020_20%20Anpassad.pdf.
47 The Government of Denmark, *Ét Danmark uden parallelsamfund: Ingen ghettoer i 2030* ["A Denmark Without Parallel Societies: No Ghettos By 2030"] (Copenhagen: Government of Denmark, 2030), https://oim.dk/media/19035/et_danmark_uden_parallelsamfund_pdfa.pdf.
48 See Heidi Svenningsen Kajita, Jennifer Mack, Svava Riesto, and Meike Schalk, "Between Technologies of Power and Notions of Solidarity: A Response to the Danish Ghetto Plan and Swedish Vulnerable Areas Documents," in *Architectures of Dismantling and Restructuring: Spaces of Danish Welfare 1970-Present*, eds. Kirsten Marie Raahauge, Deane Simpson, Martin Søberg, and Katrin Lotz, (Zürich, Switzerland: Lars Müller Publishers, 2022), 148–59.
49 Loïc Wacquant, *Urban Outcasts: A Comparative Sociology of Advanced Marginality* (Cambridge: Polity, 2008).
50 Ibid., 137.
51 Dianne Harris, *Little White Houses: How the Postwar Home Constructed Race in America* (Minneapolis: University of Minnesota Press, 2012), 92.

52 Allan Pred, *Even in Sweden: Racisms, Racialized Spaces, and the Popular Geographical Imagination* (Berkeley: University of California Press, 2000).
53 Herbert Gans, *The Levittowners: Ways of Life and Politics in a New Suburban Community* (New York: Alfred A. Knopf, Inc. and Random House, 1967), 165.
54 Mark Clapson, *Suburban Century: Social Change and Urban Growth in England and the USA* (London: Berg, 2003), 125.
55 Sophie Hochhaeusl, "From Vienna to Frankfurt Inside Core-House Type 7: A History of Scarcity through the Modern Kitchen," *Architectural Histories* 1, no. 1 (2013), DOI: 10.5334/ah.aq.
56 Ibid.
57 This can be linked to Dolores Hayden's analysis of earlier, nineteenth century feminists' architectural interventions, which were meant to make housework and childcare communal. See Dolores Hayden, *Grand Domestic Revolution: A History of Feminist Designs for American Homes, Neighborhoods, and Cities* (Cambridge: MIT Press, 1981).
58 See Ingrid Dalén and Lennart Holm, eds., *Bättre bostäder: Bostadsbyggnadsutredningens huvud-betänkande Höjd bostadsstandard* (Stockholm: Prisma, 1965).
59 Heidi S. Kajita and Jennifer Mack, "Hertopia: Women's Swedish Welfare Landscapes during the 1960s and 1970s," manuscript under review (2023).
60 Central Intelligence Agency, "The Kitchen Debate – transcript" (July 24, 1959), https://www.cia.gov/readingroom/docs/1959-07-24.pdf.
61 Clapson, *Suburban Century*, 126.
62 This misapprehension has been investigated, for example, by Tim Retzloff in his work on the "Association of Suburban People," a group of gay men living in suburbs near Detroit in the 1970s. See Retzloff, "The Association of (Gay) Suburban People."
63 Ibid., 126.
64 Mattsson, "Where the Motorways Meet." See also Mack, "Hello, Consumer!".
65 Betty Friedan, *The Feminine Mystique* (New York: W. W. Norton & Company, 1963), 15.
66 Richard Gordon, Katherine Gordon, and Max Gunther, *The Split-Level Trap* (B. Geis Associates, 1961); Gans, *The Levittowners*.
67 "Disturbia" was later used as the title of a 2007 cinematic thriller about a suburban serial killer and was also the title of a 2008 song by the artist Rihanna.
68 Amy Bix, "Creating 'Chicks Who Fix': Women, Tool Knowledge, and Home Repair, 1920-2007," *Women's Studies Quarterly* 37, nos. 1–2 (2009): 44.
69 Alice Friedman, *Women and the Making of the Modern House* (New Haven: Yale University Press, 1998).
70 Mack, "Hello, Consumer!".
71 Christos Makridis and Michael Ohlrogge, "Moving to Opportunity? The Geography of the Foreclosure Crisis and the Importance of Location," *Journal of Economic Geography* (2021): 2, fn.1.
72 See Aron Chang, "Beyond Foreclosure," in *Places Journal* (September 2011), DOI: 10.22269/110914; Alex Schafran, "Discourse and Dystopia, American style: The Rise of 'Slumburbia' in a Time of Crisis," *CITY* 17, no. 2 (2013): 130–48, DOI: 10.1080/13604813.2013.765125.
73 This film, like the present essay, connects stories from different global contexts to illustrate the consequences of predatory actions by risk capitalists, and how this affects people by "pushing" them from affordable housing all over the world.
74 Raymond Williams, *The Country and the City* (London: Hogarth Press, 1973).
75 Ibid., 12.
76 Rem Koolhaas, "Countryside (Part I)," 032c (February 13, 2020). From a lecture at Oude Lutherse Kerk, Amsterdam, April 25, 2012.
77 Nicholas A. Phelps, *Sequel to Suburbia: Glimpses of America's Post-Suburban Future* (Cambridge, Mass.: MIT Press, 2015).
78 Jack Healy, "Skipped Showers, Paper Plates: An Arizona Suburb's Water Is Cut Off," *The New York Times*, January 16, 2023.

Fifth-Wave Gentrification and the Financialization of Housing

An Interview with Manuel B. Aalbers

Manuel B. Aalbers (MA)

The Editors (EDS)
Tahl Kaminer Leonard Ma

Manuel B. Aalbers is professor of human geography at KU Leuven where he leads a research group on the intersection of real estate, finance, and states. He is the author of *Place, Exclusion, and Mortgage Markets* (Wiley-Blackwell, 2011) and *The Financialization of Housing: A Political Economy Approach* (Routledge, 2016).

Fifth-Wave Gentrification

EDS[1] Manuel, you are an important contributor to research into the financialization of the built environment. We will be discussing financialization, but would like to begin by asking you to explain "fifth-wave" gentrification, particularly in terms of the way that you develop the concept in your 2019 paper "Revisiting 'The Changing State of Gentrification.'"[2]

MA The *wave* theory of gentrification is different from *phases* or *stages*. A "phase" of gentrification occurs within the same, identified, gentrifying area: first, there is decline; then, you have a phase of marginal gentrification; then, you have gentrification proper; and so on. With *waves* of gentrification, we don't see waves follow one another in a particular place. Rather than progressing over time, waves are qualitatively different in different periods: gentrification in the 1970s was different than gentrification in the 2020s. And the basic idea of this wave thinking, which comes from Jason Hackworth and Neil Smith,[3] who talked about three consecutive waves, is to identify changes in *processes* of gentrification—not in one particular case but in many different cases—and then think: what is different now, compared with a few years ago? When they wrote "The Changing State of Gentrification" in 2001, what they were trying to argue was, basically, that the role of the state, of the government, had changed during the different waves of gentrification. Gentrification had become *state-led*. So, in the literature, we see references to "state-led gentrification," which is in fact what Hackworth and Smith meant by "third-wave gentrification."

Some years later, Elvin Wyly, Loretta Lees, and Tom Slater, in their book *Gentrification*, proposed a "fourth wave of gentrification."[4] What I am suggesting in my paper from 2019 is that some additional changes in gentrification have taken place since then. One particular change is the rise of corporate landlords—large landlords that include, for instance, private equity funds, hedge funds, real estate investment trusts (REITs), and other real estate investment funds. They are now taking over a large part of the housing stock in cities. I'm not saying in all cities and I'm not saying this is a shift that we see everywhere, but this is a significant shift. Another thing we see is the rise of things like Airbnb. So we're generally speaking of what we sometimes call "platform capitalism." It's also related to "touristification." Tourists were already very important to many cities, but over time they have become even more important. Through Airbnb, booking.com, and other platforms, we can see that touristification and gentrification have become increasingly intertwined. Whereas touristification in the past was very particular—taking place in particular places like on seafronts, or if it was in cities, in specific districts, and being mostly about hotels—now, a lot of the rise in tourism infrastructure happens in residential neighborhoods that are also undergoing gentrification. Touristification adds another layer on top of that.

Something else that we see in a select number of cities is investment by transnational wealth elites—people investing in different places and buying housing somewhere else.[5] This is a phenomenon that is really big in places like London or New York, but it also happens in smaller cities such as Vancouver, Lisbon, or Amsterdam. It's also increasingly driven not just by these transnational wealth elites, who are very rich people, but also by the middle classes. If you go to a city like Lisbon, you can see a lot of apartments being bought up by middle-class and upper-middle-class French people, for instance.[6] So it's no longer just the super-rich investing in housing. And while a lot of this is quite an urban phenomenon, it's something we would also see in other hotspots, like the Gulf, for instance.

A further element of this fifth wave lies in the ongoing role played by the state. That was the key item in the third wave, and it is still very important. Another thing that's been carried on from the fourth wave is the importance of mortgage debt. In the financial crisis, we saw that places with high mortgage debt were hit the hardest—in particular in the US (in the west and southwest and also Florida), but also in Spain, Ireland, and Iceland. But what we've seen in the fifth wave is that while mortgage debt may have stabilized or even declined in some places, in a lot of places—in particular, in the global south, and especially in middle-income countries in Latin America, East and Southeast Asia, and the Middle East, as well as select northern and southern African countries—it has expanded significantly. And this is also driving gentrification. So: these are some of the elements we see in *fifth-wave gentrification*.

One thing that I could add relates to what I've called "a subsumption of alternatives." Airbnb, again, is a good example. While Airbnb started as a "sharing economy"—I know people who were using it to basically sleep on someone's sofa—it has become something that's integrated into the dominant forms of capitalism. It's no longer an alternative to capitalism. This is, of course, something that Karl Marx discussed: capitalism has this tendency to subsume the alternatives that are being offered to the system by integrating them into the system. We don't only see this in fifth-wave gentrification, we saw it in earlier waves of gentrification as well—the whole DIY movement that was important in early gentrification has also been subsumed.

Super-Gentrification

EDS You mentioned the book by Lees, Slater, and Wyly, which discusses, among other things, "super-gentrification," a term coined earlier by Loretta Lees and Tim Butler. Super-gentrification involves a gentrifier who is a high-earning figure working in financial services, thereby suggesting an "upgrading" of the gentrifying figures of the artist and the yuppie—but here, there seems to be an overlap between super-gentrification and the fifth wave in the sense that finance capital is placed at the center of both.

MA We see super-gentrification in specific cities: in places where gentrification has already occurred, a new layer of gentrification is applied on top of that, whereby very rich people gentrify an already gentrified place. I think that this process is very specific to places like New York, London, probably Singapore, Tokyo, and maybe Paris, but probably that's about it. Super-gentrification requires a lot of gentrification to already have happened and a lot of rich people to move into a place that is already gentrified. So, I don't think that this is a general trend, whereas many of the trends that I mentioned as part of the fifth wave are, I think, quite general, and we also see them occurring in smaller cities and in large parts of the global south—Airbnb is an issue there as well.

What is key here is that super-gentrification is a *stage* or *phase* of gentrification, which follows on from gentrification proper, not a wave! Where super-gentrification enters into the fifth wave is through this element of transnational wealth elites and middle classes investing somewhere else. But the big difference is that in the original formulation of super-gentrification, the focus is on rich people from a particular city investing in those cities, whereas with the transnational wealth elites and middle classes, we focus on rich people investing in cities in other countries. In that sense, it is quite different. I think that it is still possible to see super-gentrification during the fifth wave.

EDS If we think of gentrification in 1964 and the work of Ruth Glass,[7] and compare it to the process witnessed in the 2000s, are we using the same term to describe something that is qualitatively too different?[8]

MA If you consider the definition of gentrification put forward by Neil Smith—gentrification as an investment or a movement back into the city by capital rather than people,[9] I think what we now see is a very intensified form of gentrification. We could invent a new term for it, but I'm not sure if that would help us because then we would have to be very clear about the point at which gentrification became something else. I'm not sure if that was during the 1990s or during the financial crisis of 2008, 2009… Whereas with the wave theory, one wave dissipates and the next one comes. The waves are always overlapping a little and they can merge. If there's a problem with the fourth wave not being different enough from the third, then it can be dealt with: for instance, if you stand at the shore, sometimes you see two waves catching up with each other and in the end merging into one. In that sense, the metaphor of the waves is a bit more flexible than saying, "Oh, all of a sudden, we're now in something new that's no longer gentrification."

Using Neil Smith's rent-gap theory, we could say, "Well, there are new waves in which rent gaps exist." There are a few papers that conceptualize touristification and Airbnb as the opening up of new rent gaps and the creation of opportunities to fill them.[10] I published a paper recently with Zac Taylor in which we argued that something similar is happening with climate gentrification or eco-gentrification—something new is being created that opens up the rent gap further and then it gets filled.[11] In that sense, Neil Smith's original conceptualizations have been very useful. I would even say that some of the original language advanced by Ruth Glass is still quite applicable to the changes that we are seeing today. I've never particularly liked the fact that in her definition she says that, little by little, the *whole* population, the *whole* district, changes. I think that has seldom been the case. In many neighborhoods, we see people with a protected rental status and a low income who can keep on living in now-gentrified neighborhoods. So that element of the original conceptualization wasn't entirely correct, in my opinion. But a lot of other things you've seen in the 1960s are still applicable to what we see today. In short: no, we don't need a new term.

The Financialization of Housing

EDS We're talking about the fifth wave as a wave driven by global flows of capital, the financialization of housing, and so on. But there is a question here about what happens with investment homes, whether they remain empty, and, if rented out, whether a new class of gentrifiers occupy them. If we don't discuss that—and much of the literature of financialization does not—then where is *class*? And without class at its center, where is gentrification?

MA The class element is very important. If you look at the literature, some papers talk much more in terms of displacement, therefore centering more on class-related issues. Some may not necessarily use the term "class" very much, but if you have an analysis of displacement, then implicitly, you're talking about class. In my opinion, there are a lot of studies which are very good at understanding the *consequences* of gentrification, but not always very good at understanding its *roots*. Many papers provide excellent case studies about local gentrification processes without tying them into the larger process. I'm not saying that this process is necessarily global, but what I find quite striking in the entire gentrification literature is that if you actually put all those case studies of places in the world that are so different together, they have many things in common regarding the gentrification processes being described.

I think it's okay to focus somewhat more on those real estate processes, as long as other people do the displacement and the class analysis. Not everyone can do everything in one paper. It's important to emphasize specific parts that are understudied. For instance, this idea of the corporate landlord has only very recently been discussed in relation to gentrification, even though in some places they're so active that they are very hard to ignore. There's a risk, if you leave that research to critical real estate studies, that it will be disconnected from gentrification. So I think it's better that within the gentrification debates, some people focus more on the supply, some people focus more on the lifestyle, and some people focus more on the displacement.

EDS Among the more unique phenomena in recent years are these so-called "safe deposit box" investments. Yet what we've seen is that these kinds of investments—for example, in Vancouver or London—have also been the best performing. Do you see the transnational wealth elites as risk-averse or safety-seeking? Where is the risk in housing as an investment?

MA Different groups invest for different reasons. When we use the term "safe deposit box," we're suggesting that some very rich people are parking their money in real estate because it's convenient. It can be a tax-optimized way to do it. In some cases, it's very easy not to pay your tax when your money is parked in real estate. And for some of these investors, it's not necessarily about making a lot of money. It's about storing it safely. And these—especially if you look at these transnational wealth elites that use real estate and global cities as a safe deposit box—are very often the ones leaving these properties empty. There were reports in London about this. At night, you don't see any lights on in some streets because those homes are not inhabited. This is very different from people investing in a condo tower on the Thames or the Upper West Side, a two-bedroom flat of 80 square meters, and renting it out for thousands of dollars or pounds. That is a different thing. Those are people trying to maximize their return on investment by investing in something that they consider to be low risk. So I think there are different things here that happen alongside each other. For those very rich people who leave the properties empty, clearly the return on the investment is not the most important concern, it is just about parking the money safely—I hear that in some cases, the cost of the upkeep of the properties is so high that they might be losing money, whereas when we talk about upper middle-class investors buying expensive apartments, they want a return on investment.

EDS Before 2007, a lot of the riskier investments in housing happened in places such coastal areas in Spain, Greece or Romania—in big housing schemes that were speculative. But considering the high returns from the non-risky investments in big cities, is there still risk investment in housing?

MA Are safe, good returns available, in fact? A lot of people don't want to put their money in stocks. Stocks are down now, whereas real-estate prices are not. People say, "Now we have rising interest rates, so a mortgage loan is going to be more expensive." Housing prices might go down if it's harder to get a mortgage, but at the same time, we now see high inflation. That means real estate is considered a safe investment, stocks less so. What we've seen in recent years is that when there was a low interest rate, real estate was attractive because other investments just didn't get you anything. It's not always the case that people try to get super-high profits from real estate investments. People could realize returns on investments in housing that are somewhere between 3% and 8%, or maybe 10%. That is a very nice return but less than what stocks would give, until half a year ago. People do it because they consider housing to be a safe investment. Even investments in Spanish coastal towns, in the end, if people are able to hold out, a lot of those properties are sold in the end. Many of those prices have gone up in the meantime.

If you invest your money in places where there is a constant demand for housing, you're very likely to rent out your property for a decent price. Pension funds invest heavily through corporate landlords. Many of them promise a return on investment anywhere between 3% and 8%. Of course, if there's a global crisis, this is still risky, but then stocks will also be down. Other investments are also potentially risky. I'm not trying to underplay the riskiness of housing. I'm trying to describe how these investors think and why they consider housing, and more broadly speaking real estate, to be attractive investments.

EDS In Berlin in the 1990s, private equity investment was already happening. Yet there seems to be this renewed energy in it now, from the likes of Blackstone; it feels like they have rediscovered that there's "no floor" to the market, because rental housing supply is so constrained. Do you see a way to counter this?

MA There are ways to counter it. The former UN rapporteur on housing rights, Leilani Farha—the protagonist in the documentary *Push*[12]—has just released human rights directives on housing to tackle the financialization of housing.[13] Others have written papers on this.[14] Such actions do not necessarily mean that housing is no longer an attractive investment, but that there could be ways in which you can protect tenants better. A lot of countries don't have proper tenant protection. If I speak to people in government, I always tell them that one of the first things you have to regulate is your private rental market. The good news is it doesn't cost you. Building social housing or supporting nonprofits, community land trusts, all cost money. Regulating the private rentals is so easy and most places don't do it. It's very easy for the government to limit landlords to raising rents by no more than inflation. Even if that's all the investors are allowed to do, they can still make a profit because that means they can make as much as they did in the previous year. What are the consequences? The investors sell the properties if they are unhappy with their profits? No problem. Other investors then buy up the housing. Or they lower the prices and then people who want to buy a home can actually buy and live there themselves. Many governments want higher homeownership rates. So if they limit rent increases, it will just make rental housing less speculative.

There are also specific types of investors that try to make a quick buck, like Blackstone and some of the private equity funds, buying housing cheap and selling it for a higher price.[15] Even in a narrow definition, that's speculation. But there are also many investors that have a middle-to-long-term interest in keeping the housing on their books. Most real estate investment trusts hold housing for at least 10 years. That doesn't necessarily make them the best landlords, but it does suggest that their interest is in the long-term rental of these housing units, which also means that their interest is in getting a good return on investment through rents. They might still be interested in increasing their rents, but they're not necessarily after a quick buck because a real estate investment trust does only one thing. They may sell some of their housing and buy new properties, but by definition they want to rent out housing or other forms of real estate. Typically, a real estate investment trust does either housing *or* offices *or* malls.

Countering Financialization

EDS There is a lot of discussion about the financialization of housing focused on the role of corporate landlords. It's easy to criticize institutional ownership of real estate, but that still makes up a relatively small percentage of tenure forms. Why hasn't there been a similar backlash against earlier waves of finance-led gentrification, for example, the deregulation of finance and the expansion of home ownership incentivization, and so on?

MA Locally, there has been a backlash against this. In Berlin, people who bought apartments in gentrifying neighborhoods would get paint bombs on their windows. Berlin might be more activist than most cities, but there have been many local protests. I think what is new is that this has become a much more internationally organized protest. Whereas a Berlin homeowner is probably someone who is working in Berlin and potentially was already living there, Blackstone is doing this globally, so the actor is international. And I think the movement itself has become much more global. In the past, all these movements were very locally organized. This is also a consequence of digitization and the communication part of globalization.

One thing that's also different is that many people, politically speaking, support homeownership. So it's more difficult to organize people against the idea that homeownership would be expanding in the gentrified neighborhood. But if you say, "A global corporate landlord is buying up all the housing," a lot of people in the center, politically speaking, who would otherwise support homeownership, would say "Whoa, what's happening here?" I notice this too with right-wing politicians who are very much in favor of more homeownership: they're very much supporting state-led gentrification but are a little bit afraid of Blackstone coming.

EDS (LM) I come from a generation and context that has internalized the ideal of homeownership. Even potentially affordable rents and social housing are seen as stepping stones towards homeownership. What steps can we take to address the stigma towards social housing within this kind of context of financialization? Because it's not just a social stigma. It's also about social housing not being an *end destination* for people.

MA Well, it's partly because governments treat homeownership preferentially. If renting gives you insecurity (if renting gives you a poorly maintained home, if your landlord can kick you out or raise the rent with only a few months' notice) and if, on the other hand, your mortgage loan is being heavily subsidized by the state (for example, by people deducting their interest payments on their mortgage loans from their income), I understand why people want to be homeowners: because in most countries it gives you better conditions than renting. It gives you more security. I'm not sure that we need to get into a situation where renting is more attractive than ownership, but we need to do something. For example, a 10-year "neutral" housing policy, which does not favor homeownership.[16]

One other problem is with social housing. If it's built for the poorest of the poor, it's almost by definition going to be stigmatized. It's going to be in less attractive locations, it's going to be smaller, it's going to have less quality, it's going to have a certain look to it. Whereas if you build social housing for a larger segment of the population, it's necessarily going to be more diverse in terms of design, location, and tenant profile, which means it probably won't seem as unattractive to people.

In the Netherlands, homeownership has increased to well over 50% of the housing stock, but in the big cities, 40% of the housing stock remains social housing—it's still a very attractive option. I studied in Amsterdam and remember that by the end of my time there as a student, some of my friends were able to get into social housing and these were big victories for them, because getting into social housing was what you wanted. And this was also with an eye on the future. It was not perceived just as temporary solution for students with no or low income. If you have an attractive social housing sector, it doesn't have to be stigmatized.

We know that from studies that have looked at what kind of housing has been sold in the UK through the Right to Buy scheme, and the result is pretty obvious. On the more attractive housing estates, more people have bought their own home. In some places where Right to Buy has been very successful and most of the housing has been sold off, many people live quite happily in places that were designed as council housing. We have to rethink what we mean with social housing, who gets to live there, who doesn't, where we build it and at what quality. But I think there are many places in which social housing was built on a larger scale and where it has been relatively successful. And it's good that there still is an alternative. It's great that people can also buy their own home if they want to. Next to social housing, for instance, we should be stimulating more alternative solutions to housing, more collaborative forms of housing based on limited equity cooperatives, community land trusts, and mutual housing associations. There's a whole range of alternatives that offer ways of focusing on different income groups or a mix of different income groups. It doesn't need to be exclusively social housing.

EDS For about a century, since the beginning of the model housing of the 1840s onwards, one thing reformers and their architects constantly debated is the question of quality and quantity. When you look into these discussions, they tended always to fall back on the same solution: a compromise, which was to build for the skilled laborers. The "filtering up" idea suggests skilled laborers vacate their homes and the unskilled laborers move one tier up. The problem with this was how to build enough but also to build quality housing. And then of course once you reach that moment of universalizing social housing, this changes the dynamics of the discussion.

MA Originally, social housing was more for skilled laborers. Then it catered to a large part of the population and then, little by little, in many places, it became just for poor people. Another thing that I often tell people in government that what they can do to improve the housing market is to say to developers: "We want 25% or 30% of the housing to be affordable." That doesn't mean that we're building for the middle classes. It actually means you're building for moderate income. And what it provides is not just more affordable housing, it also gets you more of an income mix. You demand within each development that there should be a minimum percentage that should be set at a certain price. It could also be subsidized home ownership. The price could be discussed—these are all political choices. But it's very easy for a government to do. This is another way to destigmatize social housing because this housing would be within the same projects as the housing that is more expensive.

Other Forms of Financialization

EDS The period you describe as "fifth-wave gentrification" also saw the rapid increase of other financial assets. If we consider the period post the 2008 financial crisis, there was significant quantitative easing, low interest rates, easy access to capital. This led capital to be funneled into real estate but also into other assets such as tech stocks, cryptocurrency, and so on. How should we view housing financialization in relation to these other currents within the financialization of the economy?

MA Definitely, there's a wider financialization trend and real estate is not the only option. I think what makes real estate not unique but significant is that it is the biggest investment class. Investment in real estate is just bigger than anything else. If you look at real estate compared to stock-market capitalization, real estate is huge. If you look at what sovereign wealth funds and pension funds have together and compare it to real estate, the latter is still huge. Maybe some of those other options have grown faster. I mean, cryptocurrencies didn't exist 20 years ago, so of course the growth in relative numbers is much larger.

The deeper trend leading towards real estate financialization has led to other forms of financialization as well. Within my research group, we've also looked at the financialization of big tech, big pharma.[17] We're now looking into mining and energy, and we see some similar trends there. We see, for instance, in big pharma that a lot of those investments are coming from private equity funds, the same funds that are doing some of the investing in housing. Some of this has to do with a larger structural shift in the economy that has given private equity funds, hedge funds, a very specific role.

What is important here is that a lot of those investments are backed by pension funds. Pension funds' capital increases much faster per year than the total amount of money on earth, as a percentage.[18] A lot of this money is being invested through private equity funds. Private equity funds exist partially because pension funds have to put away so much money that they need to find outlets. And it's not just the case that pension funds are growing in the global north, which is definitely the case, but also that they're increasing in some middle-income countries where there is a similar pension fund system set up, whereas two decades ago, they didn't. Brazil for instance, has a significant pension fund system, and didn't have one in the past. Chile has had one for a longer period of time. But in countries like Brazil, that have growing pension funds, capital needs to be invested somewhere.

Whatever pension funds do, they almost always have to put most or all of their money in risk-averse investments. Again, we can have a discussion about whether investing in real estate is risk-averse or not, but the fact is that it seems that way to the pension funds, to the rating agencies, and to most governments, and by and large this holds up quite well. It is a good investment against inflation, as we see right now; it has a decent return on investment, which is higher than other low-risk investments. As long as this is the case, a lot of these funds are going to invest in real estate, which is called "high-quality collateral" in financial markets. There are only a few investment opportunities that are high-quality collateral and real estate is the big one.

EDS Why wasn't private equity similarly investing in real estate prior to 2008?

MA In real estate in Germany they were investing in offices, but from 2001 onwards, they began investing heavily in housing in Berlin. The private equity firms are interested in buying up large packages of housing. Such packages didn't really exist in most places before 2008. Germany was quite specific because it privatized its housing by selling off entire housing associations. That brings to the markets such packages. The largest one was 93,000 units. This was unique. There are not so many places where you can buy 93,000 units in one transaction.

And then what changed in the global financial crisis was that banks started to repossess homes, and then they had all these housing units on their books that they didn't want to keep, for good reasons, so they started to sell them off. The governments started to do the same. In specific places that were hard hit by the crisis, places like Spain and places like the US, but again, mostly states like Nevada, California, and Florida, not so much in the Midwest or the northeastern states, you then see that all of a sudden thousands of housing units were available. It's not really a mass market, but there needed to be large packages on offer. Earlier, it was much more difficult.

Some private equity firms, like Blackstone, work with smaller agents that buy units here and there, and then bring them together and sell them. And some of those agencies, some of those firms, exist only because an actor like Blackstone will buy from them. But it's not a subsidiary, it's a firm that only has one client, which will buy up the units. I think private equity firms only started doing that because they realized that though the pipeline of the large portfolios is drying up, there's still money to be made. In effect, it's a bit more complicated because it's partly a story of transaction costs. If you can buy 93,000 units in one transaction, you don't have to place many of your staff on it, but buying 93,000 individual units, that takes a lot of time, lawyers' time. It's more costly. But I think that explains why it took a while before private equity became heavily interested in housing.

EDS Manuel, thanks again for your time!

1 The interview was conducted via Zoom on June 21, 2022. Manuel Aalbers, Tahl Kaminer, and Leonard Ma were present.

2 Manuel B. Aalbers, "Revisiting 'The Changing State of Gentrification' Introduction to the Forum: From Third to Fifth-Wave Gentrification," *Tijdschrift voor Economische en Sociale Geografie* 110, no. 1 (2019): 1–11, DOI: 10.1111/tesg.12332.

3 Jason Hackworth and Neil Smith, "The Changing State of Gentrification," *Tijdschrift voor Economische en Sociale Geografie 92* (2001): 464–477.

4 Loretta Lees, Tom Slater, and Elvin Wyly, *Gentrification* (New York; London: Routledge, 2008).

5 Rodrigo Fernandez, Annelore Hofman, and Manuel B. Aalbers, "London and New York as a Safe Deposit Box for the Transnational Wealth Elite," *Environment and Planning A* 48, no. 12 (2016): 2443–461.

6 Agustin Cocola-Gant and Ana Gago: "Airbnb, Buy-to-Let Investment and Tourism-Driven Displacement: A Case Study in Lisbon," *Environment and Planning A* 53, no. 7 (2021): 1671–88.

7 Ruth Glass, "Aspects of Change" [1964], in *The Gentrification Debates: A Reader,* ed. J. Brown-Saracino (London; New York: Taylor and Francis, 2010), 19–29.

8 Neil Smith, "The Evolution of Gentrification," in *Houses in Transformation: Interventions in European Gentrification*, eds. Jaap-Jan Berg, Tahl Kaminer, Marc Schoonderbeek, and Joost Zonneveld (Rotterdam: NAi Publishers, 2008), 15–25.

9 Neil Smith, "Toward a Theory of Gentrification: A Back to the City Movement by Capital, not People," *Journal of the American Planning Association* 45, no. 4 (1979): 538–48, DOI: 10.1080/01944367908977002.

10 David Wachsmuth and Alexander Weisler, "Airbnb and the Rent Gap: Gentrification Through the Sharing Economy," *Environment and Planning A* 50, no. 6 (2018): 1147–170; Ismael Yrigoy, "Rent Gap Reloaded: Airbnb and the Shift from Residential to Touristic Rental Housing in the Palma Old Quarter in Mallorca, Spain," *Urban Studies* 56, no. 13 (2019): 2709–726.

11 Zac Taylor and Manuel B. Aalbers, "Climate Gentrification: Risk, Rent, and Restructuring in Greater Miami," *Annals of the American Association of Geographers* 112, no. 6 (2022): 1685–701.

12 *Push*, directed by Fredrik Gertten (WG Film, 2019), 1 hour 32 minutes. https://vimeo.com/ondemand/pushthefilm.

13 "Make the Shift," accessed September 19, 2022, https://make-the-shift.org.

14 Some examples: #housing2030, "Effective policies for affordable housing in the UNECE region," last modified October, 2021, https://www.housing2030.org/reports/; and Daniela Gabor and Sebastian Kuhl, "My Home is an Asset Class: Study About the Financialization of Housing in Europe" (The Greens/EFA in the European Parliament, 2022), https://www.greens-efa.eu/en/article/document/my-home-is-an-asset-class. See also: Gertjan Wijburg, "The De-Financialization of Housing: Towards a Research Agenda," *Housing Studies* 36, no. 8 (2021): 1276–293; Michelle Norris and Julie Lawson, "Tools to Tame the Financialisation of Housing," *New Political Economy* (2022): 1–17.

15 Desiree Fields and Sabine Uffer, "The Financialisation of Rental Housing: A Comparative Analysis of New York City and Berlin," *Urban Studies* 53, no. 7 (2016): 1486–502.

16 A housing policy that avoids nudging citizens towards a particular tenure through directed incentives and disincentives (the editors).

17 Tobias J. Klinge, Rodrigo Fernandez, and Manuel B. Aalbers, "The Financialization of Big Pharma," *Revista Internacional de Sociología*, 78, no. 2 (2020), DOI: 10.3989/ris.2020.78.4.m20.006; Tobias J. Klinge, Reijer Hendrikse, Rodrigo Fernandez, and Ilke Adriaans, "Augmenting Digital Monopolies: A Corporate Financialization Perspective on the Rise of Big Tech," *Competition & Change* (June 20, 2022), DOI: 10.1177/10245294221105573.

18 Rodrigo Fernandez and Manuel B. Aalbers, "Financialization and Housing: Between Globalization and Varieties of Capitalism," *Competition & Change* 20, no. 2 (2016): 71–88.

I.
AMSTERDAM

“Creative” Regeneration and the Dissipation of Amsterdam’s Suburbs

Tahl Kaminer

> Not only is Amsterdam one of the creativity project's most receptive and resonant locations, it has also become one of many "translation spaces" between the generic model of creative growth, qua model, and adaptive regimes of European urban governance.
> —Jamie Peck[1]

In the 1970s, the municipalities of Western cities were faced with an unfamiliar crisis in their inner cities for which they were unprepared and lacked "oven ready" solutions: the de-industrialization of the inner cities in the postwar years had led to growing deprivation, falling real-estate values, population shrinkage, rising crime, and physical dilapidation. By this era, wholesale slum clearances common in the postwar years were no longer acceptable, and heritage and resident groups mounted increasingly successful opposition to the demolition of pre-twentieth-century buildings. Government retrenchment, initially the result of an economic downturn ("stagflation") and later as a result of monetarist policies and "roll-back neoliberalism,"[2] further limited the options available to municipalities.

Consequently, municipalities experimented with new forms of urban regeneration. Among the "trial and error" remedies applied by cities were large-scale, commercial projects, such as the development of city-center shopping malls, convention centers, and sports or performance arenas, in support of which municipalities could pool their limited resources in the hope that these would trigger a "snowball effect." "Theme park urbanism," including branding certain central areas as, for example, "cultural quarters," were likewise rolled out, and since the 1992 Barcelona Olympics, "mega events" were leveraged for ambitious regeneration projects. But a more sophisticated and pernicious culturally infused form of regeneration gradually emerged from cities in northern Europe. Arguably, three key conditions could be found in these cities: strong planning, in a sense that either never existed or had been eroded in other Western countries; relatively small gaps between rich and poor; and enough resources, despite their overall contraction, to allow municipalities to invest more in regeneration than other Western counterparts could.

In the 2000s, Amsterdam became the face of this form of culturally infused regeneration. From Richard Florida's "creative class" to Charles Landry's "creative cities," and from Neil Smith's discussion of Amsterdam's squatters to Jamie Peck's critique of the "creative" narrative,[3] Amsterdam has been at the fore of these discussions ever since, even while similar forms of regeneration could be found in other Dutch, Danish, or Swedish cities. This section of *Urbanizing Suburbia* documents and critiques the mutation and diversification of "cultural" regeneration in the 2010s, following and in response to the financial crisis of 2008. It

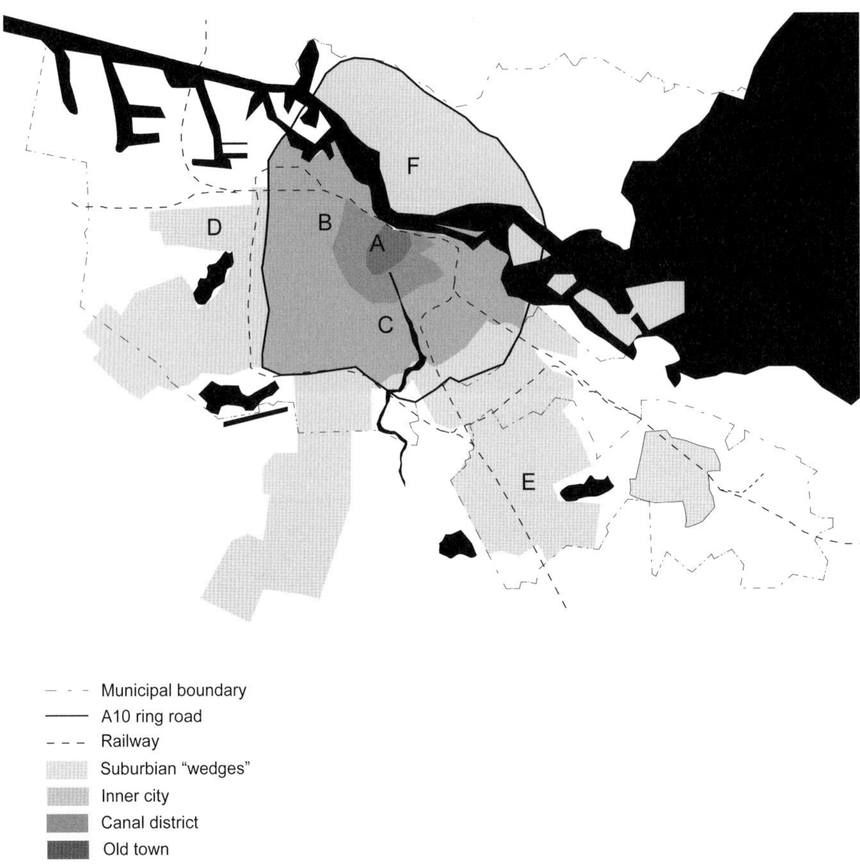

Figure 1: A map of Amsterdam showing the "wedge" shape of the built up area. A. Old town; B. Inner-city Jordaan neighborhood; C. Inner-city Pijp; D. The Western Garden Suburbs of the Nieuw-West; E. Bijlmer; F. Noord. Map by the author.

highlights the city's decision to eliminate its suburbs by increasing outer-city densities, reducing car dependency, scaling town centers, changing the tenure balance and demographics, altering the live/work ratio, and introducing "urban" morphologies and typologies—moves that spell, in effect, the end to Amsterdam's suburbs.

This introductory chapter offers a critical study of the recent application of "creative-led" regeneration, which was initially developed as an inner-city remedy, to Amsterdam's suburbs. As such, the chapter sets the stage for the section by providing an overview of housing and regeneration in Amsterdam over the decades, identifying the development of forms of "creative" regeneration in the inner city in the 1990s, and discussing the application of those strategies to Amsterdam's suburbs in the 2000s and particularly the 2010s. It ends by interrogating recent policy changes that deliberately target the suburbs for radical overhaul—and in effect, for eradication.

Alternative City

In the postwar years, Amsterdam (Figure 1), like other Western cities, was subjected to Fordist forms of development, redevelopment, and regeneration, including: the development of sprawling suburbs in the Nieuw-West (New West) in the 1940s and 50s, based on van Eesteren's original plan from the early 1930s, or the experiments in the Bijlmer in the city's southeast in the 1970s; demolitions in the inner city; and the carving of arteries for traffic east of the Amstel River. While the new suburbs were being realized, the municipality's concerns increasingly focused on the inner city, with its loss of population, dilapidated housing, and overall decline.

Resistance to postwar redevelopment and regeneration emerged relatively early in Amsterdam, with the Provo movement of 1965–66 being the first significant manifestation of opposition to the dominance of the car and technocratic planning processes.[4] Provo and its successor, the Kabouters, radical as they were in the late-1960s, provided an early articulation of a form of urbanism which would become hegemonic. "[T]he inner-city districts should retain their typically urban and social character," said at the time Provo founder Roel van Duijn. "Despite their dilapidated nature, [...] they are more livable than suburbs."[5]

The 1970s placed Amsterdam at the center of the burgeoning international counter culture, due to the city's tolerance of alternative lifestyles. In the mid-1970s, squatters spearheaded the fierce struggle against the demolition of the central Nieuwmarkt area for the construction of a metro line, a struggle that pushed tensions between the municipality and grassroot organizations into outright adversity. The protests were followed in 1981 with clashes between the police and squatters over the planned demolitions in Waterlooplein, an area located at the eastern corner of the city center.

Between the mid-1970s and the mid-1980s, and in response to the demands of protest groups, tighter controls were created to prevent speculation in housing, subjugating all rental tenures to controls and, in effect, de-commodifying the free-market rental sector while expanding the provision of social housing. Rents and rent rises were thus controlled and tenure protections strengthened. Social housing was considered a universal right and made available to the middle class as well as the working class and poor.[6] During this period, the Kabouters and their allies brought about a shift in municipal priorities and policies, and particularly in practices of urban redevelopment and regeneration.[7] Several plans for new metro lines were put on hold. "Compact city" ideas came to dominate municipal urban approaches; accompanied by an emphasis on city-center living, this signaled an early acceptance of the arguments of the nascent "back to the city" movement.

Inner-city working-class neighborhoods such as the Jordaan had lost population in the previous decades and their housing stock was considered dilapidated. These areas were devalued, creating a rent gap. The Jordaan's gentrification kicked off hesitantly in the late 1960s through the arrival of young "alternative" newcomers and their bohemian lifestyles.[8] Heritage advocates from 1960 onwards actively battled comprehensive redevelopment by purchasing and renovating housing, including through a foundation focused on buying and renovating homes for artists' accommodation. "In the period of 1960–90," write urban historians Tim Verlaan and Aimée Albers about the success of the protest groups, "... gentrification was to a large extent the ultimate consequence of citizen protests against comprehensive urban redevelopment."[9] The tight controls of the housing market limited the speed and extent of gentrification until it was incorporated into regeneration policy in the 1990s. Until then, gentrification was primarily focused on devalued inner-city areas with a relatively high percentage of free-market rental homes.

"Creative" Regeneration

Amsterdam's municipality, then, adapted its approaches to accommodate the logic and demands of the urban protestors of the 1960s and 1970s: demolitions within the inner city were minimized; respect for heritage increased; a "back to the city" process was supported through policy; a focus on densification and *the compact city* replaced the traffic-centric, dispersal-focused Fordist logic; and comprehensive urban regeneration was replaced by more "delicate" forms of urban intervention. Beginning with the 1989 Housing Policy, central government in the Hague began pursuing an increase in the number of owner-occupiers and the residualization of social housing. Its policies and ideas gradually impacted Amsterdam in the 1990s and 2000s.[10]

The bulk of housing in Amsterdam was owned by housing associations, many of which were originally founded in the late nineteenth century as professional associations and later became a key organ for delivering government housing policies and targets. These housing behemoths became market-based non-profits in the 1990s, selling social housing units as a means of funding new build and refurbishments. Their overall regulation and control by government was sharply reduced, yet, in comparison to similar organizations in the UK, they are today still significantly larger, more powerful, and work in closer collaboration with local government. In effect, no substantial regeneration project can be undertaken without close collaboration and agreement between the municipality, local boroughs, and the housing associations. By 2001, social tenure was down by around 10% compared to a decade earlier, yet at 54% of all housing it still formed the majority of Amsterdam’s housing stock, compared to 32% private rental and 14% owner-occupied.[11]

Whereas redevelopment projects such as the Holland Casino in the city center experimented with commercially focused development as a means of attracting investment, inner-city regeneration took another shape. The regeneration of Staatsliedenbuurt in Amsterdam’s Old West in the 1990s, for example, addressed an area notorious at the time for its deprivation, dilapidation, and rowdy squats. The regeneration included refurbishment of the existing housing stock as well as new build. The squats that were perceived to be troublemakers were removed, whereas others, which were key local hubs for cultural activities, were left untouched. The regeneration thus produced incremental change, yet the change was substantial enough to alter the neighborhood’s demographics and trajectory by improving its reputation and attracting middle-class families. In this process, the extant squats not only offered a certain continuity to the area, but also guaranteed cultural programming and vitality.

Through such experiences, a “cultural component” entered regeneration plans, and this took diverse forms, ranging from municipal investment in a cultural institution to temporary subsidies or grants for local cultural organizations that were awarded by the borough or by developers, from temporary studios for artists to the funding of one-off large-scale art or cultural projects. Such investments in cultural activities brought vitality and cultural content to areas of regeneration. They attracted a middle-class cultural elite, whether in the form of artists working or residing in the area or art connoisseurs visiting the neighborhood’s art or cultural events. The cultural elite brought its cultural capital and contributed to increased positive media coverage of the neighborhood, aiding in overturning negative perceptions and stigma. The “discoveries” of the potency of culture and “creatives” in transforming cities were trumpeted in a 2002 publication by the Dutch Ministry of Housing and Spatial Planning (VROM), titled *Creative Cities!*.[12]

The housing associations, in turn, were responsible for refurbishing the housing stock. In the process, they were permitted to reduce the overall amount of social housing in a regeneration area, selling units to raise funds for investments. In many of the cases, the reduction in social housing was not significant enough to instigate a backlash—in the regeneration of the inner-city Indischebuurt in east Amsterdam, which kicked off in 2003–04, for example, social housing was reduced from 87% to 70%, an amount substantial enough to alter the area's demographics and yet small enough to avoid mass protest. Tellingly, it was the original plan to demolish two early twentieth-century blocks designed by Hendrik Berlage that generated protest and the squatting of these buildings.[13] Again and again, the argument by the Amsterdam municipality and boroughs was that the reduction in social housing was aimed at creating a better social mix. "[S]ocial mix," wrote geographer Wouter van Gent, "is a vision of place by governing elites rather than that of residents . . . focused on nurturing a new middle class."[14] The reduction in provision of social housing was typically carried out by the sale of social housing and therefore was, in effect, tenure conversion. Needless to say that the requirement for a better social mix was never directed to the more affluent neighborhoods.[15]

A program that attracted significant attention abroad was the municipality's Broedplaats ("breeding grounds") program. Officially, the program helped to create dozens of "cultural incubators" around the city—organizations offering spaces for design and artists' studios and cultural programming. It was launched without much fuss in the late 1990s. One of its original, unstated aims, it could be argued, was to resolve the problem of squats, which were tolerated and yet illegal, through a municipal program that legalized them. In the long run,[16] the program helped protect the city's cultural vibrancy in the 2000s and 2010s, decades in which rents rocketed and squatting was criminalized (2010). More specifically, Broedplaats were often supported in areas of regeneration and redevelopment, as in the case of the NDSM in Amsterdam Noord (North), in effect a component of such projects.

The publication of *The Rise of the Creative Class* and Florida's keynote talk at an Amsterdam conference in 2003 heralded a more hands-on approach to culture and creativity by the municipality, including an assimilation of Florida's approach, rationale, and language (culture as key to urban competitiveness and focus on economic benefits of creativity) through a string of policies and publications.[17] Much of this, though, according to geographer Jamie Peck, was hot air and rhetoric: the sums actually invested in culture by the city were small and the leverage and impact of the "creative" policies were limited. If the Broedplaats were, as argued above, initiated primarily to resolve the illegality of squats, and the processes of "cultural" regeneration were indeed initially conceived as a pragmatic solution to specific situations and conditions, then it becomes clear that these forms of "creative" city policies were only later identified as a model to emulate—once someone like Florida could articulate such an understanding.

Culture, then, ranging from "lifestyle" to art, was fully integrated into Amsterdam municipality's regeneration policies and practices. It was part of a process that included the curtailing of social housing, upping the real estate values of homes, and "middle-classing" deprived neighborhoods. Art and culture were shielded from the excesses of the market through diverse supports, appreciated not only for their cultural capital but also for their "sweat equity," social capital, and impact on demographics. Squatters, in the emerging "creative" narrative of the 2000s, were seen as the city's saviors, through their choice of occupying city-center buildings in an era in which the middle class fled; through their cultivation of cultural and "creative" activities; and through their contribution to the battle against demolitions. Subsequently, with squatting criminalized in the 2010s, its history was coopted by a quasi-official, convenient narrative of urban renaissance—the adversity and tensions of a previous era now willfully forgotten.

The Outer City

The success of the "back to the city" movement and its backers became visible by the early 2000s in the influx of capital (in the form of investments in properties) and the middle class to the inner city. Data from 2002 shows that those in cultural and "creative" fields of employment (e.g., media, architecture, advertising) in Amsterdam primarily resided in the city center or inner city, whereas middle-class employees in fields such as IT and accounting resided in suburbia or in commuter towns, confirming extant stereotypes of city versus suburbs.[18]

With the crisis of inner-city neighborhoods resolved or en route to resolution, and with mounting pressures to address housing shortages and rocketing housing prices in the 2000s, the city increasingly began paying more attention to its suburbs. Earlier regeneration projects in the 1970s and 1980s in the suburbs had increased the amount of social housing in these areas.[19] The immigrant population of these neighborhoods grew during this period. The high proportion of immigrants and social housing stigmatized suburbs such as the Nieuw-West and Bijlmer. Bijlmer, in particular, had been an ongoing concern for the city, never quite receding from vision, its troubles exacerbated by the disaster of the 1992 El Al airplane crash (the *Bijlmerramp*).

The main difference between the regeneration projects of the inner city in the 1990s and 2000s and those of the suburbs in the 2000s and 2010s was demolitions: in contrast to inner-city regeneration, the demolition of postwar housing estates was a key feature of the suburban regeneration plans. Nowhere has this been more visible than in the Bijlmer, in which the honeycomb behemoths of the 1970s have been systematically demolished and replaced with "respectable" terraced housing and the like.

In the Nieuw-West, the "garden city suburbs" regeneration projects of the 2000s included demolitions, new build, and refurbishment (Figure 2)—and a reduction of the overall proportion of social housing. In effect, the same remedies that had been applied to the inner city, including the cultural component, were now being applied to the suburban belt, despite the differences in location, demographics, and overall character—and despite

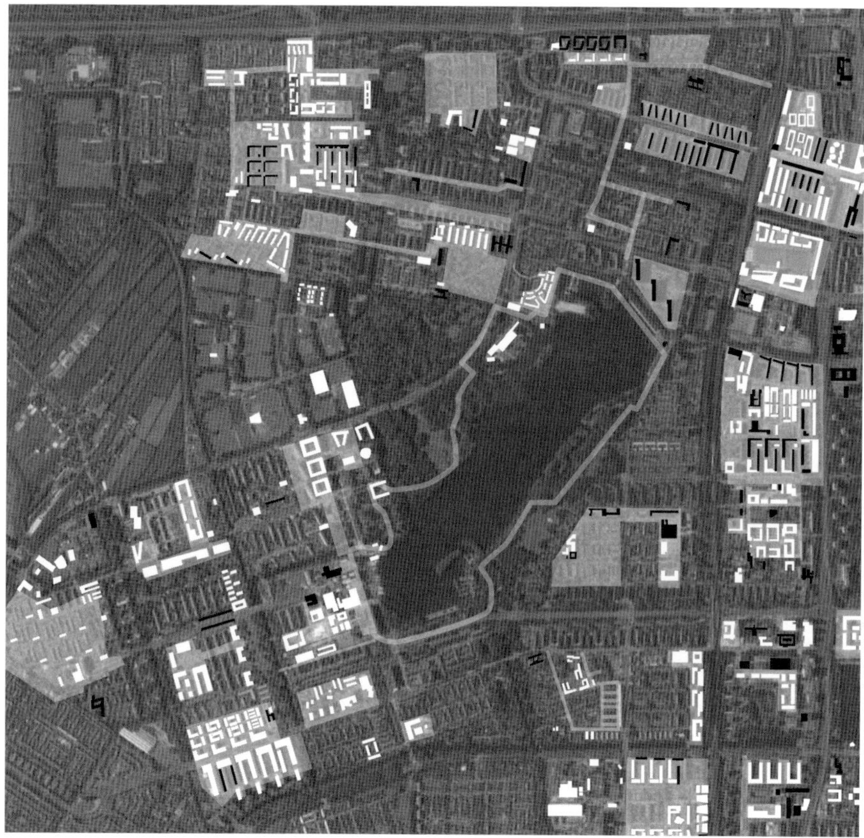

Figure 2: Urban renewal in Amsterdam's Nieuw-West, 2000–21: in black, refurbished buildings; in white, new build; refurbished public spaces in light translucency.

Drawn by T. Kaminer based on a map by MUST Urbanism, published in: Maurits de Hoog and Anouk de Wit (eds.) *SuperWest 2000-2021: Vernieuwing van de Amsterdamse Tuinsteden* (Bussum: Uitgeverij Thoth, 2022). By kind permission of Maurits de Hoog. Aerial photograph © Google, 2022 Aerodata International Surveys, CNES/Airbus, Landsat/Copernicus, Maxar Technologies.

the concentration of cultural-sector employees and connoisseurs in the inner city. A new typology, named the "hybrid complex," was introduced through the regeneration, whereby, for instance, a café, library, neighborhood center, and social housing could occupy a single building. In 2000, social housing in the Nieuw-West comprised 65% of the area's total housing stock; by 2021, and as a result of the renewal projects, it comprised only 49%.[20]

Ambitious plans were being made in the 2000s for sleepy Amsterdam Noord, located on the northern bank of the body of water called the IJ. Initially, these plans replicated the type of regeneration projects familiar from the inner city: new build and refurbished housing delivered by the housing associations, a reduction in social tenure "to improve the social mix" (basically, a high percentage of free-market housing aimed at "young professional families," the same demographic that was the focus of much inner-city regeneration), a cultural component (the relocation of the Film Museum from the center to Noord), improvements to infrastructure (first-and-foremost a new metro line), new-build offices close to transport connections, and so on.

The financial crisis of 2007–08 brutally disrupted some of these plans. A key housing association in the Nieuw-West faced bankruptcy. Funding was no longer available. Plans and projects were frozen. The city faced years of uncertainty and stagnation, of delayed and cancelled projects. Subsequently, the municipality showed a new openness to doing things differently, arguably as a means of progressing urban redevelopment within the constraints of the crisis and its aftermath. One innovation was a self-build program (in Dutch, *collectief particulier opdrachtgeverschap* (CPO)), which satisfied different demands: a desire to make sure housing construction continued despite the housing associations' financial difficulties; a local campaign by middle-class residents to facilitate self-build; and general support for self-build and ownership by central government. The new CPOs as well as other programs—including the Broedplaats—were a means of attracting non-conventional investments at a moment in which the more regular streams dried up. The economic rationale of a post-2008 regeneration project was emphasized. A new tier of housing tenure was introduced in 2017: "intermediate," which is similar to the British "affordable housing." New build was expected to provide 40% social housing, 40% intermediate, and 20% free market.

The photo-essay "Integrating Amsterdam Noord" in this volume provides a documentation of Noord in 2022, highlighting the radicality of these changes. Less visible by 2022 was the quirkiness of the regeneration projects of the 2010s, which cranked up the "creative" component to 11, becoming a caricature of sorts. One example is the case of Shell's Overhoeks Tower, a landmark on the northern bank of the IJ, part of the area vacated by the energy company. A group of investors linked to the summer music festival circuit converted this 80-meter-high office tower into the A'dam Tower, housing music-industry offices, creatives, a hotel, and a gym. A revolving restaurant was added, as well as an observation deck with swings at the top (see page 309), which contribute a quirky, "over-the-top," brash, and trashy twist to the development. Another quirky development was the de Ceuvel area. Originally a contaminated former shipyard, it was developed into an area of creatives' studios and a major café through a tender as part of the Broedplaats program; as with the Shell Tower, relying on private investors beyond the typical developers. The redevelopment avoided expensive de-contamination of the land, and instead introduced elevated jetties with the studios located in grounded boats. The café and its environment were designed and built to resemble the look and ambience of a squat—like the Shell Tower, the sought-after expression was one of excess and make-believe. The Tolhuistuin, a cultural center located in a postwar building which had formally housed the Shell research center, is right across the IJ from Amsterdam Central Station, near the ferry pier; it came into being following Shell's relocation and was supported by city funding. To exacerbate the excess, numerous "creatives" were recruited to occupy vacated buildings during the interim period of regeneration, to the extent that certain parts of Noord in the 2010s appeared to be overrun by young artists and designers. All this turned the regeneration of Noord into an extreme version of the more familiar and subtle "creative-led" regeneration.

The project, at the time, also reeked of panic—of a worry that the "tried and tested" regeneration model may have run out of steam post-2008. To a degree, such panic could be expected in the aftermath of the financial meltdown and in light of the limited funding available for new build and for culture. It may also reflect, however, the emergence of doubts regarding the prowess of culture as a motor of change. As Peck demonstrated, Amsterdam's much lauded "creative" policies received relatively minor funding. Hard evidence regarding their impact has been difficult to come by. The political atmosphere circa 2010 certainly did not provide confidence: the coalition government, headed by the neoliberal

VVD party and supported by the ultra-right PVV of Geert Wilders, targeted the cultural budget for sweeping cuts and accompanied this by the type of derogatory comments and hyperbole more typical of the American "culture wars," indicating, in effect, that culture and its funding were not necessarily still within the Dutch consensus. Throughout the Netherlands, funding for the arts was substantially reduced—a shift that impacted art and cultural institutions, cultural-producers, and communities alike. Amsterdam Noord's almost comic excess, in this context, certainly betrays a lack of confidence, if not outright trepidation.

The End of Suburbs?

The 2010s, then, brought some confusion to what had seemed a robust process of regeneration and encouraged skepticism towards the "creativity" narrative. The regeneration model developed for the inner city was now applied to the suburban belt with only marginal "corrections" to account for the different settings. Cool cafés and boutique hotels, pop-up beaches and "meanwhile" shops began emerging outside the A10 ring road—the boundary separating the inner from the outer city.

Amsterdam's *Vision 2050* was published in 2021, following its ratification by the municipality.[21] The document discloses the plans and thoughts of the city's planners and councilors regarding Amsterdam's trajectory and future form. A major policy shift announced in the document—one that suggests a reconceptualization of the city—is the move away from a centric towards a polycentric city. Such a reconceptualization entails a shift from a "roll out from the center" approach, which drove the application of inner-city solutions to the suburbs in the 2000s and 2010s, to the idea of neighborhoods' internal logic as the major driver of their own development.

In this document, the city rejects future spatial expansion, meaning that no new urban extensions, whether suburban or not, are to be realized in coming decades. The current boundaries of the built areas will remain as they are. Throughout the document, the suburban belt is repeatedly identified as the focus for growth, for housing supply and generally for change. "Back to the city" is absent, suggesting that this particular project has been completed. "Most new developments will take place in the Nieuw-West, Noord and Zuidoost," announces the document.[22] The suburbs will absorb some of the tourism infrastructure to reduce pressures on the center. More workplaces will be created near suburban district centers and the larger rail stations surrounding Amsterdam, and areas with inner-city live/work ratios will be developed in the suburbs.[23]

In effect, the vision suggests that the outer city will densify and hence urbanize. Its tenures and demographics will change as a result of the city's "social mix" policies; their morphologies and typologies will change in order to increase densities—less detached and semi-detached housing, more multi-unit residential buildings, perhaps perimeter blocks; densities will go up, whereas live/work ratios will go down. Suburban centers will become more substantial. There will be less car dependency. Consequently, without spatial expansion but with a densifying outer city, what will emerge over time is an Amsterdam with fewer and fewer low-density suburbs, as the outer city transforms into an area with inner-city densities and characteristics. The *Vision 2050* document prescribes the death of Amsterdam's suburbs.

Such a "suburban eradication" approach should be seen not as a radical shift in policy, but as an enhancement of an approach that has animated Amsterdam's planners since the adoption of *the compact city* doctrine at the end of the 1970s. Yet until the 2000s or 2010s, focus had been placed on inner-city infill and the reuse or redevelopment of inner-city brownfields and ex-industrial complexes and buildings, as in the cases of the Entrepotdok, the KNSM/Java islands, and Borneo Sporenburg. Now that the outer city is the focus of densification, however, the consequences of the urbanization of suburbia are becoming visible, and their relation to *the compact city* doctrine is clearer.

The interviews in this section with Paco Bunnik and Flora Nycolaas, planners within the municipality's Planning and Sustainability Department, interrogate the *Vision 2050* document and shed light on the thoughts from inside the municipality itself regarding the last decade and the new trajectory. Nycolaas argues that residents interested in low-density, car-dependent forms of habitation have many such areas to choose from in the Netherlands—Amsterdam does not need to be one of them. Bunnik focuses on the regeneration of Noord, whereas Nycolaas on the Nieuw-West. Timothy Moore's contribution to this section takes a closer look at Amsterdam Noord and specifically studies a local Broedplaats, the Tolhuistuin, which came into being with the regeneration, whereas the photo-essay "Integrating Amsterdam Noord" documents the radicality of Amsterdam Noord's makeover.

This chapter has discussed the emergence of a particular form of urban regeneration that was tailored for Amsterdam's inner-city neighborhoods, aspects of which have been mythologized by the city council and distant admirers. The application of inner-city remedies to the outer city should be understood within the context of a broader trajectory whereby monofunctional, low-density suburbs are transformed into areas resembling the inner city. Nycolaas and Bunnik both highlight a recent change in thought in the municipality, moving away from the "roll out from the center" approach that animated regeneration projects in the suburbs during the 2010s towards one in which the future transformation of suburban areas will be guided by their own internal logical—the premise of a newly adopted polycentric city model. Yet, by now, so much has already been put in motion, that the transition of Amsterdam into a "suburbless"—even if polycentric—city may be inevitable.

1 Jamie Peck, "Recreative City: Amsterdam, Vehicular Ideas and the Adaptive Spaces of Creativity Policy," *International Journal of Urban and Regional Research* 36, no. 3 (2012): 464, DOI: 10.1111/j.1468-2427.2011.01071.x.

2 Jamie Peck and Adam Tickell, "Neoliberalizing Space," in *Spaces of Neoliberalism: Urban Restructuring in North America and Western Europe*, eds. Neil Brenner and Nik Theodore (Oxford: Blackwell, 2002), 33–57.

3 Richard Florida, *The Rise of the Creative Class: and How It's Transforming Work, Leisure, Community and Everyday Life* (New York: Basic Books, 2002); Charles Landry, *The Creative City: A Toolkit for Urban Innovators* (London; Sterling, VA: Earthscan; New Stroud, UK: Comedia, 2008); Neil Smith, *The New Urban Frontier: Gentrification and the Revanchist City* (London; New York: Routledge, 1996); Jamie Peck, "Recreative City."

4 The Provo movement is particularly remembered for its White Bicycle plan, proposing free bikes to city residents. Richard Kempton, *Provo: Amsterdam's Anarchist Revolt* (New York: Autonomedia, 2007).

5 Harm Kaal, "A Conceptual History of Livability," *City* 15, no. 5 (2011): 539, DOI: 10.1080/13604813.2011.595094.

6 Justus Uitermark, "An Actually Existing Just City? The Fight for the Right to the City in Amsterdam," in *Cities for People, Not for Profit: Critical Urban Theory and the Right to the City*, eds. Neil Brenner, Peter Marcuse, and Margit Mayer (Oxford: Blackwell, 2011), 197–214.

7 Kaal, "A Conceptual History of Livability"; Smith, *The New Urban Frontier*, 165.

8 Tim Verlaan & Aimée Albers, "From Hippies to Yuppies: Marginal Gentrification in Amsterdam's Jordaan and De Pijp Neighbourhoods 1960–1990," *City* 26, no. 2–3 (2022): 496–518, DOI: 10.1080/13604813.2022.2054223; Smith, *The New Urban Frontier*, 168.

9 Verlaan and Albers, "From Hippies to Yuppies": 498.

10 Hugo Priemus, "How to Abolish Social Housing? The Dutch Case," *International Journal ofUrban and Regional Research* 19, no. 1 (1995): 145–55; Uitermark, "An Actually Existing Just City?," 206.

11 Sako Musterd, "Amsterdam as a Creative Cultural Knowledge City: Some Conditions," *Built Environment* 30, no. 3 (2004): 233.

12 Zef Hemel, *Creatieve steden!* (The Hague: VROM, 2002). See also Peck, "Recreative City."

13 The agreement reached with the squatters preserved the blocks as student housing–a major boost to gentrification through increasing the number of middle-class residents and preserving heritage.

14 W.P.C. van Gent, "Neoliberalization, Housing Institutions and Variegated Gentrification: How the 'Third Wave' Broke in Amsterdam," *International Journal of Urban and Regional Research* 37, no. 2 (March 2013): 507.

15 Willem R. Boterman and Wouter P.C. van Gent, "Housing Liberalisation and Gentrification: The Social Effects of Tenure Conversions in Amsterdam," *Tijdschrift voor economische en sociale geografie* 105, no. 2 (2014): 140–60.

16 See also Peck, "Recreative City": 468.

17 Peck, "Recreative City."

18 Musterd, "Amsterdam as a Creative Cultural Knowledge City": 229–30.

19 Kaal, "A Conceptual History of Livability."

20 Maurits de Hoog and Anouk de Wit (eds.) *SuperWest: Vernieuwing van de Amsterdamse Tuinsteden* (Amsterdam: Thoth, 2022), 20–21.

21 Gemeente Amsterdam, "Omgevingsvisie Amsterdam 2050: Een menselijke metropool" (Amsterdam: Gemeente, 2021).

22 Amsterdam, "Omgevingsvisie Amsterdam 2050," 75, my translation.

23 Amsterdam, "Omgevingsvisie Amsterdam 2050," 53.

The View from the City: Amsterdam Noord, Self-Build, and Broedplaats

An Interview with Paco Bunnik

Paco Bunnik (PB) *Tahl Kaminer (TK)*

Paco Bunnik is the lead urban designer at the Planning and Sustainability Department of the City of Amsterdam. He has been involved in the regeneration of Amsterdam Noord and developed the master plan for Buiksloterham.

TK The first thing I'd like to start with is the history of the regeneration of Amsterdam Noord. The plans were in place before the 2007–08 crisis, and then the crisis put things on hold and reset everything. Do you recall how those earlier plans emerged and how the crisis impacted them?

PB If you allow me, I'll take a step further back, because originally Amsterdam Noord used to be open waterfront. All the ships sailed out to the sea, and the north was non-existent, under water. Slowly it was turned into agricultural land for feeding the growing city. And then, in the age of industrialization at the end of the nineteenth century, the north was all industry. It was just farmland, no buildings, nothing. Criminals were hanged here, that was the only thing happening in Noord. The gallows were opposite the waterfront. So the south of the river IJ was all harbor and Noord was industry. And then, slowly, industry began to move west and the harbor moved out. But during that era, industry was connected to the "garden hamlets" (*tuindorpen*) in the north. Garden hamlets in the sense that they were low-rise, characterized by sloping roofs, and green, but at the time these were laborers' dwellings. Except for these factory or shipyard laborers, nobody wanted to live in Noord.

Once the heavy industry disappeared, the area combined more elements, such as suburban housing for lower-income people, or industrial estates for garages, workshops, and light industry. The regeneration started with the waterfront. Opposite the Central Station, Shell had a large waterfront area. Shell moved and enabled the redevelopment. We made it a mixture of housing and culture, with the new Film Museum. So then, slowly, the city "leaped" over the IJ to the north.

TK The relocation of Shell was vital. Was that purely an internal decision of Shell driven by the company's needs or achieved through negotiation with the city?

PB I think it was a negotiation. A real estate developer was initially involved, but then it went bankrupt, and the city stepped in with a new plan. All this made the negotiation more complicated. Instead of a one-on-one private-led development, it became a more standard big city plan. The city started to rethink the whole North waterfront. It made plans, started to develop, and build. And then indeed, as you said, the crisis came, but before the crisis there was already an ongoing debate in the city. Remember, the north was non-existent for people living elsewhere in Amsterdam. Nobody went there to do anything, but slowly it became more popular. The people who lived there for dozens of years felt like, "Oh no, the money is coming and the city is coming"—though that was already happening for a longer period before the crisis. The debate was about gentrification.

TK Caused by the housing crisis in the inner city?

PB Also by the change of character of Noord because it is like a village, and the residents start to feel that, "Okay, now the big city is coming and the identity of the area is changing," and many people didn't like the changes.

TK And a lot of the newcomers were young professional families?

PB Definitely. It's a standard kind of regeneration and gentrification discussion. But then the economic crisis came, and the whole city was in standstill, no construction anymore from 2007–09. The city itself started to think about re-starting through self-build communities [CPOs].[1] And then the city sold property or leased land to groups to self-develop their own homes or co-housing.

The city itself initiated the self-build program. We wanted to keep on developing the city. But maybe it's a combination of media and people wanting something and taking initiative. There were around 30 places where you could self-build in the city. In Houthavens, on the south waterfront, a plot would go for 200,000 euros, while a similar plot in Noord would be 75,000 euros. You can see the opportunity: it would be a row of houses in the middle of nothing, but it was very popular. It was like a lottery: first come, first served. For the first batch [of self-build plots], people hired students to camp for a week or so to be first in queue. It started with self-build single-family terraced houses, but then the crisis went on and on for a few years, and the city expanded the program to include other kinds of housing such as co-housing, and architects reinvented themselves as half-developer/half-architects and as residential building groups.

TK Some of these projects, such as the self-build CPOs, co-housing, and the Shell Tower all involved not the typical developers but residents or, in the case of the Shell Tower, music industry investors.

PB The city said, "What shall we do with that tower?" Because it was abandoned and it's on the most beautiful spot. And it said, "Okay, you can buy it for one euro, but then you have to provide a good plan as to how to develop the tower program-wise, finance-wise, and in terms of what the tower gives back to the city." I think six or seven plans competed, and the party that won was indeed from the music industry. The creative entrepreneurs were from the summer dance festival industry. They grew up as kids in Amsterdam Noord. So they really had a connection with that area.

TK Then you have the case of de Ceuvel, the space for creatives and a café in Noord. I understand it was a contaminated area and this was a self-initiated proposal.

PB Well, de Ceuvel is in the same area where the self-build homes were developed, the bachelor homes, a project I supervised. It was also a competition by the city for a sort of green-tech hub. So it was not exactly the group's own initiative, but their reaction to the city's competition brief.

They came up with the best plan and they became a really important incubator for new sustainable approaches and also for urban development.

TK: To what extent were these three examples (the self-build program, the Shell–A'dam–Tower, and de Ceuvel) in fact solutions to the crisis condition?

PB Originally, the self-builds were very successful, but not large in number. We're talking about a few hundred homes in total, when we made a mass plan for 8,000 homes. Once we were out of the crisis, many big, standard developers and housing associations entered the field again, but we tried to protect the values that were created during the financial crisis, because what had happened was quite innovative. And the quality of building was very high because the self-build was not a commercial enterprise. The program also produced innovative buildings for working and living, models that are now applied in the new plan.

TK I am curious about the application of regeneration strategies, which were originally developed for inner-city neighborhoods such as Staatsliedenbuurt in the 1990s, to outer city areas such as Noord. To what extent have they evolved or changed to accommodate the suburban conditions?

PB Historically, the city evolved in two periods. In the first, the city extended from one central point. In the second, you get the A10 ring road and beyond. Everything outside of the A10 was not popular with the young urban professionals. But now it's quite popular to live outside the ring because it is less overcrowded. More recently, there has been a paradigm shift in thinking of Amsterdam as a polycentric rather than centric city, also in residents' mental perception. This shift, I think, is really a good, healthy one. It's a more balanced kind of arrangement now, and it's not just Amsterdam but the whole metropolitan region that is starting to develop into a clearer, better balanced system.

TK To what extent has the regeneration introduced more urban morphologies and typologies to Noord? Considering the city is not planning urban extensions but is densifying its suburbs, does the *Vision 2050* plan not spell the end of the suburb?

PB Every 10, 14 years or so, we prepare a long-term vision plan. The prior one was in 2011. But in a sense, the "wedge" or "hand with fingers" form of the city was developed from van Eesteren's original 1934 plan, and for years we've been filling it in. That form remains a sort of sacred cow.

There has been a gradual shift of focus over time, we were looking at places like the Zuidas and now we look beyond. In the Nieuw-West, 30,000 new homes were built in the last 20 years. It was a silent revolution, it just happened. Noord is like an add-on; where there was industry, now there's new housing, but the old garden hamlets have been kept as they are. They didn't change too much. So Noord is like a crazy collage of all styles.

TK Since the 1980s, regeneration in the inner city has been very careful with demolitions. The regeneration of Nieuw-West, however, included significant demolitions of housing.

PB It's been a combination of refurbishing or restoring and demolishing and building back in higher densities.

TK Any large-scale regeneration needs to satisfy very different objectives and demands. From what you've seen, what have been the major drivers of key decisions such as densification? Is it primarily driven by the need for housing?

PB What I've seen is the willingness to extremely densify the City of Amsterdam within its own perimeter without sacrificing the green spaces and parks. We now have a policy that really protects green or open spaces, and it puts more pressure on the existing urban fabric. There have been studies about how many people use the parks, and over 12, 15 years the use grew exponentially.

When you go outside here, the way people live and use public space has really been changing in the city.

TK The appropriation of public space in Amsterdam has a particular history, whether the appropriation of the Old Town stoops, or neighbors dining on the pavement outside their home in summer evenings.

PB It's also the typology, because the typology of [suburban] Osdorp or the modernist stretches, building strips with a lot of green in between, without a classic street, discourage this. When you enter your house, you meet each other there, and it's a kind of typology which tends to encourage private living, like detached houses. These places are quite popular for families now, and that's a gentrification discussion, because there is much social housing there. In the north, I worked on a project with 72% social housing and a shopping center in the middle, and we made a new plan for the densification and for the shopping center. In general, people were quite happy with the plan because we also added new squares and new programs; nothing was happening there before. But there was also a group of people who felt like, "Oh no, the money's coming really close now." Even in Amsterdam Noord, some of these areas are protected. So while in Nieuw-West there were extensive housing demolitions, in Noord there are less because of [heritage] protection, which is good because the built environment is part of your history.

TK Culture has played an important role in regeneration in the last decades in Amsterdam. To what extent did the budget cuts to the arts and culture in 2010–11 have an impact on the form of regeneration? Did the political animosity towards culture in those years alter the thinking regarding the place of culture within regeneration?

PB Culture is really, really important economically, but it is also a social driver for the city. It has always been and always will be, and Amsterdam tends to be, within Netherlands, as they say, "the Republic of Amsterdam." The city tends to be out of sync with the national mood. The Netherlands has been very neoliberal for some time, while Amsterdam does things differently and is more left-wing. We try to protect, within our possibilities, the cultural landscape, but culture also needs financial support from the Hague—and that was stopped at the time. The city was unable to finance it all by itself. The subsidized culture took a real hit under that government. But the city itself is so strong in culture, it's also international and a hub. We built *broedplaats*, incubation spaces for artists and cultural producers, as a way of reserving space for them. *Broedplaats* are a way of protecting the original DNA of the city.

Small industrial estates with places for workshops and small creative enterprises have really been disappearing, but then there are also responses, like the NDSM, the huge hanger in Noord with a "city" of creatives inside. Planning the future of the area, we won't allow this cultural front to change, it will remain a cultural place for the city—we won't smash it down or redevelop it. You have to protect these places. These places are actually the most popular places right now, and they even appear in *Lonely Planet*. So many tourists visit them!

TK The NDSM and de Ceuvel seem to be cultural signifiers that point towards the Amsterdam squat, now relegated to a historic moment and memory.

PB I really agree with you. They are like well-behaved squats; they offer subculture. The squatting scene has been extremely important to the inner city in Amsterdam, it really saved the city from demolition. The squats occupied neglected areas, then they became hubs for interesting artists, and then slowly became popular.

TK That string of events, leading from squatting to the revitalization of the city, is something of a semi-official history of Amsterdam. The antagonism between the squatters and the city municipality and police vanishes in this story.

PB Maybe Amsterdam has the tendency to like the artistic side of the story. We have an ongoing discussion in city planning about how top-down planning is in Amsterdam. There's no place left for imagination or free space for unplanned things. These places, like NDSM, are like unplanned places, which are innovative in their own way. In the master plan I made for the Buiksloterham area in Noord, where the self-build and de Ceuvel are, we said 10% of these projected 8,000 houses should be developed in an alternative way, to avoid programming everything, to allow new housing typologies and so on. Just to be surprised by the results.

TK It is going to be fascinating to watch the area evolve in the forthcoming years. Thanks for the discussion!

1 *Collectief particulier opdrachtgeverschap*, see introductory chapter in this section.

The View from the City: Vision 2050 and the Nieuw-West

An Interview with Flora Nycolaas

Flora Nycolaas (FN) Tahl Kaminer (TK)

Flora Nycolaas is an urban designer at the City of Amsterdam's Spatial Planning and Sustainability Department. She has worked on the city's *Vision 2050* plan and is currently working on the Nieuw-West (New West) regeneration. She recently contributed to the book *Super West*, which addresses the redevelopment of the area in the past twenty years.[1]

TK Hi Flora, thanks for meeting me. The *Vision 2050* plan includes many references to the city's suburbs. Nieuw-West and Noord are mentioned a lot. The document is pretty clear in rejecting the physical expansion of the city, and instead promotes the densification of the outer city. Does this mean that in the long run, the low-density suburbs of today will vanish as these areas will become denser, more urban?

FN One thing I think is very important in the definition of the suburbs is that there's not a lot of mixture on the level of program and function: they primarily consist of housing. I think the quality of an urban area depends on having a mix of uses in the neighborhood. The aim [of the *Vision 2050* plan] is very much to create resilient areas, which also offer something of quality to the people living there: in livelihood, in opportunities to go to work nearby, to shop nearby, for example, to go to school nearby. To make your daily urban routines very easy. I think that's why it's a big task for us to urbanize these areas in terms of more density, better public transport network and to make it feasible to have amenities nearby.

As for [spatial] growth, in Holland, the idea of the compact city is strong—you don't [spatially] expand into the greenbelt. There is of course the need for more housing to accommodate population growth, so there was an aim to accommodate growth of population as well as an aim to strengthen the [suburban] areas, and we use densification to satisfy both.

Saying that we lose suburban quality, a certain housing type, or, maybe, quietness—partially, it might be so, but if you really look at the Amsterdam suburbs, many of them do not offer such a high-quality living environment. Many of the postwar areas don't offer that. The dwelling itself and its floor plan, some of the greenery: those things are quite good. But these suburbs are very often car-orientated, without eyes on the street, and the public space is messy. We should be able to do better.

Amsterdam has a very exclusive position in the Netherlands in being a strong urban area with a strong urban character, which is quite rare. When looking at the quality of living, the quality of the cultural amenities, access to and proximity to work, and interactions between people, there are only a few Dutch towns that have the ability to offer such an environment. And we think we shouldn't use the area that we have to develop neighborhoods for cars, for a public space with little public value. This can take place elsewhere in the Netherlands. We should use the special quality of the city—we can strengthen it, expand it, inside the city borders. That is the goal rather than to keep car-centric sorts of living environments here, when those can be found elsewhere in the Netherlands.

TK The decision to apply inner-city forms of regeneration, including densification, change of work/live ratios, "population mix," a focus on "young professional families" as housing purchasers and incomers and so on—to what extent was this a reaction to demands by local residents of the suburbs and to what extent was this driven by housing pressures, concerns for sustainability, and more general strategic concerns?[2] Has local opinion affected decision-making in this process?

FN I wouldn't say it's all aimed at these young urban professionals from the inner city. The aim was mixture. The suburbs' demographics were very one-sided. In a sense, social mix is the solution we always come up with, but I do very much believe in it—in the long run, mixing [populations] helps, in the sense that schools become more mixed, that there are some people who have the luxury to have time to invest in the neighborhood. So the aim was not so much to make space for the young urban professionals in the suburbs, but to create more mixed areas. Apart from that, most of the housing there is owned by the social housing associations, and those are the big players that do the work on the renewal. It is the blocks they own that are renewed. And they always have to ensure the right of residents to return [to the area]. We densify by adding houses to the current amount. The absolute numbers increase.

We know that the children of people living in the suburbs actually want to stay in these areas, want to have their own family at a certain point, and they care about these areas. We're trying to address this by providing people living in the area with a first choice [within the system of allocation of social housing]. Currently, the new coalition in the municipality demands that 25% of the housing should be reserved for people already living in this area. So there's much more nuance in the idea of for whom this regeneration is actually meant.

In the *Super West* book to which I contributed, there were maps showing every additional building in the area in the past twenty years. And it's more than we were aware of. It was done in little steps, without realizing how wide-reaching it actually was. All this, let's say, happened under the radar in the past twenty years.

In sociological research undertaken in the area, which included interviews with local residents, people said that "Okay, it's nice that the whole neighborhood looks better, that the public space is renewed." But there's not so much happening *between* these people—they still are in their own separate communities. There's so much that has already been renewed, but in character, it has not changed so much. It was easier, of course, to address one neighborhood at a time than changing the whole urban structure, but then, fundamentally, these neighborhoods don't change very much because the overall structure stays the same. Now, we say we really need to add a new structural layer, and we will use the Nieuw-West's large avenues for it. Such an intervention would mean there's also mobility change and the car is not so dominant anymore. There is more focus on public space where you meet; you place buildings on the street with their front doors facing it. So that's a big step we are taking, in contrast to the past regeneration.

TK When comparing the regeneration and renewal projects of the 1990s and 2000s in the inner city to those of the 2010s in the outer city, what are the main differences?

FN Well, I think the programmatic mixture, maybe it's comparable, right? In the sense that we support such cultural amenities. The process in inner and outer city has been similar, but the physical interventions are different. In the suburbs, we allow a greater physical intervention compared to the limited intervention in the built environment of the inner city. The renewal in the inner city in the 1990s and 2000s was less of a grand project compared to the 1980s in the inner city or recently in the outer city.

TK The demolitions stand out for me as the biggest difference; in the inner city, Amsterdam has been—for a long time—very careful. More so than a lot of other cities. Is this willingness to demolish in the outer city driven by a perceived lack of heritage value, a perceived lack of quality, or a more economic rationale?

FN Now there's a strong heritage movement [in the Nieuw-West]. There have indeed been discussions about whether we are demolishing buildings that are actually of cultural heritage. But as I said before, in the case of postwar Nieuw-West, a lot of this housing is technically not of quality. On the other hand, the floor plans of this postwar housing have quality, and many homes are large, which is rare in the city and in demand, and some of the greenery was carefully designed.

There is also the case of cultural heritage in the Southeast (*Zuidoost*, including the Bijlmer). The regeneration there included very big structural changes, let's say, especially the demolition of the famous honeycomb housing blocks of the Bijlmer. Many have been demolished and replaced with terraced houses in a very different type of urban setting. Only lately, voices calling to be careful with this heritage have been listened to. So now part of it is protected.

TK Regarding changes of structure and lifestyle in the suburbs, the suburbs' dependency on cars is of course a huge issue, but the design of the Nieuw-West, which accommodates pedestrians and traffic, has qualities.

FN Of course. The public transport network is getting worse, actually. Bus and tram lines are cancelled because they aren't used enough, so people need their car more. This is a really big challenge, but I think it is necessary if we want to make our city ready for the next century. Regarding the existing qualities, as I said, I think we should be very careful with certain postwar urban blocks because their housing layout is very good.

When I think of the design of the Nieuw-West, I think of it as an intellectual plan. It's very well thought out. It's very smart. It's really interesting in that sense, but it's interesting for professionals in the field, right? And then one has to think about how it is for people living there. There's still a lot of trouble in the area. We spoke with women there, mothers who said, "Yeah, I just don't want to have my kids playing outside here. There are boys walking around here involved in crime." We should not be naive or too optimistic, and neglect what's happening on the ground; on the other hand, it's also very important to realize there are many people living their lives in these neighborhoods—it's their home.

TK Can you tell me about how Amsterdam went about consulting residents? Did the community have a voice in the regeneration of the Nieuw-West?

FN We organized this whole process of talking to people, and there were many different voices. Of course, people that run a business typically emphasized that they need their car. People voiced different opinions, different needs, but overall, I must say, there's a shared idea of what is a nice, good city: safe, lively, a place where you're not in a barren landscape.

There are ongoing discussions with industry and commerce about whether, if we identify the city with housing and offices, we end up losing a big part of that economic sector that doesn't fit in the city anymore. Could we combine such sectors with housing and offices? If you can combine them, it would be a more productive economy. There are many experiments going on in this field at the moment.

TK The *Vision 2050* plan posits a clear ambition and what looks like a draft plan of traffic reduction, particularly within the A10 ring road.

FN "Car-low," rather than "car-free," according to the Vision. Relocating the traffic that uses the A10 ring road to bypass Amsterdam, diverting that traffic to an outer ring. That will become the regional ring road so that everything that is in the city or on the A10 is traffic for the city itself. And then there's the idea that a large part of Amsterdam will be totally car free, preventing the use of the city center as a thoroughfare. Another aspect is preparing for and encouraging the use of shared mobility. The biggest question regards people living on the outskirts of the city, who have limited access to the public transport network.

TK It is interesting to observe the change of focus of architects, urban designers, planners, and city councilors, who have been so focused on the inner city for so many years.

FN One thing is that the urban plan came ahead and before the structural Vision, in 2014. The big idea there was the expansion or "rollout" from the city center. We had this idea of using the way the inner city works for the regeneration of the outer areas. The same sort of areas, the same sort of feel. Trying to make a nineteenth-century city out of a postwar city. And I think we made a really big step with the new, current *Vision*, with the move to the idea of a polycentric city. Using the existing character of the areas themselves. Develop the outer city areas "from themselves." With the polycentric city, we add complexity to the radial structure of Amsterdam.

All of this is related to how we are organized in the municipality. Before, we had a central city planning department, which did the big urban projects such as Ijburg, the Zuidas (South Axis), and the shores of the IJ. The city boroughs were more focused on services provision. And now we are one big organization. By changing the structure of the organization, I think our view of the city changed greatly as well.

TK Thanks for pointing that out, it totally makes sense. Thanks for your time!

1 Maurits de Hoog and Anouk de Wit (eds.) *SuperWest: Vernieuwing van de Amsterdamse Tuinsteden* (Amsterdam: Thoth, 2022).

2 The term used in the Netherlands is *Stadsvernieuwing*, which translates to "urban renewal." Here, I use "urban regeneration" because it is the common term currently in use in the UK, even though it loses some specificities.

Rolling Out the Center: The Temporary Use of Tolhuistuin in Longer-Term Urban Development in Amsterdam Noord

Timothy Moore

Welcome to Amsterdam Noord

"I get so bored in Amsterdam Noord," sang Harry Slinger in the late 1970s. "What it's like to live in the north? It takes a lot of time to get into town. Few bars, no movie theatres... For young people, [it's] an uninhabitable place." Written with the help of some community center attendees in Amsterdam Noord, the minor Dutch schlager hit "Ik verveel me zo" by Drukwerk reflected the social, cultural, and physical disconnection of the north from the city proper, a condition that still permeates the area today. Amsterdam Noord, stretching over 6,000 hectares, is Amsterdam's largest borough, and at the start of the 2010s, it was also one of its poorest, with four of its twenty neighborhood areas considered to be socioeconomically deprived, with high unemployment rates, and low incomes compared to national levels.[1] Amsterdam Noord was not only segregated from the wealthier center by these socioeconomic indicators. A large waterbody, the IJ, must be crossed by ferry, car bridge, or tunnel in order to reach the area. This sees it branded with the affectionate moniker of "Amsterdam's backyard." But the municipality has undergone tremendous transformation. In 2016, *The Guardian*, *The New York Times*, and *BNE Magazine* all declared Amsterdam Noord a must-see on any visit to the Netherland's largest city, even if—as one writer for *The New York Times* jested—"You can't see the cows anymore for all the BMWs."[2] This capitulation to market forces has increased since then, with average housing prices in the southern part of Amsterdam Noord in 2020 matching those of the southern side of the IJ, a development that follows the recent completion of the new metro extension.

Amsterdam Noord underwent rapid gentrification in the 2010s and much of the area's transformation has been influenced by a top-down planning approach that has combined landmark buildings, new housing builds, social housing regeneration, and smaller citizen-led projects. This chapter looks at the case of Tolhuistuin, a temporary-use project orchestrated by citizens and the municipal government; this project has been leveraged within longer-term urban development plans to both support and signify a transition in the urban realm of the north of Amsterdam. This reflects the translation, or rollout, of inner-city regeneration strategies to the city's outer boroughs. In doing so, the project foreshadows the increasing densification of these neighborhoods and the introduction of inner-city lifestyles that accompany the changes in the population mix.

The Emergence of the Breeding Grounds Policy

The intensification of the capital invested in urban development in the late twentieth century has seen the core of many wealthy cities, including Amsterdam, transform.[3] Similar to the patterns identified by Hackworth and Smith, who outlined a theory of successive and evolving "waves" in the gentrification that occurred in the second half of the twentieth century,[4] in the 1970s and 1980s the gentrification of Amsterdam took place in the eighteenth-century city core, whilst in the 1990s this was followed by a public policy that promoted middle-class homeownership in both the postwar and nineteenth-century neighborhoods of the city.[5] Urban geographer Wouter van Gent refers to this phenomena as the "rollout of the city center" (paraphrasing a municipal government document of that era) through the promotion of high-density housing, amenities, and cultural venues by the state in neighborhoods close to the historical core.[6]

A unique government-led policy emerged at this time as part of Amsterdam's urban renewal: buildings were to be rehabilitated in order to keep creative services and the cultural sector, which were being pushed out by a lack of affordable space, in the inner city. Since 2000, the Broedplaatsenbeleid, or "breeding grounds" policy, has been part of the city's suite of rigid spatial development controls.[7] From the inception of the Broedplaats model, over 113,000 square meters on over 50 sites, and 3,500 living and working places, have been brokered in council-owned and private property. Each project has, however, been unique in terms of its site, level of government involvement, governance model, and outcomes. The ambitions of the policy are achieved through a range of measures, including making loans available, providing subsidies and expert advice to create spaces, making property assets available, and connecting artists to temporary housing.[8] In 2022, there were sixty-three *broedplaatsen*, with over 1,000 artist studios,[9] in operation in Amsterdam—16 were located outside of the A10 ring road and 9 were located in Amsterdam Noord.

In the 2010s, the Broedplaats policy shifted focus, from the rehabilitation of property towards the "cultivation of talent." Entrepreneurship therefore lies at the crux of this unique policy. Jaap Schoufour, former head of the Broedplaats office, explained in an interview: "In the beginning we paid a lot of money to get real estate. Nowadays we regard artists and *broedplaats* initiatives as entrepreneurs."[10] He remarked that:

> each *broedplaats* has a vision document [which asks:] what is the added value for the city on economic and cultural and social and spatial perspective? Cultural is: *you need to house artists*. Social is: *what do you do for the neighborhood?* Economic is: *are there any start-ups involved?* . . . They have to express themselves in terms of added value. After that, we make all these calculations about what the subsidy should be.[11]

Urban regeneration is outsourced in the short-term to the creative workers, who are asked to deliver community engagement programs in return for the use of space, and even submit a business case in relation to the opportunity.

The Broedplaats model formalizes the temporary use of space—that is, the use of a building or land in the interim, in-between the time when the previous function of a site ceases and the site is redeveloped.[12] The acclaim accorded to temporary use—which has been documented *ad nauseum* in popular literature—demonstrates the diversity of temporary-use projects in terms of their uses, sites, durations, construction, users, financing, and purpose.[13] They can provide affordable space, laboratories for new economies and cultures, and spaces for consumerism alike.

They can also be strategic instruments for mainstream actors like property developers and local governments in bolstering consensus for urban transformation and jumpstarting urbanity in the suburbs. Read crudely, the model may constitute *a form of social control*. This is evident in the origins of the Broedplaats policy, which developed out of confrontations between the city and squatters in the 1990s, particularly along the southern part of the IJ, over demands for affordable space for living and working. Rather than working against the squatters, the city decided to learn from the experience.[14] When interviewed, Schoufour acknowledged this: "We took the lessons of the squatting movement into our policy, so the squatting movement showed us that getting into a building, reconstructing it, reorganizing it, managing it, is not explicitly a job which may be done by government. The group can do it themselves. That is what the squatters showed us."[15] Through the lawful inhabitation of buildings through government-sanctioned temporary use, squatters are potentially transformed into occupants who are less likely to challenge dominant property regimes because they now benefit from legal occupation (despite the instability of short-term contracts). In parallel to the rise of *broedplaatsen*, squatting became illegal in the Netherlands in 2010.

There is another acknowledged advantage to such policies, which lies in the potential of longer-term cultural capital to also provide economic benefits. The Broedplaats policy was supported by thinking around the creative city, and in particular the influence of Richard Florida, author of *The Rise of the Creative Class* (2002), who defined and documented the creatives—who may be artists, architects, managers, professional workers, or even dentists or tax collectors—that make cities more attractive and marketable, despite the lack of evidence that this creative class significantly stimulates urban growth.[16] Florida's tantalizing mantra of tolerance, talent, and technology already suited the existing Dutch scheme of reorienting cultural funding towards entrepreneurship.[17] Schoufour commented that "[t]his Broedplaats instrument was already fitting within this concept of Richard Florida. We continued this policy, creating affordable space for artists, as then the city would be attractive for young artists to settle down. It all fitted in the Florida idea: you facilitate talent."[18] The government support of temporary use is thus also part of a longer-term strategy to make the city more attractive to global businesses and their workforces.

The Broedplaats model provides affordable space in the interim. These small-scale projects, which have small-scale impacts on the built environment, should not, however, be dismissed as lacking power to affect the everyday lives of people that come into contact with them. This makes them valuable. At their best, temporary-use projects provide places of assembly to reimagine other lifestyles, reappropriate urban space, and maybe even rethink society. But at their worst, they can be mobilized in the service of exclusion and displacement.[19] Temporary users can move in while property development plans are cold, but can be moved on when the market heats up again after being used as a place-marketing and change management tool within an urban development project.

Supercharging the City-Center Rollout

Over a decade after the initiation of the Broedplaats model, and following the global financial crisis of the late noughties, in the early 2010s urban renewal and development in Amsterdam's center was supercharged by "fifth-wave gentrification"—a process of gentrification led by the state, which is supplemented by financial institutions, whereby housing becomes an asset class for transnational investors.[20] In Amsterdam, the penetration of global capital has been supported by processes of "touristification" and the growth of "platform capitalism."[21] This new wave of gentrification may take place at the center of wealthy cities, but it has had a rippling effect, shifting the middle class to the suburbs, forced out of the inner city by actors within global finance. This has not only seen the transformation of Amsterdam's center, such as in De Wallen or in the nineteenth and early twentieth-century rings, it has also shifted outwards to De Biljmer in Amsterdam's southeast and also northwards to Amsterdam Noord. The rollout of the city center continues today.

Dramatic changes in the Dutch housing market have paved the way for equity to flow across the city, in particular through the shift, initiated in the early 2000s, from social housing policy towards the promotion of homeownership via new mortgage lending, tax deductions, and cuts to social housing subsidies,[22] which altered the housing mix in many neighborhoods. This state-led intervention saw an increase in owner-occupiers, which also translated to the outer boroughs of Amsterdam across the IJ and outside of Amsterdam's ring road with an increase to the number of owner-occupied homes that was matched by a decrease in the share of social renters.[23] In Amsterdam Noord, the share of owner-occupied housing increased from 19% to 27% of the housing stock between 2005 and 2016.[24]

One component of the increase in owner-occupied homes was through new builds rather than classic displacement. New builds were aided in Amsterdam Noord by the lack of comparable density to other boroughs: the borough is predominantly low-rise, housing one-tenth of the city's population despite being a quarter of its area. (It also has a high availability of brownfield sites.) The scale of new builds is evident in increases in Amsterdam Noord's population, which grew more than 7% between 2011 and 2016. This also results in old-timers becoming increasingly outnumbered by newcomers: in 2016, 27% of the population had only lived in the North since 2013, with high concentrations of new Northerners around NDSM, Elzenhagen Zuid, Buiksloterham, Papaverweg, and Hamerstraat.[25] The slight majority, although far from all, of these new arrivals came from across Amsterdam. More space has thus been created for the middle-class.

Another component that arrived from the inner city at this time was a focus on the restructuring of social housing through renovation, rent increases, the sale of parts of the stock, and low rates of new construction. This is evident, for example, in Bloemenbuurt in Amsterdam Noord where social rental apartments have been renovated and partly merged with larger, market-sector rental houses. This has occurred in parallel to a broader change in the mix of social housing tenants across Amsterdam: tenants have become more economically homogeneous through a change in means testing that has led to a greater representation of low-income households in social housing.[26]

While new builds and the restructuring of social housing have both been part of the landscape of urban regeneration for some time, the deployment of artist studios, entrepreneurial hubs, and cultural attractions in Amsterdam Noord (including the cultural center NDSM, which became a *broedplaats* in 2007) are newer parts of a larger strategy whereby the city government applies inner-city regeneration strategies to its peripheral boroughs. Temporary-use projects like *broedplaatsen* can be entangled within broader political decisions where the city government actively tolerates and promotes temporary-use activities for the purpose of city branding, and can therefore become "unwitting players in processes of symbolic gentrification."[27] In doing this, these projects not only act as soft-branding exercises—they also foreshadow the increasing infill of these neighborhoods through new development and a rise in the inner-city, middle-class lifestyles that accompany it.

The Case of *Broedplaats* Tolhuistuin

Situated at the gateway from Amsterdam Noord to Amsterdam, at the ferry terminal, lies Tolhuistuin, or the Toll House Garden, which is a patchwork of heritage buildings and gardens. The use of this site was made possible when Shell decided to vacate 20 of its 27-hectare Amsterdam Noord locations in 2002, which left large tracts of land and buildings available for redevelopment. Guided by the *Projectbesluit Shellterrein* (2004), which was updated in 2005, the twenty-hectare redevelopment plan for the Overhoeks area contained a high-density building program with 70,000 square meters of new office space that were incorporated within a high-rise strip. The redevelopment plan was also steered by the master plan *Noord aan het IJ: Masterplan Noordelijke IJ-oever* (2003) and the Amsterdam Structural Plan 2003-2010 (2003), the latter of which set out a long-term strategic framework to introduce 13,000 homes in Amsterdam Noord, including nearly 9,000 along the northern IJ bank. Typical to many large, mixed-use urban redevelopment projects, landmark developments were planned, including the EYE Film Museum and a makeover of the Overhoeks Tower as an entry point to the district. The site of Tolhuistuin, a slither of land adjacent to Overhoeks between the NoordHollandsch and Buiksloter canals, was marked as "green space" in the master-planning documents.

While development plans were warming up along the IJ shoreline—at NDSM, Overhoeks, Buiksloterham, and Hamerstraat—and as capital ebbed and flowed just before the Dutch financial crisis of 2008, the redevelopment of Tolhuistuin

Figure 1: The former Shell canteen is transformed into a restaurant and events space (2015). Photograph by the author.

remained ambiguous due to its overlooked status on planning documents. Former Amsterdam Noord mayor Rob Post remarked, "We had a blueprint for the Overhoeks: The Tolhuistuin was in-between. In fact, the city hardly knew that it existed."[28] The origin of temporary-use projects can be found in-between spaces, in the cracks, or on seemingly undervalued land.

The *broedplaats* Tolhuistuin was jumpstarted by the local government in order to utilize vacant land and buildings on the site before the rollout of the adjacent landmark icons of the EYE Film Museum and the renovation of the Overhoeks Tower. In 2006, the City of Amsterdam advertised for expressions-of-interest through a tender process for the site, looking for a group that could demonstrate an operational plan for a "temporary interpretation" that contained cultural activities for the north[29] in line with the site acting as a "bridge between Amsterdam and Amsterdam North."[30]

The winning team was led by Chris Keulemans, renowned cultural director, curator, and writer in Amsterdam. Three ideas were key in the success of the winning proposal. The first was the establishment of a restaurant in the old Shell canteen, approximately half of the profits of which would go to Tolhuistuin's cultural agenda. Second, the project would provide a place for people in the neighborhood to work and engage in leisure activities. And third, Amsterdam's popular cultural venue Paradiso was proposed as an anchor tenant in the bid. The local government understood the value of introducing new commercial and cultural operators.

Local government may benefit from temporary cultural activity, but so do the temporary users who gain short-term access to affordable working spaces. In 2008, several buildings in Tolhuistuin were handed over to the cultural trust Stichting Tolhuistuin for a limited period. These buildings, which included the former Shell infirmary (Staalvilla), canteen (Kantine), and port building (Portgebouw), have been rented out to various creatives, such as architects, writers, artists, and independent cultural organizations, and have hosted cultural events since 2008. (I also worked from this complex in the office of Archis between 2010 and 2011.) This introduced inner-city cultures to the area across the river, bringing them into a neighborhood with a strong working-class history.

Despite Tolhuistuin being geared towards creative Amsterdamers, Tolhuistuin also contributed to the local economy by employing people from, and delivering cultural programming for, the neighborhood. One of the pioneers at Tolhuistuin, Joost Janmaat, remarks, "There are handymen, cleaners, gardeners, cooks, guards, all people from this neighborhood. That is the lasting effect: they change the lives of 100-plus people that have meaningful work."[31] Tolhuistuin also took care of "programming, putting things on stage from different groups from the neighborhood - Moroccan music, Dutch schlager."[32] A celebrated element of temporary-use projects, as an alternative form of urban development, is the way in which they involve people outside dominant property development interests, including citizens, community groups, and artists.

Temporary-use projects provide many benefits for their users: they provide a place of assembly, affordable workspace, and employment. When viewed in isolation, they may appear as informal, creative, or community spaces, but they can simultaneously be the outcome of very precise institutional apparatuses and legislative frameworks that emerge to produce a subjectivity that looks and feels participatory. Flexibility can be a calculated practice that is performed by structures of state power.[33] Users can be entangled within broader political decisions where the city government actively tolerates and promotes temporary-use activities for the purpose of city (and neighborhood) branding. In the sophisticated turn of gentrification from the city center to places that are further afield, temporary use can affect the different types of people that new urban development brings together and as such can fulfill a "gateway" function in relation to the area.

Figure 2: The former port building operates as studios for creative businesses (2015). Photograph by the author.

Temporary-use projects have become a strategy employed by mainstream actors such as government and property developers to symbolize and stimulate change. That the introduction of creative people and cultural activities to Tolhuistuin was instrumental in re-orientating the identity of the North is clear, according to former Amsterdam Noord mayor Rob Post, who championed the project. He commented in an interview that, "[t]he main thing I wanted to do was change the image of Amsterdam North, and to change the idea that it was something different from the rest of Amsterdam. That it's an integral part of Amsterdam."[34] The former alderman was aware of this challenge from the outset but says that the neighborhood needed to change. "Improving an area does mean the cost of living does increase. I don't know how you can do it otherwise. Of course, when you see where we came from, we were the absolutely bottom ... It will be another 20 years [before

Amsterdam Noord improves its standings]."[35] Temporary-use projects are leveraged as a symbol of urban renewal, regeneration, and transition during a lengthy and often invisible process of property and policy development, providing legitimacy to the process.

Cultural development is a component of economic development, and temporary-use projects have a role to play. Post believed that the introduction of creative people to the site was instrumental in the scheme of re-orientating the identity of the north. He remarked: "I think we can say that if we get the creative people in with ideas, and cultural people, the rest will follow."[36] Or as he once said in Dutch: "*Geld volgt cultuur, zo simpel is het*"—money follows culture, it's that simple.[37] In the interim, a temporary-use project becomes a landmark to reorientate the branding of the neighborhood through the entanglement of local and cultural actors. Further, by increasing the value of a site through its rehabilitation via creative actors and attracting new uses and users, temporary-use projects are part of a process of economic transition in neighborhoods. Creative users reinforce existing market conditions.

Short-term temporary-use projects are implicated in longer-term urban development, but as time goes on, the vision and goals of projects can undergo reorientations. This was evident at Tolhuistuin, when macroeconomic conditions changed: in the third quarter of 2008, as the tenants were moving into Tolhuistuin, the global financial crisis was in full swing, and larger redevelopment plans at Overhoeks were suddenly put on hold. (At Overhoeks, a small number of developers with large plots and preset outcomes were not able to adapt. ING dropped out of the project in 2010; as a result, the municipality took control of parts of the development.) This extended the project with many tenancy contracts being renewed yearly.

From 2014, a second wave of tenants began to arrive at Tolhuistuin, as the precinct was put on a new ten-year contract, which extended its life far beyond what was originally planned and offered protection to tenants from redevelopment in the meantime. The old port building opened, while the former Shell canteen was finally renovated and opened up as a new restaurant and performance venue, an outpost of Paradiso. Tenant Lilet Breddels, from architecture publisher Archis, remarked in an interview, "[g]radually the other buildings opened, the Poortgebouw is there, everything became bigger, and they made rental arrangements with the others—and they all paid relatively more per square meter more than we did."[38] But it also meant that the city could recoup the money that it had invested in the buildings' maintenance. Former Tolhuistuin director Keulemans remarked in an interview: "The city understood they had to invest more, and in order for us to make it possible to pay back investments through rent, the rental contract was extended for ten years and possibly longer."[39] Temporary users contribute value in providing upkeep and maintenance, a service that government would otherwise pay for with their own building assets.

As this interim period extended, rents increased. The old Shell canteen, now Restaurant THT and Paradiso, formerly empty spaces for tenants to use, charged higher fees for the use of their spaces. Golfstromen's Jeroen Beekmans, who ran Amsterdam's PechaKucha, authored the aforementioned blog Pop-Up City, and was one of the original tenants, remarked that he once held Pecha Kucha in the Tolhuistuin garden. "We could get it for free in 2010. Now [in 2015] it's 1,200 euros for a night. Our type of event never earns a lot of money, we can't afford it."[40] What creative users may have gained in the short term (in terms of privileges like subsidies) is lost in the long run. It can be sobering for the Tolhuistuin pioneers to feel the effects of the market-driven processes behind urban development.

The preference for (and rhetoric of) the creative as a miracle worker in stimulating economic growth, or at the least, an unknowing proponent in processes of symbolic gentrification through the urban regeneration of local neighborhoods, also creates another familiar dilemma. These "cultural actors involved in place shaping are exposed to the risk of becoming the victims of their own success"[41] as their "critical forms of urban activism and intervention provide alibis (or, worse, seed-funding and ground-breaking) for more conventional rent-seeking urban development."[42] This may lead to their displacement with the gentrification of a neighborhood.[43] The inner-city lifestyles that were punted across the IJ risked also being fleeting.

The extension of time at Tolhuistuin demonstrates that temporary-use projects may reinforce existing market powers by shifting from their original spirit of social concerns to economic relations. The municipal real estate company took over ownership of the site from the local borough around 2018; today, the place is no longer a *broedplaats*.[44] A consistant condition over this time is the value of creatives within the urban development process, which has been championed for over two decades in Amsterdam, and Tolhuistuin is a continuation of this positive approach by local government, which has created favorable conditions for temporary use via policy and financial assistance. "Amsterdam has learnt to value the art of bottom-up, improvisation, temporary—it has learnt," remarked Keulemans.[45] But this is a one-sided affair. "You have to improve, one, more mental things, especially younger pioneers. That somehow learn to look at the bigger picture rather than their own success and development."[46]

This highlights one final dilemma: The privileging of the creative middle class over the working class, or the disenfranchised over the marginalized, in urban development processes. The disparity between the everyday experience of the creative users at Tolhuistuin and the Northerners is vast. While the urban development project and its associated temporary projects may bring short- and longer-term value to a property owner and to temporary users, locals may not see any benefit unless they are themselves property owners and profit from property price rises as their neighborhood undergoes a makeover, renaissance, redevelopment, or capitulation.

Conclusion

The transformation of Amsterdam's inner city has seen government initiatives to stimulate economic growth shift to the other side of the IJ, which has engendered the erosion of difference between the urban development processes deployed in the inner city and those seen outside the city core. The policy of the Broedplaats, or "breeding grounds," saw the temporary-use project of Tolhuistuin used as tool by local government to re-orientate Amsterdam Noord towards new urban development and the different types of people that such development brings—in particular, artists, architects, cultural organizations, and creative entrepreneurs in the short-term, and middle-class residents, who will inhabit the surrounding housing (re)development projects, in the long-term. The instigation of Tolhuistuin as a gateway project to future urban development in Amsterdam Noord was embroiled in a larger policy framework that took in the whole of Amsterdam and was part of a larger trend amongst local authorities, which saw them grappling and experimenting with the potential of temporary use as a radical component of urban regeneration. Tolhuistuin demonstrates a broadening of focus on cultural amenities from the provision of hero buildings, such as museums, towards the inclusion of the middle class people and programs, which, when inserted into existing buildings, became their own kind of landmarks in the era of ubiquitous gentrification.

1 Robin Boelsums, "Living next to a Flagship Development: Research on Creating Mutual, Local Benefits between the Residential Neighbourhood Van der Pekbuurt and the Contemporary Flagship Area Overhoeks Amsterdam, in Socioeconomic and Spatial Terms" (thesis; Delft: Technical University of Delft, 2012).

2 Russell Shorto, "Amsterdam, Revisited," *The New York Times*, August 30, 2016, http://www.nytimes.com/2016/09/04/travel/amsterdam-revisited.html.

3 Manuel Aalbers, "Revisiting 'The Changing State of Gentrification': Introduction to the Forum: From Third to Fifth-wave Gentrification," *Tijdschrift voor Economische en Sociale Geografie* 110, no. 1 (2018): 1–11, DOI: 10.1111/tesg.12332.

4 Jason Hackworth and Neil Smith, "The Changing State of Gentrification," *Tijdschrift voor Economische en Sociale Geografie* 92, no. 4 (2001): 464–77, DOI: 10.1111/1467-9663.00172.

5 Wouter van Gent, "Gentrification of the Changing State," *Tijdschrift voor Economische en Sociale Geografie* 110, no. 1 (2018): 35–46, DOI: 10.1111/tesg.12331.

6 Wouter van Gent, "Neoliberalization, Housing Institutions and Variegated Gentrification: How the 'Third Wave' Broke in Amsterdam," *International Journal of Urban and Regional Research* 37 (2013): 503–22, DOI: 10.1111/j.1468-2427.2012.01155.x.

7 The City of Amsterdam translates a *broedplaats* as an arts factory in its English language documents.

8 Bureau Broedplaatsen, *Policy Framework: Studio & Art Factories Programme Amsterdam Metropolitan Area 2012-2016* (Amsterdam: City of Amsterdam, 2012).

9 Koen Boswinkel and Edwin van Meerkerk, "Creative Hubs: An Anomaly in Cultural Policy?," *International Journal of Cultural Policy* (2022), DOI: 10.1080/10286632.2022.2107636.

10 Jaap Schoufour in discussion with the author, August 26, 2015.

11 Ibid.

12 See Florian Haydn and Robert Temel, *Temporary Urban Spaces: Concepts for the Use of City Spaces* (Basel: Birkhäuser, 2006); Philipp Oswalt, Klaus Overmeyer, and Philipp Misselwitz, *Urban Catalyst: The Power of Temporary Use* (Berlin: Dom Publishers, 2013); Francesca Ferguson (ed.) *Make_shift City: Renegotiating the Urban Commons* (Berlin: Jovis, 2014).

13 Including on blogs (Rebel Art; Wooster Collective; Urban Shit; The Pop-Up City; We Make Money Not Art) and in exhibitions (*Unplanned: Research and Experiments at the Urban Scale* at the Superfront Gallery in Los Angeles (2010); *Actions: What You Can Do With the City* at the CCA in Montreal (2008); *DIY Urbanism* at Mission Street Urban Center in San Francisco (2010)).

14 This was covered extensively over a decade ago. See Jamie Peck, "Recreative City: Amsterdam, Vehicular Ideas and the Adaptive Spaces of Creativity Policy," *International Journal of Urban and Regional Research* 36, no. 3 (2011): 462–85, DOI: 10.1111/j.1468-2427.2011.01071.x; Justus Uitermark, "The Co-Optation of Squatters in Amsterdam and the Emergence of a Movement Meritocracy: A Critical Reply to Pruijt," *International Journal of Urban and Regional Research* 28, no. 3 (2004): 687–98, DOI: 10.1111/j.0309-1317.2004.00543.x; Kate Shaw, "The Place of Alternative Culture and the Politics of its Protection in Berlin, Amsterdam and Melbourne," *Planning Theory & Practice* 6, no. 2 (2005): 149–69, DOI: 10.1080/14649350500136830; Lynn Owens, "From Tourists to Anti-Tourists to Tourist Attractions: The Transformation of the Amsterdam Squatters' Movement," *Social Movement Studies* 7, no. 1 (2008): 43–59, DOI: 10.1080/1474283080196 9340.

15 Jaap Schoufour in discussion with the author, August 26, 2015.

16 Richard L. Florida, *The Rise of the Creative Class: And How It's Transforming Work, Leisure, Community and Everyday Life* (New York: Basic Books, 2002). See also: Ann Markusen, "Urban Development and the Politics of a Creative Class: Evidence from a Study of Artists," *Environment and Planning A* 38, no. 10 (2006): 1921–940, DOI: 10.1068/a38179.

17 Jamie Peck, "Recreative City."

18 Jaap Schoufour in discussion with the author, August 26, 2015.

19 Amelia Thorpe, Timothy Moore, and Lee Stickells, "Pop-up Justice? Re-thinking Relationships in the Temporary City," in *Transience and Permanence in Urban Development*, ed. John Henneberry (New Jersey, USA: Wiley-Blackwell, 2017), 151–69.

20 Manuel Aalbers, "Revisiting 'The Changing State of Gentrification'."

21 Ibid.

22 Federico Savini, Willem Boterman, and Wouter van Gent, "City Profile: Amsterdam in the 21st Century: Geography, Housing, Spatial Development and Politics," *Cities* 51 (2016): 103–13, DOI: 10.1016/j.cities.2015.11.017.

23 Eva Bosch, "Gentrification in all Boroughs of Amsterdam: Increasing Land Values and Socio-spatial Change, Little Direct Displacement," *Territorio* 73, no. 2 (2015): 23–29, DOI: 10.3280/TR2015-073004.

24 Hester Booi and Annika Smits, *Veranderend Noord. Ontwikkelingen in de bevolkingssamenstelling en de woningvoorraad van Noord* (Amsterdam: Gemeente Amsterdam: Onderzoek, Informatie en Statistiek, 2017).

25 Ibid.

26 Wouter van Gent and Cody Hochstenbach, "The Neo-liberal Politics and Socio-spatial Implications of Dutch Post-crisis Social Housing Policies," *International Journal of Housing Policy* 20, no. 1 (2019): 156–72, DOI: 10.1080/19491247.2019.1682234.

27 Claire Colomb, "'DIY Urbanism' in Berlin: Dilemmas and Conflicts in the Mobilization of 'Temporary Uses' of Urban Space in Local Economic Development" (Paper presented at Transience and Permanence in Urban Development, University of Sheffield, January 14–15, 2015), 10.

28 Rob Post in discussion with the author, August 26, 2015.

29 Projectbureau Noordwaarts, *Tolhuistuin: Tenminste Houdbaar tot 2013 Werkboek* (Amsterdam Noord: Projectbureau Noordwaarts, 2006).

30 Rob Post in discussion with the author, August 26, 2015.

31 Jaap Schoufour in discussion with the author, August 25, 2015.

32 Chris Keulemans in discussion with the author, August 31, 2015.

33 Ann Varley, "Postcolonialising Informality?" *Environment and Planning D* 31, no. 1 (2013): 4–22, DOI: 10.1068/d14410.
34 Rob Post in discussion with the author, August 26, 2015.
35 Ibid.
36 Ibid.
37 Jeroen Junte, "Noord, Toevluchtsoord," *De Volkskrant*, January 25, 2014.
38 Lilet Breddels in discussion with the author, August 25, 2015.
39 Chris Keulemans in discussion with the author, n.d.
40 Jeroen Beekmans in discussion with the author, August 31, 2015.
41 Panu Lehtovuori and Sampo Ruoppila, "Temporary Uses Producing Difference in Contemporary Urbanism," in *Transience and Permanence in Urban Development*, ed. John Henneberry (New Jersey, USA: Wiley-Blackwell, 2017), 58.
42 Fran Tonkiss, "Austerity Urbanism and the Makeshift City," *City* 17, no. 3 (2013): 318, DOI: 10.1080/13604813.2013.795332.
43 Sharon Zukin, *Loft Living: Culture and Capital in Urban Change* (Baltimore: Johns Hopkins University Press, 1982).
44 Tolhuistuin was not technically operating as a *broedplaats* in the mid-2010s. Jaap Schoufour, former head of the Broedplaats office, explained: "For a *broedplaats*, at least 40% of the square meters should be used by professional artists. At this point, Tolhuistuin is running, but 40% of its floor space is not used by artists. It's not a *broedplaats*" [since the introduction of the commercial operations such as the restaurant THT]. Jaap Schoufour in discussion with the author, August 25, 2015.
45 Chris Keulemans in discussion with the author, August 31, 2015.
46 Ibid.

II.
BERLIN

Culture in the Trenches: Housing and Resistance in Berlin

Maroš Krivý and Leonard Ma

In 2021, the new club venue RSO opened in Berlin's Schöneweide. The techno club is situated in the former Bärenquell Brewery—a suitably atmospheric building, albeit in an unlikely urban context. The riverfront neighborhood is located at a straight-line distance of some 10 kilometers from Alexanderplatz, well outside the S-Bahn ring that has traditionally defined the "center" of Berlin. Prospective clubbers, who disembark at the Schöneweide station, trek through a sprawling landscape of big box stores and parking lots to reach the venue.[1] Under a massive motorway sign, a long queue forms opposite a Renault service center; muffled techno reverberates through the weathered brick walls of the once abandoned brewery. RSO was founded by the team behind Griessmuehle, after the cult underground techno club was forced to vacate its former waterfront site in Berlin-Neukölln. Since opening in 2012, Griessmuehle had relied on temporary half-year leases, the last of which was not renewed as the landlord made way for new office developments along the Spree.[2] The fate of Griessmuehle and its subsequent reincarnation as RSO presents a by now familiar story, whereby cycles of pioneering action and displacement act as precursors to the intensification of real estate investment. Yet, while techno clubs, and along with them galleries, cafés, and subcultural bookstores, have flourished in vacant inner-city sites of Berlin, what might this latest migration to spaces located at a growing distance from the city center reveal about contemporary urban change in the German capital?

The premise of our contribution to *Urbanizing Suburbia* is that this change cannot be put down to the standard narrative of arts- or culture-led gentrification but reflects broader linkages and tensions between urban cultures, housing policy, and international finance.[3] While, at the turn of the millennium, Berlin's comparatively affordable rents attracted a generation of artists and creatives to its flourishing cultural scene, the recent decade and a half was characterized by an unprecedented influx of global capital in real estate. Since 2008, Berlin has come to pernicious prominence as the paradigmatic example of what former UN special rapporteur on housing Raquel Rolnik terms a "new wave" of financialization.[4] With around 85% of its residents in some form of rental tenure, Berlin has become a playground for corporate landlords, private equity funds, and other institutional investors in real estate. In 2018, for example, Berlin had the fastest growing property prices in the world, outpacing other destinations for international investment such as New York, Hong Kong, or Vancouver.[5] It is true that the rise of Berlin as both a cultural capital and as a real estate investment capital follows the familiar trajectory of real estate speculation pushing out the same artists that helped bring the city to prominence in the first place. However, the causality at work in the story, lies in the role of global political economy and how it has intersected with the specificities of Berlin's housing policy and political culture.

Through the case study of Schöneweide, we explore the transforming role of culture in relation to the financialization of housing. Having attracted a plethora of international artists and education institutions, this former industrial suburb is undergoing a renaissance as a hub not only for clubbing but also for other cultural activities. As financial players shift from the speculative "flipping" of investments to long-term "buy and hold" value-added strategies, culture becomes a means of adding value in the process of "urbanizing" Schöneweide. Our analysis, however, aims to expand the narrow conception of *culture* that defines it in terms of *the arts* to an expanded definition based on Raymond Williams's theorization of culture as "a whole way of life."[6] This perspective allows us to avoid the extremes of explaining gentrification as a process that is either "led" by artists or that can be put down solely to an autonomous logic of capital: the neighborhood change being witnessed at an urban periphery cannot be understood, we argue, without understanding how cultures of politics, housing, and protest shape the wider urban arena. A cultural materialist perspective draws attention to the role played by local cultures, in their broader definition, in anchoring and resisting financialization and other globalizing processes.[7]

From "Poor but Sexy" to Deutsche Wohnen

In 2003, then Berlin Mayor Klaus Wowereit announced "*Berlin ist arm, aber sexy*" ("Berlin is poor but sexy"). Tapping into Berlin's cultural legacy and ongoing economic difficulties, the Social Democratic Party (SDP) mayor sought to make a compelling pitch for Berlin on the world stage. With its relatively low cost of living for a major European city, Berlin was a culturally vibrant and dynamic city that was also affordable to live in. Wowereit's announcement reframed Berlin as a potential hub for artists and creatives. Drawn to the city's rich history, flourishing contemporary arts scene and the untapped potential of unique vacant spaces for studios and galleries, the ensuing years saw many emerging artists establish themselves in Berlin. Aided by specific policy initiatives, such as Berlin's special residence permit for self-employed artists, a particularly "Berlin" model for contemporary art was established.[8] Emerging artists could hope to eke out a sustainable living in a competitive industry by utilizing the networks of Berlin's rich cultural scene and the city's cheap rents, while selling their work on an international art market.

In comparison to its more affluent counterparts—cities like Frankfurt, Munich, or Hamburg, with established finance, trade, and manufacturing sectors—Berlin has historically had a lower-income population. The influx of creative workers throughout the 2000s, however, did not translate directly into an economic boom. A 2011 report estimated that the average income for artists in Berlin was 11,612 euros, with less than 1,000 artists earning sufficient income from artistic activities alone to live on. The remainder need to supplement their income from other sources, with nearly 50% relying on service work to make ends meet.[9] While artistic work remains a precarious form of work in Berlin, it has come to play a significant role in making Berlin attractive for investment, especially for private equity firms investing in real estate.

To understand this, the branding of Berlin's vibrant and cosmopolitan culture must be seen as occurring in step with transformations in housing policy. As housing scholars Desiree Fields and Sabina Uffer recount, housing provision in Germany's postwar economy was typically managed by large private or municipal companies, with affordable housing seen as a key component of the "social market economy."[10] In the late 1980s, however, the Helmut Kohl administration challenged state support for social housing, and the "common interest principle" (*Gemeinnützigkeit*), which guaranteed that social housing companies could be exempt from taxation, was abandoned in order to reduce public expenditure in the housing sector.[11] At first, Berlin's government continued to invest in housing construction and renovations: in 1991, Berlin held over 480,000 housing units in public ownership, roughly 28% of the housing stock. However, this policy was undermined by the mid-1990 fiscal crisis, after which municipal housing companies in Berlin were instructed to sell off 15% of their housing units to pay off municipal debts and to attract private investment for refurbishments. These sales were initially meant to be directed at sitting tenants, but the poor macroeconomic situation in Berlin meant that many tenants simply could not afford to buy their homes.[12] As a result—and unlike Right-to-Buy privatizations implemented in the UK and across most former state-socialist countries—Germany, and Berlin in particular, privatized municipal housing *en bloc*, transferring ownership to private equity funds.

Private equity funds began buying municipal housing to capitalize on the gap between subsidized and market rent levels, by vacating, upgrading, and renting out flats. The number of large, *en bloc* sales from municipal housing companies to institutional investors increased dramatically between 2004 and 2007.[13] For example, in 2004, more than 60,000 units owned by Berlin's GSW were sold to a Goldman Sachs-led consortium for the steeply discounted price of 405 million euros (for a shocking price of 6,230 euros per unit).[14] In 2007, Deutsche Wohnen—the company most emblematic of Berlin's housing crisis and a subsidiary of Deutsche Bank—took over almost 30,000 rental units from Berlin's GEHAG, including those in the Hufeisensiedlung, an iconic modernist housing estate designed by Bruno Taut and put on the UNESCO World Heritage List in 2008 (the municipality first sold this particular group of units to a Hamburg-based real estate company in 1998).[15] Together with a drastic decrease of interest rates in the early 2000s (after the dot-com bust), transactions such as these triggered what Field and Uffer call a "herd-like movement of international investment firms" into Berlin's residential real estate.[16] Overall the municipal housing stock was reduced from 370,000 units in 1993 to less than 150,000 in 2012.[17]

Although housing prices in Berlin are still lower than in comparable German and European cities, Berlin rents more than doubled between 2009 and 2019 (from 5.70 euros to 11.60 euros per square meter).[18] Expanding on the role of international financial players, urban researcher and planner Laura Calbet i Elias introduced the concept of the "financialized rent gap": a gap between local ground rents and an "abstract international rent level" that leads to the perception that Berlin properties are comparatively undervalued and therefore attractive as an investment.[19] A danger inherent in the financialized rent gap is that it connects with a cultural imaginary that sees Berliners as undeserving. For example, an American real estate investor recently complained that paying "30% of your income for your rent is not exorbitant" considering that "people in the US pay 50% for their rent," adding that "people in Berlin still go on vacations" while "many Americans cannot afford vacations."[20]

What God-Given Right Do You Have to Live in Berlin-Mitte?

Private equity funds typically operate as highly leveraged entities, operating with little equity and instead relying on strategic loans to make investments. Between the mid-1990s and the mid-2000s, private equity investors chased short-term gains through "buy-low, sell-high" and other highly leveraged financial strategies. From 2008 onwards, however, their focus shifted towards securing lower but stable income streams through rent extraction and management optimization.[21] Wijburg, Aalbers, and Heeg identify this as "financialization 2.0," distinguishing it from the earlier waves of financialization focused on speculation. After the turmoil of the global financial crisis, many private equity firms sold or spun off their housing portfolios into separate real estate income trusts or listed companies. Today, institutional investors in Berlin primarily take the form of long-term "buy and hold" landlords, with 12 companies owning more than 3,000 apartments in

Berlin, with institutional investors owning almost a quarter of a million rental units. Most of these actors are publicly listed companies with complex global shareholder structures, dominated by powerful asset management firms such as Blackstone, and pension funds.[22] Notably, Norwegian and Danish pension funds have also entered this market, either by owning shares in these listed companies or directly expanding their own real estate holdings. In 2018, for example, a Danish pension fund bought a portfolio of 140 apartments in Neukölln for 1.2 billion euros.[23] While Denmark has successfully resisted Blackstone's attempt to buy up residential properties in Copenhagen, the country's welfare system is built on similar real estate investment strategies, the social repercussions of which are exported to locales such as Berlin.[24]

In 2013, a new rental law was introduced in Berlin, which allowed private landlords to pass on up to 11% of modernization costs to their sitting tenants. Many landlords were therefore motivated to perform modernizations, often in excess of what the sitting tenant required. The advantages were two-fold. Firstly, modernization costs allowed for rent increases that could bypass strict regulations that cap rent increases yearly. Secondly, these (often dramatic) spikes in costs tended to be beyond sitting tenants' budgets, putting into motion "renovictions" (eviction through renovation), whereby long-time sitting tenants with protected rents could be forced out with increased rents due to modernization expenses. The rental price could then be further increased by being listed on the private rental market. Furthermore, specialized real estate management companies emerged in this period, oftentimes owned and operated by the institutional landlords themselves. Utilizing economies of scale across large portfolios of housing under their management, landlords were thus able to optimize, or even worse, neglect management demands. Strategies of cost-optimization are not new to private landlords, but as Anne Kockelkorn observes, the coherence, scale, and systematization of these strategies point towards a "new model of housing of the twenty-first century: an ideal city of financialization which promotes the destruction of social cohesion for the sake of shareholders' interest."[25]

These changes have not gone uncontested. In 2019, the Berlin Senate approved legislation for a five-year rent cap (*Mietendeckel*), after which rent increases would be limited to the rate of inflation.[26] Additionally, new leases would be capped according to building age and condition, limiting excessive modernization and renovictions. In 2018, the initiative Expropriate Deutsche Wohnen & Co (*Deutsche Wohnen & Co. Enteignen*) was launched, with the aim of organizing a referendum to expropriate corporate landlords with over 3,000 units in their portfolios. With almost 60% of votes in favor, the September 2021 referendum was a resounding success, far exceeding the combined number of votes for the red-red-green coalition government (the SDP, the Left and the Greens) in the local elections (which were held on the same day as the referendum). The challenges and implications will be unpacked later in this section. Ultimately, however, these victories are just the first in an ongoing struggle over not just urban political economy, but also an intellectual struggle over the power to define the terms of a political debate. With Berlin having flourished under the inflow of global investment, and now facing a housing supply shortage (vacancy rates remain around 1% as of 2021),[27] there is significant political opposition towards initiatives that may scare off investors.

A lobbying group led by Deutsche Wohnen contested the *Mietendeckel* in the Federal Court, which deemed it unconstitutional and overturned it. The case was backed by politicians from the Christian Democratic Union and the pro-business Free Democratic Party, who argued that the rent cap would discourage investment, decrease housing supply, and increase rents.[28] The current Mayor of Berlin, Franziska Giffey (SDP) has been critical about the expropriation referendum, apparently playing for time by pushing the decision on to an expert commission that must first decide if it is constitutional.[29] Just days before the referendum, Berlin's city government bought an estimated 15,000 homes from Deutsche Wohnen and Vonovia (for 2.46 billion euros).[30] The purported message was that expropriating these companies is unnecessary because the City is already taking back ownership of the apartments. However, as critics point out, by buying these homes at an inflated market price, the municipality intervened in favor of big capital, the bitter irony being that their overall condition was now worse than two decades ago when they were privatized for a steeply discounted price.[31]

Berlin's gentrification was once likened to a spiral, targeting up-and-coming neighborhoods that are further and further away from the center: from Mitte and Prenzlauer Berg, to Friedrichshain and Kreuzberg, to Wedding (that, as the joke goes, "never comes").[32] However, as Fields and Uffer observe, the arrival of private equity real estate investment in the early 2000's makes a "property's location and conditions of negligible importance."[33] Since these investors operate by leveraging capital—taking loans to make short term investments—any potential property can generate a profitable return, not just those in up-and-coming neighborhoods. Gentrification therefore comes to be dispersed over a large territory like a "cluster bomb" as described by gentrification scholars Andrej Holm and Matthias Bernt.[34] With increasingly few affordable neighborhoods in the inner city, it is only by moving to the urban periphery that one can hope to find reliably lower rents, vividly encapsulated by a landlord's lengthy complaint about housing regulations:

> What's the problem of moving out [of Berlin] to the outside areas in Brandenburg? The fringes of Brandenburg are shrinking ... This is a real chance for these towns, 30-45 minutes from Berlin, to revitalize ... This is a chance for young families to move out to the edges of Brandenburg ... This is a chance for suburban Berlin areas to grow again ... Why can't people commute 45 minutes? ... What is so abnormal about commuting from outside the city? What God-given right do you have to live in Berlin-Mitte?[35]

Schöneweide on a Road to the Future

The parallel development of an increasingly unaffordable urban core and the shift towards financialization 2.0 strategies is consistent with an imaginary of urbanizing suburbia, one where value added "buy and hold" strategies begin to appear on the urban periphery. This poses a particular challenge for a study of gentrification and the urban periphery. With our opening vignette, which described the move of Griessmuehle to an apparently suburban location in Schöneweide, we do not necessarily claim that

Schöneweide is undergoing gentrification, but rather that extreme inner-city prices have triggered a series of transformations on the periphery, whose more precise political and economic implications call for further consideration. An emphasis on the cultures of gentrification therefore doesn't mean reverting to an idealist conception of art as a driver of gentrification. Rather, we focus on Schöneweide—a suburban neighborhood of 35,000 inhabitants in the Treptow-Köpenick borough—to consider how the role of "culture" as a financial asset shapes strategies and imaginaries at the local level.

First developed by the AEG electric company around the 1900s with several buildings by Peter Behrens, the industrial waterfront developed throughout the prewar, interwar, and postwar periods with a focus on components for electric power production. The housing stock consisted of late-nineteenth century, interwar and post war low-rise multi-family buildings primarily intended for local workers. After German reunification, most production disappeared, with a loss of over 20,000 jobs in Oberschöneweide.[36] Over the years, there have been sporadic investments in new production (notably Samsung between 1993 and 2005), but unemployment in the area remains high. The neighborhood has also been infamous as the center of Berlin's neo-Nazi scene. Between 1993 and 2006, a significant portion of Schöneweide was designated as an urban redevelopment zone (*Sanierungsgebiet*)—one of few off-center locations to be designated as such.[37] While the rents remain affordable, the neighborhood has been identified as "up-and-coming" by the real estate industry: one company described it as the "most potential loaded future spots in Berlin."[38]

This narrative is echoed by local policy makers, who have made it their highest priority to bring investment and transform the neighborhood's image. Along with Schöneweide's industrial architectural heritage (Industriesalon, a museum of local industry, was opened in 2019), the main cornerstones of the revitalization efforts are the smart/tech economy and the arts and culture. A placemaking brochure has referred to this amalgam of strategies as "the 'Schöneweide mix' . . . unique in Berlin."[39] The future of the neighborhood has been imagined as, on the one hand, a "container" for artists and cultural producers priced out from the center and, on the other, an "incubator" for the emerging start-up scene. This entrepreneurial ethos is unsurprising considering that Schöneweide has lost most of its economic base. However, revitalization is at the same time seen as a tool to fight right-wing extremism by promoting urban culture. According to Head of Urban Development in Treptow-Köpenick Rainer Hölmer (SPD), the fact that "Schöneweide's image is currently changing from a haven for right-wing extremists to a hip neighborhood" should be welcomed and promoted "because it brings kindness, but also because culture is always an attraction in Berlin".[40] The housing question and gentrification are addressed primarily through conservation (*Milieuschutz*) and other "soft" regulatory policies, along with an emphasis on new construction.

Situated halfway between the city center and the new airport, Schöneweide has been positioned as the site of a new R&D cluster. Since 2011, the neighborhood has been the focal point of a PPP-led economic development program, a collaboration between the local district and a Berlin state-affiliated innovation manager/urban developer (WISTA), which has been financed through private investments and federal, state, and district support. The program is part of a larger regional development strategy for southeast Berlin (Regionalmanagement Berlin Südost), focused primarily on the forthcoming Berlin-Brandenburg Airport and Adlershof Park (the largest science and technology park in Germany, operated since the reunification on a former GDR Academy of Sciences campus). The University of Applied Sciences (HTW) moved in in 2009, and it plans to move all its campuses to the neighborhood—a move described by a journalist as demonstrating Schöneweide's role as a "road to the future."[41] Additionally, there are plans for start-up incubators and close collaboration in the green energy field between education, research, and industry. Much has been made of the AEG's legacy in the neighborhood: the Industriesalon museum promotes it as an "Elektropolis," while other placemaking efforts focus on the idea that Schöneweide "has been a 'smart city' since [the nineteenth century]."[42] The impact on Schöneweide of the recently announced Tesla factory and design center—to be built near the recently opened Berlin Brandenburg Airport—still remains to be seen.

Independent co-working spaces established in one of the former factories such as KAOS (Kreativen Arbeitsgemeinschaft Oberschöneweide) provide a link between the culture and tech scenes. The nucleus of the renovation, however, is a cluster of industrial buildings. One of these, Reinbeckhallen, was sold to a private investor in 2004 for the symbolic price of one euro, and opened in 2017 as an exhibition complex with studios, a printing workshop, and a residency program.[43] When it opened, the studios were provided at a comparatively affordable rent; a 40-square-meter studio cost 651 euros per month (compared to 905 euros in Kreuzberg).[44] Reinbeckhallen sits next to the warehouse that was converted into a studio by the internationally prominent Icelandic artist Olafur Eliasson.[45] Another converted space is Spreehalle, an old factory hall redeveloped and carved up into 14 modern studio spaces by the Canadian musician-turned-photographer Bryan Adams, which is occupied by the Polish-German sculptor Alicja Kwade, among other influential artists.[46] There had also been rumors that the high-profile art dealer Johann König was negotiating a takeover of a nearby former cable factory.[47]

Ich Liebe Dich / I Love You Too

Within this political climate, the pioneering arts and cultural activities that were the vanguard of gentrification, clearing the way for further development, are now a key part of the charm offensive being launched by corporate landlords. In contrast to the two-decades-old “poor but sexy” image of Berlin, the presence of established figures in Schöneweide such as Adams, Eliasson, or Kwade points to the changing nature of arts and culture in relation to real estate investment. Rather than struggling artists trying to establish themselves in the cracks and abandoned sites of Berlin’s industrial past, the courting of internationally prominent figures also comes with a speculative stake in the pioneering developments. For example, Adams’s investment was expected to transform the dark atmosphere of the former industrial zone into a supportive space for arts and culture.[48] However, with the price tag of upward of 800,000 euros for a bare-shell studio (in 2018), the investment clearly caters exclusively for an elite artistic clientele, reflecting the changing relationship between art and finance in the German capital.[49]

While it remains to be seen whether the mediatized presence of art-market heavyweights will put Schöneweide on the cultural map of Berlin, this is consistent with the vision that local authorities refer to as the "Master plan for Art and Culture" (*Masterplan Kunst und Kultur*). A journalist summarized this vision as a "Meatpacking District approach" to industrial revitalization, referring positively to the ongoing transformation of New York's Meatpacking District.[50] Neighborhood festivals such as the annual Kunst am Spreeknie, along with landmark venues in the wider area such as Funkhaus, fit under this approach. However, consistent with the vision for Schöneweide seems to be also the real estate dynamics in the neighborhood, such as plans by an Irish developer to convert Rathenau Halls, one of the neighborhood's most iconic industrial buildings named after the AEG founder, into luxury flats.[51] Across the river, a former iron smelting works has been demolished to make way for a 60,000-square-meter development by the Austrian real estate company BUWOG.[52] The BUWOG site is bracketed by Novella, a cultural center located in the former Hasselwerder villa. The prosperous, if uneasy, alliance between arts and culture-based regeneration and the aims of value-added strategies of financialization is illustrated by two graffiti messages sprayed nearby on opposite banks of the river: "*Ich liebe dich*" and "I love you too."

The club RSO, unlike its predecessor Griessmuehle, is now the centerpiece of the Bärenquell Brewery development. Led by the real estate development company Home Center Management, the motto of the new brewery development is "creating space," leveraging the industrial heritage and cultural amenities—such as a weekly flea market, beer garden, and RSO itself—to market the development as a high-end creative hub.[53] The development website reads: "As an old brewery it is naturally associated with culture, leisure, and recreation on one hand and with industrialization, technology, and innovation on the other. A perfect mix for the home that is being created there."[54] The property is owned by Aroundtown, a publicly listed real estate company registered in Luxembourg, with a focus on generating "value-add potential in central locations in top-tier European cities."[55] The case of a techno club being a driving force of a suburban redevelopment scheme is therefore of particular significance. The company purchased the brewery with the hopes of utilizing its unique architectural qualities and waterfront location to develop the site into over 70,000 square meters of rented office spaces as well as micro- and student apartments.[56] The "value extraction potential" of the site is expected to achieve market rents of 14.5–17.5 euros per square meter, with sale prices ranging between 4,000 and 5,000 euros per square meter, a rate comparable with inner-city prices.[57] The development is emblematic of the shift that occurs under financialization 2.0, which moves away from "flipping" for a quick return and towards optimizing management and increasing rent levels. Rather than being hostile to long-term goals, corporate involvement in "neighborhood development" now operates in tandem with forms of local planning to promote culture and urban livability.

The developments in Schöneweide follow a by now familiar turn towards the arts and culture as part of a value-added strategy that can be seen in cities around the world. The growing presence of these strategies on the urban periphery, however, poses a particular challenge for the study of gentrification and financialization 2.0. As specialized artistic and creative cultural activities such as galleries, clubs, and artists' studios play an increasingly prominent role in cementing Berlin's cultural status on an international stage, they need to be understood not only as gentrification's pioneers or sympathetic victims but as financial assets in their own right. Support for the arts serves to help frame new developments as responsible actors, one that is further intensified in the urban periphery. After all, who would disagree with transforming a struggling industrial suburb marred by a neo-Nazi reputation into a hub for arts, culture, and education? Nevertheless, such a transformation cannot be neatly detached from the wider set of cultural processes through which gentrification is anchored and resisted.

Culture as Double-Edged Sword

For the neo-Marxist critic Raymond Williams, the popular contemporary definition of "culture," which relates the term to the arts, emerged as part of a broader critique of industrialization. After the Industrial Revolution, "culture" came to be identified with a specialized process of creative effort, elevating it in relation to its more humble origins—what Williams described as "a whole way of life."[58] The emphasis on "ordinary cultures" forms the basis of Williams' pioneering work on cultural materialism, wherein culture is understood not in the limited sense of art as superstructure, but in a broader sense as a means of production that therefore belongs to the economic base. Culture refers in this regard to a shared "structure of feeling" that makes production possible, but also a site of alternative imaginaries and resistance.[59] Struggles around culture are political and economic struggles. Beyond its direct products, it is the *preconditions* of Berlin's flourishing as an arts scene that therefore call for closer analysis.

The affordable rents that attracted the first wave of artists and creatives to Berlin can be attributed in part to the unique status of Berlin as a city predominantly made up of renters. Even now, Berlin has roughly 85% of all residents in some form of rental tenure, a far higher proportion than other Western European cities where homeownership is the norm.[60] If the cultural scene of Berlin is increasingly embraced under the auspices of financialization 2.0, it is the "ordinary culture" of tenancy that appears increasingly under threat. Pressure to participate in the asset economy through homeownership has intensified in recent years in line with the advent of historically low interest rates. In the drive to bypass rental restrictions while also satisfying the supply-side demands of politicians, there has also been a marked growth in the proportion of owner-occupied housing being constructed. Since 1991, the number of owner-occupied dwellings constructed in Berlin has been more than double the number of new rental apartments.[61] The conversion to owner-occupation is one of the latest investment strategies that investors have utilized. Owner-occupiers are afforded particular privileges within the rental regulations, allowing existing tenants to be evicted if the apartment will be for personal use.

Investors now see the opportunity to divide their en bloc properties into smaller units for owner-occupiers, transforming relatively decommodified rental housing protected by strong regulations into commodified private investments.[62]

Beyond the increasing financial advantages that it offers, owner-occupation is also seen as a more secure form of tenure. The artist Alicja Kwade, mentioned above, purchased a studio in the warehouse redeveloped by Bryan Adams after the rent for her previous studio in Kreuzberg had been dramatically increased.[63] Kwade's story is featured in a *New York Times* article on a "creative paradise" springing up in and around Schöneweide: the article reads as an updated version of the "poor but sexy" narrative, documenting several prominent artists that have taken over and refurbished properties along the Spree, having moved on from Mitte, Prenzlauer Berg, and Kreuzberg. Yet these artists are all well-established, and now have considerable resources at their disposal to purchase and develop properties of their own. As rent hikes increase in frequency and intensity, they in turn threaten not just displacement but the culture of renting as a secure and viable form of housing tenure.

At the same time, Berlin's reputation as a renter's paradise reflects the city's strong tenant culture, which serves as a wellspring of resistance to housing financialization. While market reforms and the reduction of state subsidies has opened up the floodgates to corporate landlords, they are also caught in a cat-and-mouse game with Berlin's complex system of tenant protections. Rents in Berlin are not directly regulated—rather, more affordable rents come from tightly controlled regulations regarding evictions and rent increases. Many of the innovations introduced by corporate landlords over the years have focused on bypassing these regulations and finding loopholes such as the aforementioned excessive modernization and renovictions. Matthias Bernt, in his summary of the German housing system, describes these regulations as "a system of bastions and trenches built into a market economy."[64] Though these regulations are the sources of potential closures of "commodification gaps" to increase investment yields, they are also the battleground for a new generation of activists, politicians, and others who are not content to remain dug in but have mobilized around the idea of expropriation and other new avenues of struggle.

When the Griessmuehle team was served the notice of contract termination, it launched a campaign to support it under the slogan "embrace our culture." Approaching Schöneweide on the S-Bahn, one can get a good glimpse of the slogan still painted in large white letters above the club's former location at Neukölln's edge. Yet what is the culture asking to be embraced? As outsiders conducting research in Berlin, we were drawn to the particular lines of political discourse, activism, and resistance to the forces of global capital. More than the flourishing of the arts and club scene in reused industrial spaces, it is the shared culture around housing and right-to-the-city discourses that continued to call for attention. What started as an exploration into the increasing significance of culture as a financial asset has led us to appreciate the role of place-based meanings and values in driving the opposition to gentrification. It may turn out that the city's ordinary culture may be extraordinary after all.

In this section, architectural historian and Berliner Anne Kockelkorn provides an opening vignette of the Hufeisensiedlung, the iconic modernist housing estate which, in passing into the hands of Deutsche Wohnen, became emblematic of the transformations described in this chapter. Following this vignette are three interviews. The first is with urbanist and gentrification scholar Matthias Bernt, who opens up about the bridge between scholarship and activism, and the role played by the particular conditions of Berlin in fostering such connections. The second is with Katalin Gennburg, a directly elected member to the Berlin House of Representatives for the Treptow-Köpenick district and the Left party. Among other insights, Gennburg introduces us to Berlin's dynamic political landscape a year after the referendum. The last interview is with Jenny Stupka and Berta Del Ben, representatives of Expropriate Deutsche Wohnen & Co's Right to the City For All working group. This interview captures an activist movement in transition responding to shifts in the strategic terrain. With these interviews, we hope to extend beyond an account of the ways that the creative arts and culture have defined Berlin's meteoric rise in order to focus on the conditions of its possibility.

1 Schöneweide consists of two administrative districts (*Ortsteil*), Oberschöneweide and Niederschöneweide, which are situated at either side of the river Spree.

2 Deutsche Welle, "Endangered Subculture," October 12, 2019, video, https://www.dw.com/en/endangered-subculture/video-49386650.

3 Compare Sharon Zukin, *The Cultures of Cities* (Blackwell, 1995); Carl Grodach, Nicole Foster, and James Murdoch, "Gentrification, Displacement and the Arts: Untangling the Relationship Between Arts Industries and Place Change," *Urban Studies* 55, no. 4 (2018): 807–25.

4 Raquel Rolnik, *Urban Warfare: Housing under the Empire of Finance* (London: Verso, 2019), 267.

5 Knight Frank, "Berlin Bucks Global Trend as Urban House Price Growth Slows" (London: Knight Frank, 2018), https://content.knightfrank.com/research/1026/documents/en/global-residential-cities-index-q4-2017-5413.pdf.

6 Raymond Williams, *Culture & Society, 1780–1950* (Columbia University Press, 1983).

7 Katharine N. Rankin, "Anthropologies And Geographies of Globalization," *Progress in Human Geography* 27, no. 6 (2003): 708–34.

8 City of Berlin, "Residence Permit for a Freelance Employment - Issuance," accessed January 27, 2023, https://service.berlin.de/dienstleistung/328332/en/.

9 Institut für Strategieentwicklung, *Studio Berlin II* (June 2011). https://ifse.de/Pdf/Studio-Berlin_II_IFSE.pdf.

10 Desiree Fields and Sabina Uffer, "The Financialisation of Rental Housing: A Comparative Analysis of New York City and Berlin," *Urban Studies* 53, no. 7 (2016): 1486–502. The following paragraphs rely on this analysis.

11 For a detailed analysis on the Kohl administration's version of "The Great Moderation" see Wolfgang Streeck, *Re-forming Capitalism: Institutional Change in the German Political Economy* (Oxford: Oxford University Press, 2009).

12 With market reform and the end of state subsidies, many industrial enterprises either collapsed or were sold off, leading to the loss of over half a million industrial jobs. In 2003, Berlin's GDP had contracted 0.7%, while the unemployment rate hovered at 18.1%. Fields and Uffer, "The Financialisation of Rental Housing," 1452.

13 Large en-bloc sales are defined as single transactions that involve 800 or more units. Fields and Uffer, "The Financialisation of Rental Housing," 1493. The original source is Bundesinstitut für Bau-, Stadt- und Raumforschung, *Anstieg großer Wohnungstransaktionen in 2012, BBSR-Analysen Kompakt 12/2012* (Bonn: Bundesinstitut für Bau-, Stadt- und Raumforschung, 2012).

14 Gertjan Wijburg, Manuel B. Aalbers, and Susanne Heeg, "The Financialisation of Rental Housing 2.0: Releasing Housing into the Privatised Mainstream of Capital Accumulation," *Antipode* 50, no. 4 (2018): 1098–119.

15 A detailed overview of these and other transactions is in Stefan Haas, *Modell zur Bewertung wohnwirtschaftlicher Immobilien-Portfolios unter Beachtung des Risikos* (Berlin: Springer, 2010): 178–186.

16 Fields and Uffer, "The Financialisation of Rental Housing," 1493.

17 Andrej Holm, "Berlin's Gentrification Mainstream," in *The Berlin Reader: A Compendium of Urban Change and Activism*, eds. Matthias Bernt, Britta Grell and Andrej Holm, (Bielefeld: transcript Verlag, 2013), 171–87.

18 According to a study by Immowelt, cited in Tobias Buck, "Berlin approves drastic measures to curb surging housing costs," *The Financial Times*, 22 October 2019.

19 Laura Calbet i Elias, "Financialised Rent Gaps and the Public Interest in Berlin's Housing Crisis: Reflections on N. Smith's 'Generalized Gentrification'," in *Gentrification as a Global Strategy: Neil Smith and Beyond*, eds. Abel Albet and Núria Benachl, (London: Routledge, 2018), 165–76.

20 Erik Kirschbaum in Soraya Sarhaddi Nelson, Barbara Steenbergen,Wibke Werner, Kalle Kunkel, and Erik Kirschbaum, hosts, "Episode 63: No Place to Call Home: An Update on Berlin's Housing Crisis," Common Ground (podcast), August 29, 2022, https://commongroundberlin.com/podcast/episode-63-no-place-to-call-home-an-update-on-berlins-housing-crisis/.

21 Wijburg, Aalbers, and Heeg, "The Financialisation of Rental Housing 2.0."

22 See also Manuel B. Aalbers, Zac J. Taylor, Tobias J. Klinge, and Rodrigo Fernandez, "In Real Estate Investment We Trust: State De-Risking and the Ownership of Listed US and German Residential Real Estate Investment Trusts," *Economic Geography* (2022): 1–24.

23 Nik Martin, "Entire Stretch of Berlin Street Bought by Investment Fund," *Deutsche Welle*, August 12, 2018.

24 Hettie O'Brien, "The Blackstone Rebellion: How One Country Took on the World's Biggest Commercial Landlord," *The Guardian*, September 29, 2022.

25 Anne Kockelkorn, "Financialized Berlin: The Monetary Transformation of Housing, Architecture and Polity," *Architectural Theory Review* 26, no. 1 (2022): 76–104.

26 Philip Oltermann, "Unaffordable Cities: Berlin the Renters' Haven Hit by Green Fog of Eco-Scams," *The Guardian*, February 11, 2014.

27 Engel & Völkers, "Berlin: Strong Demand and Limited Supply Lead To Further Price Increases on Residential Market," *Engel & Völkers*, accessed January 27, 2023, https://www.engelvoelkers.com/en/blog/property-insights/market-trends/berlin-strong-demand-and-limited-supply-lead-to-further-price-increases-on-residential-market/.

28 Kate Connolly, "Berlin's Rent Cap Is Illegal, Germany's Highest Court Rules," *The Guardian*, April 15, 2021.

29 There are disagreements between the party leadership and the rank and file on this issue. In summer 2022, the SPD's local annual congress voted in favor of carrying out the referendum. Dave Braneck, "Berliners voted for a radical solution to soaring rents. A year on, they are still waiting," *Euronews*, September 26, 2022. On the ambiguous role of the commission see Leander Jones, "After Berliners Voted to Nationalize Housing, City Hall Isn't Delivering," *Jacobin*, May 2, 2022.

30 Iain Rogers and Agatha Cantrill, "Berlin Buys Vonovia, Deutsche Wohnen Apartments for $2.9 billion," *Bloomberg News*, September 17, 2021.

31 Nikos Vrantsis, "What Is at Stake After Berlin's Referendum for the Expropriation of Big Corporate Landlords," *Medium*, October 28, 2021, https://medium.com/@nikvrantsis/what-is-at-stake-after-berlins-referendum-for-the-expropriation-of-big-corporate-landlords-f432a2c5ae4.

32 Holm, "Berlin's Gentrification Mainstream."

33 Fields and Uffer, "The Financialization of Rental Housing," 1490.

34 Matthias Bernt and Andrej Holm, "Gentrifizierung in Ostdeutschland: der Fall Prenzlauer Berg," *Deutsche Zeitschrift für Kommunalwissenschaften* 41, no. 2 (2002): 125–50.

35 Erik Kirschbaum in Kirschbaum et al., "Episode 63."

36 Matthias Dunger, "Bewahrung der Denkmale der Industrie und der technischen Infrastruktur: eine Zwischenbilanz," in *Sowjetische Avantgarde der 1920er und 1930er Jahre* (Moscow: Rudenzowych, 2014), 68, https://issuu.com/kvagit/docs/sovetskii_avangard1/141.

37 Both Oberschöneweide and Niederschöneweide were included in Berlin's first post-unification redevelopment program (*Gesamtberliner Stadterneuerungsprogramm*), introduced in 1993, as "rehabilitation areas" (*Sanierungsgebiet*). Senatsverwaltung für Stadtentwicklung, *23. Bericht über Stadterneuerung, 01.01.2000–31.12.2001. Mitteilungen des Präsidenten des Abgeordnetenhauses von Berlin, Drucksache Nr. 14/821* (2000), https://www.stadtentwicklung.berlin.de/staedtebau/foerderprogramme/stadterneuerung/de/download/23StB-00.pdf.
38 Bato Group, *The Future of Schöneweide: Under Construction* (2014), www.batogroup.com/newsletter/news_attachment_550_1393855694.pdf.
39 *Magazin Schöneweide* (2016), 9.
40 Dietrich von Schell, "Gentrifizierung, Asylbewerber und Beamte am Limit," *Der Maulbär*, October 5, 2015.
41 Karin Schmidl, "Auf dem Weg in die Zukunft: Neue Eigentümer wollen neue Industrien nach Schöneweide bringen," *Der Maulbär*, October 11, 2019.
42 *Magazin Schöneweide* (2016), 9.
43 Gunda Bartels, "Kunstquartier in Oberschöneweide: Heimkehren heißt anfangen," *Tagesspiegel*, May 1, 2017.
44 Statista, "Rent costs in Berlin areas by apartment size, 2017," *Statista*, accessed January 27, 2023, www.statista.com.
45 Bartels, "Kunstquartier in Oberschöneweide."
46 Andrew Blackman and Birgit Jennen, "Surging German property prices are haunting Merkel," *Bloomberg News*, July 2, 2018; Thomas Loy, "Kunstquartier im Berliner Südosten: Kühler Empfang für Bryan Adams," *Tagesspiegel*, November 6, 2016.
47 Gisela Williams, "In Berlin, A Creative Paradise That's Easiest to Reach By Boat," *The New York Times*, October 11, 2019.
48 Thomas Loy, "Treptow-Köpenick Atelierhaus von Bryan Adams ist fertig," *Tagesspiegel*, January 2, 2018.
49 Blackman and Jennen, "Surging German Property Prices Are Haunting Merkel."
50 Schmidl, "Auf dem Weg in die Zukunft", Reinhart Bünger, "Berlin-Treptow-Köpenick: Rathenau-Hallen vor dem Verkauf," *Tagesspiegel*, February 11, 2019.
51 Brian Carey, "Irish companies are making millions in the German property market," *The Sunday Times*, May 23, 2021.
52 The plot sits empty as of 2022. Buwog was acquired by Vonovia in 2018.
53 "Home Center Management," Home Center Management, accessed January 27, 2023, https://home-center-management.de/.
54 "History," Bärenquell, accessed January 27, 2023, https://baerenquell.eu/history/
55 "Aroundtown," Aroundtown, accessed January 27, 2023, https://www.aroundtown.de/.
56 Aroundtown, *9M 2022 Financial Results* (2022), https://www.aroundtown.de/fileadmin/user_upload/04_investor_relations/downloads/2022/AT_9M_2022_financials_presentation.pdf.
57 Statista, "Average Asking Rent of Apartments in Berlin, Germany from 2019 to 2021, By District," *Statista website*, https://www.statista.com/statistics/800765/rent-expenditure-apartments-berlin-germany-by-district/; JLL, "Office market braces itself against recessive trends," JLL Research, October 20, 2022. https://www.jll.de/en/trends-and-insights/research/office-market-overview.
58 Williams, *Culture & Society*.
59 Raymond Williams, *Culture and Materialism: Selected Essays* (Verso, 2005).
60 Christoph Trautvetter, *Who Owns the City? Analysis of Property Owner Groups and Their Business Practices on the Berlin Real Estate Market* (Rosa Luxemburg Stiftung, 2021), https://www.rosalux.de/fileadmin/rls_uploads/pdfs/Studien/Studien_6-2021_Who_Owns_The_City.pdf.
61 JLL, *The Berlin Market for Newly Constructed Condominiums Market Relevance and Spatial Shifts in Completions* (Berlin: JLL, 2021), 7, https://www.jll.de/content/dam/jll-com/documents/pdf/research/emea/germany/en/Newly-Constructed-Condominiums-Berlin-JLL-Germany.pdf.
62 Matthias Bernt, *The Commodification Gap: Gentrification and Public Policy in London, Berlin and St. Petersburg* (Hoboken, NJ.; Wiley: 2022).
63 Gisella Williams, "In Berlin."
64 Bernt, *The Commodification Gap*, 98.

Hufeisensiedlung as Financialized World Heritage

Anne Kockelkorn

Since the mid-1990s, the rental housing market in Germany has undergone a process of financialization that has, especially in the last decade, affected social cohesion in urban centers like Berlin.[1] Through its privatization and financialization, the former social housing stock of the twentieth century now facilitates an upward redistribution of wealth in Germany, a development that comes at the expense of community-building, well-being, and sustainability. Berlin's *Siedlungen* from the interwar period exemplify this fundamental reversal of societal ambitions related to housing provision.

A key example to illustrate this shift is Bruno Taut's Horseshoe Estate (Hufeisensiedlung) in the Britz neighborhood (1925–33). With its iconic horseshoe-shape of apartment blocks, which enclose an existing pond, the project is part of the DNA of architectural education in Germany, Europe, and beyond. The project includes an entire urban ensemble of about 1,000 housing units, organized in a neighborhood of two-storey row housing, with small front yards and large backyards following an axisymmetric pattern. The subtle power of its urban design makes it outstanding. The monumental apartment ring embodies the notion of community within an urban neighborhood and opens up towards the east with a small neighborhood center. To the west, the central horseshoe form finds its counterpart in a diamond-shaped square lined with ground-level dwellings, which takes on the proportions of a village green. Between these two central squares, streets run diagonally, forming broken lines which, due to their individual orientation, colors, and planting, accord each plot its own identity despite and within the repetition of aesthetic features. These ground-level machines for living carefully balance between community building and the articulation of individuality, combining access to recreational green space and dense living within an urban neighborhood.

The second outstanding feature of the Horseshoe Estate and other modernist *Siedlungen* of Berlin lies in their regulatory underpinnings. They result from a decades-long struggle to provide high-quality housing for lower income groups. After World War I, Berlin experienced a housing shortage in the order of 100,000 flats that demanded urgent action from public officials. One of the measures taken was the introduction of a property tax (*Hauszinssteuer*) in 1924, which called private landlords—who were hardly affected by the hyperinflation of 1923—to invest in public housing. In 1924, the German Salaried Employees' Union also founded the non-profit housing developer GEHAG (Gemeinnützige Heimstätten-, Spar- und Bau-Aktiengesellschaft), which was instrumental in developing *Siedlungen* in the periphery of newly established Gross-Berlin. Overall, 60,000 new housing units were built in the urban region between 1925 and 1928, 40% of which were developed by municipal housing companies and funded by public investments—including the 1,000 units of Hufeisensiedlung and the 2,000 units of Waldsiedlung Zehlendorf, designed by Bruno Taut and developed by GEHAG. As a form of modern welfare provision, the urban and architectural design of these *Siedlungen* was on the one hand dedicated to improving the quality of life and residents' conditions of social reproduction. On the other hand, the design concepts were based on public ownership and relied on the establishment of municipal and cooperative housing developers that were committed to non-speculative modes of housing production.[2]

It is the interplay of these social, political, and aesthetic features that qualified the Horseshoe Estate for its UNESCO World Heritage status, which it was awarded in 2008, together with three other GEHAG housing estates: the Wohnstadt Carl Legien in Prenzlauer Berg (1928–30), also designed by Bruno Taut; the Siemensstadt settlement in Charlottenburg, designed by Hans Scharoun (1929–31); and the "White City" in Reinickendorf, designed by Otto Salvisberg (1928–31).[3] As the UNESCO website states, these settlements express "a broad reform of housing construction and *Siedlungsbau*" that combined "esthetic research with new social and hygiene standards" and served as "guidelines for social housing in Germany and beyond."[4] The German UNESCO webpage also emphasizes that two of the six *Siedlungen* still operate under a cooperative mode of housing tenure, a model of human cooperation added to UNESCO's Intangible Cultural Heritage register in 2016. However, what the website fails to mention is that four of the six *Siedlungen* were already owned by a financialized housing provider at the time of their listing—i.e., a provider using a significant amount of debt leverage, bundled in mortgage-backed securities that can be traded on global capital markets.[5]

In 2003, GEHAG was privatized through a sale to the American hedge fund Oaktree, only to be resold to the real estate developer Deutsche Wohnen SE (which was founded in 1998 by Deutsche Bank) in 2007. In 2013, Deutsche Wohnen SE also bought shares in GSW (Gemeinnützige Siedlungs- und Wohnungsbaugesellschaft Berlin mbH), formerly Berlin's largest social housing company, which had already been privatized in 2004. One year prior to the acquisition, GSW estimated the value of its real estate portfolio at 3.3 billion euros—around four times the 2004 sales price.[6] Ownership of GEHAG and GSW combined turned Deutsche Wohnen SE into the largest real estate company in Berlin and the second largest real estate company in Germany. In 2015, the company's profit amounted to 1.2 billion euros. In the same year, the salaries of the executive board increased from 2.5 to 6.5 million euros.[7] In 2020, Deutsche Wohnen SE was recognized by the German share index DAX as one of the most valuable stock corporations in the country. Valorization of market capitalization continues to date, as the sale and resale of company shares remains an important generator of fictitious capital gains. The most striking example of this strategy is the successful 2021 takeover of Deutsche Wohnen SE by Germany's largest housing company, Vonovia SE, who also originated from en-bloc sales of former social housing stock. This takeover resulted in the formation of an enormous rental housing provider, which, in owning 550,000 units, was able to dominate the German rental market, including all 4 of the UNESCO World Heritage *Siedlungen* in Berlin. In fact, according to Deutsche Wohnen SE's 2020 Annual Report, 39.72% of the company's housing stock was built between 1919 and 1979; 8.6% was built prior to 1919, 18% percent was built between 1980 and 1999; only 0.9% of the company's housing stock was built after 2000. Vonovia's annual report does not provide such data, but just like Deutsche Wohnen SE, its portfolio grew through en-bloc acquisition of former social housing stock from the twentieth century.

The financialization of rental apartments reverses the goals and mandates of a housing association. The aim of a private equity fund or publicly listed housing company is to satisfy investors' expectations of profit, not to provide tenants with high-quality housing at a low cost. An important tool in increasing the asset value of the housing stock is to ensure a continuous increase in rents, to be achieved through the strategic assessment of rent gaps.[8] Another instrument for securing rental increases is the modernization of amenities—that is, the comprehensive renovation of housing to increase its energy efficiency and comfort, the costs of which, unlike maintenance, can be passed on by raising the rent. In the case of financialized world heritage, modernization can be combined with "patrimonialization"—that is, the targeted renewal, staging, and commodification of cultural heritage, as described by the sociologists Luc Boltanski and Arnaud Esquerre.[9] Both strategies were implemented in Berlin's financialized *Siedlungen*. Energy modernization offered the opportunity to save taxes and pass on the costs of modernizations to rents, followed by "renoviction"—that is, the displacement of low-income households from the neighborhood. [10] On the one hand, modernization according to heritage standards contributed to an instrumental symbolic upgrading: the horseshoe layout of the Hufeisensiedlung was chosen as Deutsche Wohnen SE's logo and the non-listed Waldsiedlung by Bruno Taut in Zehlendorf labeled an "architectural jewel" on Deutsche Wohnen SE's website.[11]

The Hufeisensiedlung thereby no longer operates as a machine for living that sets urban green space, everyday routines, and an urban neighborhood in relation to each other. It has become, rather, a machine for value extraction through continuous rental increases. In 1938, Bruno Taut claimed in his *Architekturlehre* that both sociospatial and aesthetic innovation ensues by developing the appropriate form for the appropriate budget.[12] For a financialized housing developer, however, appropriate innovation must be geared to maximize shareholder value and thus commodifiable floor space. This take on appropriateness renders the design of a large horseshoe courtyard around an existing pond unthinkable—unless it was paid for by public budgets—and happens to be charged with the symbolic power of World Heritage.

This reversal calls for a rethinking of the meaning of heritage, and of the way in which existing housing stock contributes to inscribing power relations into living routines. It also calls for a parallel rethinking of the exclusive attribution of World Heritage status to the *Siedlungen's* urban form, as opposed to recognizing that status as resulting from a coherent ensemble of urban politics, housing tenure, and urban design. If a *Siedlung* is owned by a financialized company, only the shareholder benefits from the value added by the expectation of future rental income accrued as a result of the symbolic value of a World Heritage listing. Seen as a sociopolitical ecology, the heritage listing thus contributes to undermining the very conditions upon which the listing is based. These conditions include: a concept of citizenship that is inseparable from the right to high-quality, affordable dwellings; an art of governing that supports a non-profit notion of collective benefit in housing policies, alongside the cooperative housing associations that implement that notion; and an architectural response to housing needs, care, and social reproduction, which, according to the political theorist Nancy Fraser, is not only a matter of private households but of neighborhoods, civil society, and state agencies.[13]

A tourist walking through the Hufeisensiedlung today witnesses the urban form as Bruno Taut designed it 100 years ago, while trimmed trees and bright colors on renovated facades indicate the ongoing process of financialization. Which kind of value is generated here, and for whom? Following the argument advanced by Boltanski and Esquerre, value translates into the *taking place* of constructed events; and this *taking place* concerns both the monetary price of land and housing as well as the lived experience of dwelling. What is at stake today is not only an understanding of the differences between these political constructions and the possibility of establishing a framework that relates them, but also our ability to identify who profits from these constructed events and why.

1 This text is based on the paper "Financialized Berlin. The Monetary Transformation of Housing, Architecture, and Polity," which investigates the historic trajectory of housing financialization in Berlin. See Anne Kockelkorn, "Financialized Berlin. The Monetary Transformation of Housing, Architecture, and Polity," *Architectural Theory Review 26*, no. 1 (2022): 76–104.

2 See Catherine Bauer, *Modern Housing* (Minneapolis, MN: University of Minnesota, 2020 [1934]).

3 Two other housing estates by Bruno Taut that were also included on the World Heritage List are the Schillerpark Siedlung in Wedding and the so-called "Tuschkastensiedlung" in Treptow, both of which are still owned by the Berliner Bau- und Wohnungsgenossenschaft von 1892 eG. Only two other housing estates in Berlin from the 1920s received UNESCO listings in addition to the Museum Island in the city center and the Babelsberg Palace near Potsdam.

4 Author's translation: "Modernität und soziales Denken im Berlin der Weimarer Republik," Deutsche UNESCO-Kommission, accessed February 27, 2022, https://www.unesco.de/kultur-und-natur/welterbe/welterbe-deutschland/siedlungen-der-berliner-moderne.

5 Both private equity firms and listed companies (German: AGs) in German housing real estate utilize commercial mortgage-backed securities (CMBS) to manage their debt, which is why they can be defined as financialized. Philipp P. Metzger, *Die Finanzialisierung der deutschen Ökonomie am Beispiel des Wohnungsmarktes* (Münster: Westfälisches Dampfboot, 2020): 207–18; Knut Unger, "Mieterhöhungsmaschinen: Zur Finanzialisierung und Industrialisierung der unternehmerischen Wohnungswirtschaft," *Prokla* 191, no. 2 (2018): 211–12.

6 GSW, "Jahresgeschäftsbericht/Geschäftsbericht 2012," accessed July 7, 2022, http://www.gsw.ag/websites/gswimmobilien/German/2020/corporate-news.html?newsID=1325383.

7 Gunnar Hinck, "Privatisierung auf dem Wohnungsmarkt: Belohnung in Millionenhöhe," *die tageszeitung*, June 14, 2016, http://www.taz.de/Privatisierung-auf-dem-Wohnungsmarkt/!5312757.

8 Laura Calbet i Elias, "Financialised Rent Gaps and the Public Interest in Berlin's Housing Crisis," in *Gentrification as a Global Strategy: Neil Smith and Beyond*, eds. Abel Albet and Núria Benach (London: Routledge, 2018), 165–76.

9 Luc Boltanski and Arnaud Esquerre, *Enrichment: A Critique of Commodities* (Hoboken, NJ: Wiley & Sons, 2020).

10 https://www.berliner-mieterverein.de/magazin/online/mm0406/040611a.htm; https://www.zeit.de/2006/02/Wohnungen_Head; https://www.berliner-mieterverein.de/magazin/online/mm1122/einwurf-von-barbara-von-boroviczeny-klein-beigeben-kam-fuer-mich-nicht-infrage-112210b.htm, accessed February 9th, 2023.

11 "Berlin—Waldsiedlung," Deutsche Wohnen, accessed October 11, 2021, https://www.deutsche-wohnen.com/bauen-wohnen/neubau-und-quartiere/berlin-waldsiedlung.

12 Bruno Taut, Architekturlehre (Hamburg: VSA, 1977 [1936–38]), 65.

13 Nancy Fraser and Rahel Jaeggi, *Capitalism: A Conversation in Critical Theory* (Cambridge: Polity, 2018): 31–32.

Theorizing Gentrification from Berlin

An Interview with Matthias Bernt

Matthias Bernt (MB)

Maroš Krivý (MK) *Leonard Ma (LM)*

Matthias Bernt is the acting head of the research focus "Politics and Planning" at the Leibniz Institute for Research on Society and Space and an adjunct lecturer at the Department of Social Sciences at the Humboldt-Universität zu Berlin. This interview took place in November 2022.

LM In the Berlin section of *Urbanizing Suburbia*, we ask how local forms of activism and resistance address global conditions. How has the experience of living in Berlin shaped your understanding of gentrification?

MB I lived in Prenzlauer Berg back in the early 1990s, when gentrification was taking off here. It was a new topic in Germany—only a handful of sociologists and geographers were familiar with the term, it was more common to call it "restructuring" or "Yuppiefication," or to use untranslatable terms such as *Schickimickisierung* (referring to conspicuous fashion and luxury types of people). While studying political science and sociology, I came across studies of gentrification, mainly in New York City—like the texts written by Neil Smith, Sharon Zukin, or Robert A. Beauregard—that illuminated what was happening on my doorstep. These brought me to urban studies and a career in academia, but also oriented my interest and engagement in grassroots politics. This inspired my interest in comparative gentrification and resulted in *The Commodification Gap*, a recently published monograph that compares gentrification and public policy in London, Berlin, and St. Petersburg.[1]

LM Your work is particularly significant because it bridges research and activism. How do you think about that bridge?

MB Let me respond by saying how research and activism differ. A key difference is that research and activism operate with different notions of time. Producing academic knowledge is a slow process. I started writing *The Commodification Gap* in 2014, completed the first manuscript in 2018, and it took another four years to get the book out. No activist is interested in that, are they? When you face a problem now, you need knowledge *now*. You need help *now*. Moreover, academic knowledge doesn't easily translate in the policy arena. Many of the problems that activists struggle with have intellectually been well understood for quite a while. So, what is needed is not so much new scientific knowledge but education, knowledge transfer, and application. At the same time, designing scholarship in a way that it fits the needs of activism is not a solution either: my academic background gives me an analytical stance and distance that enables me to develop new perspectives and find out new things, and this can be helpful for activism too. Both roles are clearly interconnected, but they can't be conflated. I wouldn't generalize by saying that my role as a scholar serves my role as an activist or the other way around.

MK Do housing researchers, activists, and left-of-center politicians cooperate in Berlin?

MB There are networks, but they are based on a handful of individuals who are in touch with and talk to each other. Andrej Holm, a friend of mine, is a good example. We studied together; we went to Prenzlauer Berg neighborhood initiatives together. Holm became a prominent, mediatized figure after he was imprisoned in 2006 on dubious charges. One of the charges was that he used the term "gentrification." The police found it in a declaration by a terrorist organization and because the term was relatively unknown, they thought Holm must be the author. Ironically, his imprisonment led to the popularization of the term in Germany, and many journalists asked me to explain it to them. Their reaction was: "Oh, you mean like what happened in Prenzlauer Berg?" Holm has brought housing research in contact with grassroots initiatives and parliamentary politics. When in 2016 The Left (*Die Linke*) gained control of the Berlin Senate's Department for Urban Development, Building, and Housing, he was appointed as State Secretary for Housing but was ousted after four months. In Berlin, the exchange between politics, activism, and academia is largely due to Holm and maybe half a dozen other individuals like Ulrike Hamann, Lisa Vollmer, Armin Kuhn, or Joanna Kusiak who have moved and shifted their roles between the academic world and activism and, in some cases, professional careers outside academia but with close relation to housing policies. This is, however, not widespread.

LM In cities such as Vancouver, there are heated discussions on housing affordability. However, critical housing scholars haven't been able to influence the public debate in ways comparable to Berlin.

MB Contrary to the appearance, housing studies are weak in Germany. There's no professorship and hardly any institutional basis for the field. Although it is gradually changing, German academia has been dominated by the notion that research has to be objective. As an academic, you steer clear of policymakers and especially grassroots initiatives because they are biased.

MK Can you broadly describe the most recent developments concerning gentrification in Berlin?

MB First, it is no longer bound to the spiral movement in the inner city—the effects are now spread out almost everywhere, at least everywhere inside the S-Bahn circle and even in some neighborhoods outside that, where it wouldn't have been expected before.[2] Overall, gentrification is no longer bound to a particular neighborhood where artists move in, then the middle class moves in, and so forth. It has become more fluid. Still, it hasn't happened everywhere; there are districts in the periphery that haven't been gentrified. A second observation concerns Berlin's increasingly cosmopolitan character. More and more, demand for upmarket housing comes from abroad, and often it is combined with temporarily locating in Berlin during a kind of transitory stage in life. Many people come to live in Berlin at a particular period in their life, for half a year or for five years, and then leave, which poses challenges for housing policy and activism. Third, investment behavior has also internationalized and, in contrast to the past, international investors play a growing role in Berlin's housing market. Fourth, and most importantly, housing affordability has become the top priority in local politics: housing policy is therefore more contested than ever before. This, effectively, makes gentrification a battlefield.

LM How do you assess the impact of international capital and rising real estate prices? Has buying become more popular than renting? What is the impact on housing tenure demographics?

MB The proportion of households living in rental apartments has decreased only very slightly, from around 85% to around 83%. In the former urban redevelopment areas [*Sanierungsgebiete*] in Prenzlauer Berg, 20% to 30% of the apartments have been converted to owner-occupation.[3] However, we don't know how many of these are inhabited by the people who bought them: many apartments that have been transformed from rental to ownership status are then rented out again. A frequent practice has been that an apartment owner claims personal use, kicks out the tenant, renovates the apartment, and then rents it out again for a higher rent. This has now become more regulated, but there are still ways of bypassing the strict rent increase regulations. So, in a nutshell, the trend towards owning a home is still somewhat restricted, and transforming a rental flat into an individually owned home is often done to make use of the loopholes of rent regulations.

LM Has there been a rise in small private landlords?

MB There has been a rise in the influence of institutional investors. *Who Owns the City?* has tracked obscure landlords, registered in the Cayman Islands or similar places, who own thousands of apartments.[4] The biggest landlord in Berlin, with close to 160,000 apartments is now Vonovia, a stock-listed institutional investor with large shareholders such as Blackrock, the Norwegian State Fund, and others. We don't know how many apartments are owned by small landlords, and we don't know how much apartments that are registered as owner-occupied are rented out.

Until very recently, tenement houses with 20 to 40 units, such as those in Prenzlauer Berg, would have been owned and rented out by a single person, who would often also live in the house. This was often a family thing. For around a decade and half now, institutional investors have been buying these properties to sell or rent them. Often, this went hand in hand with changing the status of the flats to owner-occupation. As a consequence, many of these buildings now have 20 to 40 different owners. For example, in the 2000s, Taekker was a big name in Berlin's housing market and their business consisted of buying up properties in neighborhoods such as Kreuzberg, getting the tenants out, transforming the units into owner occupation and selling them to individual buyers (often from Scandinavia) who wanted to buy a home in Berlin as an asset. All this points to the internationalization of housing and financial markets but also to the role of new technologies. Nowadays, you can find out which neighborhood fits you on your smartphone, without even visiting the city. You can buy a property and get legal advice using your smartphone. Altogether, this has had a profound effect on the ways in which housing is produced, bought and sold, and valorized.

MK In September 2021, the historic referendum to expropriate large corporate landlords in Berlin, organized by the *Deutsche Wohnen & Co Enteignen* initiative (Expropriate

Deutsche Wohnen & Co, DWE), was passed with 59,1% of votes. Who supported the referendum?

MB What made the referendum extraordinary was that it was a grassroots initiative that came from outside of party politics. Housing affordability has become an important issue for a large number of Berliners, including the middle class. There is a widespread dissatisfaction and a sense of urgency about changing the system. The support for the referendum doesn't neatly correlate with support for specific parties.

MK The referendum was supported by many more people than those who voted for The Left and The Greens (*Die Grünen*), the two government coalition parties in favor of expropriation. What has been the impact of the referendum in the urban arena? It does not seem that much has happened more than a year after the referendum.

MB Berlin is governed by a red-red-green coalition, made up of the Social Democratic Party (SDP), The Left and The Greens. These three parties have very different opinions on expropriation. The Left has supported the referendum campaign from the start. Among The Greens, some politicians support expropriation, others don't, and still others see the referendum as a form of political leverage that can be used to negotiate with the big investors, but they don't want to actually expropriate them. The SDP is against expropriation. These three parties have had a tremendous problem finding a consensus. Eventually they founded an expert commission, but it remains unclear whether the rationale was to assess the legality of expropriation or how to implement it. It's unclear what the committee members discuss because the meetings are not public.[5] Some people hope the initiative will just fizzle out.

MK Does DWE have seats on the commission?

MB There are 12 members: each party nominated three experts and DWE nominated three experts. I expect that there won't be consensus on any issue and the final report will be useless. Eventually, the government will have to make up its mind anyway. And if they go ahead with the expropriation, it will almost certainly go through the courts. So it is a long way to go, even in the most auspicious case.

The commission reflects the SDP's, and especially Mayor Franziska Giffey's, dilemma: they wish the issue would go away, but they also need to demonstrate that they acknowledge and address the result of the referendum.

At the same time, Berlin's government has held roundtable talks with big housing investors, tenant representatives, and other stakeholders, chaired by the mayor. These have ended up in a "Coalition for new construction and affordable rents"—which has been largely used for PR, but in practice turned out to be a huge flop. The goals were set so low with regard to rents, that Berlin's tenant association withdrew from the discussion. Interestingly, the same goes for some major landlords for whom even the most modest targets were too much. Thus, the idea to get the problem solved on the basis of voluntary agreements has been largely discredited by now.

LM Corporate landlords and private equity investment already appeared in Berlin's housing market during the 1990s, and pioneered many of the investment strategies of corporate financialization that has become such a big topic in housing today. After the expropriation referendum, have there been new strategies developed by these types of large-scale landlords?

MB In 1991, Berlin had something around 350,000 social housing units, now it has less than 100,000 units. "Municipal housing" refers to the housing stock owned by municipal housing corporations, much of which has been privatized. In the first wave, in the 1990s, many nineteenth and early twentieth-century tenement buildings in areas such as Prenzlauer Berg were restituted to their prewar owners, who quickly sold the buildings to commercial investors, who in turn "renovicted" the tenants (evicted them by renovating the apartments). The second wave, in the 2000s, was marked by the internationalization of housing investments. A combination of municipal fiscal difficulties and shrinking population (in the former East) created a situation when city officials desperate for money sold off large portions of the municipal housing stock. For example, Berlin's municipal housing company GSW, which owned around 75,000 apartments, was sold to a US investor.

Today, the cities are no longer selling their housing stock. Thus, the third phase is marked by a concentration process within the stock held by private investors. We see a pattern of one investor selling to another selling to a third one, then the third one fuses with a fourth one, like the takeover of Deutsche Wohnen by Vonovia in 2021. In the urban studies literature, this is called "financialization 2.0."[6] The concept describes a shift from the opportunistic model of buying cheap, renovating, and selling high to one of holding and raising rents. Financialization 2.0 equally involves economies of scale such as streamlining administration and operation costs. As a result, tenants of companies such as Vonovia wait for hours on the phone when they need to speak with a housing manager. Requests for repair are often ignored. There have been scandals such as the heating being broken for weeks during the winter. Photographs of freezing people dressed in jackets and anoraks inside their apartments have circulated in the media. All this signals an emerging business strategy: these investors are here to stay.

MK Your recent book contributes a new concept to gentrification theory: the commodification gap. You highlight the limits of a logic of capital argument, asking how capital flows into the housing market are regulated. Can you elaborate the concept and the context in which you developed it?

MB I became interested in gentrification in the early 1990s. I read gentrification literature and went to New York for the first time in 1994. Back then, the gentrification frontier was Avenue A in the Lower East Side. And I thought: "This is just like Kollwitz Platz."[7] I attended some tenant meetings in New York and understood there are many similarities in how gentrification unfolds but also major differences in policy. Getting to grips with gentrification being simultaneously a general and particular concept has occupied me ever since.

There are two main gentrification narratives. One focuses on the presence of artists and yuppies to explain why the neighborhood is becoming fancy and expensive. The other is about capital: as soon as the potential rental income is higher than the current one, this view suggests, capital flows in, the rent gap is closed, prices go up. Both narratives tend to represent gentrification as a natural process. The idea behind the commodification gap is to focus on housing regulations and other institutional contexts that enable gentrification: the *politics* of gentrification. The ground rent that is potentially achievable on commodified (unregulated) land is different from the ground rent that is potentially achievable on (partly) decommodified land.

How was the concept developed? I compared the politics of commodification and decommodification in London, Berlin, and St. Petersburg with respect to gentrification dynamics and patterns in these cities. Interestingly enough, I was recently told that only a German could write this book. In a way, this is true, because Berlin has a highly regulated rental market. It would have been a different book if I wrote it from Texas.

MK The commodification gap highlights the comparative experience of European, American, and other urbanisms and exposes the limits of general theory.

MB The postcolonial urban scholar Jennifer Robinson talks about "geographies of theory": theories are developed against a particular background.[8] This is all the more true for gentrification studies. The idea of "gentrification pioneers" reflects the experience, in the 1970s US, of white, educated, middle-class kids moving into black neighborhoods. It captures a cultural fascination with the apparent reversal of the "white flight." The rent gap theory similarly reflects under-maintained, abandoned inner cities as the reality of the 1970s' US. Conversely, the value gap of Chris Hamnet can be traced to the "flat break-up market" in 1970s and '80s in London, while the functional gap of Luděk Sýkora was developed against the example of post-communist Prague.[9] All these concepts have been generalized, but they reflect specific experiences or regimes of regulation and valorization.

LM What role does *context* play in homeownership? In London, for example, homeownership and the asset economy have been extremely significant. But welfare states across Europe have been rolled back, while homeownership, and the idea of home equity as a safety net, have been encouraged. Germany is unique in that regard in having high levels of tenancy. Is there a pressure to buy in Germany, and specifically in Berlin?

MB The process of *assetization*—using assets to make up for reduced welfare protection—is, among other things, driven by the lack of affordable housing. Finding an affordable rental apartment, and thereby benefiting from regulations that protect sitting tenants, can be very difficult. For example, if you are from Munich and get a job in Berlin, you compete with a hundred other people willing to pay the same overpriced rent. Ownership is a way of bypassing that system. But if you are lucky enough to have lived in a flat for a long time, your rent is relatively protected, and it is economically disadvantageous to buy an overpriced home. This "dualization" of the housing system hasn't been studied to a satisfactory degree.

LM And how does assetization sit with the commodification gap theory?

MB It concerns what I call the "tenure transformation gap." Landlords can extract only a very limited profit from existing rental contracts because these are strongly protected. However, if as a landlord you manage to get the tenant out and sell the apartment, the difference between the tenanted value and the untenanted value can easily reach 1,000 euros per square meter. As a middle-class buyer, you then get a chance to purchase the apartment as an asset and exit from the more and more competitive rental market. You can eat the cake and keep it too, so to speak. You can live in your own apartment, but once you get old, you have something to leave to your children. This is becoming an increasingly normal calculation for middle-class households. People wouldn't have thought like that 20 years ago, especially not in tenement house neighborhoods such as Prenzlauer Berg.

LM Is there now pressure to climb the housing ladder?

MB Totally, but it's also driven by internationalization. Because many people are coming to Berlin from environments where buying and selling an apartment is a totally normal thing. You know, in Germany for a long time, the idea was that when you buy an apartment, it's a once in a lifetime decision. But, you know, to enter a market for maybe five years, buying an apartment and selling it and planning to go back to New York City, I mean, that's really a new thing. But it's really complicated for people to get into the rental market now, and I think these moments work together.

LM Maybe this leads to the next question. You have private landlords, you have pension funds investing in corporate landlords, and then you have a large contingent of homeowners. This would appear to blur the lines of housing activism across different class lines. How do you see activism and political decision-making reflecting this?

MB The role of traditional class lines in housing change has decreased, partly because even the middle classes are affected by affordability issues. Expropriation is a popular idea because more than 80% of the households in Berlin rent. But it is also due to a mass-oriented campaign not limited to particular population strata or a particular neighborhood. At the same time, the fragmented nature of neighborhoods such as Prenzlauer Berg complicates grassroots housing organizing. There are "Ossis" who went through the renovation phase in the 1990s and are tired of speaking to "Wessis," there are people who are fine with rent increases because "I mean, face it, rent was really low," and there is the one quarter to one third of international tenants who don't even know that there are rent regulations in place and will leave soon anyway, so they don't have a reason to get involved. Alongside this, you face many different landlords with different strategies, so that one tenant would say, "I already have a lawyer because my landlord is ruthless," while another would say, "My landlady is a very nice woman, we talked over coffee and she promised not to increase the rent very much." Such fragmentation cannot be easily explained by class and makes organizing tenants very difficult.

LM What strategies do you see to address these challenges?

MB There is a widespread agreement among tenants around key issues such as the rent cap (*Mietendeckel*) and the expropriation of large property investors. Other issues, such as the expiring housing subsidies or the commercial rent regulation, are not unimportant, but they affect only certain neighborhoods or social groups. The challenge is how to build a broad-based protest movement without fragmenting it.

Unfortunately, this challenge comes together with a dramatic lack of resources, e.g., in the form of time and money on the side of the activists. Andrej Holm and I have been interviewing housing activists to understand how their different everyday life situations affect the amount of time they can dedicate to activism. And the outcome has been really sobering: most activists are totally overworked and they can hardly mobilize the resources that would be necessary for sustained lobbying, organizing, and mobilizing over a longer period.

MK You have suggested that the effects of gentrification are now spread out almost everywhere in Berlin. How does it affect the urban periphery and the suburbs? If Neil Smith's classic definition of gentrification is a back to the city movement by capital, do you observe in Berlin a process of capital moving to suburbs with the intent of "urbanizing" the suburbia? Can we think of outer neighborhoods such as Schöneweide as a kind of "frontier"?

MB The frontier metaphor reflects the US urban form: the CBD, the zone in transition, and the suburbs. It only translates with difficulties to the ways in which the urban fabric appears here. What I would refer to as suburbs here are places with lakes and forests in Brandenburg such as Erkner, one-hour outside of Berlin. If gentrification was to go there, it would need to leapfrog quite a huge area. This doesn't seem to be the case.

Moreover, around 30% percent of the Berlin housing stock is municipally or cooperatively owned, and the number is even higher in the outer neighborhoods. These are the places where gentrification can hardly take place, or only in spots here and there. So the high percentage of non-market housing limits the applicability of the frontier metaphor. I would rather describe Berlin's gentrification as a *cluster bomb*, the effects of which are dispersed over a wide territory.[10] The neighborhood-level gentrification of the 1990s and early 2000s has given way to a more dispersed dynamic, where latte macchiato places now appear in places such as Lichtenberg or Schöneweide.

LM You referred to Schöneweide in a half-joking way. But there's a planned massive residential development by BUWOG, suggesting that these outer neighborhoods are attractive for investors.

MB I wouldn't connect that necessarily. Oberschöneweide has been an industrial suburb since it was founded in the late nineteenth century, with factories and some residential developments for the workers. In the 1990s, it was a polluted, noisy, badly maintained place with high unemployment and population loss. Oberschöneweide lost one third of its population. Up until very recently, there were only a few penny stores and few döner stores.

Artists, DJs, and cultural producers are moving out of the center because there is less and less space for them there. Due to its industrial heritage, Oberschöneweide can provide space for them. A typical example is the RSO club in the former Bärenquell Brewery. In the 1990s, the clubs were all in Mitte and Prenzlauer Berg. Even the idea of going to the outer part of Friedrichshain sounded suspect because you wouldn't be able to get back by bike. Clubs having to move to Rummelsburg and now even to Oberschöneweide baffles me. The idea of Oberschöneweide becoming an artsy neighborhood seems just bizarre. The more famous clubs such as Tresor or Yaam managed to secure their central locations through lobbying, but others will have a hard time staying or finding new places. The same goes for galleries. Not unlike Soho in the 1970s, the availability of gigantic former industrial buildings through deindustrialization makes Oberschöneweide attractive for these users. And that might create some residential demand. Additionally, the University of Applied Sciences (HTW) opened a campus in the neighborhood. A decade or two ago, students wouldn't have lived in Oberschöneweide, but now the chances to get a flat in Kreuzberg are very limited, so they are more willing to live in the neighborhood, thus potentially contributing to residential demand. Despite all these signs of a gentrification culture, I haven't studied Oberschöneweide, therefore can't assess the impact on social structure.

The building project by BUWOG in Niederschöneweide is due to investors looking for sites that are large enough and have good public transport access. The presence of industrial brownfields in the area can be a factor behind their decision to invest there. But similar residential developments take place in other places such as Buch or Blankenfelde that do not have any artsy reputation. It remains an open question whether the transformations in culture and housing can be put together under a gentrification umbrella or whether the cases of RSO and BUWOG reflect processes that happen simultaneously in the same area but have different causes.

1 Matthias Bernt, *The Commodification Gap: Gentrification and Public Policy in London, Berlin and St. Petersburg* (Wiley: 2022).

2 The spiral movement refers to the spatial dynamics of gentrification theorized by Andrej Holm. See Andrej Holm, "Berlin's Gentrification Mainstream," in *The Berlin Reader: A Compendium of Urban Change and Activism*, eds. Matthias Bernt, Britta Grell and Andrej Holm (Bielefeld: transcript Verlag, 2013): 171–87.

3 The reference is to the city-level urban redevelopment program introduced in the 1990s.

4 Christoph Trautvetter, *Who Owns the City? Analysis of Property Owner Groups and Their Business Practices on the Berlin Real Estate Market* (Berlin: Rosa Luxemburg Stiftung, 2021), www.rosalux.de/fileadmin/rls_uploads/pdfs/Studien/Studien_6-2021_Who_Owns_The_City.pdf.

5 On December 15, 2022, the committee released an interim report, which stated that expropriation is legally possible in principle.

6 Gertjan Wijburg, Manuel B. Aalbers, and Susanne Heeg, "The Financialisation of Rental Housing 2.0: Releasing Housing into the Privatised Mainstream of Capital Accumulation," *Antipode* 50, no. 4 (2018): 1098–119.

7 An emblematic square in Berlin's Prenzlauer Berg.

8 Jennifer Robinson, "Comparative Urbanism: New Geographies and Cultures of Theorizing the Urban," *International Journal of Urban and Regional Research* 40, no. 1 (2016): 187–99.

9 Chris Hamnett and William Randolph, "The Role of Landlord Disinvestment in Housing Market Transformation: An Analysis of the Flat Break-Up Market in Central London," *Transactions of the Institute of British Geographers* 9, no. 3 (1984): 259–79; Luděk Sýkora, "City in Transition: The Role of Rent Gaps in Prague's Revitalization," *Tijdschjrift voor Economische en Sociale Geografie* 84, no. 4 (1993): 281–93.

10 Matthias Bernt and Andrej Holm, "Gentrifizierung in Ostdeutschland: der Fall Prenzlauer Berg," *Deutsche Zeitschrift für Kommunalwissenschaften* 41, no. 2 (2002): 125–50.

The Question Is No Longer Whether to Expropriate, but Why It Hasn't Happened Yet

An Interview with Katalin Gennburg

Katalin Gennburg (KG)

Maroš Krivý (MK) *Leonard Ma (LM)*

Katalin Gennburg is a German politician of *Die Linke* (The Left) who has been an elected member for the Treptow-Köpenick district in the House of Representatives of Berlin since 2016. This interview took place in December 2022.

MK What are the most important recent milestones concerning housing financialization in Berlin? What is your perspective on the political context leading up to and following the successful 2021 referendum on the expropriation of corporate landlords?

KG The referendum and the political situation reflect the ongoing crises in the housing market and capitalism more broadly. As the recent downfall of the Adler Group illustrates, the entire building sector is falling to pieces. The crisis in the real estate industry has led to further rent increases—similarly to what happened in Spain during the European debt crisis. However, the political pressure for housing market regulation is increasing as a result. The outsized role that the global real estate investors play in Berlin, and their effect on residential housing, is a background against which to see the rise of housing and right to the city movements. The Deutsche Wohnen & Co Enteignen (DWE) initiative to expropriate large corporate landlords has succeeded in injecting the idea of expropriation into the public debate: the question is no longer whether to expropriate, but why not—*why has it not happened already*? (The ongoing war in Ukraine and the energy crisis are compounding factors that pose the question of large energy companies as the next candidate for expropriation.) Tomorrow, the expert commission assessing the legality of expropriation will release an interim report, probably stating that it is possible—what a surprise!

The expropriation initiative accelerated the political debate, but the reality demands an even faster response. As a political party, The Left (*Die Linke*) was confronted with a yes/no question, at a time when it was easy to dismiss it as too radical. We decided to support the referendum. It's fascinating how quickly expropriation stopped being just a crazy idea, so that there is now an ever stronger focus on regulating the housing market, and a profound debate on the role of banks in the housing crisis. For a left politician, this is a terrific development.

MK For us as outsiders, it's exciting to see the extent to which the idea that the market is the best instrument of housing policy has been challenged in Berlin. The onus is now on your conservative political opponents and social-democratic coalition partners, as they have to accept expropriation as a new terrain of political struggle. What challenges and opportunities for local politics do you see being opened by the ongoing real estate market crisis?

KG The entire logic of market-driven housing construction is now collapsing. An important question for the near future is whether the big housing corporations will be deemed "too big to fail": I'm quite certain that they will be bailed out as banks were during the previous financial crisis. At the same time, the crisis casts a shadow over the policies of the Christian Democratic (CDU) and Social Democratic (SDP) parties to increase housing supply rather than to expropriate or regulate. A new opportunity has now opened up to build social housing in the inner city, on sites that were previously given away by the municipality to private corporations. Look at the case of the Adler Group, which is now selling plots in Berlin, and I think in other cities too. For instance, they owned a plot next to the Brandenburg Gate, where they wanted to build 600-square-meter apartments with pools and stuff like that. We can get undeveloped plots such as these back into municipal ownership and use them to build affordable public housing. The plummeting share prices of companies such as Adler or Deutsche Wohnen represents a momentous opportunity to act instead of allowing these companies to accelerate rent increases to get their payback. This is the situation in which 60% of Berliners said "yes" to expropriation.

LM After the 2021 elections, you campaigned against the proposed coalition agreement, citing concerns about housing and development policies. Could you give some insight into your position at that time.

KG During the campaign, we stated that our policy is to support and combine various forms of housing regulations: new constructions by public housing enterprises, rent regulation by the state, and public-oriented and participatory city planning. This is in contrast to the SDP's support for market solutions to increase housing construction, which has led to a confrontation during the election campaign and coalition negotiations. The SDP had a well-rehearsed position, doubting the legal viability of expropriation and instead emphasizing the need to have cooperation instead of confrontation. To that end, they launched a forum where public representatives and representatives of housing and construction companies would sit together and discuss how to solve the crisis. This platform is really undermining the power of public reregulation. It is the opposite of our approach. We have always stressed the importance of regulation and confrontation: "It's capitalism, baby, and you cannot negotiate with capital!" As a state, you have to *regulate*, not negotiate. You can negotiate politically but not with capital. However, the coalition agreement is largely based on the SDP's position; we haven't been able to influence it to a significant extent. There are some points that The Left and The Greens (*Die Grünen*) managed to get through, such as getting back hotel plots for a model housing program.

The main disagreement is on the expropriation referendum and breaking the private power in the housing market, which the coalition agreement doesn't support. I said we cannot be part of a coalition that negotiates rules and laws with private companies, because that's the end of democracy and the democratic state. But my party said that we should try it first: be part of the governing coalition in order to use the window of opportunity created by the referendum.

MK Considering that even many leftists oppose expropriation, how do you explain the landslide victory in the referendum? Which social groups support it, considering that the "yes" votes in the referendum (59.1%) outnumbered the combined votes for the three coalition parties (52.4%)?

KG The consensus around expropriation relates to Germany's postwar transformation. The expropriation proposal is based on Articles 14 and 15 in the German Constitution, which were codified after the Second World War. To make sure that fascism would not ever happen again, there was a broad alliance across the political spectrum, including the conservatives, in support of enshrining in the Constitution an article on the possibility of expropriating those who might support fascism.

There's still a widespread agreement, including by the liberals as well as classic conservatives, that financial speculation should be reined in. In Germany, there's a deep connection between democracy and state regulation, a common sense about the state, so to speak, which might explain the widespread support for expropriation, especially among older generations. But we have a crisis of political representation—the electoral system is very volatile. This crisis also concerns The Left. Many people who are for expropriation don't believe that our party can make socialism happen.

MK You pointed out the difference between The Left and SDP as one of confrontation versus cooperation, with the referendum being a source of major disagreement between the two parties. Why are the Social Democrats against expropriation?

KG The SDP is responsible for the crisis of political representation. It is unclear what they fight for. We even have an expression in Germany, "socialdemocratization" (*Sozialdemokratisierung*), to describe the abandonment of labor politics. They have a strong connection to moneyed interests and an ambivalent position on housing policy that could be summed up as, "It's not good, but it could be worse." Instead of reclaiming the state's political power, they responded to the dismantling of the state by seeking to improve cooperation with private investors.

LM The ideological shift towards third-way politics also seems to correlate with the prioritization of attracting investments.

KG Yeah! And we need to talk about this: why are third-way politics in such a crisis as well? I mean, they are not successful with this story, and it's not successful doing politics like this. An important part of their narrative, which hasn't been successful, is to promote the role of experts and big money in politics: "These people know things better," as they say. But I, as a left politician, say, "Why not let the people do it better? Focus on what the people said in the referendum." The Social Democrats really don't want people to participate in decision-making, and this lack of democratic representation is the crucial hurdle in the coalition.

MK You represent one of the six electoral districts in the southeast borough of Treptow-Köpenick. In the 2021 elections, the SDP was victorious in the other five, including in Schöneweide, our case study. There's a strong emphasis in the neighborhood on using the arts and culture as placemaking tools, even as it seems that real estate speculation is widespread and poverty and other social issues are given little consideration. Is this an example of *Sozialdemokratisierung*?

KG Schöneweide is a very interesting spot to discuss global capital and real estate speculation. Large international corporations are buying up what might be one of the most important industrial areas in Europe. Often it's unclear where the capital comes from. And our regional mayor says, "Well, it's good that Schöneweide is now so important for the world." And what happens is that nothing happens: classic land speculation. It isn't good. Take the old Bärenquell Brewery, which has a new owner after having been abandoned for 30 years. One of the tenants is the techno club Griessmuehle, they try to cooperate with the investor. The investor is Aroundtown, a big real estate investment company. They have big plans, but we don't know what they will do in the future. What happens most of the time is that an investor comes and presents their plans, and local politicians say, "Oh, this sounds very interesting," and the investor gets the permission to build. And then the investor says, "Oh, well, we are not doing anything, we are selling it again." But we know that investors are not our friends. I don't want to cooperate with Aroundtown.

The investment flows in the neighborhood are not sufficiently understood. In general, Schöneweide is a place with a lot of criminal money, there are many bad players. Mostly poor and unemployed local people suffer as a result. There has been high unemployment in the neighborhood since the Wall came down. You can say that Schöneweide is emblematic of East Germany's history and transformation.

I am not sure whether the placemaking story will work. I worked on Schöneweide and urban change, but it is politically very challenging—the problem is simply too big for local representatives. The older-generation politicians have struggled with Schöneweide's urban and social issues since 1990 and are tired of it. They say, "Go away with this shit, we don't want to deal with it anymore." Which of course leads to the question: why has Berlin been sold? And a very strong argument in favor of privatization has been that "this shit" will go away indeed. What I mean is that the complexity of challenges for local politicians is so big that privatization seems like a convenient escape. But skyrocketing prices resulting from this only make the problem worse.

LM So instead of confronting these difficult urban and social challenges, municipal real estate is unloaded onto the market?

KG The dominance of capital over the city has been enabled by the weak, circumscribed city planning we have today. Planners no longer see social regulation and redistribution as their goals, they avoid confrontation. There is a big loss of competence in this area. The crisis of rental affordability has been talked over for years now, but it needs to be seen against the backdrop of the crisis in city planning.

LM What's the driving force behind real estate speculation in Schöneweide? You mentioned non-transparent international investments, even criminal money. At the same time, there are widely reported investments by prominent figures such as Canadian singer Bryan Adams. There is also the new airport, Tesla's gigafactory, and other developments in the southeast that might contribute to putting Schöneweide on the map as an investment opportunity.

KG The speculation has to do with rental gaps in Schöneweide and the opportunity to profit from developing an underdeveloped area. This has an international dimension because developers compare local rents with rents in other global cities such as London. Berlin is also a place where tax haven companies are very active, such as the real estate group Signa, which owns the city's main department store chains. That there are many shady players in Berlin's real estate arena has to do with the legacy of the 1990s, when the city lost a lot of land and properties to privatizations. As a result, the municipality's capacity to regulate urban development has been eroded. Once real estate is lost, it is difficult to get it back, which is why the expropriation referendum is of such historic significance. Housing policy cannot be only about keeping rents affordable—it must also ask, "Who owns the city?"

LM A big part of what makes Berlin attractive for international investment is its status as a global cultural capital. Does your party have a perspective on working-class politics as they relate to cultural production (versus a working-class politics that is rooted in industrial production, say)?

KG Our position on this issue as a party is yet to be developed, but a crucial conflict is the pressure of international competitiveness that forces cities to behave like corporations. In the 1990s, the neoliberal urban policy combined two paradigms for competing in the international economy: the global city and the creative city. I would say now that the most challenging question is how to have a socialist urban policy within a globalized economy. I must do more work on these questions as my homework.

LM If you work in the field of cultural production, it's likely that you identify as a worker and have a shared sense of solidarity and precarity with fellow workers. So could urban cultural policy also be a call for a working-class politics?

KG In reality, it's a compromise of sorts. The Left has the seat of the Senator for Culture, Klaus Lederer, and he is responsible for promoting big events and keeping Berlin on the cultural radar. I had an argument with him concerning tourism regulation, especially how to regulate Airbnb and its impact on the city. I see this as a social and ecological question.

LM Since we previously talked about ownership, your office recently published research on the financialization of housing in relation to digital platforms such as Airbnb. Is there a tension between corporate landlords and private owners who are renting out via Airbnb? How does this factor into your political discussions?

KG The impact of Airbnb, hotels, and other short-term rentals is yet to be publicly debated, but it is something that personally interests me very much. We are confronted with a form of digitally enabled housing financialization. This goes back to the founding of Deutsche Wohnen as an expression of the banking sector's adaptation to digital capitalism. It connects to new opportunities on the stock market related to digital finance, and to what is now called "PropTech." Even as we ask "Who owns the city?" it is necessary to ask "Who programs the city?"—to see the capitalist housing market against the backdrop of digital capitalism. Because Deutsche Wohnen is an expression of global digital capitalism as much as

Airbnb or BlackRock are, the expropriation campaign has international significance.

MK To conclude, can you tell us how you personally, and The Left as a political party, have approached the cooperation, on the one hand, with grassroots movements such as DWE and, on the other, with urban scholars, heterodox economists, academics, and critical researchers to create concrete policy objectives around housing? Are there established institutional channels for these kinds of cooperation or is it a matter of a couple of individuals active across and connecting these spheres?

KG It's both. Personally, I am very close to critical urban research, and this has influenced my approach to housing politics. I am interested in broader questions about the role of housing politics in urban change and the role of conflict in socialist politics. Traditionally, our Left politicians did housing politics by informing tenants about their rights. They saw their role as similar to tenants' associations (Mieterverein). By contrast, a new generation of Left politicians have embraced a much more activist approach to housing politics. This generational shift in The Left has led to disputes inside the party. For instance, after the DWE campaign was launched, we had a long debate within the party on what our position on expropriation is—I am glad that we came to the right decision to support it! As a left party, it is our responsibility to support left urban movements, to amplify ideas coming from the grassroots and help introduce them in politics.

If you think about urban politics in this way, it widens the scope for urban researchers to participate. For instance, many cities internationally have now implemented, or are considering implementing, various rent regulation policies, and comparative urban research plays an important role in this. I just came back from a housing conference in Barcelona: two days of presentations on rent regulation strategies and experiences from all around the world. Rent regulations are now being discussed in Spain, in Scotland, and many other countries. At the same time, these political changes open up new avenues for urban research so that there is a mutual responsibility between political and academic work. If you yourselves want to organize politically next to research, let me know!

Playing Our Match to Win Battles All Over the World

An Interview with Berta Del Ben and Jenny Stupka

Berta Del Ben (BD) *Jenny Stupka (JS)*

Maroš Krivý (MK) *Leonard Ma (LM)*

Berta Del Ben and *Jenny Stupka* are activists with *Deutsche Wohnen & Co Enteignen* (DWE), the movement aiming to expropriate large corporate landlords in Berlin. This interview took place in December 2022.

LM We first met with representatives from your organization in 2019, and at that time you were engaged in preparing for a historic referendum to expropriate large institutional landlords. Could you first tell us a bit about the background to the organization and how it developed its political strategy?

JS I think it really started after the financial crisis, against the backdrop of post-1989 reunification. A lot of houses on both sides of the wall were in a really bad condition after the unification, and rents were very low even in the western part of the city. My parents lived in West Berlin and they spent one tenth of their income on rent, or even less. There was so much flexibility. They usually tell me that people used to move a lot just to get closer to their friends or their favorite bar even. And then after the financial crisis of 2008, and after the Berlin municipality sold a lot of the public housing it held previously, things felt very different and the situation slowly started to change. Around 2012, a landscape of initiatives started to form, focused on resistance to specific building projects. Also an initiative against evictions was gaining momentum. By 2013–14, there was already a huge plurality of initiatives in Berlin, addressing different issues with their respective landlords, and they started to connect more and more.

Some weeks ago, I heard Andrej Holm speaking, who you may know as he is an activist and important scholar regarding the development of rents in Berlin and the tenants' movement. His research backs up our activism. Many scientists want to help activists in their work. But Holm's research stands out in that it has had a real impact on activist work for almost a decade now. He put it nicely: for some time, the dominant approach to the analysis of gentrification focused on cultural aspects and experiences of gentrification; but then the analysis turned towards the more systemic issues behind Berlin's gentrification, and the role of new actors buying themselves into the German rental market.

LM What would you say precipitated this shift away from the cultural aspects of gentrification and towards these more systemic issues?

JS Several different factors, but one important shift regarding the growth of the movement was when the tenants of Deutsche Wohnen formed a Berlin-wide coalition. Earlier initiatives were limited to particular apartment blocks: they would organize locally to, for example, fight a rent increase. These initiatives worked hard to draw public attention to these issues, which helped activists realize that they are facing a common enemy. In 2017, they formed a coalition of Deutsche Wohnen tenants from all over Berlin. As I said, it was well backed up by scientific research, which started in parallel to move away from a cultural perspective on gentrification. For example, at a university class in political science that I took back in 2013, the financialization of housing was not discussed even though the class was given by some serious Marxists.

LM You mentioned this specific demand to expropriate. Could you give a summary of what this means and how it should be enacted.

BD Based on our previous experience with the campaign, it is very important that the proposal is in accordance with the law. That's why this referendum is not a legally binding referendum, but it's a referendum with a proposal for the Senate to take action. What we need is actually two steps. The first step is the expropriation of profit-oriented big landlords (we are talking about the ones that have more than three thousand apartments in Berlin). The second step is that we want the way we manage these houses to be a democratic process. This relates to what is called *Vergesellschaftung*, "resocialization" or "socialization," and to how we build and manage these buildings so that the people can say something about their house.

LM This aspect of democratic decision-making feels extremely important. One can imagine that lack of transparency is what leads to the privatizations in the first place. Is the governing structure of these councils also rooted in some kind of legal framework?

JS Some examples are the television companies held by the counties of Germany, administrative bodies entrusted with a public task assigned to it by public law or by statute (Anstalt des öffentlichen Rechts). We chose this legal form as it is particularly open to different institutional designs. For the administration of flats we suggest a kind of council system.

BD When the goods are public but the administration is not, it's only partly public. We want to push for a form of democratic participation. Not every public institution has this, and we want to propose it.

LM This is also a very broad form of participation, especially in regard to non-Germans who are living in rental housing.

MK Can you tell us about the organizational structure of Deutsche Wohnen & Co Enteignen (DWE) and more specifically about the working group Right to the City (R2C)?

BD If we want to imagine having a campaign, we need to imagine it big. You need to organize the work, and we have two systems of how we organize activities. One is thematic—we have, for example, the task forces "Actions" which takes care of rallies and demonstrations etc. When you join the campaign, you can decide if you want to join something where your specific talent can shine. Say you're good at social media, you may join that group, or you want to organize demonstrations, you go in the other group. Alternatively, you can organize starting from where you live and go into the Kiez (neighborhood) teams.

Kiez teams are the local neighborhood groups in which you collect signatures in your area with people you know or you get to know people living in the same neighborhood while meeting them for the activities of the group. We have around 14 of these groups all over Berlin, and then we have a system to coordinate all of this, wherein there are delegates for every task force. And one or two people from each group go into a coordination group. This is called Ko-Kreis, which is like a coordination circle. Then, finally, we have the big plenum, the main organ of decision-making for the campaign, which everybody joins; this is held every two weeks.

So this task force—Right to the City for All—actually came from the work of other task forces which were thinking about strategies such as collecting signatures and organizing. In Berlin, there are a lot of people who are non-German, and one group was organizing tenants at Akelius and did not have the know-how to connect with the other tenants because of language barriers, but also because of different backgrounds or perceptions of themselves. It's also a problem that the majority of the people that are in this condition are not German. They can't vote on the referendum, but they can still participate and do a lot of other stuff: they can still fight.

So Right to the City came about from the need of organizing people with different backgrounds.

LM There are such large numbers of non-German Berliners, it's really great that there's this attempt to reach out to them to be part of this movement. But within this broad coalition, how do you build solidarity?

BD To make a distinction, R2C doesn't work with all the migrant communities living in Berlin. R2C represents people who feel the need to join the campaign but have a hard time going into a German assembly or understanding how the campaign works. What happens is that people who have lived in Berlin for a while and experienced the challenges of trying to find a home, especially an affordable home, have a tendency to feel that that's simply how it works. That's a problem that everybody has but especially people coming from outside of Germany. And so we are trying to shift the discourse to see that this is not your personal problem. It's not you—it's a systemic problem, there are political and economic conditions that make that process happen. And that's the work that we are trying to do, to shift the narrative for such people.

It's also made up of a lot of people who feel that this is a good way to start initiatives. For example, what was cool was that we went to clubs to collect signatures because some members were DJs. Berlin has a big community of queer spaces, and it happens that a lot of people who feel better in Berlin than somewhere else are also from this cultural, queer, music background. And then we really had DJs who put on our song every night to say, "Go vote for expropriation if you can!"

JS When we first started in 2018, we were around 20 people. Then we started to set up the working groups because we knew that we needed the thematic structure so other people could join. There was one very annoying summer when I was with the actions group and we met every two weeks, but we would see each other in different contexts anyway, yet we would still have to go for that specific date, that time, so other people could probably join. It took some time until they started coming. And then in different "waves" we became more and more. We really understood that we would need additional structures for the second phase where you have to collect many, many signatures. One person came up with the idea of local groups and this was really a game changer, because before mostly male activists were leading the way and "naturally" putting themselves forward as spokespersons and so on. And then these people that were organizing in the local groups formed really strong social bonds. In the thematic working groups, people don't always become friends, they don't always treat each other very nicely because of all the stress and so on.

But in those local working groups, people really get along, they go on holiday together, like several times a year actually. Then after the referendum, those people actually started getting more involved in the other structures. They would join the plenum more, for example. And in the beginning, people mentioned to me a lot that they were shocked by the male-dominated political culture in those structures and that they were discouraged by the way in which we lead strategic discussions. So the local groups really initiated a cultural change concerning how people treat each other, what standards exist for a good discussion, the way that we prepared discussions. All these people that came from the local groups kind of made those changes.

BD I think the key issue is the welcoming culture. We ask the people what they can do and don't tell them what they should do. It's about what we can do together, and not that you need to hit a certain bar of "this is activism." That you need to do it like this, or like this, or like this. Now "this" is you and me. That's why this is kind of working. We have people who have experience and they can support others, but it's also about trying to start from the people that come to join, instead of from a standard that is somewhere above.

MK One of the most fascinating aspects of the campaign is how the expropriation referendum was won by quite a significant margin, 59.1%, more than any single political party achieved. Who are the people who support your campaign? Who do they vote for? And how does the expropriation campaign translate in terms of party politics?

JS There was a poll prior to the election in reference to people's voting inclinations. It showed that up to 20% of the conservative voters would actually consider voting in favor of our campaign. So that was a quite shocking number to us also and very interesting. I'm sure you know the text of Engels regarding the housing question where he just says, "Okay, this question gathers interest, public interest, because it's the middle classes who are affected too." Even people who are of higher middle income have the problem of finding appropriate housing, so I think that people really see that there is a structural problem.

In our strategic press work, we stress that the large majority of people voted in favor of the referendum. However, in our internal analysis and strategic planning, it's important to acknowledge that only a percentage of those voters are really in favor of socialization, others just want to make a symbolic gesture to call politicians to action. I think this distinction is important when what we now strategically need is power to actually make it happen when we analyze with whom we can actually build strong coalitions.

LM We're very much interested in the role the Social Democrats play in relation to this campaign because one would assume that they'd be mobilizing the progressive vote, but many of the party leaders have been quite outspoken against the expropriation. For example, Mayor Franziska Giffey is well known for her anti-expropriation stance. How does this affect your work?

BD In February 2023, there will be new local elections in Berlin. So there is a chance that the consensus around Giffey is not going to be confirmed. In June 2022, I think, at their annual conference, the Social Democrats approved a decision that if the expert commission finds the expropriation constitutionally legal, the party will be in favor of expropriation. So there is tension inside the party. So that's still a question mark how much the SPD is willing to implement the referendum and respect the democratic process of it. I would also say that they have particular interest in not expropriating because of the politics they did before: ten years ago, Andreas Geisel was responsible for a lot of the decisions that have created the problems we have today.

JS The neoliberal political framework in which we operate as activists consists of an entire political landscape of habits, values, and ideology. In this manner, the expropriation referendum has been a success: it has changed the dominant discourse in German society and actually convinced people that alternative solutions to economic and political problems are possible, other than just more privatization. There's always a kind of strategic mapping that you have to do. There are people that you can draw to your side and have to bind to yourself and your politics more and more.

LM It's really interesting you bring up this neoliberal framework within which you operate because this poses particular challenges, as simultaneously you have to focus on building these broad coalitions of support, but also you have to always be adjusting to strategic conditions. So how do you discuss strategy and how do you maintain momentum between political moments?

BD It's a very complex thing to discuss strategy because things constantly happen and there is not much time: in the main plenum, for example, we have just two hours. So what we did recently was also to make a weekend where we said, "Okay, we're gonna get together. We have these four themes. We do workshops and we try to put them together, and now this is our strategy weekend." We came out with a big calendar, which is like a big piece of paper with the timetable for the next four months written on it.

So what do we do in between? We have ups and downs in energy. I think another thing that is fair to ask is how do we sustain ourselves? How do we do activism in a way that also takes care of our life, of our health, that cares? So this is where we try to have a caring environment, but it's still work and we are all volunteers and activists. So I would also say that in the down phases, we try to rest because it's a long process.

JS I think there's a phase right now of DWE forming some kind of organization. As Berta said, there's still new people coming in, but there's also a base of 60 to 80 people that are deeply involved, where their lives are very much led by this kind of activist identity, and DWE has become the political home for it. That's why I said it's kind of a stage of forming an organization where people feel connected with the organization in a way that transcends the current political situation, or, let's say, the expert commission pursuing a new report or something. Sometimes friends of mine ask me about this—for example, in the phase after the referendum, they were like, "Oh, okay, and are you relaxing now after all this time?"—And this surprises me so much, because that's such a misconception about how social movements work. And, actually, I think it's part of how journalists and even scientists cover social movements—there's this misconception of fluidity and spontaneous gathering and so on, whereas it's really like hard work, organizing and putting in place an organizational structure and making people feel at home in the longer term.

Regarding the strategic question, it is really a situation that I feel is very difficult, because before we won the referendum, it really worked very well as a threat to politicians. You could really notice it in their rhetoric and how they would engage with the possibility of us winning the referendum. Even housing companies, or at least the lobbying institutions of the housing companies, seemed really stressed. And it's really weird how we just lost the leverage after winning the referendum. So hopefully with us doing good press work, it'll become clearer that Social Democrats are taking a political stance and not one of like legal questions or economic issues. But I think one of the questions that is most interesting right now is how to come up with a strategy that is a genuine, radical left strategy to obtain power.

LM From an international perspective, you are doing amazing work and I think we are already seeing others being inspired by you. You can really see a shift in the kind of language and thinking spreading around.

BD I think that's something that we need to do to keep building layers together. People who need to move every two years from place to place are not really represented. I can't vote. So I really don't care about politicians because they don't represent me because they can't represent me. Can the expropriation campaign also become a network that builds power with others against speculation and financialization? The challenge for us is also how to play our match so well that we win other battles all over the world. That's really something that I want. I can't lose enthusiasm for this because we have the big picture to consider.

III.
LONDON

The Transformation of London's Outer City

Tahl Kaminer

> [M]uch of what is now happening in London's suburbs involves processes of class change and de facto replacement of existing populations, which was not the case when suburbanization was at its height half a century ago.
> —Tim Butler[1]

Traveling on the London Docklands Light Railway from Stratford via Silvertown and London City Airport to Woolwich, the overwhelming magnitude of development and redevelopment is impossible to miss: new glass towers, dense neighborhoods, and infrastructure appear everywhere, often in stark contrast to low-rise terraced housing and decrepit, single-story industrial estates, now in a clear state of retreat and wholesale demolition. London's eastwards impetus is underlined by vision documents and plans issued since the early 2000s by the Greater London Authority (GLA) and boroughs in the area, as well as by PR material by developers. "East London's transformation cemented two distinct personalities," argues a developers' brochure, in effect mythologizing the eastward trajectory: "the luxury life of canary wharf [sic.], and the cool credentials of the 'other' east."[2]

The largest redevelopment and regeneration projects of the 2010s are located along the corridor of the River Lea, the eastern boundary of the inner boroughs, and the East Thames, and include areas such as Stratford, Leamouth, Beckton, Barking, Woolwich, and Thamesmead—areas that have been battered by de-industrialization. The Thames area of this corridor is incorporated into the huge Thames Gateway project, stretching eastwards along the river's estuary beyond Greater London. In 2015–16, the London Mayor's office identified this corridor as an area of opportunities, a "City in the East."[3] In the recent 2021 London Plan,[4] an ambition for 194,000 new homes in these areas is outlined.[5] These areas fall within the Plan's transport-associated Opportunity Areas (OAs): "Crossrail 2 North," "Thames Estuary North and South" areas, and one additional OA along the corridor "Elizabeth Line East." As the titles of the OAs suggest, the development of the Crossrail (Elizabeth Line) train link is a key catalyst for much of this redevelopment.

Many projects in the River Lea Valley were launched ahead of the 2012 Olympics, but the radical transformation of these areas through major completions, new infrastructure, and the initiation of new projects was not widely experienced until later in the 2010s. The scale of these projects dwarfs not only the very limited redevelopment that took place in outer boroughs in the previous two decades, but also the ambitious projects of the 2000s in the nearby, inner-city boroughs of Hackney and Tower Hamlets, which at the time experienced a major wave of redevelopment and gentrification.

A long-term impact of East London's redevelopment, which is rarely mentioned in policy papers or research literature, is the urbanization of London's outer boroughs—of London's suburban belt. London consists of inner boroughs and a ring of outer boroughs. The inner boroughs, which include the city center and inner-city areas, originally formed the area of the London County Council (LCC), which was replaced in 1965 by the far-larger Greater London Council (GLC). The statutory inner London boroughs are Camden, Greenwich, Hackney, Hammersmith and Fulham, Islington, Kensington and Chelsea, Lambeth, Lewisham, Southwark, Tower Hamlets, Wandsworth, and Westminster.

The change of focus from Tower Hamlets to Barking is profoundly different from previous shifts in focus, such as, for example, that from Islington to Hackney: a whole new London is imagined through these changes, in which the differences between the inner and outer city are eroded over time and London, as a whole, urbanizes. Areas with suburban characteristics in London will shrink as outer boroughs become more urban; more workplaces will be created in the outer boroughs, modifying the live/work ratio of these areas; and the relationship between London and its commuter towns will necessarily alter. The demographic changes in London's suburbs are gentrifying certain areas,[6] yet they have also introduced poverty and deprivation in suburban boroughs where these issues were previously minimal.[7]

The London neighborhoods that are considered today to be "inner city" areas, such as Islington, were often enough created as extensions of the city center; they were first suburban or proto-suburban in character, only later becoming densified as the city grew.[8] The current process of suburban transformation in London certainly shares some characteristics with these historic changes, yet is not driven by outwards spatial expansion: whereas some expansion certainly exists, it is limited in its scale and in its capacity to address the housing crisis, and is dwarfed by other processes in contemporary London. In effect, the trajectory of the current processes leads to an overall reduction both in the absolute area size and in the proportion of areas within Greater London that can be considered suburban.

The description of London's outer boroughs as "suburban" requires some explanation. No London borough stands as an equivalent of, say, New Jersey's Levittowns or Amsterdam's Western Garden Suburbs—the scale is radically different. Each borough has the population of a medium-sized European city, manifesting multiple diversities—in land uses, densities, morphologies, typologies, and demographics—within its area. The outer boroughs have multiple town centers, as well as high-, medium- and low-density housing areas. All boroughs have employment areas: the East London outer boroughs of Newham and Barking and Dagenham all had substantial industrial areas along the Thames. These boroughs can nevertheless be considered suburban because their overall densities are lower than those of the inner boroughs; they have a higher percentage of owner-occupiers and fewer free-market rentals, more detached and semi-detached housing, and their live/work ratios and car dependency are higher. The somewhat recent term "post-suburban" perfectly captures the variegated character of London's outer city.[9]

This chapter discusses the process of suburban urbanization underway in the British capital as an introduction to the London section, providing an overview of the process as it has manifested in the last decade and offering an understanding of the specific conditions at play in London. It is in the particular context of London's housing crisis, which is distinct though not disconnected from the larger British housing crisis, that this chapter will discuss the process of suburban restructuring. This chapter will study outer London and the transformation underway there, highlighting Newham's role as a "bridge" of sorts between the inner and outer city. But before that, it will begin by flagging recent decisive historical moments in the development of London.

London, Transforming

As in other Western cities, processes of automation in London in the 1950s and 1960s led to an exodus of industries and skilled laborers from the inner city.[10] Unskilled laborers, in contrast, mostly remained in the inner city but increasingly depended on insecure jobs and were prone to unemployment as a result. The London Docks closed, and new, automated facilities were opened further east of London, in Tilbury; local industries dependent on the docks relocated or vanished. As automation was rolled out in the postwar years, the London County Council actively relocated residents of inner-city areas such as the East End to the New Towns being built around London, reducing overcrowding in the process but leading to a hollowing out of the inner city.[11] Deprivation and long-term unemployment were concentrated in boroughs such as Hackney and Tower Hamlets. The loss of population and resulting decreases in housing pressure discouraged investment in and the maintenance of the older housing stock, which continued to dilapidate. Real estate values decreased, empty homes were squatted, and, in effect, a rent gap was created.[12]

Out of the ashes of the industrial city, a new city emerged over time. The "back to the city" movement, hesitantly launched in the 1970s,[13] brought capital and the middle class back into inner-city neighborhoods, exploiting the rent gap and thereby causing gentrification and the displacement of local population. Throughout the 1980s, 1990s, and 2000s, the inner-city areas of London were the center of attention and a focus of regeneration and redevelopment projects, the largest of which was the Docklands—the transformation of the ex-industrial docks to an abode for financial services.[14]

Since gentrification was first identified in London's Islington in 1964, the processes involved have intensified and mutated.[15] In Britain, gentrification has been mostly market-led, yet government has contributed to and exacerbated this process, welcoming it as a solution to the "problem" of inner cities. The Right to Buy policy, introduced at the onset of Thatcher's premiership, dramatically reduced council housing stock and discouraged local authorities from building new housing. The 1988 Housing Act removed protections for free-market renters, making price hikes and evictions easier, and encouraged Buy-to-Let investments. Responsibility for building housing for the poor was thus transferred, in effect, to housing associations—an amalgam of relatively small charities and nonprofits, which struggle to build at scale. An alternative route to affordable housing was through Section 106 agreements with for-profit developers; these agreements, however, incessantly failed to deliver the amount and quality of housing units necessary.[16]

In the 1990s, large-scale international development firms of the type previously involved in big, high-end projects (shopping malls, sports arenas, speculative office complexes) increasingly took on extensive housing redevelopment projects in London's inner-city areas. The predecessors of the contemporary Australian Lendlease, Chinese Knight Dragon, or Irish Ballymore were attuned to the interests of investors, in contrast to "home builders" such as Taylor Wimpey or Barratts, which were primarily focused on urban extensions and urban sprawl and were attuned to local middle-class homebuyers' preferences and financial capacities. By the late 1990s, international capital began investing in housing in London in earnest. Investments originating in hedge funds, pension funds, and other sources increased speculative dynamics and, inevitably, housing prices in London, just as they had in other global cities.[17] The 2008 financial crisis further intensified these pressures. Capital was redirected from precarious investments in insecure conditions in cities such as Madrid or Athens to the safety of London, and the city became a refuge for investments. As a result, housing prices have become less dependent on local wealth and earnings, and increasingly become caught up in international flows of capital. Not all reinvestment of transnational capital in London has been aimed at speculation or the extraction of land rent. In the case of some "safe," low-risk investments, homes have remained unoccupied.[18]

These pressures have brought about an acute housing crisis, which is focused on the inner-city boroughs. Free-market renters, with very limited tenure protection, were the first to be displaced—initially from the city center. But the implementation of austerity in the 2010s meant that boroughs, suffering from budgets depleted by 25–50%, were encouraged to demolish council housing and sell the land for redevelopment for luxury housing, relocating council-tenure residents elsewhere.[19] The benefit cap and "bedroom tax," introduced by the UK Government in 2013, further exacerbated the situation, reducing the housing options available to the poor.[20] In parallel, borough councils have been "dumping" welfare recipients in outer boroughs, thereby moving the "problem" elsewhere.[21] Unprecedented numbers of unemployed, working poor, and lower-middle-class residents have been banished from central locations to the periphery and beyond. *The Independent* put the number of poor families that had to leave London in the years 2011–14 alone at 50,000.[22] Homeowners have been bought out through compulsory purchases at values which require their relocation to more distant areas. Middle-class residents soon discovered that they too could no longer purchase or rent homes in the inner city and likewise have been relocating further afield. Inner-city property prices became totally detached from local income. As the comfortable middle class is now faced with similar pressures to those experienced by the poor and lower-middle class, housing and gentrification have increasingly become major political issues. All tenures appear precarious when faced with the present dynamics of London's property market.

In this context, which likens an inner-city pressure cooker, a shift of perspective not only towards London's east, but more generally towards the suburban outer boroughs is hardly surprising, whether understood as a means of alleviating the stress on housing or as an opportunity for developers. A 2013 report by the Future of London think tank identified the manner in which the benefit cap and general unaffordability of housing in the inner city were driving the housing programs of the GLA to increasingly focus on the outer boroughs.[23] The major regeneration projects that are either planned or underway along the eastern Thames in Barking, Thamesmead, and elsewhere are all outer-city projects. The London Plan 2021 explicitly targets the outer boroughs for densification and "intensification," for new housing, for tourism infrastructure, and for places of employment.[24] It encourages decreasing allocation of car parking in these suburban boroughs, particularly in their town centers. It identifies the outer boroughs as a site of "incremental" change, and the OAs, whether inner or outer city, are described as sites of "significant" transformation.[25]

The exodus of middle-class and poor residents from overpriced inner-city boroughs is already remaking London's outer city: the newcomers, in search of affordable housing, bring with them specific expectations and demands for urban forms of living; the outer-borough councils are focusing on attracting economically active residents and development as a means of bolstering their reputation and income; and the real estate sector is discovering new

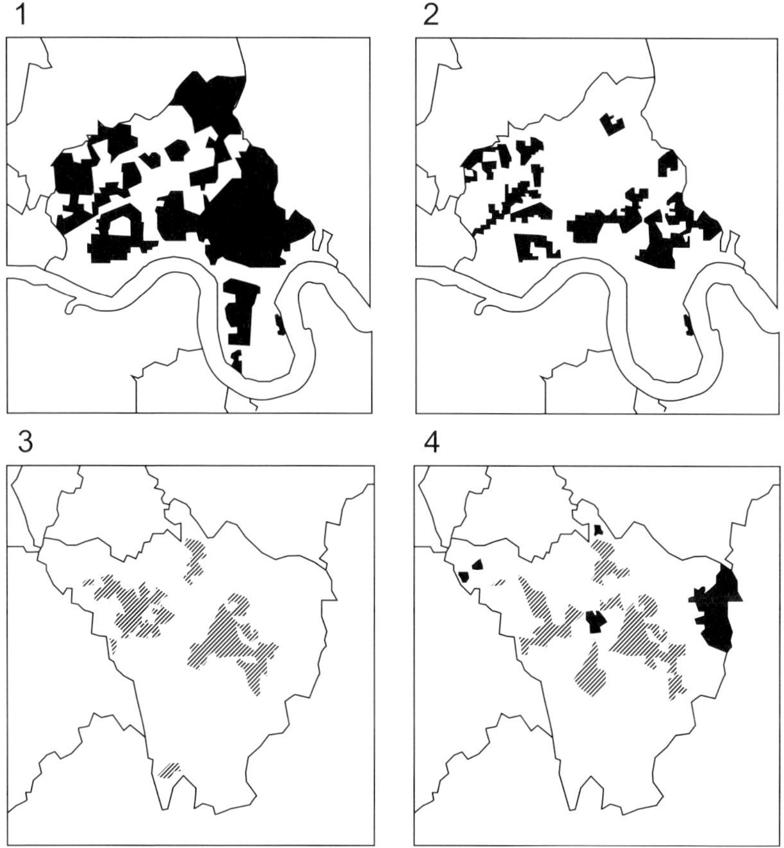

Figure 1: Changes in deprivation in (inner city) Tower Hamlets between 2004 (1) and 2015 (2) and (outer city) Bromley between 2004 (3) and 2015 (4). Black: most deprived; hatched: least deprived.

Drawings by Miritte Ben Yitzchak, based (by kind permission) on mappings by Alasdair Rae.

opportunities for profit creation. All of these factors together are remaking London's suburbia. Higher densities are being created, urban morphologies and architectural typologies atypical of suburbia are now standard in suburban new build, and artist and "creatives" enclaves, so long associated with the inner city, can now be found as far as Bexley. Entrenched deprivation in inner-city boroughs such as Hackney and Tower Hamlets has declined as their poorer residents have been pushed out, while significant deprivation has appeared for the first time in outer boroughs such as Barnet, Bromley, Havering, Sutton, and Redbridge, as those expelled settle in their new neighborhoods (Figure 1).[26]

Tenure Change and Newham

Inner-city neighborhoods typically maintain a higher percentage of private rental homes and a lower percentage of owner-occupied homes compared to suburbs, reflecting as well as inducing the higher resident churn and the transitory character of dwelling in the contemporary inner city.[27] The researchers Antoine Paccoud and Alan Mace identified significant levels of tenure conversion in outer London already in the period of 2001–11:

> Buy To Let [sic.] gentrification in Outer London can thus be understood as an over-spill into areas affording a semblance of metropolitan milieu in Outer London by… [managers, professionals] tenants uninterested, or unable to access, ownership and priced out of high house price Inner London.[28]

Office of National Statistics (ONS) data confirms the rise in free-market rental tenures in outer London since then: in 2006, the percentage of private rental dwellings in outer London was 15.5% in comparison to 23.5% in inner London; by 2020, it was 21.2% in outer London (a 36% increase) and 28.9% in inner London (a 23% increase).[29] Overall, the percentage of private rental has gone up—but more so in the outer city, reducing the gap between the two. The 2021 census data confirmed this trajectory, which was highlighted by *The Guardian*, which commented that "[o]uter London boroughs as well as parts of Greater Manchester and the West

Midlands recorded the largest increases in renters compared with homeowners."[30]

Inspecting the numbers for four boroughs—Newham and Tower Hamlets, the adjacent Olympic duo of outer and inner city; Barking and Dagenham, an outer borough further afield; and Islington, the ex-working-class inner borough in which gentrification was first identified—shows that the percentage of owner-occupied dwellings has remained stable in the years 2006–20 (circa 40% for Newham and Islington; 27–30% for Tower Hamlets), with the exception of Barking and Dagenham, in which this figure collapsed (54% in 2006 to 28% in 2020).[31] In the latter borough, the percentage of private rentals doubled between 2006 and 2020, but at 19% it remains the lowest among these four boroughs. The figures for Newham and Tower Hamlets are very similar, with both experiencing a growth in the private rental sector from circa 25% in 2006 to circa 35% in 2020.

The transformation of London's suburbs is led by Newham and Haringey, which are statutorily outer boroughs but share characteristics with the inner city and are consequently categorized by the ONS as "inner boroughs." Due to Newham's similarity to the inner city, its proximity to over-priced Tower Hamlets and Hackney, and the impact of the redevelopment of the River Lea Valley for and since the Olympic Games, it has become a locus of "over-spill" from the inner city: new, dense housing in Stratford, the Royal Docks, and elsewhere has been developed and directed at potential Buy-to-Let landlords, and at young professionals, for whom relocation from areas such as Bow in Tower Hamlets is no longer experienced as a significant psychological, geographic, or lifestyle change.[32] Whereas such processes have been catalyzed in Newham by the redevelopment of the River Lea Valley, similar processes can also be identified in north and south London.

In Newham in 2001, private rental dwellings comprised only 18% of the total number of dwellings;[33] this figure rose to 25% by 2006. That year, Newham's percentage of private rental placed it 6th among London boroughs, trailing Westminster (33.2%), Camden (28.1%), Wandsworth (28%), Kensington and Chelsea (27.3%), and Lewisham (25.7%), all of which are inner boroughs.[34]

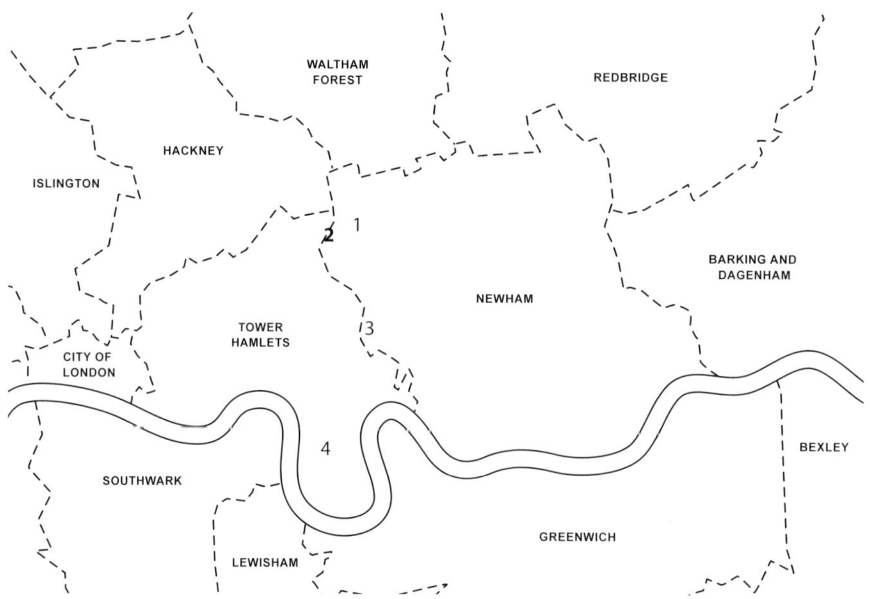

Figure 2: Newham and adjacent boroughs. The River Lea runs along the boundary between Newham and Tower Hamlets (3), through the Olympic Village (2) and to the West of Stratford (1). The Docklands (4) are to the southwest of Newham.

Drawing by the author.

By 2020, it was joint first (34–35%) with Tower Hamlets and Wandsworth, both of which are inner boroughs.

Private rental has not enjoyed linear growth. It peaked in Newham in 2015, reaching 41.4%, which was highest in London at the time and significantly higher than its closest competitor, Westminster, with 35.6%.[35] The UK Government's 3% additional tax on second homes, which was implemented in early 2016, was arguably the cause for the decrease in Buy-to-Let and consequently in the free-market rental sector in Newham in following years, echoing the impact of the policy elsewhere.

Newham, which is home to 355,266 residents in an area of 36.2 square kilometers, is hardly uniform, displaying many contradictions that limit the accuracy of any overall characterization. Furthermore, considering the size of the area, some changes are easily veiled within numbers and statistics for the entire borough. Newham's density has somewhat increased from 9,234 residents per square kilometer in 2015 to 10,043 in 2020. It is not dissimilar to inner borough Southwark's density of 11,339.[36] Newham, in fact, has the highest density among outer boroughs; Bromley, in comparison, has a density of only 2,240 and Ealing, the "queen of the suburbs," of 6,514. The numbers show a moderate yet substantial increase in density. Signs of the change are nevertheless visible in new developments, whether in Stratford or the Royal Docks, all of which have high densities. As new developments proliferate, Newham's density will increase. Newham has improved its standings in diverse indices of deprivation and poverty, changes that not only indicate gentrification, but also a greater similarity to the conditions of Tower Hamlets and Hackney, where inequalities within the boroughs themselves have been growing. The significant growth in private rental tenures that is discussed above, from 18% in 2001 to the apex of 41% in 2015 or 35.4% in 2020, is the strongest indicator of the de-suburbanization in Newham as a whole. This tenure has not only doubled, but its growth has outperformed inner-city boroughs.

Research carried out in 2006–08 in the outer London areas of Leyton, northeast Newham, Barkingside and Central Redbridge, and inner London near Victoria Park (in Tower Hamlets and Hackney), found that only the latter, the one inner-city area, was clearly gentrified.[37] In 2013–14, Bernstock could already identify gentrification that was caused by the regeneration of Stratford, i.e. early signs of the "Olympic Bounce."[38] Since then, development and regeneration have reached other parts of Newham. Examples of recent major projects beyond Stratford include developments at the Royal Docks, an OA and an Enterprise Zone earmarked for 4,000 homes, and in the Canning Town area, such as the ongoing Hallsville Quarter (to be completed 2024) and the rental housing tower Fizzy Canning Town. New projects are emerging on the site of the former Upton West Ham Stadium, such as Barratt's Upton Gardens (which boasts 25% affordable housing and no social housing).[39] Further in the east of Newham, in Beckton, a project called Beckton Parkside is underway. "Beckton has undergone large scale regeneration over the past few decades and is now firmly establishing itself as a desirable new area of London," announces the project's brochure, exposing its target clientele: "Its close proximity to the city and great transport links have made it a popular home for young professionals seeking an easy commute to Canary

Wharf."[40] Every new project in Newham, and similarly across most of the outer city, is medium to high density. Every new project in the outer city alters the demographics and tenure balances in its neighborhood. Every new build uses urban morphologies and typologies. In effect, every new project in the outer city means *less suburbia*.

De-suburbanization

The previous passages outlined some of the evidence of the transformation of London's suburban belt, with a particular focus on Newham, a borough that can be seen to be spearheading the process, as a bridge between the inner and outer city. In this London-focused section of the book, Paul Watt discusses the narrowing gaps between inner and outer London over the last decades, with particular emphasis on the suburbanization of poverty. Juliet Davis and Penny Bernstock take a closer look at the redevelopment of the Lea River Valley and Stratford, which is at the heart of the "breaching" of the boundary which separates the inner and outer city. They demonstrate how the redevelopment led not only to residents' displacements, but also to a loss of the workplaces which employed locals. And lastly, "The Normalization of Thamesmead" takes a closer look at the regeneration of Thamesmead by Peabody, at the time London's largest regeneration project, demonstrating that the road presently being traveled leads to the deployment of familiar, dense inner-city morphologies in suburbia. A snapshot of an early moment in the process, it documents an area undergoing radical urbanization.

The urbanization of the outer city is a slow process; the size of London's suburban belt dwarfs even the large-scale Thames Gateway development. But the trajectory of this process has become clearer in recent years: the de-suburbanization of London is reducing the differences between inner and outer city and making the outer city, in effect, more *urban*. This project increases outer-city densities and private-rental tenures and results in "the suburbanization of poverty" and the displacement of residents to, and in some cases from, the outer city. Every new project in the outer city marks a further retreat of suburbia. Particularly concerning is that—and arguably as a result of the focus on East London—the restructuring of London's outer city is taking place under the radar, with scant discussion and debate, while it ought to be a focus for planners, academics, London politicians, and London activists.

1 Tim Butler, "Re-urbanizing London Docklands: Gentrification, Suburbanization or New Urbanism?" *International Journal of Urban and Regional Research* 31, no. 4 (2007): 762, DOI: 10.1111/j.1468-2427.2007.00758.

2 Ballymore, London City Island, accessed June 18, 2015, http://www.londoncityisland.com/brochures/city-island-brochure, 23.

3 Mayor of London, "Mayor Launches 'City in the East' Masterplan," October 22, 2015, accessed 28 January 2023, https://www.london.gov.uk/press-releases/mayoral/new-city-in-the-east.

4 Local authorities in UK prepare statutory Urban Plans (or Urban Development Plans) every 4–5 years. These documents include policies regarding housing, environment, economic development, and more.

5 GLA, *The London Plan 2021* (London: GLA, 2021), https://www.london.gov.uk/sites/default/files/the_london_plan_2021.pdf, 36.

6 Antoine Paccoud and Alan Mace, "Tenure Change in London's Suburbs," *Urban Studies* 55, no. 6 (2018): 1313–328.

7 Jonathan Owen, "Gentrification Pushing Some of the Poorest Members of Society Out of Their Homes, Says Study," *The Independent*, October 15, 2015, https://www.independent.co.uk/news/uk/home-news/gentrification-pushing-some-of-the-poorest-members-of-society-out-of-their-homes-says-study-a6695926.html; Paul Watt, "'It's Not For Us': Regeneration, the 2012 Olympics and the Gentrification of East London," *City* 17, no. 1 (2013): 99–118, DOI: 10.1080/13604813.2012.754190.

8 Chris Hamnett, *Unequal City: London in the Global Arena* (London: Routledge, 2003), 149; see also Jean Gottmann, *Megalopolis: The Urbanized Northeastern Seaboard of the United States* (Cambridge, Mass.: MIT Press, 1964).

9 Roger Keil, *Suburban Planet: Making the World Urban from the Outside In* (Cambridge; Medford, MA: Polity, 2018); Nicholas A. Phelps and Fulong Wu (eds.) *International Perspectives on Suburbanization: A Post-Suburban World?* (New York: Palgrave Macmillan, 2011); Nicholas A. Phelps, Nick Parsons, Dimitris Ballas, and Andrew Dowling, *Post-Suburban Europe: Planning and Politics at the Margins of Europe's Capital Cities* (Basingstoke; New York: Palgrave Macmillan, 2006).

10 Peter Marcuse, "Do Cities Have a Future?," in *The Imperilled Economy: Through the Safety Net*, eds. Robert Chery, Christine D'Onofrio, Cigdem Kurdas, et al. (New York: Union of Radical Political Economists, 1988), 189–200.

11 Michael Young and Peter Wilmott, *Family and Kinship in East London* (Abingdon, Oxon: Routledge, 2011).

12 Neil Smith, *The New Urban Frontier: Gentrification and the Revanchist City* (London; New York: Routledge, 1996).

13 Neil Smith, "Toward a Theory of Gentrification: A Back to the City Movement by Capital, Not People," *Journal of the American Planning Association* 45, no. 4 (1979): 538–48.

14 Sue Brownill, *Developing London's Docklands: Another Great Planning Disaster?* (London: Paul Chapman Publishing, 1990); Tahl Kaminer, *The Efficacy of Architecture: Political Contestation and Agency* (London; New York: Routledge, 2017), 70–71, 162–65.

15 Ruth Glass, "Aspects of Change" [1964], in *The Gentrification Debates: A Reader*, ed. J. Brown-Saracino (London; New York: Taylor and Francis, 2010), 19–29; Tom Slater, "Gentrification of the City," *The New Blackwell Companion to the City* (Blackwell, 2011), 571–85; Neil Smith, "The Evolution of Gentrification" in *Houses in Transformation: Interventions in European Gentrification*, eds. Jaap-Jan Berg, Tahl Kaminer, Marc Schoonderbeek, and Joost Zonneveld (Rotterdam: NAi Publishers, 2008), 15–25; Smith, *The New Urban Frontier*.

16 Oliver Wainwright, "The Truth About Property Developers: How They Are Exploiting Planning Authorities and Ruining Our Cities," *The Guardian*, September 17, 2014, https://www.theguardian.com/cities/2014/sep/17/truth-property-developers-builders-exploit-planning-cities.

17 Loretta Lees, "Super-Gentrification: The Case of Brooklyn Heights, New York City," *Urban Studies* 40, no. 12 (2003): 2487–509; Manuel B. Aalbers, "Introduction to the Forum: From Third to Fifth-Wave Gentrification," *Tijdschrift voor Economische en Sociale Geografie* 110, no. 1 (2019): 1–11, DOI: 10.1111/tesg.12332. Aalbers suggest that the dot-com crash of 2000 led to redirection of investments from IT into real estate.

18 Rowland Atkinson, "Necrotecture: Lifeless Dwellings and London's Super-rich," *International Journal of Urban and Regional Research* 43, no. 2 (2019): 2–13, DOI: 10.1111/1468-2427.12707.

19 Paul Watt and Anna Minton, "London's Housing Crisis and its Activisms," *City* 20, no. 2 (2016): 204–21.

20 The benefit cap accompanied the introduction of Universal Credit and was a means of limiting overall benefit payments to individuals and families. The "bedroom tax" was imposed on residents of council housing who had a spare room, e.g., a couple, occupying a two-bedroom flat after their child had grown up and left. For many benefit-dependent residents of inner London, these changes meant they could no longer afford living in the inner city. See Shelter, "Briefing: What's Wrong with the Bedroom Tax?" (London: Shelter, 2013), https://england.shelter.org.uk/professional_resources/policy_and_research/policy_library/briefing_whats_wrong_with_the_bedroom_tax.

21 Paul Watt and Penny Bernstock, "Legacy for Whom? Housing in Post-Olympic East London," in *London 2012 and the Post-Olympics City: A Hollow Legacy?* eds. Phil Cohen and Paul Watt (London: Palgrave Macmillan, 2017), 91–138; Graeme Demianyk, "A Housing Emergency: 50,000 Homeless Households Moved Out of Their Communities in Five Years," *Huffington Post*, October 25, 2018, https://www.huffingtonpost.co.uk/entry/homeless-households-placements_uk_5bbb9099e4b01470d053d2a6.

22 Anonymous, "Over 50,000 Families Shipped Out of London Boroughs in the Past Three Years Due to Welfare Cuts and Soaring Rents," *The Independent*, April 29, 2015, https://www.independent.co.uk/news/uk/home-news/over-50000-families-shipped-out-of-london-in-the-past-three-years-due-to-welfare-cuts-and-soaring-10213854.html.

23 Andrew Heywood, "The Affordable Rent Model in London: Delivery, Viability, Potential" (London: Future of London, 2013), 10.

24 GLA, *The London Plan 2021* (London: GLA, 2021), https://www.london.gov.uk/sites/default/files/the_london_plan_2021.pdf, 16, 29, 83, 167, 170, 241, 266, 273–74.

25 GLA, *The London Plan 2021*, 29, 429.

26 Jonathan Owen, "Gentrification Pushing Some of the Poorest Members of Society Out of Their Homes, Says Study," *The Independent*, October 15, 2015; Butler, "Re-Urbanizing London Docklands": 764; Nick Bailey and Jon Minton, "The Suburbanisation of Poverty in British Cities, 2004–16: Extent, Processes and Nature," *Urban Geography* 39, no. 6 (2018): 892–915.
27 Hamnett, *Unequal City*, 151.
28 Antoine Paccoud and Alan Mace, "Tenure Change in London's Suburbs: Spreading Gentrification or Suburban Upscaling?", *Urban Studies* 55, no. 6 (May 2018): 1325.
29 ONS, "Housing Tenure by Borough," London Datastore, accessed February 4, 2022, https://data.london.gov.uk/dataset/housing-tenure-borough.
30 ONS, "Housing, England and Wales: Census 2021," January 5, 2023, https://www.ons.gov.uk/peoplepopulationand-community/housing/bulletins/housingen-glandandwales/census2021; Robert Booth and Michael Goodier, "Number of Households Renting Has More Than Doubled Since 2001, Census Reveals," *The Guardian*, January 5, 2023, jan/05/number-households-renting-more-than-doubled-2001-census-england-wales?C-MP=Share_AndroidApp_Other.
31 ONS, "Housing Tenure by Borough."
32 Penny Bernstock, *Olympic Housing: A Critical Review of London 2012's Legacy* (London: Taylor & Francis, 2014).
33 Bernstock, *Olympic Housing*.
34 ONS, "Housing Tenure by Borough."
35 ONS, "Housing Tenure by Borough."
36 LBN, "Population Per Square Kilometre," accessed February 15, 2022, https://www.newham.info/data-catalog-explorer/indicator/I24609?view=table.
37 Tim Butler, Chris Hamnett, and Mark Ramsden, "Gentrification, Education and Exclusionary Displacement in East London," *International Journal of Urban and Regional Research* 37, no. 2 (March 2013): 559.
38 Bernstock, *Olympic Housing*.
39 Watt and Bernstock, "Legacy for Whom?"
40 Bellway, "Beckton Parkside: Grove Court," accessed February 14, 2022, https://www.bellway.co.uk/new-homes/thames-gate-way/beckton-parkside#, 10.

Housing and Social Change in Outer London

Paul Watt

Introduction

This chapter examines housing in outer London with reference to various social changes which have impacted London during the last thirty years. The chapter begins by providing an overview of the development of suburban outer London, a place which is traditionally associated with middle-class, semi-detached homeownership, even though this was always only ever a partial aspect of outer London's twentieth-century story. The chapter moves on to examine the contemporary London housing crisis and how this has impacted upon outer London with an emphasis on affordability. The chapter then sketches the impacts of gentrification and regeneration in outer London, and includes a discussion of social housing estate demolition and redevelopment. Finally, it considers suburban affluence, but also the growing "suburbanization of poverty" which is reshaping outer London and transforming both its place image as well as its sociological reality.

Suburban Outer London

Suburban outer London is popularly associated with neat rows of 1920s–30s' semi-detached houses with gardens, as typified by Kenton, in north west London, which Paul Barker singles out as "the kind of place I want to celebrate" in his eulogistic book *The Freedoms of Suburbia*.[1] Suburban London represents what is often called "the Anglo-American model" of twentieth century suburbanization in the US, UK, Canada, and Australia—i.e., middle-class residential areas consisting of white nuclear families living in owner-occupied houses.[2] In these societies, the spatial movement out from the city to the suburbs is associated with a process of social mobility whereby those *moving out* also *move up* the social hierarchy, as in the notion that suburbia represents a "bourgeois utopia."[3] This centrifugal movement outwards and upward is a significant aspect of early/mid-twentieth-century US and UK suburbanization, which involved intertwined processes of middle-class formation and suburban homeownership.[4] Culturally, the Anglo-American suburbs involve a "suburban way of life" based on maintaining social order, reinforcing class, status, gender, and racialized distinctions, as well as conforming to middle-class norms of respectability.[5]

This dominant place image of the London suburbs reflects and reinforces the powerful notion that outer London is the representational symbolic "other" to the more socially problematic inner London and its longstanding association with poverty. Whereas inner London, and especially inner East London, has long been known for its concentrated poverty and deprivation, large rental sector, and multi-ethnic population, outer London has had much lower levels of poverty, majority homeownership, and was also much whiter.[6] London's suburbs were seen as the epitome of the middle-class "good life," and the popular 1970s TV sitcom *The Good Life* was indeed set in suburban Surbiton in the Royal Borough of Kingston-upon-Thames in southwest London.[7]

The sociological reality of outer London was, however, always more variegated in housing, class, and ethnic terms than the above binary inner-outer representation suggests. Indeed, suburbia is generally far more socially differentiated than its dominant place image implies.[8] Parts of outer London have had a long-standing working-class presence dating back to the development of the interwar suburbs, fueled by speculative housebuilders and cheap mortgages.[9] Outer London was also the site of large "out-county" local authority cottage estates, including the massive Becontree estate built by the London County Council during the 1920s and located in the present-day borough of Barking and Dagenham. During the postwar period, council housing estates were built in many parts of outer London. These include Grahame Park and West Hendon estates in suburban Barnet, both of which are partway through regeneration programs, as discussed below. However, council housing provision in often Conservative-dominated outer boroughs never reached the same high levels as seen in Labour-dominated inner London boroughs;[10] Barnet had just 19% of all households living in council housing at the 1981 peak, compared to 82% in the inner east London borough of Tower Hamlets.[11]

If outer London was historically more socially differentiated than the dominant place image of a middle-class and largely white "leafy suburbia" implies, it's also the case that it has become more differentiated over time such that, "The suburbs of London have become not just more ethnically and religiously diverse, but also remarkably complex social and political spaces more generally."[12] Many contemporary outer London suburbs have a prominent Black, Asian, and minority ethnic (BAME) presence and identity.[13] Not only are London's suburbs more demographically multi-ethnic, they are also more socioeconomically diverse than they once were, as discussed further below, and hence suggestive that outer London maybe experiencing the withering of suburbia, as the editors argue.

London's Housing Crisis

London is experiencing a chronic housing crisis characterized by housing shortages, rocketing house prices and private rents, alongside a rising tide of homelessness, evictions, and displacement.[14] One response to the housing shortage has been to build new homes at a higher density, and especially in the form of residential blocks of flats including large towers. Although this has tended to be associated with central London developments, it's also the case that it is becoming more prominent in outer London.[15] Such high-density developments have contributed towards the erosion of the suburban low-rise distinctiveness of outer London, and have also proved politically controversial, feeding into current debates regarding the environmental and social sustainability of outer London.[16]

In his 2013 study on the London suburbs, Mace highlights how between 70 and 80% of the new-build properties in the boroughs of Bromley, Havering, and Harrow were flats rather than houses, whereas their 2001 existing stock consisted of between 72-81% houses.[17] Ealing Council in outer west London has been particularly assiduous in terms of applications for new residential blocks of flats in meeting the challenges of providing new housing supply.[18] This "tall buildings" approach has prompted resident opposition in Ealing via the well-organized "Stop the Towers" campaign.

In terms of affordability, Hamnett and Reades have analyzed house price data from 1969 to 2016 and they conclude that: "The past 45 years have seen the emergence of a marked Regional House

Price Gap (RHPG) in Britain that is characterized by a sharp and growing difference between average prices in London and those in the peripheral regions."[19] Indeed, this house price gap has widened since the Great Financial Crash (GFC) in 2007–08. In 2015, the mean property price was £277,000 in the UK and £291,000 in England, but £514,000 in London (ibid.). London has also increasingly pulled away from South East England, the next most expensive region, where the mean price was £351,000 in 2015. Within London, clear patterns are emerging, especially in the increasing differentiation of the "prime" London area, consisting of the two central London boroughs of Kensington and Chelsea, and Westminster, plus the City of London. Average prices in 2016 stood at a staggering £1.9 million in Kensington and Chelsea, and £1.5 million in Westminster (ibid.). In other words, while prices in London were 2.06 times greater than the national average (England and Wales) in September 2016, prices were 6.76 times greater in Kensington and Chelsea and 5.35 times greater in Westminster (ibid.).

If central London is by far and away the most expensive metropolitan area, Hamnett and Reades also identify a significant gap between inner London and outer London, such that inner London prices reached 268% of the UK average compared to just 194% in outer London by 2016 (ibid.). Table 1 shows median house price changes in inner and outer London from 1996–2014, as well as in England and Wales. This indicates a widening house price gap over the entire period both between London and England and Wales, but also between inner and outer London. In 1996, median London house prices were 135% above the England and Wales median, but this widened to 148% by 2009 and 190% by 2014. Outer London house prices have shrunk relative to inner London prices over the same period, since they were 85% of inner London prices in 1996 but just 68% by 2014. Indeed, since the GFC, inner London has pulled further away from England and Wales, and also from outer London in absolute and percentage terms. Table 1 shows how house prices increased from 2009–14 by an average of £139,000 in inner London (43%), but by only £80,000 in outer London (34%), and by a mere £23,000 (13.6%) in England and Wales.

	1996	*2009*	*2014*	*2009–2014 N increase*	*2009–2014 % increase*
London	77,000	250,000	364,000	114,000	45.6
Inner London	87,000	323,000	462,000	139,000	43.0
Outer London	74,000	235,000	315,000	80,000	34.0
England and Wales	57,000	169,000	192,000	23,000	13.6

Table 1: Median house prices in London, England, and Wales, 1996–2014.

Adapted from Joel Marsden, *House Prices in London: An Economic Analysis of London's Housing Market* (London: GLA), 13.

There are several reasons for the widening, between the 1990s and the mid-2010s, of the house price gap between inner London and outer London. One major reason is linked to global capital flows into inner London and especially central London.[20] Central London is the preferred location for global property investors hoping to capitalize on the ever-rising house prices—made more attractive through the easing of transactional flows into the UK and the relative political safety of London (the "cash-box in the sky"). Data on London from 2014–16 indicates how overseas sales account for the largest percentage of total sales in the three central London local authority areas: 41% in the City of London, 38% in Westminster, and 32% in Kensington and Chelsea.[21] Nine of the ten boroughs (with the exception of Merton) with the largest overseas' sales percentages were in inner London. By comparison, nine of the ten boroughs with the lowest percentage of overseas' sales (minus Haringey) were in outer London—all below 5% of sales, with Havering and Sutton having no overseas sales at all (ibid.). This suggests that outer London is generally less attractive to overseas homebuyers compared to inner London, and especially central London. One estate agency estimated that nearly half of all home sales in the second half of 2019 for "Prime Central London" were to overseas buyers.[22]

In sociological terms, we can link the growth of overseas property sales to the rise of the global "superrich" in London—aka High Net Worth Individuals (HNWIs) who own US$1 million or more in investable assets (excluding primary residence, collectibles, consumables, and consumer durables)—or the elite, the 1%, or just "serious money."[23] Not only are the UK superrich spatially concentrated in London, but within the city they cluster in those central and north London neighborhoods which have traditionally functioned as exclusive wealthy enclaves, such as the West End, Belgravia, Mayfair, Kensington, Chelsea, and Hampstead, but also within new spaces of affluence such as new-build luxury private developments like Vauxhall Nine Elms and The Shard.

The rise of the overseas superrich, plus the growth of domestic Buy-to-Let landlordism since the 1990s, has undoubtedly contributed towards the housing unaffordability of inner London, and especially central London.[24] Official data indicates that there were no areas in London where private rent was "affordable" for low-medium income groups in 2020 (i.e., 30% or less of gross monthly income).[25] Therefore, only London households in the higher income quartile would be able to rent a property without spending more than 30% of their income on rent. Private rents have increased more in inner London than outer London.[26] (Table 2) shows monthly median private rents for England and London from April 2021 to March 2022. It includes data on the South East (the most expensive region after London), and the North East (the cheapest region in England). Rents in inner London were £1,625

	Median monthly private rents £
London	1,450
Inner London	1,625
Outer London	1,300
South East	950
North East	505
England	795

Table 2: Median monthly private rents for all bedroom categories, England and London, April 1, 2021 to March 31, 2022.

Adapted from ONS, "Private Rental Market Summary Statistics in England: April 2021 to March 2022" (2022), https://www.ons.gov.uk/peoplepopulationandcommunity/housing/bulletins/privaterentalmarketsummarystatisticsinengland/april2021tomarch2022.

per month, over double the England average, and 25% greater than in outer London.

Median private rents for two-bedroom properties in 2021–22 vary from £2,535 per month in Kensington and Chelsea down to less than half that figure at £1,150 in the outer borough of Havering.[27] Indeed, monthly median rents for two-bedroom homes are higher in every inner London borough compared to every outer London borough with the two exceptions of inner London's Lewisham (£1,350 per month) and outer London's Richmond-upon-Thames (£1,650) which we discuss further below.

In 2016–18, a slowing down occurred in house price growth in London, which was generally sharper in inner rather than outer London. Indeed, seven inner and two outer London boroughs witnessed negative growth rates during 2017–18.[28] Increased taxation and regulation of the Buy-to-Let market have probably contributed to this. COVID-19 and lockdown seemed to deepen these trends such that "London was the property market laggard in 2021, outperformed by every other region."[29] Whereas several inner London boroughs witnessed price falls during 2021, the 13 boroughs with the greatest price growth were all in outer London, with the strongest being Redbridge (8.1%), Waltham Forest (7.5%), and Harrow (6.9%). Homebuyers' search for greater space and more affordable properties undoubtedly contributed towards the outer London price increases, while overseas buyers were restricted due to lockdown which particularly affected central and inner London. The most recent HMRC data for November 2022, shown in Figure 1, indicates that there has been a narrowing of the average inner/outer London house price gap to 80% (£626,890 and £499,970) from the mid-2010s. Figure 1 also shows that there are six outer London boroughs which have house prices above the London average of £542,311, but only one of these—Richmond-upon-Thames—is well above the inner London average at £764,789. We discuss this expensive outer borough further below.

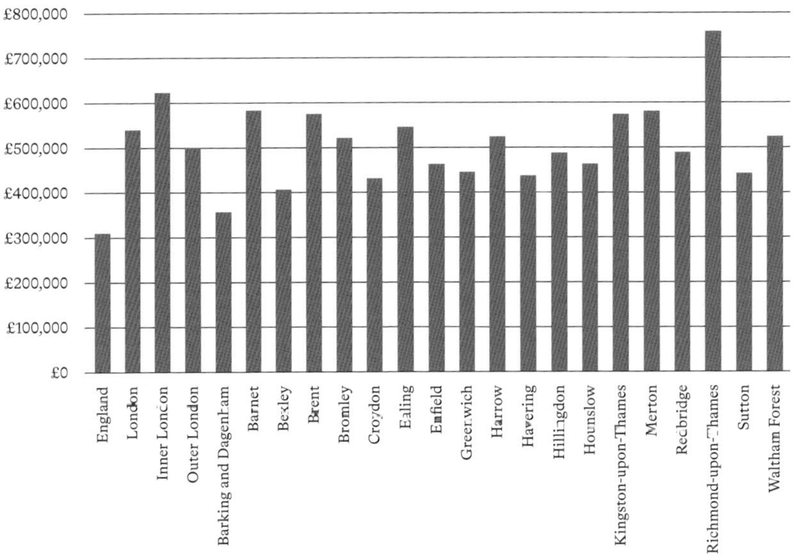

Figure 1: Average property prices in England, London, and outer London boroughs, November 2022.

Contains HM Land Registry data © Crown copyright and database right 2020. This data is licensed under the Open Government License v3.0. HM Land Registry, "UK House Price Index" (November 2022), https://landregistry.data.gov.uk/app/ukhpi?utm_medium=GOV.UK&utm_source=england&utm_campaign=section8&utm_term=9.30_18_01_23&utm_content=UK_HPI_toolSource.

Gentrification and Regeneration

Another aspect of how and why private housing has become so unaffordable in London, and especially inner London, is the spread and intensification of gentrification. Gentrification was first identified in the 1960s by the sociologist Ruth Glass in relation to the class transformation of previous working-class areas of Camden and Islington in north London. Since then, gentrification has spread way beyond its north London origins into many parts of the city, including some outer London neighborhoods.[30] As Watt argues, "London's gentrification has taken an intense corporate form—'gentrification on steroids' (Watt and Minton, 2016: 218)—characterised by accelerating house prices, rents, capital flows and displacements which has no equivalent in the rest of the UK."[31] Hence London, and especially inner London, is subject to "hyper-gentrification."[32] Gentrification contributes towards rising house prices and private rents, and hence makes much of inner London and even parts of outer London unaffordable.

Contemporary inner London is already heavily gentrified, as numerous studies attest.[33] Almeida's recent study has calibrated a mean gentrification score for the 2010–16 period which indicates that gentrification is generally more prominent in inner rather than outer London boroughs.[34] Nevertheless, among the ONS outer boroughs, Ealing, Waltham Forest, and Brent have above-average gentrification scores. Furthermore, gentrification is spatially variable *within* each borough. Thus, while Waltham Forest is the twelfth most gentrifying borough in London, gentrification is particularly intense in the Walthamstow and Leyton areas, while gentrification in Brent (the fourteenth most gentrifying borough) aka Northwick Park as well as parts of Willesden (ibid.). More generally, Paccoud and Mace have identified the phenomenon of "Buy-to-Let Gentrification" in parts of outer London, whereby professionals and managers move into the private rental sector (PRS) as a way of escaping high house price inner London.[35]

State intervention in the form of urban regeneration has played an increasingly important role in generating gentrification—"state-led" gentrification—in London, including in parts of outer London. This includes major regeneration projects, such as the 2012 London Olympic Games, which centered upon six inner and outer east London "host boroughs." The Games have contributed towards house price increases in east London.[36] Over the August 2012 to May 2021 period, three of the Olympics' boroughs experienced the highest property price increases in London: Waltham Forest (first at 106%), Barking and Dagenham (second at 86%), and Newham (third at 81%), compared to 61% for London as a whole.[37] In Newham, there are significant post-Games gentrification effects connected to the new upmarket housing developments which are especially prominent in the Stratford area.[38]

Another prominent aspect of regeneration qua state-led gentrification in London is associated with the controversial policy of demolishing and rebuilding social housing estates as mixed-tenure neighborhoods including some re-provided social housing, but also with large numbers of market properties for sale or private rent.[39] Much academic, policy, and activist attention has focused on inner London demolition schemes, and in particular on two now infamous examples in the south London borough of Southwark: the now-demolished Heygate estate which is being rebuilt as “Elephant Park,” and the long-running regeneration at the nearby Aylesbury estate.[40] Despite this focus, estate demolition is by no means restricted to inner London. Although Southwark Council demolished 1,178 of its homes from 2011–12 to 2020–21 (at the above two estates), demolition has been greater at each of the three outer boroughs of Ealing (2,008 properties), Greenwich (1,896 properties), and Barking and Dagenham (1,895 properties), as Figure 2 shows. Over the ten-year period from 2011/12 to 2020/21, a total of 11,900 local authority homes were demolished in London, and of these 71% (8,408) occurred in outer London compared to 29% (3,492) in inner London.[41] Just four outer London boroughs (Ealing, Greenwich, Barking and Dagenham, and Barnet) accounted for 58% (6,848) of the city-wide demolition total over this period.

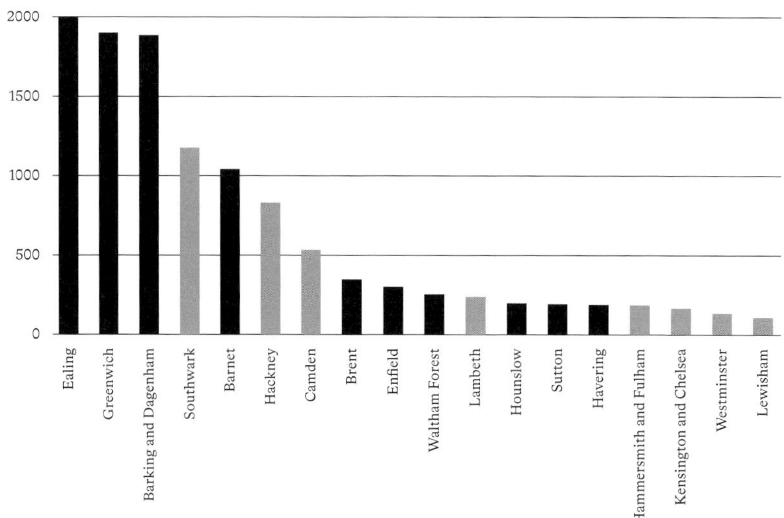

Figure 2: Demolition of local authority properties by London borough and number, 2011/12–2020/21, (showing 18 local authorities which demolished at least 100 of their properties).[42] Outer London boroughs in black, inner London boroughs in grey.

Source: GOV.UK

One reason for the high level of local authority demolitions in the outer borough of Greenwich (Figure 2) is the demolition of the over-1,900-unit Ferrier estate which was completed in 2013. The Ferrier estate was built by the Greater London Council from 1968–72, and was demolished and rebuilt as Kidbrooke Village under a £1 billion regeneration project undertaken by Greenwich Council in partnership with the GLA and Berkeley Homes, the upmarket developer. The intention behind the regeneration was to "create a new mixed-tenure, mixed-used community of 4,800 homes, schools, shops, health facilities, restaurants, offices, community facilities, and new open spaces."[43] Several research reports and papers have examined this redevelopment. Some are highly positive in arguing that Kidbrooke Village is a model for "social sustainability" with a strong sense of place identity, and residents generally very happy with their new homes and open spaces, as well as feeling safer in the area.[44] This *Living at Kidbrooke Village* report was commissioned by the developer, as was the later *New London Villages: Creating Community* report.[45] The latter report emphasizes how Kidbrooke Village represents a model for a "New London Village" in the suburbs defined by six criteria: small and intimate, unique, designed for social interaction, locally driven and locally responsive, functional, and comprising a mixed community. According to the report, all six criteria were either achieved or were in progress at the time of the research.

On the other hand, Smets and Watt argue that the *New London Villages* report's "rationale and overall aims are predicated on a mythical, pastoral notion of 21st century London as a 'city of villages'."[46] In addition, these honorific reports airbrush out the large loss of social renting (around 57%).[47] It's noteworthy that despite their general positive assessment of Kidbrooke Village, Woodcraft and Bacon do acknowledge that "it is also important to note that some residents from the Ferrier Estate were unable to return to Kidbrooke Village because they could not afford higher rents and higher council tax payments compared to the costs of their previous homes."[48] In other words, the Ferrier/Kidbrooke regeneration scheme resulted in a significant loss of social rental homes, as well as the physical displacement of some of the original low-income residents probably to cheaper areas in outer London or even outside London altogether.

Similar issues of displacement and estate regeneration functioning as state-led gentrification in outer London can be identified in the north London borough of Barnet, where the council has enacted a large-scale demolition program at its largest estates since 2002. As Figure 2 shows, Barnet was the fifth highest in terms of local authority housing demolitions from 2011/12 onwards. Its two largest estates—Grahame Park (1,777 units) and West Hendon (649 units)—are both part-way through long-running demolition and rebuild programs. When complete, there will be a net loss of around 45% social housing at each regeneration scheme, but a fourfold increase in private homes for sale or rent at Grahame Park and an equivalent ninefold increase at West Hendon.[49] Even those West Hendon social tenants who managed to return to the redeveloped and rebranded "Hendon Waterside" often expressed a place attachment and community relative to when they were previously living at the old West Hendon estate.[50] Given that the London-wide loss of social rental homes resulting from demolition/regeneration schemes from 2004–14 was 27%,[51] the Ferrier/Kidbrooke Village, Grahame Park, and West Hendon/Hendon Waterside regeneration examples represent well-above-average losses of social housing in the two outer London boroughs of Greenwich and Barnet.

If social housing has been lost at these outer London estate regeneration schemes, their extensive provision of expensive apartment blocks for sale to affluent professionals has directly contributed towards gentrification, and very likely towards the recent rising costs of homebuying in outer London since the mid-2010s (Figure 1). Like all London's premium "villages," the cost of buying a property at Kidbrooke Village is way beyond what the average London household could afford. At the time of writing (February 2023), Foxtons, the upmarket estate agents, had 1–2 bedroom apartments at Kidbrooke Village for sale between £460,000 and £652,500: "Offering a bespoke collection of beautifully finished luxury apartments each with outside space, Kidbrooke Village boasts a vibrant lifestyle within the Royal Borough of Greenwich."[52] However, even the cheapest 1-bedroom flat at Kidbrooke Village is over 13.5 times the annual median gross pay in London at £33,970.[53] One-bedroom apartments at Hendon Waterside are slightly cheaper, but nevertheless currently range from £408,000 to £431,000, again way beyond average Londoners' earnings.[54]

Suburban Affluence and Poverty

As noted above, inner London has traditionally been poorer, on average, than outer London, and it still has extremely high levels of poverty by national standards: "inner East boroughs still have the highest proportions nationally of children and old people living in poverty [in England]."[55] Recent data for 2015/16 to 2019/20 confirm this broad picture of higher rates of poverty in inner London compared to outer London boroughs, as seen in Figure 3. Seven out of the ten poorest boroughs are in inner London, with Tower

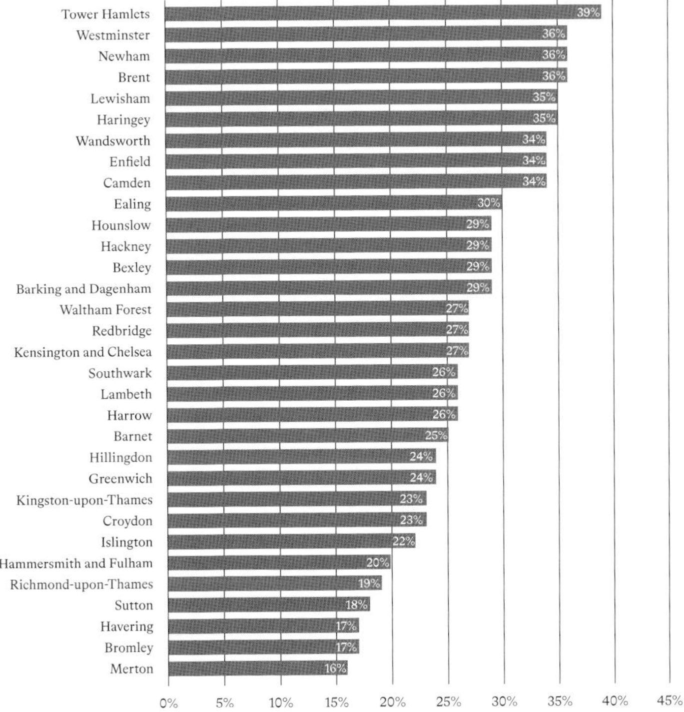

Figure 3: Poverty rates by London borough, 2015/16–2019/20 (%).

Trust for London, "Poverty Rates by London Borough, 2019/20," https://www.trustforlondon.org.uk/data/poverty-borough/.

Hamlets having the highest rate at 39% of households in poverty after housing costs. At the other end of the scale, eight out of the ten boroughs with the lowest poverty rates are in outer London, with the five lowest (Merton, Bromley, Havering, Sutton, and Richmond-upon-Thames) having rates below 20% and all with less than half the Tower Hamlets' rate.

The 2019 Index of Multiple Deprivation (IMD) shows similar results, with eight out of the least deprived boroughs (by IMD rank of average score) being in outer London and Richmond-upon-Thames being the least deprived borough.[56] Drilling down to the ward level shows an even starker picture since 19 out of the 20 least deprived wards are located in outer London, with five of these being in Richmond-upon-Thames alone.[57]

In fact, the suburban west London borough of Richmond-upon-Thames has been identified as one of the epicenters of London's superrich, as seen in Caroline Knowles' walking tour of "plutocratic London."[58] While plutocratic London has its epicenter in central London and is primarily inner London based, it also has suburban outposts in the more affluent parts of outer boroughs such as Richmond-upon-Thames, Barnet, Bromley, and Harrow.[59] A recent study of "the geography of elite residential basement development in London" identifies such large basements as being spatially concentrated in central and inner London, but Richmond-upon-Thames contains almost 10% of the Greater London total, again suggesting that this outer borough has a sizeable superrich presence.[60] Richmond-upon-Thames can be clustered alongside the more expensive inner London boroughs (such as Camden and Hammersmith and Fulham) as having both high mean house prices and house price increases over the 1995–2016 period.[61] Figure 1 above shows Richmond maintaining its high house prices in 2022. As seen above, Richmond-upon-Thames is also distinctive in having the highest median monthly private rent in outer London for a two-bedroom property at £1,650 in 2021–22, the same cost as the heavily gentrified inner London boroughs of Hackney, Southwark, and Tower Hamlets.[62]

The above discussion suggests that parts of outer London have retained their leafy suburban affluence, and are even centers of the superrich elite as in the case of Richmond-upon-Thames.

Nevertheless, the long-term social-spatial gap between more affluent outer London and impoverished inner London has narrowed during the twenty-first century, prompting the notion that London is experiencing the "suburbanization of poverty." In their study of changing income deprivation across 25 UK cities from 2004 to 2015/16, Bailey and Minton identified how poverty became less centralized and less concentrated in almost every city. However, the pace of change was especially marked in London: "It is a unique city in the UK in terms of its scale and housing market pressures, and it is here that the impacts of welfare reform were expected to be greatest."[63] Other recent reports, using somewhat different datasets and methodologies, have come to very similar conclusions regarding the changing spatial distribution of poverty in London:

> "Poverty rates have increased in outer London and decreased in inner London."[64]
>
> "The housing crisis is therefore turning London's poverty map inside out ... [there is] a consistent picture of decreased poverty rates in inner London and increased rates in outer London."[65]
>
> "... for much of the post-war period concentrations of poverty and the worst forms of multiple deprivation were to be found in inner London. Even if poverty rates are still higher in inner London, this simple description is no longer the case. As this report and related research by the Trust for London shows, poverty rates in outer London have been increasing."[66]

From 2001–11, nine out the 13 inner London boroughs witnessed a fall in poverty rates, while 15 of the 19 outer boroughs saw an increase.[67] Whereas only one outer London borough was among the ten poorest boroughs in 2001,[68] Figure 3 shows that this had increased to three outer boroughs by 2019–20: Brent (fourth poorest), Enfield (eighth poorest), and Ealing (tenth poorest). Given Ealing's affluent place image as "The Queen of the Suburbs,"[69] its current high average poverty level suggests that underlying social changes are occurring in suburban outer London.

There are several causes for the suburbanization of poverty in London, but here we will focus on just five.[70] First is the increased private housing costs and unaffordability of inner London:

low-to-middle-income households simply cannot afford to buy a property in inner London and increasingly cannot afford to rent there, making buying or renting in outer London their only feasible option unless they move out of London altogether. Second is the changing occupational distribution between inner and outer London, whereby inner London has witnessed an increase in professional and managerial occupations. This is one of the major reasons for declining poverty in inner London rather than an improvement in living standards among lower-income groups.[71] In other words, the influx of those occupational classes most associated with gentrification has contributed to area-based poverty reduction in inner London. Conversely, "the negative change in occupational level in several outer London boroughs suggests a movement of poorer, less skilled households into these areas."[72]

Third are tenure shifts between inner and outer London. Although outer London remains predominantly owner-occupied, this has reduced from 67% in 2001 to 60% in 2011, while private renting increased from 12% to 21% over the same period.[73] The numbers of private renting households who were in poverty in outer London increased by 208,000 from 2001 to 2011 (or 1%).[74] The trend towards greater private renting in outer London has increased further from 2011 to 2021, as Figure 4 shows based upon census data on the size of the PRS. London experienced an increase of 3.7 percentage points in the proportion of private renters (from 26.4% in 2011 to 30.1% in 2021), higher than the 2.4 percentage points in England (from 18.2% to 20.6% respectively). The equivalent increase was lowest at 0.9% in Waltham Forest, although this was from an already high level, and second lowest at 1.7% in high-rent Richmond-upon-Thames. However, the percentage point increase was higher than the London average of 3.7% in 13 out of 19 outer London boroughs and was greatest in the four boroughs of Hillingdon (6.9%), Redbridge (6.7%), Harrow (6.5%), and Hounslow (6.5%). While by no means all current outer London private renters are on low incomes, it's likely that those who are will be lured by the generally cheaper rents to be found in outer London.[75]

Fourth, there are the direct displacement impacts of social housing estate demolition which has resulted in the movement of

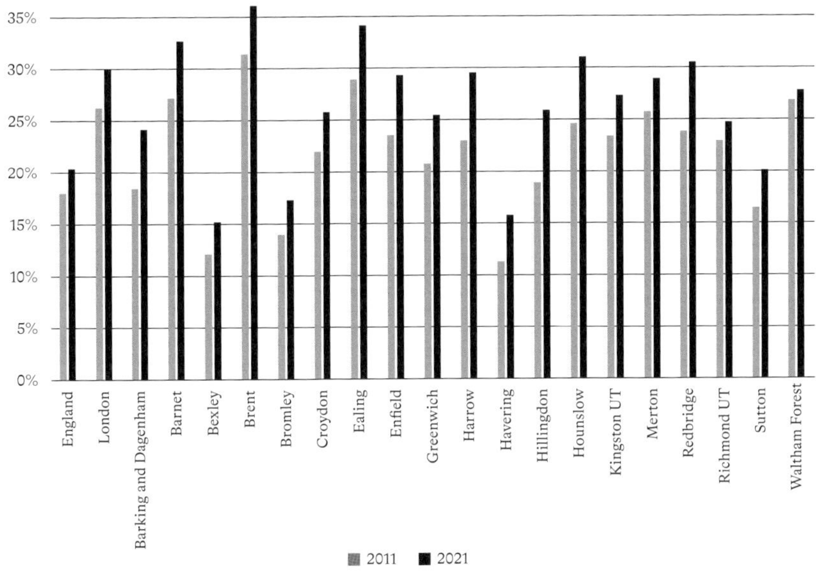

Figure 4: Percent living in private rented or rent-free housing in England, London, and outer London boroughs, 2011–21.

Source: Census 2011 and Census 2021.

estate residents (council/social housing tenants, but even more so owner-occupiers and temporary tenants) to cheaper areas, including from inner to outer London but also within outer London.[76] Fifth are austerity-related welfare changes, which have contributed to the displacement of lower-income people away from inner London areas and into the cheaper areas of outer London or even further afield into South East England. This partly results from Housing Benefit/Local Housing Allowance cuts but also from the relative contraction in social housing provision such that renting from the PRS becomes the only—i.e., forced—"option" for low-income Londoners.[77]

Conclusion

This chapter has highlighted the housing changes which are repositioning the social character of outer London vis-à-vis inner London. The latter has become much more expensive in terms of house prices and rents due to the rise of speculative property investments, many from overseas, and the housing-related impacts of the increased presence of the superrich, Buy-to-Let landlords, and affluent gentrifiers. Inner London is increasingly a hostile place for low-income households. Whereas the latter could access social renting during most of the postwar period, this has become increasingly difficult due to the long-term shrinkage of this sector, combined with the shorter-term impacts of austerity welfare policies. Moving out to the cheaper parts of outer London is therefore a prominent trend. Parts of outer London, such as Richmond-upon-Thames, have however retained and even enhanced their well-heeled suburban chic, and indeed contain a superrich demographic. Nevertheless, the PRS is growing in outer London, as is suburban poverty. Although London is currently a "long way from [the] European model" whereby outer urban areas are markedly poorer than inner areas, as in the case of Paris,[78] it's nevertheless clear that the place image of outer London as an affluent, suburban, home-owning Shangri-La is increasingly at odds with its sociological reality.

Acknowledgements: Thank you to Tahl Kaminer and Chris Hamnett for their very helpful comments on earlier drafts of this chapter.

1 Paul Barker, *The Freedoms of Suburbia* (London: Frances Lincoln, 2009), 15.

2 Mark Clapson, *Suburban Century: Social Change and Urban Growth in England and the USA* (Oxford: Berg, 2003); Paul Maginn and Katrin B. Anacker (eds.) *Suburbia in the 21st Century: From Dreamscape to Nightmare?* (Abingdon: Routledge, 2022).

3 Robert Fishman, *Bourgeois Utopias: The Rise and Fall of Suburbia* (New York: Basic Books, 1987).

4 Clapson, *Suburban Century*; Paul Watt, "Moving to a Better Place? Geographies of Aspiration and Anxiety in the Thames Gateway," in *London's Turning: the Making of Thames Gateway*, eds. Phil Cohen and Michael J. Rustin (Aldershot: Ashgate, 2008); Paul Watt, Gareth Millington, and Rupa Huq, "East London Mobilities: The Cockney Diaspora and the Remaking of the Essex Ethnoscape," in *Mobilities and Neighbourhood Belonging in Cities and Suburbs*, eds. Paul Watt and Peer Smets (Basingstoke: Palgrave Macmillan, 2014).

5 M.P. Baumgartner, *The Moral Order of a Suburb* (New York & Oxford: Oxford University Press, 1988); Clapson, *Suburban Century*.

6 Chris Hamnett, *Unequal City: London in the Global Arena* (London: Routledge, 2003).
7 Marie-Hélène Bacqué, Gary Bridge, Michaela Benson, Tim Butler, Eric Charmes, Yankel Fijalkow, Emma Jackson, Lydie Launay, and Stephanie Vermeersch, *The Middle Classes and the City: A Study of Paris and London* (Basingstoke: Palgrave Macmillan, 2015).
8 Maginn and Anacker, *Suburbia in the 21st Century.*
9 Clapson, *Suburban Century*.
10 This chapter mainly uses the ONS definition of inner and outer London boroughs. The ONS classifies Greenwich as outer London, and Haringey and Newham as inner London.
11 Paul Watt, *Estate Regeneration and Its Discontents: Public Housing, Place and Inequality in London* (Bristol: Policy Press, 2021).
12 David Gilbert, Claire Dwyer, and Nazneen Ahmed, "Ethnic and Religious Diversity in the Politics of Suburban London," *The Political Quarterly* 90, no. 1 (2019): 73.
13 Alan Mace, *City Suburbs: Placing Suburbia in a Post-suburban World* (London: Routledge, 2013); Gilbert et al., "Ethnic and Religious Diversity in the Politics of Suburban London."
14 Paul Watt and Anna Minton, "London's Housing Crisis and its Activisms," *City* 20, no. 2 (2016): 204–21; Anna Minton, *Big Capital: Who is London For?* (London: Penguin Books, 2017); Paul Watt, "This Pain of Moving, Moving, Moving: Evictions, Displacement and Logics of Expulsion in London," *L'Annee sociologique* 68, no. 1 (2018): 67–100; Tom Gillespie, Kate Hardy, and Paul Watt, "Surplus to the City: Austerity Urbanism, Displacement and 'Letting Die'," *Environment and Planning A* 53, no. 7 (2021): 1713–729.
15 Mike Raco and Frances Brill, *London* (Newcastle upon Tyne: Agenda Publishing, 2022).
16 Paul Hunter, *The Unspoken Decline of Outer London. Why is Poverty and Inequality Increasing in Outer London and What Needs to Change?* (London: The Smith Institute, 2019); The Suburban Taskforce, *An Inquiry into the Future of the Suburbs* (London: All-Party Parliamentary Group for London's Planning and Built Environment, 2022).
17 Mace, *City Suburbs*, 134.
18 Raco and Brill, *London*.
19 Chris Hamnett and Jonathan Reades, "Mind the Gap: Implications of Overseas Investment for Regional House Price Divergence in Britain," *Housing Studies* 34, no. 3 (2019): 402.
20 Alison Wallace, David Rhodes, and Richard Webber, *Overseas Investors in London's New Build Housing Market* (York: Centre for Housing Policy, University of York, 201); Hamnett and Reades, "Mind the Gap."
21 Wallace et al., *Overseas Investors in London's New Build Housing Market*, 100.
22 Hamptons, "Capital Gains: How the London Market Is Springing Back," (March 2022), https://www.hamptons.co.uk/research/articles/capital-gains-how-the-london-market-is-springing-back#/.
23 Rowland Atkinson, Roger Burrows, Luna Glucksberg, Hang Kei Ho, Caroline Knowles, and David Rhodes, "Minimum City? The Deeper Impacts of the 'Super-Rich' on Urban Life," in *Cities and the Super-Rich: Real Estate, Elite Practices and Urban Political Economies*, eds. Ray Forrest, Sin Yee Koh, and Bart Wissink (New York: Palgrave Macmillan, 2017); Rowland Atkinson, *Alpha City: How London Was Captured by the Super-Rich* (London: Verso, 2020); Caroline Knowles, *Serious Money: Walking Plutocratic London* (London: Allen Lane, 2022).
24 Watt and Minton, "London's Housing Crisis and its Activisms."
25 Office for National Statistics [ONS], "Private Rental Affordability, England: 2012 to 2020" (2021), https://www.ons.gov.uk/peoplepopulationandcommunity/housing/bulletins/privaterentalaffordabilityengland/2012to2020.
26 Tony Travers, Sam Sims, and Nicolas Bosetti, *Housing and Inequality in London* (London, Centre for London, 2016).

27 Greater London Authority [GLA], *Housing in London 2022: The Evidence Base for the London Housing Strategy* (London: GLA, 2022).

28 ONS, "Exploring Recent Trends in the London Housing Market" (September 19, 2018), https://www.ons.gov.uk/economy/inflationandpriceindices/articles/exploringrecenttrendsinthelondonhousingmarket/2018-09-19.

29 Hamptons, "The London Market: A Strong End to a Tough Year" (December 2021), https://www.hamptons.co.uk/research/reports/market-insight-winter-2021-2022/the-london-market#/.

30 Adam Almeida, *Pushed to the Margins: Gentrification in London in the 2010s* (London: Runnymede Trust, 2021); Joshua Yee and Adam Dennett, "Stratifying and Predicting Patterns of Neighbourhood Change and Gentrification: An Urban Analytics Approach," *Transactions of the Institute of British Geographers* 47, no. 3 (2022): 770–90, DOI: 10.1111/tran.12522.

31 Watt, *Estate Regeneration and Its Discontents*, 25.

32 Loretta Lees, Hyun Bang Shin, and Eduardo López-Morales, *Planetary Gentrification* (London: Polity Press, 2016).

33 Tim Butler and Gary Robson, *London Calling. The Middle Classes and the Re-Making of Inner London* (Oxford: Berg, 2003); Bacqué et al., *The Middle Classes and the City*; Yee and Dennett, "Stratifying and Predicting Patterns of Neighbourhood Change and Gentrification."

34 Almeida, *Pushed to the Margins*, 10.

35 Antoine Paccoud and Alan Mace, "Tenure Change in London's Suburbs: Spreading Gentrification or Suburban Upscaling?," *Urban Studies* 55, no. 6 (2018): 1313–328.

36 Paul Watt and Penny Bernstock, "Legacy for Whom? Housing in Post-Olympic East London," in *London 2012 and the Post-Olympics City: A Hollow Legacy?*, eds. Phil Cohen and Paul Watt (London: Palgrave Macmillan, 2017).

37 Property Observer, "Olympic Legacy is Still Benefitting the London Property Market in These Boroughs," *Property Observer* (June 5, 2022), https://www.propertyobserver.co.uk/tips/olympic-legacy-is-still-benefiting-the-london-property-market-in-these-boroughs/.

38 Penny Bernstock, *Olympic Housing: A Critical Review of London 2012's Legacy* (Farnham: Ashgate, 2014); Piero Corcillo and Paul Watt, "Social Mixing or Mixophobia in Regenerating East London? 'Affordable Housing', Gentrification, Stigmatisation and the Post-Olympics East Village," *People, Place and Policy* 16, no. 3 (2022): 236–54.

39 Watt, *Estate Regeneration and Its Discontents*.

40 Jerry Flynn, "Complete Control," *City* 20, no. 2 (2016): 278–86; Phil Hubbard and Loretta Lees, "The Right to Community? Legal Geographies of Resistance on London's Gentrification Frontiers," *City* 22, no. 1 (2018): 8–25; Almeida, *Pushed to the Margins*; Watt, *Estate Regeneration and Its Discontents*.

41 GOV.UK, "Local Authority Housing Data" (2022), https://www.gov.uk/government/collections/local-authority-housing-data.

42 These account for 98% of the London total for this period.

43 Saffron Woodcraft and Nicola Bacon, *Living at Kidbrooke Village* (London: Berkeley Homes, 2013), 11.

44 Woodcraft and Bacon, *Living at Kidbrooke Village*.

45 Kath Scanlon, Emma Sagor, Christine Whitehead, and Alessandra Mossa, *New London Villages: Creating Community* (London: Berkeley Group/London School of Economics, 2016).

46 Peer Smets and Paul Watt, "Social Housing and Urban Renewal: Conclusion", in *Social Housing and Urban Renewal: A Cross-National Perspective*, eds. Paul Watt and Peer Smets (Bingley: Emerald, 2017), 471.

47 Calculated based on figures included in Loretta Lees, "The Death of Sustainable Communities in London?", in *Sustainable London? The future of a Global City*, eds. Rob Imrie and Loretta Lees (Bristol: Policy Press); Emily Rogers, "Ferrier Estate Reborn", *Inside Housing* (June 19, 2014).

48 Woodcraft and Bacon, *Living at Kidbrooke Village*, 64.

49 G15, *Meeting the Challenge of Urban Renewal: The G15's Contribution to Regenerating London's Estates* (London: G15, 2016), 48; Watt, *Estate Regeneration and Its Discontents*, 102.
50 Paul Watt, "Displacement and Estate Demolition: Multi-Scalar Place Attachment Among Relocated Social Housing Residents in London," *Housing Studies* 37, no. 9 (2022): 1686–710.
51 Watt, *Estate Regeneration and Its Discontents*, 86.
52 Foxtons, "Kidbrooke Village" (February 2023), https://www.foxtons.co.uk/newhomes/kidbrooke-village.
53 ONS, "Earnings and Hours Worked, Place of Residence by Local Authority: ASHE Table 8" (October 26, 2022), https://www.ons.gov.uk/employmentandlabourmarket/peopleinwork/earningsandworkinghours/datasets/placeofresidencebylocalauthorityashetable8.
54 Barratt London, "Hendon Waterside" (February 2023), https://www.barratthomes.co.uk/new-homes/dev000147-hendon-waterside/?gclid=EAIaIQobChMI76nOqJL6_rTtCh2xkgGjEAAYASAAEgKOLvD_BwE&gclsrc=aw.ds.
55 Kat Hanna and Nicolas Bosetti, *Inside Out: The New Geography of Poverty and Wealth in London* (London: Centre for London, 2015), 9.
56 Ministry of Housing, Communities & Local Government, *English Indices of Deprivation 2019* (September 26, 2019), https://www.gov.uk/government/statistics/english-indices-of-deprivation-2019.
57 City Intelligence, *The Indices of Deprivation 2019: Ward Level Summary Measures for London* (London: GLA, April 2020), 4.
58 Knowles, *Serious Money*.
59 Atkinson et al., "Minimum City?"
60 Roger Burrows, Stephen Graham, and Alexander Wilson, "Bunkering Down? The Geography of Elite Residential Basement Development in London," *Urban Geography* 43, no. 9 (2019): 1372–393.
61 Robert Webb, Duncan Watson, and Steven Cook, "Price Adjustment in the London Housing Market", *Urban Studies* 58, no. 1 (2021): 113–30.
62 GLA, *Housing in London 2022*.
63 Nick Bailey and Jon Minton, "The Suburbanisation of Poverty in British Cities, 2004-16: Extent, Processes and Nature," *Urban Geography* 39, no. 6 (2018): 910.
64 Hanna and Bosetti, *Inside Out*, 6.
65 Travers et al., *Housing and Inequality in London*, 11 & 37.
66 Hunter, The *Unspoken Decline of Outer London*, 4.
67 Travers et al., *Housing and Inequality in London*, 37.
68 Hanna and Bosetti, *Inside Out*.
69 Gilbert et al., "Ethnic and Religious Diversity in the Politics of Suburban London."
70 Hanna and Bosetti, *Inside Out*; Travers et al., *Housing and Inequality in London*; Bailey and Minton, "The Suburbanisation of Poverty in British Cities, 2004-16"; Hunter, *The Unspoken Decline of Outer London*.
71 Hanna and Bosetti, *Inside Out*.
72 Hanna and Bosetti, *Inside Out*, 11.
73 Hanna and Bosetti, *Inside Out*.
74 Travers et al., *Housing and Inequality in London*.
75 Watt, "This Pain of Moving, Moving, Moving."
76 Flynn, "Complete Control"; Hubbard and Lees, "The Right to Community?"; Watt, "This Pain of Moving, Moving, Moving"; Watt, *Estate Regeneration and Its Discontents*.
77 Watt, "This Pain of Moving, Moving, Moving"; Paul Watt, "'Press-Ganged' Generation Rent: Youth Homelessness, Precarity and Poverty in East London," *People, Place and Policy* 14, no. 2 (2020): 128–41; Gillespie et al., "Surplus to the City."
78 Gilbert et al., "Ethnic and Religious Diversity in the Politics of Suburban London," 75.

From Inclusive Legacy Promises to Exclusive Realities: Planning, Design, and Displacement in Post-Olympic East London

Juliet Davis and Penny Bernstock[1]

Introduction

A link between the production of the elaborate stages and infrastructures required by megaevents and the displacement of the existing residents from the sites of those events has been firmly established in the field of urban studies. Much of the related literature presents this as the outcome of the application of neoliberal strategies that aim to attract private capital and market-oriented development as a means to transform devalued and/or low-income urban areas, often involving the forced relocation of existing communities.[2] Much of this work, however, focusses on a key period: typically, the moment when cities are *preparing* to host megaevents and state-led displacements, forced evictions, and demolitions are *paving the way* for spectacular parklands and venues. There is a relative dearth of literature on displacements associated with legacy planning, design, and development in and around megaevent sites in the years *after* the event. Further, the focus of analysis has been almost exclusively on displacement associated with housing, with a more limited focus on employment and no attention paid to the intersections between housing and employment-related displacement.

These lacunae in current research are addressed in this chapter, which depicts the analysis arising from longitudinal research into displacements and replacements connected to the development of London's 2012 Olympic Games and its planned "regeneration legacy" from 2005 to 2022. We utilize the dual lenses of *displacement* and *replacement* to illuminate the process of restructuring taking place over this period. We show that the displacement of low-income residents living in affordable housing and of unskilled and semi-skilled workers employed in traditional manufacturing jobs prior to the Games has made way for their replacement with mainly market housing and employment opportunities targeted at professional groups from outside of the area. This replacement has occurred despite a clear and laudable policy commitment to regenerate "an entire community for the direct benefit of everyone that lives there."[3] We argue that the process has been enabled by a set of policy assumptions, planning policies, and urban designs that may be read as state-led gentrification unfolding in the anticipation of Olympic legacy development. Over the course of the chapter we show why focusing on housing and employment together is crucial, given not only the existence of important historical connections between traditional manufacturing jobs and low-income residents in East London but the ways in which both have been the focus of regeneration plans for a post-industrial east London since the days of the Olympic bid.

Through the chapter, we will reveal displacement as a process unfolding through three main stages in the planned urban transformations with which London's Olympic Park (hereafter, the Park) has been associated. Through our analysis, we draw on the concepts of displacement first established by Peter Marcuse to characterize different forms of displacement involving different interactions between the state and markets, along with insights from gentrification studies.[4] First, we show, in the period between 2005 and 2007, "direct displacement" emerged as a feature of land assembly and a planning process predicated on tabula rasa redevelopment. Second, between 2008 and 2012, indirect "exclusionary displacement" processes and forms of anticipated replacement became embedded in regeneration plans and policies. The third stage extends from 2012 to 2022. In this period, we see the gradual materialization of legacy development and the emergence of major issues of affordability that are the outcome of a combination of regeneration plans, policies, and market forces, exacerbating exclusionary displacement dynamics and shaping patterns of replacement in terms of land uses and population.

Displacement and Redevelopment, 2005–07
New Opportunities or Just a Familiar Tale of Eviction?

In 2004, the site designated for the 2012 Olympic Games in London's Lower Lea Valley was largely an employment zone at the cusp of four London Boroughs (Figure 1). Across its 266 hectares, 284 businesses were accommodated, largely SMEs (Small and Medium-sized Enterprises), employing in the order of 5,000 people within a total floor space estimated at around 330,000 square meters.[5] Businesses, without exception, fell into commercial and industrial categories of use as defined by the 1987 Town and Country Planning Order B1c (Business: light industrial), B2 (General industrial), and B8 (Storage and distribution). Viewed at a finer scale of resolution, these use categories comprised of a rich mix of activities including manufacturers of clothing and textiles, food, theatre sets, furniture, glass, concrete, and metal products. There were also waste management and recycling firms, printers, motor vehicle repairers and second-hand vehicle part merchants, bus depots and garages, and wholesale suppliers of foods from all over the world.[6]

These activities were and remain important to many different aspects of London's life and metabolism—from its waste

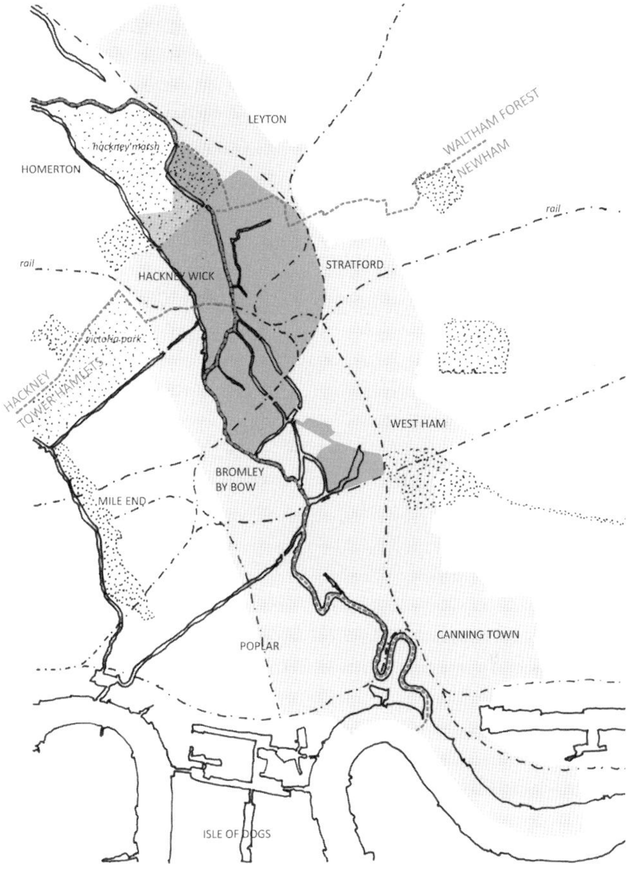

Figure 1: The Olympic site in the Lower Lea Valley (the pale grey describes the Lower Lea Valley Opportunity Area which the site, in dark grey, formed part of).

© the authors.

removal to its markets for fine food, its international restaurants, and its cultural industries. The origins of their concentration in the Lea Valley lies, however, in the nineteenth century when the area, which is close to London's docks, industrialized. Between the 1800s and 2005, the profile of industries evolved continually, and the fortunes of firms were affected by changing commodity markets and manufacturing processes as well as by broad geo-political forces. Reflecting this churn, most of the firms active on the site in 2005 had arrived from the early 1990s onwards. They reflected the diversity and, to an extent, the regeneration of East London's manufacturing base in the wake of the decline of earlier industries.[7] They relied on the relative cheapness (by London standards) yet centrality of the site, with tenants paying in the order of £5 per square foot per annum for basic industrial premises and with the area designated as industrial land (which was one eighth of the price of residential land). The employment opportunities which the firms provided were, typically, for unskilled and semi-skilled workers.

There is a clear historical relationship between local employment and housing in the Lower Lea Valley, with typically private, though working-class, housing springing up along the fringes of the Lea Valley concurrently with industrialization. The Olympic site itself had little housing before the 1960s, though, largely owing to unfavorable ground conditions, flood risk and the proximity of industry. In the 1960s, the Carpenters Estate adjacent to the site was built to ensure a supply of high-quality low-cost housing for those working in manufacturing industries in the area at that time.

By 2005, there was an eclectic mix of residential land uses on the site, providing an opportunity for low-cost housing in a city that was already becoming increasingly unaffordable. This included student accommodation and two permanent Romani and Travelers' sites. One Travelers' site was based in Hackney and was home to 20 Irish Traveler families who had lived there since 1993 and the other site was based in Newham, where 15 English Romani families had lived since 1972. The site also included Europe's second largest housing cooperative. Clays Lane Housing Cooperative was designed and developed in 1984 to provided 452 tenancies for single people. Housing here was genuinely affordable, with rents set at around £200 per calendar month. There were long-standing residents living there in 2005 and the area was imbued with a strong sense of community.[8]

The direct displacement of these businesses and residents to make way for the Games was led by the London Development Agency (LDA) through a Compulsory Purchase Order aligned to a comprehensive redevelopment strategy. The aim was not just to free up land for a suite of sporting venues, but to more radically reorder land uses in East London, closing the "edgy" seam which the Lea Valley formed between inner and outer East London with high-density, mixed-use development and by relegating industry, seen as incompatible with housing and no longer as a route to local prosperity, closer to the periphery of Greater London.[9] These activities were viewed by LDA leaders and by the Greater London Authority as imperative for the site to "realise its full regeneration potential," offering many more employment opportunities as well as homes and high-quality amenities in the future.[10]

And yet, numerous commentators documenting the compulsory purchase process have noted the overlap between London's relocation strategy and the aggressive displacements and sometimes violent "un-homing" of working-class and/or precarious populations observed in other megaevent host cities.[11] These, after all, have often been located in poor and deprived areas, with these attributes used as a justification for radical, top-down intervention. Key observations included that this state-led, direct displacement process was underpinned by a "wasteland" narrative that served within official accounts of regeneration benefits and promises to conceal or ignore the true variety of SMEs occupying the site, and the attachment to place and dependency on the warmth and care that residents experienced in their communities.[12] Also noted were: the lack of opportunity for landowning stakeholders (typically businesses) to participate in the process and benefit from an uplift in values connected to planning for mixed-use development, and the tendency of officials to refer to the process as a negotiated relocation, whereas many occupants experienced it as eviction.[13] Questions were raised about the feasibility of moving such a large number of firms and the potential knock-on consequences for rental values, though the LDA had insisted that "similar premises at similar rents/values could be found elsewhere" within industrially-designated land in East London.[14] The displacement process, further, was far from straightforward, resulting in adverse consequences for both residents and employers who were forced to make compromised decisions within an accelerated timeframe because of the need to clear the site.[15] A significant consequence of this was that some firms were not able to recover, closing shortly after being uprooted. In turn, though many residents were satisfactorily resettled, the aspirations of a significant proportion who expressed a desire to move as a group was not realized, housing costs increased, and an important source of community-led housing was lost.[16]

Imagining the Landscape of Change—An Emerging Urban Topography of Replacement, 2008–12

We now turn to explore the emergence and evolution of key principles underpinning plans for replacement housing and employment on the Park in the post-Games period. The earliest master plans for the Games were produced at the time of the bid in 2003–04. These established the key spatial principles of an Olympic Park that would transform after the Games into a set of compact urban neighborhoods gathered around a grand public space. However, it was the Legacy Masterplan Framework (LMF), launched in 2008, just as the displacement of former occupants was completing, that established the range and balance of land uses, densities, and tenures in detail, describing in the process the objectives and goals underpinning these strategies in terms of "regeneration." The LMF included detailed spatial proposals for six neighborhoods and a socioeconomic strategy for housing, employment, and social infrastructure that drew on a wide array of data including legacy promises, planning and housing policies, population surveys, and analyses of local deprivation.

The master plan responded to five "legacy promises" formulated by London Mayor Ken Livingstone, which established the goals of providing a significant uplift in housing and employment opportunities through the site's transformation.[17] It also responded to The London Plan 2004, which set out an aspiration of 50%

affordable housing on all new developments. Thus, "around 9,000" homes within the site boundaries were to be accommodated, 35–50% of which, it was claimed, would be "affordable" (with a 60% social-rented/40% intermediate housing split), significantly more than the site had previously accommodated. In turn, 9,400 employment opportunities were anticipated, almost doubling pre-2007 on-site jobs.[18]

All development would be clustered within mixed-use, mixed-tenure neighborhoods, which aimed to transform the sense of containment and isolation that characterized earlier settlement. Low-density development (the site's old one-to-two-story industrial units) and its populations of low-income residents and industrial workers would be replaced by the sort of compact, walkable, mixed-tenure urbanism that was idealized as the essence of sustainability in the context of the incumbent Labour government's "Urban Renaissance" agenda.[19]

The LMF was to be short-lived, however. With Livingstone replaced at the end of 2008 by Boris Johnson as the new Conservative Mayor of London and a new Conservative Government in Westminster in 2010, the master plan was relaunched as the Legacy Communities Scheme (LCS) under the new leadership of a development corporation in place of the LDA. Targets for both anticipated homes and employment opportunities within the planned new neighborhoods were slashed in 2011. Thus, the LCS anticipated "around 6,400" homes in total in 5 new neighborhoods with affordable housing targets set as 35% (subject to viability and now with an established minimum of 20% affordability across the site and a split of 30% social-rented/40% intermediate/30% in what was then the newly introduced "affordable rent" category that linked rental costs to market values rather than incomes). 8,000 jobs were now anticipated to replace the 5,300 lost. The declining commitment to affordable housing was motivated by four factors: austerity, the need to repay public debts and maximize land value, an ongoing belief that the legacy boroughs needed more private housing to balance out the historic predominance of social housing at the fringes of the Park, and a new predilection stemming from the new Mayor for lower-density, less "European" models of urban form.[20] A focus on clustered development, the formation of five neighborhoods, mixed-use urban form integrating housing and employment uses in a variety of ways, and the idea of sustainable walkability between different land uses persisted, however, as urban design principles in the LCS (Figure 2).

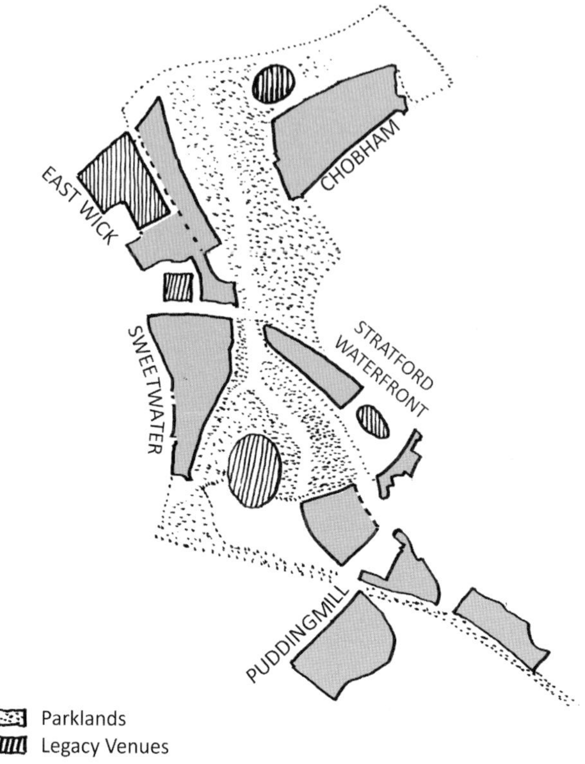

Figure 2: Legacy Communities.
© the authors.

The anticipated profile of replacement employment uses also remained constant between the LMF and LCS. While, on the one hand, employment strategies articulated the aim to cultivate a diverse range of economic sectors to align at least some of the future job opportunities with legacy borough resident populations' skillsets and qualifications, the overall direction marked a dramatic shift in the balance of employment uses from a predominance of light industry, manufacturing, transport, and storage (use classes B1c/B2/B8) to employment in such areas as retail, "banking, finance, and insurance," and "public administration, education, and health" (which are planning use classes A2-B1a/b). These are seen as higher-value jobs associated with higher levels of prosperity.[21] This range of jobs would clearly relate to a diversity of incomes, raising questions of the possible correspondence between workers' incomes and residents of the Park.

A sense of inevitability is communicated by the plans; they read as rational responses to an inexorable shift in the pattern of London's post-industrial economic transformation from an imperial, industrial capital to a global city centered on professional and financial services. It is notably a shift from blue-collar jobs to white-collar ones, suggesting an overall reduction in the sorts of opportunities that would have been available to working-class people living in either social or affordable market housing in the legacy boroughs and an accompanying escalation in demand for middle-class populations with advanced qualifications. It may be assumed that, as it would be an incoming population to whom new employment opportunities were made available, it would be to these groups that the new market housing would appeal. For existing local populations characterized by lower levels of skill and pay, the LCS highlights the importance of education infrastructure within the Park to "reduce disadvantage and to enable residents to access both work and better-paid work" and to ensure that young people resident in the legacy boroughs are able to access aspirational jobs.[22] However, issues of housing affordability raise questions of the feasibility of this plan, given that low-income families would depend on access to suitable housing within the catchment areas of the new schools.

The kinds of urban forms and approaches to tenure, social mix, and employment strategies outlined here have all been associated with processes and theories of gentrification and displacement. The compact, walkable urbanism first emerging under the progressive banner of the "Urban Renaissance" has been seen to constitute a "gentrification aesthetic" of new-build architecture on brownfield sites as well as a symbol of the re-colonization of the inner city by the middle classes in the wake of their postwar flight to suburbia and consequent direct/indirect displacement of lower-income groups.[23] In the later LCS, this symbolism becomes more pronounced than in the earlier LMF, with neighborhood forms designed to emulate, through designerly visualizations, the mixed-use topography of elite neighborhoods such as Mayfair and Belgravia. The aesthetic is also associated with indirect "exclusionary displacement" as it is aimed at generating the desirability that would lead real estate values to soar.

The strategy of creating mixed communities—which is promoted by planners and policymakers as a vehicle for increasing the life chances of the deprived tenants of social housing, and/or of creating chances for low-income residents to live in desirable areas—has been questioned by academic commentators as a form of "gentrification by stealth" that leads progressively to displacement.[24] For some scholars such as Chris Hamnett, London's changing economy can, but need not necessarily, involve displacement when people are able to gain new skills and adapt to suit emerging employment opportunities.[25] However, plans to promote white-collar jobs and higher-value employment uses generally have, in recent times, come to be seen as a distinctively, workspace-related form of gentrification, as they are often linked to forms of direct and indirect forms of small business displacement.[26] In the upcoming section, we look in detail at how replacement dynamics have actually unfolded through the materialization of legacy since 2012 and how displacement has continued to operate in tandem with them.

Realities of Replacement, 2012–22

At the time of writing, large swathes of the Olympic legacy communities anticipated by plans in the period 2004–12 have been realized. As of June 2022, almost exactly ten years after the Olympic Games, the first neighborhood to develop, Chobham Manor (see location in Figure 2), is close to completion. Neighborhoods named East Wick and Sweetwater are in part complete (including the Here East complex, which is a focus for industry and education), with Phases 2 and 3 in development and planning permission granted for Phases 4 and 5. Plans for the Pudding Mill neighborhood are advanced, with a contractor selected, and Stratford Waterfront is on site. Also complete are the transformations of the parklands and retained sporting venues from the Games into local, everyday amenities. Urban designs for each neighborhood have been developed within the parameters established by the LCS (which was awarded outline planning permission in 2012), with each neighborhood or planning delivery zone becoming the focus of a new zonal master plan which was required to demonstrate compliance with the LCS. In this section, we consider replacement largely by recourse to the following forms of data: planning and urban design strategies, official monitoring and performance reports, and some broader data around costs and property values.

Part of the planning process since 2012 has been the creation of new planning policy by the London Legacy Development Corporation (LLDC), which was incorporated as a planning authority at its establishment. In 2012, again, the LLDC produced its first Local Plan, which established strategic policies for land in the Olympic Park—the area covered by the LCS—but also for larger expanses of Olympic fringe territory. The most recent Local Plan was produced in 2020.

Apparent from this is that the idea of creating dense, mixed-use, mixed-tenure neighborhoods has survived from the earliest master plans to delivery, with walkable proximity between "live" and "work" at the heart of the LLDC's vision of sustainable places and communities.[27] The Park is positioned in the Local Plan 2020 as a magnet for "high-quality businesses and employers" offering "quality jobs," as an exciting center of "cross-sector innovation," and as a dynamic focus for the economic growth required in east London to advance prosperity. High-quality jobs across a range of sectors of the economy have remained the vision for replacing those older jobs linked in the LDA's relocation strategy to deprivation, supposedly outmoded industry, and low skill.

Looking at this at a finer scale of resolution, while the neighborhoods are all planned to be highly mixed, different amounts and proportions of various land uses are included in each, the aim being to mold subtly distinct characters of place. The LCS neighborhoods as a whole look set to deliver less housing than anticipated—i.e., around 5,200 homes of different sizes and tenures (excluding 1,800 student rooms linked to university-led development). They are likely to deliver around 132,679 square meters of floorspace related to B use classes (business, industry, distribution, or storage), a figure representing only around 40% of the "B" use class floorspace available across the site prior to 2007. Employment space now also includes significant areas of "A" use class workspace (retail, food and drink, financial and professional services), "D" use class (education and other social infrastructure, leisure), and "sui generis" (such as theatres, which fall outside the other categories), revealing a policy of economic diversification. Since the production of the LCS in 2012, the idea of a cultural and educational quarter has emerged and led to a complete revisioning of the Stratford Waterfront neighborhood. This is now a focus for the development of cultural and educational (use classes D and sui generis) institutions including the BBC, the V&A, Sadler's Wells, the London College of Fashion, and University College London (UCL), which have taken the place of previously planned residential uses. While the development of cultural and education infrastructure has become an important theme in regeneration, connected at least in part to the idea of creating broad public benefit, the loss of housing raises questions about the LLDC's priorities in the context of London's housing crisis, ongoing issues of deprivation in the legacy host boroughs, precarity, and high levels of demand for affordable workspace.

Table 1 provides an overview of residential development in the first four neighborhoods on the Park and suggests that, despite drops in housing provision since the LMF/LCS, there is clearly much more housing today than on the pre-Olympic site (see section 1 above). The mix of tenures, broadly, coheres with the LLDC's vision of "mixed communities," encompassing a range of house sizes and tenures. However, issues of affordability pertain to much of it, echoing Watt and Bernstock's analysis of the East Village (former Athlete's Village) in 2017.[28]

The table shows that most housing built in these four neighborhoods is, in fact, market housing (66%). Affordable housing comprises 34% of all housing. The figures reflect modifications to Chobham Manor, Eastwick, and Sweetwater following local campaigns and a commitment from Mayor Khan to provide more affordable housing than had been indicated in zonal master plans. For example, Chobham Manor was, at one time, to have included just

28% affordable housing, while levels of affordable housing at East Wick and Sweetwater were reduced in 2013 from 43% and 48% respectively to 30% in 2013, only to be subsequently increased back up to 34% in 2020.

Neighborhood	*Total number of units*	*Number and percentage of market units*	*Number and percentage of affordable units*	*Quasi-affordable (shared ownership units)*	*Genuinely affordable units*
Chobham Manor	859	556 (65%)	303 (35%)	98	205
East Wick and Sweetwater	1844	1226 (66%)	618 (34%)	191	427
Stratford Waterfront	600	390 (65%)	210 (35%)	210	0
Total	3303	2172 (66%)	1131 (34%)	499 (44%)	632 (56%)

Table 1: Housing provision in the first four neighborhoods.

Affordable housing is divided into two main categories. The first is labelled as "quasi-affordable" because, as we demonstrate below, although it meets the statutory policy definition of an affordable housing product, it is not affordable to residents living in the legacy boroughs. The second category is labelled as "genuinely" affordable housing because, here, costs are capped to ensure that rents are affordable to local residents.

Table 2 below provides an analysis of incomes for three of the four legacy boroughs (data was not available for Waltham Forest) and sets these against the cost of one-bedroom and two-bedroom shared ownership properties at Chobham Manor. It shows that the income requirements for these homes are above both mean and upper quartile household incomes in the boroughs. Clearly, then, this type of affordable housing would not be accessible to the majority of households. These issues are also present at East Wick and Sweetwater, where a minimum household income of £69,000 is required to purchase a share of a two-bedroom property with a total market value of £620,000. Paradoxically, then, while it is generally assumed that affordable housing reflects a policy of "anti-displacement," this quasi-affordable housing stands to exacerbate exclusionary displacement patterns. When combined with market housing, it becomes clear that 81% of all housing built in these neighborhoods is unaffordable.

Differentials between incomes and house prices are even more accentuated in private market housing both for rent and sale. Across the Park, market rental values have been rising. The Manhattan Loft Gardens development has recently launched with 1-bedroom rental apartments starting at £3,000 and increasing to £7,500 and above for 2-bedroom luxury apartments. A 2-bedroom flat at Chobham Manor is being marketed in August 2022 for £600,000, while 3- and 4-bedroom houses are set at around £1 million. According to data from the Office for National Statistics, median house prices in the small census areas intersecting the Park are in the region of £600,000, around fifteen times the mean incomes indicated in Table 2, and these prices exert a strong exclusionary displacement effect.

Of course, this is not just an issue for the Olympic Park—property values in the legacy boroughs have risen by as much as

Legacy borough	*Mean household income*	*Upper quartile household income*	*Income requirement for quasi affordable shared ownership housing at Chobham Manor*
Newham	£36,584	£48,780	1 bed = £58k 2 bed = £69k
Tower Hamlets	£41,104	£53,349	
Hackney	£38,018	£50,649	
Average legacy boroughs	£36,568	£50,649	

Table 2: Income and affordability—Quasi affordable shared ownership housing.[29]

425% in specific postcodes since 2005, and escalating property values in London constitute a key dimension of the housing crisis. The wider significance of this is not just displacement but rising poverty rather than prosperity stemming from physical and economic regeneration. Newham, for example, has the second highest number of children living in poverty in England, and most children living in what is described as "absolute low-income households" are members of "working families."[30] The legacy boroughs have some of the highest levels of housing need in England. Numbers of people on the local waiting lists for housing range from 8,379 in Waltham Forest to 27,635 in Newham, with many thousands living in unsanitary and/or overcrowded conditions. As Watt and Bernstock have shown, these figures have been on the rise since 2012.[31] The lack of housing means that a growing number of households are placed in temporary accommodation, both inside and outside of the legacy boroughs. In 2018, Newham placed more households out of borough than any other borough in England.

Issues of housing affordability have a bearing, in a range of ways, on the capacity of the Legacy Corporation agenda to genuinely reverse "local trends of unemployment and lower educational attainment, earnings and life expectancy" through the planned employment-related development described above.[32] As illustrated in Table 3 below, more than 13,000 end-use employment opportunities look set to be created through legacy development, with many more related to the construction of legacy parklands, venues, and communities—many more than anticipated. This excludes the large numbers of jobs expected in neighboring developments in Stratford–Stratford City and the International Quarter. The employment cluster of Here East alone (a focus for "B" class uses) provides the same sort of figure for jobs as the whole site provided in 2005, now within compact and environmentally sustainable development.

A key strand of the LLDC's current (2020) planning policy related to employment space and the promotion of workspaces that meet the needs of a range of businesses, from new business start-ups and micro-businesses to larger, established companies. In the development of the site, this is reflected in the provision of different sized units, but also the provision of supportive infrastructure in the form of incubator, accelerator, and co-working spaces. At Here East, for example, Plexal offers co-working spaces including hot-desking arrangements and offices, along with meeting rooms, equipment, and technology to a membership comprised of start-ups and SMEs. Hence, such spaces are conceived of as an intermediary between the two universities occupying space at Here East (Loughborough University and UCL) and enterprise. Within the former industrial areas just outside the Park, the LLDC has employed and subsequently promoted the expansion through new development of live-work models emergent within the creative communities of Hackney Wick and Fish Island.[33] Both initiatives suggest a desire to accommodate enterprise and innovation at all stages of development rather than merely focusing on established firms.

However, the affordability of workspaces, particularly in the "B" use class categories, and in new building, has rapidly become an issue on and at the fringes of the Park as elsewhere in London. In Hackney Wick and Fish Island, rising rents have been leading to the indirect or exclusionary displacement of artists and other creative, homegrown organizations, and to these areas being recognized as centers of "commercial gentrification."[34] On the Park, high costs risk excluding the very sorts of younger start-up firms with bright ideas but typically low levels of capital that the LLDC has often sought to attract. One result has recently been a policy initiative, set out within the Local Plan, to create subsidized

	Estimated 2020
Legacy communities scheme (including Stratford Waterfront)	8,000
Press and broadcasting center (Here East cluster)	5,300
Stadium/venues	254
	13,300

Table 3: Estimated jobs on the Olympic Park (Source: London Legacy Development Corporation)

affordable workspace. According to the LLDC, this is required to be designed as flexible space and defined by rental values that are "up to 75 per cent of historic market rent for the previous year for the equivalent floorspace in the same area for an equivalent B Class Use."[35] In addition, since 2012, approximately 22,500 square meters of affordable workspace have been permitted in the area over which the Development Corporation has planning powers. Notably, however, only two small areas fall within the actual Park rather than the wider territory that the LLDC controls. The rest exists at the fringes of the Park, where the LLDC has been endeavoring to protect existing pockets of historic affordability for artists and makers. Of the areas in the Park, one is designated as an interim use.[36] The other falls within Here East. Named the "Trampery on the Gantry," this area comprises a sliver of studio space of around 1,000 square meters in total, just 0.89% of the net lettable area of Here East and offered at the required rate of 75% of historic market rents (which works out at approximately £40 per square foot per annum). At Here East, floorspace rents are £25–49.50 per square foot per annum, close to the average for Grade A office space in Stratford in 2022 (£40–45), though still some way below Grade A or Grade B office space prices for areas such as Kings Cross and the City of London.[37] The significance of this is that Here East is a strategic industrial location, and elsewhere in East London, these spaces more commonly attract £10.50–13 per square foot per annum. In Plexal, the arrangement is different as members pay a monthly rent for hotdesking (£240 per month per person) or a tiny office (£1,375 per month) along with a set of membership benefits. For comparison, however, the most affordable hotdesking arrangements in the capital are around a quarter of that price at £60 per month; this is elite co-working, ostensibly inclusive because it offers different pricing options, but still high-end and hence exclusive, much as Karin Fast has found in wider research on platformed workspaces.[38]

The types of jobs emerging and projected on the Park are, as a result of the sheer range of land uses and types of spaces, highly varied, encompassing plenty of unskilled and semi-skilled jobs at former venues such as the Stadium and Aquatics Centre, in retail and in ancillary or service roles at the Cultural and Education

Quarter, and highly skilled jobs at Here East and the Cultural and Education Quarter. The LLDC and Here East have both developed systems of reporting on access to employment opportunities, though the LLDC has only focused on venues, construction, and estates to date. None of the existing data indicates whether or how many people working on the Park also live there, or how long people have lived there in order to differentiate long-standing legacy borough residents from those who have moved into these areas more recently. What is available suggests a varied picture of employment from within and outside the legacy boroughs. Within the Copper Box Arena and London Aquatics Centre, for example, 70% of the workforce are said to be legacy borough residents, while at Here East it was 30% in 2018. At Here East too, there have been indications that workers are predominantly white, strongly contrasting with the profile of workers in 2005, though we gather this picture is changing.[39] Many jobs at Here East, whether in housing, design, research, or advanced manufacturing, are likely to require a high level of skill and will therefore draw on highly competitive national and international labor markets, while unskilled jobs at the venues, in retail and in administration, are likely to draw on local labor markets.

Though all employers are required to pay the London Living Wage as a minimum, the housing data above suggests we can assume that those working in unskilled and semi-skilled jobs, whether in venues, higher education institutions, or cultural centers, and indeed many skilled and professional workers, will currently have a very limited potential to access housing in the new neighborhoods. Only those recruited to jobs with incomes in the top 10% of all earners in the UK (more than £60,000 per annum) are likely to be able to purchase or rent housing on the open market or in the quasi-affordable housing sector. Research by the London Prosperity Board indicates that, among those able to access housing, issues of “real household disposable income” exist in the Park, as housing costs consume take-home pay. Currently, we anticipate that the Park will repeat a pattern that has evolved in Tower Hamlets since the development of the Docklands, characterized by economic polarization between those living in the borough and those working in the borough.

The exclusivity of the Park has a bearing on the LLDC's strategies and measures to link younger residents from long-standing East London and underprivileged backgrounds to employment opportunities too. In planning and design terms, the most tangible evidence of this is the development of state-funded schools within the fabric of each of the neighborhoods, all framed with a mission to skill the next generation. As the neighborhoods are exclusive, though, those most in need may well not benefit from these facilities and the longer-term opportunities they connect to. Other schemes include Build East, a construction training center formed through a partnership of building contractors on the Park to promote a collaborative approach to skills training, apprenticeship recruitment, and pay rates. Another, the Good Growth Hub (GGH), is designed to be a focal point for local people seeking Park-based careers, particularly in the cultural, creative, fashion, and technology sectors, and for employers looking to recruit "local talent." It offers information, advice, and guidance to local people and supports businesses to adopt inclusive working practices. In turn, the Shared Training and Employment Programme (STEP) scheme links local young people to placements in a range of employment settings across the Park.

Laudable and ground-breaking as these initiatives may be, the number of beneficiaries per annum appears to be small, with a mere 10 young people involved in the STEP 12-month placements in 2021/22 and 35 apprenticeship starts in 2021–22 in construction. In other words, as for housing, "anti-displacement" strategies such as these fail to counteract the forces of urban changes producing exclusion.

Overall, our analysis suggests that the LLDC is cautious when it acknowledges that "without careful attention, there is a risk that [regeneration] could create a place which is quite simply out of the reach of the people who have always lived here."[40]

Discussion

This chapter has offered a detailed insight into displacement and replacement on London's QEOP. Over time, low-income communities living and working at the Olympic site and in the wider host boroughs have been replaced with an exclusive housing offer linked to employment for privileged, professional, highly skilled workers. Despite Mayor Ken Livingstone's commitment to regenerate the area for the benefit of everyone that lives there, the key beneficiaries are affluent groups who have the requisite level of skills to compete for highly competitive jobs and to access exclusive housing. Planning and design have played crucial roles in displacement and replacement, offering an imagined future that would depend on redevelopment, and a relationship between housing and employment that is by definition exclusionary, in spite of an inclusive rhetoric.

Displacement has been identified as a key feature of mega-events. However, in the case of London, a narrative was developed by policymakers that this would be insignificant long-term by comparison to the benefits that would follow in terms of new jobs and housing within a higher density, compact, mixed-use urban environment. As we have demonstrated, however, from the outset, the overall policy and planning direction could be seen as a kind of "state-led gentrification" of former industrial land at the lucrative cusp of the inner city,[41] resulting in the development of exclusive market housing under the guise of "mixed communities" and an employment strategy aimed at attracting highly skilled jobs that would inevitably draw on national and international labor markets to place the site at the cutting edge of innovation, rather than local ones. Over time, the Olympic legacy planning and development process has been associated with different stages of direct and indirect displacement, which have been countered largely ineffectively with limited anti-displacement measures.

Overall, the chapter demonstrates that the hosting of a megaevent In London has enabled a process of long-term socio-spatial restructuring that reflects continuity rather than change with other host cities. For policymakers seeking to address deprivation and regenerate low-income neighborhoods for the benefit of existing communities, there is an urgent need for different approaches to the planning, financing, governance, and marketing of development to genuinely be able to focus on local requirements for housing and employment in regeneration areas, and to genuinely address needs.

1 Davis is listed first to acknowledge a lead role in writing this chapter. However, the division of labor in research and editing has been 50:50.

2 As key examples worldwide, see: Raquel Rolnik, *Urban Warfare: Housing Under the Empire of Finance* (London: Verso, 2019); Jules Boykoff, *Celebration Capitalism and the Olympic Games* (London: Routledge, 2014); Andrew Zimbalist, *Rio 2016: Olympic Myths, Hard Realities* (Washington: Brookings Institution Press, 2017); Adam Elliott-Cooper, Phil Hubbard, and Loretta Lees, "Moving Beyond Marcuse: Gentrification, Displacement and the Violence of Un-Homing," *Progress in Human Geography* 44, no. 3 (2020): 492–509, DOI: 10.1177/0309132519830511; Gabriel Silvestre and Nelma Gusmão de Oliveira, "The Revanchist Logic of Mega-Events: Community Displacement in Rio de Janeiro's West End," *Visual Studies* 27, no. 2 (2012): 204–10, DOI: 10.1080/1472586X.2012.677506; Claudio M. Rocha and Zixuan Xiao, "Sport Mega-Events and Displacement of Host Community Residents: A Systematic Review," *Front Sports Act Living* 7, no. 3 (2022), DOI: 10.3389/fspor.2021.805567.

3 London 2012, "London Olympics Candidature File, Volume 1" (London: London 2012, 2004).

4 Peter Marcuse, "Gentrification, Abandonment, and Displacement: Connections, Causes, and Policy Responses in New York City," *Journal of Urban and Contemporary Law* 195 (1985).

5 London Development Agency (LDA), *Relocation Strategy: Lower Lea Valley Olympic and Legacy Planning Applications* (Appendix 6 to the Environment Statement), 2004, 4.

6 Marion Davies, Juliet Davis, and Debra Rapp, *Dispersal: Picturing Urban Change in East London* (Swindon: Historic England Publishing, 2017).

7 Gavin Poynter, "Manufacturing in East London," in *Rising in the East: The Regeneration of East London*, eds. Tim Butler and M. Rustin (London: Lawrence and Wishart, 1996).

8 Libby Porter et al., "Planning Displacement: The Real Legacy of Major Sporting Events," *Planning Theory & Practice* 10, no. 3 (2009): 395–418.

9 Oliver Pohlisch, "Edgelands and London 2012: The Case of the Lower Lea Valley," in *The London Olympics and Urban Development: The Mega-Event City*, eds. Gavin Poynter, Valerie Viehoff, and Yang Li (Abingdon: Routledge, 2015).

10 LDA, "Relocation Strategy."

11 Elliott-Cooper, Hubbard, and Lees, "Moving Beyond Marcuse"; Boykoff, *Celebration Capitalism and the Olympic Games.*

12 Mike Raco and Emma Tunney, "Visibilities and Invisibilities in Urban Development: Small Business Communities and the London Olympics 2012," *Urban Studies* 47, no. 10 (2009): 2069–91, DOI: 10.1177/0042098009357351; Penny Bernstock, *Olympic Housing: A Critical Review of London 2012's Legacy* (Abingdon, Oxon: Routledge, 2014).

13 Davies, Davis, and Rapp, *Dispersal: Picturing Urban Change in East London*; Paul Watt, "'This Pain of Moving, Moving, Moving:' Evictions, Displacement and Logics of Expulsion in London," *L'Année sociologique* 68 (2018).

14 LDA, "Relocation Strategy."

15 Penny Bernstock, *Olympic Housing*; Davies, Davis, and Rapp, *Dispersal*; Watt, "This Pain of Moving, Moving, Moving."

16 Porter et al., "Planning displacement."

17 Mayor of London, *Five Legacy Commitments* (London: Greater London Authority, 2008).

18 London Development Agency, *The Legacy Masterplan Framework [Output C]* (London: London Development Agency, 2009).

19 Claire Colomb, "Unpacking New Labour's 'Urban Renaissance' Agenda: Towards a Socially Sustainable Reurbanization of British Cities?" *Planning Practice & Research* 22, no. 1 (2007): 1–24, DOI: 10.1080/02697450701455249.

20 Juliet Davis, "Futurescapes of Urban Regeneration: Ten Years of Design for the Unfolding Urban Legacy of London's Olympic Games, 2008–2018," *Planning Perspectives* 34, no. 5 (2019).

21 See, for example, LDA, *The Legacy Masterplan Framework [Output C]*, 249, 50.

22 Olympic Park Legacy Company, *Legacy Communities Scheme: Employment Statement* (London: Olympic Park Legacy Company, 2011).

23 Mark Davidson and Loretta Lees, "New-Build 'Gentrification' and London's Riverside Renaissance," *Environment and Planning A* 37, no. 7 (2005): 1169–70; Chris Hamnett, *Unequal City: London in the Global Arena* (Abingdon: Routledge, 2003), 179.

24 Gary Bridge, Tim Butler, and Loretta Lees (eds.) *Mixed Communities: Gentrification By Stealth?* (Bristol: Policy Press, 2012).

25 Hamnett, *Unequal City.*

26 Jessica Ferm, "Preventing the Displacement of Small Businesses Through Commercial Gentrification: Are Affordable Workspace Policies the Solution?" *Planning Practice & Research* 31, no. 4 (2016): 402–19, DOI: 10.1080/02697459.2016.1198546.

27 London Legacy Development Corporation (LLDC), *Legacy Development Corporation Local Plan 2020–2036, adopted July 2020* (London: LLDC, 2020).

28 Paul Watt and Penny Bernstock, "Legacy for Whom? Housing in Post-Olympic East London," in *London 2012 and the Post-Olympics City: A Hollow Legacy?* eds. Phil Cohen and Paul Watt (London: Palgrave Macmillan, 2017).

29 LLDC, *LLDC Annual Planning Monitoring Report and Infrastructure Statement 2021/2022.*

30 Dave Hill, "Newham: A Profile of Poverty as Cost of Living Pressures Grow," in *On London For the Good City*, September 14, 2022, https://www.onlondon.co.uk/newham-a-profile-of-poverty-as-cost-of-living-pressures-grow/.

31 Watt and Bernstock, "Legacy for Whom?."

32 LLDC, *Legacy Development Corporation Local Plan 2020–2036, adopted July 2020, Section 4: Developing Business Growth, Jobs, Higher Education and Training.*

33 Aecom / We Made That, *LLDC Employment Space Study*, Aecom (London: Aecom, 2015).

34 Francesca Weber-Newth, Sebastian Schlüter, and Ilse Helbrecht, "London 2012: 'Legacy' as a Trojan Horse," *ACME: An International Journal for Critical Geographies* 16, no. 4 (2017): 713–39.

35 LLDC, *Legacy Development Corporation Local Plan 2020–2036, adopted July 2020.*

36 LLDC, *LLDC Corporate Performance (Jan–Mar 2022: Quarter 4)* (Stratford: LLDC, 2022), 102–3; LLDC, *Legacy Development Corporation Local Plan 2020–2036, adopted July 2020.*

37 Oktra, *London Office Rent Report, 2022* (London: Oktra Ltd., 2022).

38 Karin Fast, "Who Has the Right to the Coworking Space? Reframing Platformed Workspaces as Elite Territory in the Geomedia City," *Space and Culture* (2022), DOI: 10.1177/12063312221090429.

39 This is based on an email exchange in August 2022 with a Here East manager.

40 LLDC, *LLDC Corporate Performance (Jan–Mar 2022: Quarter 4)*, 30.

41 Davidson and Lees, "New-Build 'Gentrification' and London's Riverside Renaissance."

The Normalization of Thamesmead: Part A

Tahl Kaminer

Planned in the 1960s and located in the historic Royal Arsenal, on wetlands prone to flooding, Thamesmead constituted the eastern edge of Greater London. The area is bisected by South London's sewage pipe, which sits on top of Bazalgette's original nineteenth-century pipe (pages 321, 326) and meets the Thames at a sewage treatment facility (a pump station until more recent times) in the eastern part of the area. The late 1960s and 1970s brutalist development offered both familiar and innovative housing typologies, which connected dwellings through a system of elevated walkways in order to facilitate escape during flooding. The Southmere Lake stood at the center of the development, with towers to its south, a library to its southwest, and a cultural center on its northern bank. Ground floors throughout Thamesmead were left unoccupied due to flooding risks.

The grand plan that was prepared by the Greater London Council was abandoned before its completion—it was undermined not only by the reversal of promises made regarding a London Underground connection to the site, but also by broader doubts regarding the scheme. The completed brutalist fragments of the plan have remained at the heart of Thamesmead; nowadays, they are surrounded by suburban developments, neighborhoods of middle-class, detached, semi-detached, and terraced housing. The area's lack of a good public transport connection has continued to undermine access to workplaces and contributed to its deprivation—these issues have also protected the area from pernicious gentrification. The area's notoriety was established through its use as a backdrop for Stanley Kuberick's dystopian *A Clockwork Orange*, for which it composes a brutalist landscape of anomie and social angst.

Overall, the brutalist fragments, taken together with the Belmarsh Prison to the west, diverse brownfield enclaves, the sewage pipe, and the sewage plant to the east, create the impression of a collection of floating fragments that together lack cohesion. An edge city, Thamesmead had become a space for London's "leftovers," "over-spills," and disconnected fragments; in this, the area resembles an archipelago, its fragments constituting islands (see page 321) in similar terms to the "archipelago model" as conceived by Oswald Mathias Ungers.[1]

This chapter looks at the ongoing regeneration of Thamesmead in order to demonstrate the transformation of an outer city area into a denser and more "urban" cityscape through demolitions and new build, the latter targeting a more affluent population. It also argues that the trajectory taken by the housing association Peabody, which leads the current ambitious regeneration project, means the loss of much of what makes Thamesmead a unique environment, replacing those unique elements with "safe" morphologies and typologies, and forms of public space that are familiar from other parts of the British capital.

Despite its notoriety, Thamesmead in 2018 was a tranquil, leafy area with quality green spaces, waterways, and walkways. Many brutalist maisonettes had been personalized and diversified. The streets and walkways of Thamesmead were desolate, as there were no street-level programs or shops, yet the area offered multiple routes to pedestrians, sheltered from the wide traffic arteries. Proximity to nature and the wetlands provided a unique experience in London. The brutalist structures—particularly the long housing slabs tagged for demolition (page 324)—(still) appeared in 2018 to be futuristic, evoking a ragged beauty rather than dystopia, and contributing to the area's distinctiveness.

Urban Regeneration

Until the current regeneration, Thamesmead had not been exposed to the type of pressures that the nearby boroughs of Newham, Barking and Dagenham, and Greenwich had encountered in the 2010s. With new towers and development converging on Thamesmead from Woolwich to the west and from Barking to the north ("Barka on the Thames"), the area's future was nevertheless easy to imagine. In previous decades, the area's population had changed, a growing Nigerian community had emerged in the north of the area, but no gentrification was evident and there was limited evidence of people being relocated into the area after being expelled from inner city.[2] In 2018, however, the signs of the coming change were everywhere. Peabody's project took advantage of the planned Crossrail Abbey Wood station (which opened in 2022 as an Elizabeth Line station), a transport connection that finally offered Thamesmead quality public transport access to central London. The station would stimulate developers' interests (and hence facilitate regeneration), higher real estate values, and usher in forces from which the area had previously been sheltered.

In the preceding years, the housing association Peabody had merged with the local housing association Gallions and acquired the local community center and local community trust, becoming the major stakeholder in the area. This consolidation of ownership under a single umbrella allowed Peabody to develop a comprehensive regeneration project. The scale of the project was nevertheless daunting and presented a risk even to a large housing association such as Peabody. Using its assets to raise investments for the project, part of the Gallions Reach area in the northwest of Thamesmead was earmarked for Thamesmead Waterfront, a joint venture by Peabody and developer Lendlease. Adjacent to a potential future Dockland Light Railway station, the site for the scheme was to accommodate 11,500—primarily high-end, free-market—homes, the sale of which would be used to raise money for the regeneration project. Lendlease is an experienced inner-city developer, responsible for, among other projects, the much-criticized Elephant Park development.[3]

Peabody's plan asserted that certain areas of historic Thamesmead would be demolished and others would be retained. The four towers south of the lake—a local landmark—have indeed been retained, as were the maisonettes to their south. The library, the linear housing typologies, the elevated walkways, and the Lesnes housing area (including its six towers) have all been demolished or earmarked for forthcoming demolition. Despite flooding risks, Peabody decided to "activate" the street level with retail and housing. An initial ambition, though one that has been hindered by high costs, was to remove, or bring to ground level, the elevated Eastern Way highway that cuts the area in two. A new pier is planned for the Thames water taxi.

Ahead of the regeneration, Peabody began investing in existing properties—by way of resolving heating, installing new windows, and addressing other persistent issues in some of the historic housing, they signaled to locals that their wellbeing was being kept in mind. In parallel, Proctor and Matthews were commissioned to prepare a new town center plan for the Southmere area (page 323). At the core of the plan is a strip, located along the boundary between Bexley and Greenwich, of multi-story, hybrid buildings that are supported by a new public space. This indicates an intention to import into Thamesmead forms familiar from inner London: forms that are more dense, more pedestrian, and more urban in the conventional sense, but also more banal, more commonplace, and ultimately more alien to the area. This phase necessitated the demolition of the library and a linear brutalist housing slab to the west of the lake. The cultural center at the north of the lake was brought back to life by Bow Arts, an organization that had been castigated for its involvement in replacing council tenants with artists in Balfron Tower in Poplar. The Lakeside Centre now hosts artist studios, a nursery, a café, and a catering business, programs which it links economically and socially.

Peabody's 2019 *Lesnes Masterplan* covers the area south of the lake. It includes a few, somewhat selective comments by residents from a 2016 consultation, such as "There are too many alleyways" and "The Estate is very complex, should be easier to navigate," which disclose the master plan's intentions.[4] Space Syntax was recruited in 2017 as consultants by Peabody,[5] and, considering their past work, would probably have advised to reduce the multiple routes through the area to create a "critical mass" that could sustain retail and "lively" pedestrianization.

Familiar Redevelopment

"Making complex projects like this work requires vision, determination, and the courage to do development differently. Housing associations possess that," asserted Prime Minister Theresa May in 2018,[6] stressing the unique aspects of the plan—namely, its comprehensive and strategic approach, yet remaining oblivious to the real similarities of the overall trajectory taken here to familiar ones elsewhere in the capital.

The presence of Lendlease, Space Syntax, and Bow Arts, and the Southmere plan all emphasize the logic that is leading the redevelopment: a removal of many of the extant particularities of Thamesmead and their replacement with familiar and "tested" forms of urbanization that ultimately make Thamesmead more similar to areas found in inner London. In the process, some of the area's qualities will be lost, especially those that make the area distinctive: the innovative housing typologies, the smart pedestrian routes, and the particular relationship between the built areas and the wetlands.

This urban regeneration project can be described as an attempt to leverage the recent interest in Thamesmead by real estate actors—and consequently the availability of investments—as a means of rectifying decades of underinvestment and marginalization. A more pessimistic assessment would characterize the urban renewal as the unwitting grooming of Thamesmead through a set of improvements that will make the area more susceptible and more desirable for investors.

The involvement of agencies identified with the inner city, whether Bow Arts or Lendlease, has necessarily led to the application of inner-city "remedies" to Thamesmead. Peabody's dependency on balancing its books and raising funds limits its options. The opening up of Thamesmead to the forces that have so far spared it is not only a result of the Crossrail station but is also integral to the regeneration project itself—its need to raise money for investment in affordable housing. The forthcoming "normalization" of the area, which will be achieved by changing housing typologies, urban morphologies, densities, tenures, and demographics, reflects the logic and forces of the finance-driven property market and illustrates the impact that hyper-gentrification has had on inner-city London. Such forces necessarily steer regeneration towards safe and familiar forms of redevelopment, a "known quantity" with which investors feel comfortable. Neither Peabody nor Thamesmead's residents are empowered in such a context of limited agency and limited options. The final form of the new, emerging Thamesmead was known from the outset: an area of medium-to-high density with up-market housing and pockets of deprivation similar to so many areas of the inner city.

1 Florian Hertweck and Sébastien Marot (eds.) *The City in the City: A Manifesto* (1977) by Oswald Mathias Ungers and Rem Koolhaas; Berlin: A Green Archipelago (Zurich: Lars Muller, 2013). See also the Stockholm section in this book.

2 In 2018, The Royal Borough of Greenwich gained population from internal migration in the age groups spanning 20 to 34 but lost population in other ages, a typical process in inner city but unusual in suburbia. In contrast, Bexley has had a less clear pattern, gaining population in the ages of 20–24, 30–44, and 85 and above, but losing population in other age groups. See ONS, "People, Population and Community," dataset, accessed September 30, 2019, https://www.ons.gov.uk/peoplepopulationandcommunity/populationandmigration/migrationwithintheuk/datasets/internalmigrationmovesbylocalauthoritiesandregionsinenglandandwalesby5yearagegroupandsex.

3 The geographers Loretta Lees and Mara Ferreri suggested that Lendlease have "a controversial track record." Loretta Lees and Mara Ferreri, "Resisting Gentrification on its Final Frontiers: Learning from the Heygate Estate in London (1974–2013)," *Cities* 57 (September 2016): 15.

4 Peabody, *The Lesnes Masterplan* (London: Peabody, 2019), https://www.thameseadnow.org.uk/media/3020/lesnes-masterplan_public-consultation_july-2019_compressedxs.pdf.

5 Space Syntax, "A Planning Platform for Thamesmead," accessed September 5, 2022, https://spacesyntax.com/project-update-a-planning-platform-for-thamesmead/.

6 Theresa May spoke at the National Housing Federation Summit, September 20, 2018. See Peabody, "Theresa May Praises Peabody," accessed September 27, 2019, https://www.peabody.org.uk/news-views/2018/sep/theresa-may-praises-peabody.

IV.
STOCKHOLM

Welcome to New Stockholm: Soft Tactics and Hard Change in the Outer City

Secretary

Helen Runting, Rutger Sjögrim, and Karin Matz

Stockholm, Sweden's capital, is a city of islands: its landmass, population, and built environment are all transected by channels, canals, bodies of water, green wedges, commuter rail infrastructure, and an array of far more diffuse (although in many ways no less visible) dividing lines. Where do you live? How many square meters is your place? How much did you pay for it and when? Are you on the board of your housing cooperative? Which landlord do you have? Do you have your own washing machine, your own dishwasher, a balcony? And (most important of all) *when were your pipes last replaced*? This short survey is a social ritual that runs on repeat and could just as easily happen on the way into an important work meeting as on a Tinder date in Stockholm. The answers that you provide, whether directly or through more casual references to an upcoming board meeting or a pending complaint against your landlord, will place you in a category—a box that we might call "class," although it is partially detached from your status as a worker—which in all likelihood will influence how you are perceived and even treated in the subsequent exchange. In a society that aspires to a polite opacity around class status, housing forms an object and a space where poverty, precarity, and privilege are all bared, and exclusionary narratives around race, criminality, meritocracy, sustainability, rights, and belonging are produced and circulate.

In introducing Stockholm as a site for a uniquely Swedish, late-welfare-state *urbanization of suburbia*, we have chosen to address a series of developments that are driving change in Stockholm's outer city in the first half of the 2020s. Specifically, we are interested in reviewing *recent efforts to construct new housing arrangements* in the outer city through (i) the construction of new multi-unit residential buildings, and (ii) related, albeit far more immaterial, shifts in tenure and ownership structures, which we term, following Baeton, Westin, Pull, and Molina, "soft tactics."[1] We ask: What are the effects of these constructions in terms of the conditions that they establish for the displacement of some bodies and the aggregation of others? What kind of subject positions do they anticipate, interpolate, and deny? And, importantly, what kind of "living environments" (*livsmiljöer*)[2] are they producing?

In tackling these questions, we address two suburban settings within the outer city of the Stockholm region—the villa suburb and the block suburb—in order to identify how they are being transformed, and in some cases replaced, via the installation of new arrangements and environments. We begin the chapter by providing the reader with a brief overview of the existing building and tenure types of Stockholm's outer city, before reflecting on the changes currently being witnessed in the region.[3]

This chapter refers to empirical material in order to situate and describe the new city that is being built at present in the gaps and voids of the existing city; the snapshot offered here supplements previous historical accounts[4] by performing a cartographic function in relation to this emerging condition: it *aggregates*, bringing together descriptions of seemingly disparate things by constructing spatial relations.[5] Lingering in the space between the Swedish and English languages, we seek to construct an account of a complex network of arrangements that are all too often experienced as unrelated, disparate, or desynchronized; that are idealized as a "system" and naturalized as a "market"; or that are increasingly simply nihilistically accepted as "fate." We hope that this chapter can act as a navigation device of sorts in entering, and ultimately even contesting, the foggy, neoliberalized conditions of Stockholm's housing arrangements.

A City Divided

Stockholm is at its smallest a municipality (*kommun*)—namely, the City of Stockholm (*Stockholms stad*)—and at its largest a metropolitan region made up of 26 municipalities, which aligns with administrative boundaries of Stockholm County (*Stockholms län*). Whilst the former is home to 978,770 inhabitants and is largely bounded by the edges of the subway network, the latter is home to 2,415,139 people and relies on an extensive network of commuter rail lines, taking in nearby settlements and other small cities like Södertälje, Norrtälje, and Sigtuna. "The outer city"—a term that is central to *Urbanizing Suburbia*—straddles these two scales.

Within the City of Stockholm, we see *the outer city* as taking in neighborhoods located "outside the tollgates" (*utanför tullarna*), a term commonly used by Stockholmers to describe areas outside of the central city, or "stone city" (*stenstaden*), with its orthogonal street grid, perimeter blocks, heritage controls, and island-like structure, which broadly comprises of the neighborhoods of Södermalm, Gamla Stan, Norrmalm/City, Kungsholmen, Vasastan, and Östermalm. The outer city does not, however, stop at the edge of the municipality—rather, we understand it as extending to encompass built-up areas (*tätort*) within the "wreath" municipalities (*kranskommunerna*) that abut the City of Stockholm, including the municipalities of Botkyrka, Huddinge, Tyresö, Nacka, Lidingö, Sundbyberg, Solna, Järfälla, and Ekerö; parts of the southern municipality of Haninge and the northern municipalities of Danderyd, Täby, Sollentuna, and Upplands Väsby; and even parts of the more distant Vallentuna and Upplands-Bro.

Far from the suggestive continuity of an "urban fabric," we view this outer city as an *aggregate*: a chunky, unresolved, and at times disconnected mass that is intentionally constructed through its analysis and made up of disparate things. Like a statistical average, the outer city is an approximation; like a shadow, it is primarily conceived of in relation to its other, the stone city within the tollgates. But what happens when the antithesis begins to draw closer to its other? Staring out the window of a train—let's say the Uppsala-bound commuter train, pulling into Sollentuna station—we are met with a view that is not un-city-like. This is the center of the municipality of the same name, perhaps it is to be expected—perhaps it *is* a city of sorts. When reaching Södra Häggvik, though, less than 2 kilometers north, the visitor is confronted with a different kind of environment: a heterogenous mix of big-box retail, commercial office buildings, high-density perimeter blocks that are set tightly to street boundaries, and, just a stone's throw away, fields of pitched roofs, as detached dwellings stretch to the horizon. Is this still "suburbia," and if so, what do we mean by this word in the late-welfare-state context of the Stockholm region in the third decade of the twenty-first century?

Two Types of Modern: Block Suburbia and Villa Suburbia

In the diffuse geographic space of the Stockholm region, the term "suburb" rings in a diverse category of living environments that are highly heterogeneous in terms of their demographics and income levels; land and building ownership and management structures and tenure types; property prices and rent levels; geography; building typologies and ages; landscape treatment; and architectural aesthetics. Mobilizing the basic difference between multi-unit housing (*flerbostadshus*) and single-unit housing (*småhus*)—and in the process shrugging off the dated terms "single-family" and "multi-family"—one might argue that in aggregate Stockholm's outer city accommodates two fundamentally different types of suburbia.

The first is made up by the "villa suburbs" (*villaförorterna*). From the rich and leafy areas where the larger homes of rich industrialists were first established in the form of summer "follies" (*sommarnöjan*) and traders' villas (*grosshandlarvillorna*) to the now highly sought-after, small-scale detached workers' housing of the "build your own home" movement (*egnahemsrörelsen*) and the familiar sprawl of mass-produced detached and semi-detached dwellings (*kataloghus*), the single-unit housing that defines the villa suburb comprises 283,689 dwellings or 25% of the region's housing stock.[6]

Most Stockholmers do not, as such, live in villas: 68%, or 770,275, of the region's 1.13 million dwellings take the form of apartments in multi-unit housing.[7] Whilst a proportion of these apartments are located in the inner city and in neighboring small cities in the region, the outer city assembles a diverse range of typologies (perimeter blocks, slab blocks, short tower blocks, and high-rises), morphological constellations, and landscape conditions, defining a second type of suburb that we call the "block suburb." The latest version of the City of Stockholm's building ordinance, *Stockholms Byggnadsordning*, maps Stockholm in terms of 14 "urban development characters" (*stadsbyggnadskaraktär*), a term that replaces the older formulation of "year rings" (*årsringar*), a model which likened the city to a section of a tree trunk.[8] Although the City is not the same beast as the region, this taxonomy helps to understand the multifarious expressions of block-based suburbia that are present in the outer city. These include "narrow" functionalist apartment buildings (*smalhus*) and more experimental early modern typologies set in Garden City settings and neighborhood units (*granskapsenheter*); denser, and at times taller and thicker, prefabricated late-modern apartment buildings, many built as part of the Swedish Million Program of 1965–75, set in larger, more diffuse fields of open space connected by the subway system; and postmodern areas of perimeter blocks built as infill on greenfield and brownfield sites, which take the form of either "urban enclaves" (*stadsenklav*) or the "dense and blended city" (*tät blandstad*).

In their account of the transformation, and ultimately deterioration, of the modern Swedish housing system that was built in line with the welfare-state ideology of "The People's Home" (*Folkhemmet*), scholars Karin Grundström and Irene Molina identify three *types* of modern suburb, produced at the intersection between building typology, tenure, and class:

> Although originally constructed for "everyone and everybody", working-class neighborhoods came to consist almost entirely of (CBC[municipally]-owned) high-rise, multi-storey rental apartment buildings. Middle-class neighborhoods consisted of row houses, detached houses, and smaller apartment buildings, mainly organized as cooperatives. Finally, upper-middle-class neighborhoods consisted of privately owned villas. This organization of almost homogeneous clusters of tenure form related to building type still, to some extent, prevails.[9]

It is important to emphasize that block suburbia (with its early-modern blocks in garden settings, late-modern blocks in open spaces, and postmodern perimeter blocks) and villa suburbia (with its leafy, early modern villa areas and prefab houses in denser, sprawl-like situations) were *planned that way* and are not the result of an unregulated market. In Sweden, municipalities maintain a "planning monopoly" (*planmonopolet*), not only approving development proposals by granting them planning permission (*bygglov*), but also actively participating in the design and production of new urban areas through strategic "comprehensive plans" (*översiktsplaner*), legally binding "detail plans" (*detaljplaner*), land allocation mechanisms (*markanvisningar*), and the work of their municipal housing companies (MHCs), amongst other mechanisms.[10]

"Swedish cities now belong to the most segregated in Europe," note urban theorists Catharina Thörn and Håkan Thörn in 2017.[11] Many commentators argue that segregation was written into Stockholm's DNA through its planning codes over the past century. Design theorist Christian Björk, for instance, describes the way in which modern architects like Sven Markelius saw "social differentiation" as a desirable goal that was complementary to "functional separation" in planning modern Stockholm in the 1940s: "Outside the toll gates," Björk writes, "housing types were in principle placed in different suburbs with the ambition of producing, through planning, local and class-bound communities."[12] To some extent, the City of Stockholm's *Building Ordinance* (mentioned above) continues this work, structuring categories based on existing built form that can be applied to coming development and in so doing suggesting the possibility of continuing the modernist model *of social differentiation through homogeneous clusters of tenure form related to building type*.

Four Forms of Tenure in Sweden

In Sweden, building typology and urban morphology cannot be considered in isolation from the tenure structures (*upplåtelseformer*) that secure access to them. In combination, these two elements create what we here refer to as "housing arrangements": ways of living in housing that are predicated on particular access arrangements. Given the interrelated and co-productive nature of these categories, it is valuable, we believe, to provide the reader with an overview of the four forms of tenure that together regulate access to housing in Sweden, namely: owner occupancy (*äganderätt*), rental (*hyresrätt*), tenant ownership (*bostadsrätt*), and subletting (*andrahandsuthyrning*). We note that instead of "public" or "social" housing, Sweden maintains a rent-negotiated, non-means-tested rental system with universal access that is complemented by a system of welfare payments for housing costs; in this context, calls for the introduction of "public" or "social" housing are forcefully made by private landlords and starkly rejected by the Swedish Union of Tenants (*Hyresgästföreningen*).[13]

Private Ownership Tenures

Two tenure types requiring individual capital investment—which together constitute what we might loosely call "privately owned" housing—exist in Sweden.

"Owner occupancy" (*äganderätt*) is perhaps the most familiar of the two for an international audience: in this case, the property (land and building) is purchased on the real estate market. 90% of all single-unit dwellings in the Stockholm region conform to this tenure type, and its use in multi-unit housing is not only rare (only 880 of 770,275 dwellings in multi-unit buildings were owner-occupied in 2021)[14] but hotly debated as a tenure form that encourages subletting, precarity, and hotelerization (we will address these issues below).[15]

In contrast, "tenant ownership" (*bostadsrätt*), which is also referred to as "cooperative ownership," is, to quote Brett Christophers, more "idiosyncratic," and as such may require some unpacking.[16] With roots in the citizen-led cooperative movement of the early twentieth century, this popular tenure form allows tenants to own shares in a cooperative association (*bostadsrättsförening*), to which they pay a monthly fee (*avgift*); the association in turn owns the property and is controlled by the tenants through a board (*styrelse*). Originally conceived of as non-commodified form of housing unable to be sold on a market, it was only through a series of deregulations—first in 1968, with the abolition of transfer controls and then in the 1980s with the deregulation of the credit market—that the tenant-owned flat became an object of real estate investment and speculation.[17] In step with these regulatory shifts, between 1996 and 2017, the price of such dwellings rose by 232%, or 5.9% per year; with the repeal of inheritance tax in 2007, this created a newly wealthy generation of Stockholmers and an increasingly inaccessible housing market.[18] A tenant-occupied flat might be a mechanism to transfer intergenerational wealth through inheritance, but it is not necessarily an object of investment and speculation in the way that such properties might be in other international contexts. This is because of the "soft" regulations that lie in the statutes (*stadgar*) of cooperative boards, which commonly require the tenant to occupy their apartment permanently, radically curbing, in the process, the possibility to sublet and thus the purchase of such flats as investment properties. Almost 42% of dwellings in the Stockholm region are cooperatively owned and just over 22% of all dwellings are owner-occupied.[19] In both cases, "ownership" must be understood as mediated by credit extended in the form of mortgages; in the case of the cooperative associations, the association itself may also hold a mortgage, which is to be paid off through the monthly fees.

Rental Tenures

Two primary categories of rental tenure exist in Sweden: rental and subletting.

In the first case, often referred to as "first-hand" renting (*förstahandsuthyrning*), tenants rent either from a private company or MHC (in Swedish, public companies are also referred to as *allmännyttan*), thereby accessing universal housing at a negotiated rent level. Following a series of deregulations in the first two decades of this century, MHCs, despite being what Martin Grander describes as "the figurehead of the universal housing policy," at present exist in a state of "financialized universalism," "dependent on financial motives, institutions, tools and financial capital" (something that we will return to in a discussion of the MHC Stockholmshem in the closing chapter of this section).[20] Regardless of the landlord, this tenure form remains *universal* in the sense that access is largely non-means-tested, first-hand rental tenants are guaranteed "security of tenure" (*besittningsskydd*), and rents are regulated in the sense that they are set through yearly negotiations between the Swedish Property Federation (*Fastighetsägare*) and the Swedish Union of Tenants. Rent levels are either based on the "use value" (*bruksvärdehyra*) of a dwelling or, in the case of newly built or newly renovated apartments, "assumed" rents (*presumtionshyra*). The latter constitutes a 15-year exemption from the use value system and allows landlords to set higher rents, again in negotiation with the Tenants' Union, that provide a reasonable level of profit over the period of the exemption in order to ameliorate construction costs. Just under 20% of the apartments brokered by the Stockholm Housing Agency (*Stockholms Bostadsförmedlingen*) in 2021 were newly built and thus subject to assumed rents. The Agency brokers the majority (75%) of the first-hand contracts for rental housing through its "queue" (*bostadskö*), which one can join at the age of 18 and has an average wait time of 8–11 years.[21] In addition to the Agency's queue, several established cooperative rental companies (for instance, HSB and SKB) manage their own queues, which can be joined from birth for a member fee—in this way, the rental system favors Stockholm-born residents over the newly arrived (whether they are from abroad or from another part of Sweden). If renters want to upscale or downscale their apartments, they are allowed to "swap" apartments (*lägenhetsbyte*), as long as money doesn't change hands and both parties have permission from their landlord (this process is brokered by private websites which charge a fee). Further, in anticipation of a major renovation or demolition, landlords are able to apply to the Tenants' Tribunal (apparently with no supporting documentation) to request for permission to use short-term contracts (*korttidskontrakt*), sometimes colloquially called "demolition contracts" (*rivningskontrakt*), which are exempted from guaranteed security of tenure.[22] Finally, 95% of the region's "special housing" (*specialbostäder*)—a relatively small category that includes housing for students, older residents, and people with special needs and comprises just under 5% of the housing stock—is also rental. Rental tenure accounted for 35% of all dwellings and 42% of all multi-unit housing in the Stockholm region in 2021.[23]

Subletting, also referred to as "second-hand" renting (*andrahandsuthyrning*), is a second category of rental tenure. Statistically opaque and highly diverse in the forms that it can take, subletting is in principle regulated to the extent that tenants are represented by the Tenants' Union and can still appeal to the Tenants' Tribunal, although they do not have full recourse to security of tenure; those letting out a cooperatively owned flat are, further, subject to their association board's statutes and those letting out a rented flat must have a good reason to do so, as well as their landlord's permission. Despite these checks and balances, the subletting market is in practice highly unregulated, and subletting constitutes a "soft tactic" that is in many cases used to divest tenants of protections ensuring guaranteed security of tenure. It is common knowledge (and our personal experience) that people who sublet pay substantially higher rents than people with first-hand contracts, but it is difficult to know how much more. While the average rent paid in the Stockholm region in 2022 was 119 Swedish crowns (sek) per square meter,[24] information from the marketplace website Blocket (a popular placc to advertise sublets) suggests that the average rent for a sublet can be estimated to be closer to 220 sek per square meter[25]—a sizeable difference in affordability.

In addition to higher rents, those renting second-hand are exposed to extreme precarity through practices that include the use of "black" contracts (*svartkontrakt*), which remove or falsify documentation that might be used in an appeal; the false allocation of "lodger" (*inneboende*) status to tenants to avoid regulations; ethnic discrimination and sexual harassment in the selection of tenants; and being forced to live in spaces not intended for habitation (cellars, storage rooms, walk-in closets, hallways, and attics).[26] Carina Listerborn and Irene Molina paint a dark picture of this shadow market:

> The housing precariat solve their housing arrangement through (expensive and non-secure) short-term subletting contracts; crowding together in one apartment and sharing beds; renting space in a storage space, on a couch, or in a cellar; living with friends; or living with their parents as long as they can. The housing precariat is not uncommonly also composed by precarious workers, a group that has grown with rising short-term employment and gig jobs ... Temporary living alternates directly with homelessness.[27]

Just as one can sublet a space as small as a closet, companies can sublet entire buildings or even neighborhoods. By way of "block subletting" (*blockuthyrning*), multiple apartments are first rented to a business, which is then able to sublet them to individuals as "business apartments" (*företagsbostäder*), thereby divesting their tenants of guaranteed security of tenure. Even Stockholm's County Administrative Board (*Länsstyrelsen*) acknowledges that "it is not easy to estimate how large the region's market for subletting is," referring to a recent survey of adults in the region in which 3.5% of respondents answered that they sublet and 5.5% that they were lodgers; amongst 18 to 30-year-olds, the figures were 8% and 17%.[28] These numbers do not translate directly to the number of dwellings and are likely well under the real figures, as the survey only addressed people *registered* in the region and strong incentives exist to conceal this information if subletting illegally.

Soft Tactics: The Immaterial Construction of Housing Arrangements in New Stockholm

Cities are sites of uneven material and social transformation: while some places, structures, and populations are subjected to intensive change, others are characterized by intensive stasis. Urban change nonetheless forms patterns that can be mapped: contiguous fields, corridors, clusters, and smatterings and points emerge, each telling a particular story. Far from a natural phenomenon, these patterns evidence complex and intertwined democratic, financial, tactical, and affective processes. The Stockholm region is experiencing a period, we argue, of escalating urban change wherein existing "housing arrangements" and "living environments" are being extensively modified through the diverse efforts of a range of actors including citizens, activists, developers, landlords, municipal housing companies, municipalities, banks, courts, architects, and the state.

In 2016, Guy Baeten, Sara Westin, Emil Pull, and Irene Molina published a ground-breaking study of the displacements resulting from "renoviction" processes in Million Program areas in Sweden.[29] In that study, they employed the term "soft tactics" in order to describe "the tactics deployed by landlords to displace low-income tenants in a system that is often and generally regarded to rest on universality, egality and strong tenant rights."[30] In the coming two sections, we will attempt to provide the reader with an inventory of urban changes, which we differentiate in terms of (i) changes in the housing arrangements of individuals and populations, which are effected through modifications in tenure, ownership, and access ("soft tactics")[31] and (ii) changes in living environments through the development of new buildings (which we term "hard changes").

Modifications to Tenure

Tenure transfers (*ombildningar*) enable rental housing to be converted to tenant-owned housing, through the sale of the property to a cooperative association (which can be formed for this purpose). Proceeding by way of an application that must be supported by two thirds of the existing rental tenants in a building, this process can appear to constitute a "bottom-up" initiative. It is, however, in reality highly steered at the municipal level: in the period 2020–22, under the previous "green-blue" municipal government in the City of Stockholm—a coalition between the environmental party Miljöpartiet (MP) and the conservative party Moderaterna (M)—some 1,217 rental apartments owned by MHCs were transferred to tenant-occupied tenure in a move driven directly by conservative politicians.[32] Following the recent election of a "red-green" coalition (the social democratic Socialdemokraterna (S), the left Vänsterpartiet (V), and MP) in the City of Stockholm, a hard brake is now being placed on this development, a move that is also being advocated in the City of Sundbyberg to the north, where a coalition comprising of S, V, MP, and the liberal centrists Centerpartiet (C) has been formed.[33] These politics vary between the 26 municipalities that make up the region, but given the concentration of rental apartments in the City of Stockholm, it appears that tenure transfers will be placed largely on hold for the coming four-year mandate period (2022–26), suggesting that other soft tactics may become more prevalent.

The possibility exists for tenant-owned and owner-occupied housing to be transferred to rental; this is highly unusual but did occur in the much-discussed case of the building "The Great Wall of China" (*Kinesiska muren*) in Rosengård in Malmö in December 2021, whereby the cooperative association board members were charged with financial crimes, and the property was sold by the Swedish Enforcement Authority (*Kronofogden*) to MKB,

Malmö's largest MHC.[34] In the Stockholm region, similar controversies have arisen around mismanaged tenant-occupied neighborhoods (most recently, Malmvägen in Sollentuna).[35] This form of tenure transfer remains highly unusual and tends to be invoked only in financial or legal crises within the management structure of a particular housing area.

Modifications to Ownership Without Tenure Transfer

Existing rental housing stock can still be sold without tenure transfer: neighborhoods owned by municipal housing companies can be (and have been) transferred to private ownership while retaining rental tenure. In the well-documented case of the suburb of Husby in Stockholm's north, approximately 1,500 apartments were sold by the MHC Svenska Bostäder to private actors in the late 1990s; these apartments, subsequently bought up by D'Carnegie, were purchased as an object of financialized investment by the transnational actor Blackstone in 2014, and eventually bought by the German firm Vonovia in the form of the business Hembla, which subsequently changed its name to Victoriahem.[36] Mobilizing the "use-value" system in order to close rent gaps,[37] private landlords like Blackstone and Hembla-Victoriahem have been able to raise rents by up to 50% by engaging in "standard-raising measures" (*standardhöjande åtgärder*) through piecemeal "concept renovation" (*konceptrenoveringar*) without replacing plumbing and ventilation systems (*stambyte*).[38] This process results in documented displacement effects and is referred to as "renoviction" (*renovräkning*), which in turn has been the subject of a flurry of recent scholarship by researchers and housing activists including Ilhan Kellecioglu; Brett Christophers; Dominika V. Polanska, Sara Degerhammar, and Åse Richard; and (mentioned earlier) Guy Baeton, Sara Westin, Emil Pull, and Irene Molina.[39] Despite scholarly and popular critique of renoviction processes in suburbs like Husby, and unlike Denmark, no regulatory action has been taken at the state level to prevent this occurring in the future in Swedish cities at large or in the Stockholm region.[40]

Ownership transfers are, at least theoretically, bi-directional in the case of rental housing. Concerted campaigns from activist organizations like Ort till Ort continue to advocate for the "re-municipalization" (*återkommunalisering*) of apartments across the Stockholm region—the purchase of private rentals by MHCs—a process which successfully occurred in 2016 in the Gothenburg suburb of Hammarkullen.[41] The push for re-municipalization continues to gain momentum at present in Husby, where Victoriahem reportedly continues to neglect maintenance responsibilities, exposing them, hypothetically, to the use of existing expropriation laws.[42]

Modifications to Access
Without Changing Ownership or Tenure

The allocation mechanisms used to access rental housing are subject to an ongoing regime of adjustment, privatization, commodification, and gamification through digitalization; through the entry of private actors and platforms, prospective tenants are being asked to motivate their applications and provide an increasing amount of personal information, a move with the potential to erode the neutrality of *non-means-tested* universal housing provision. Moreover, as interfaces multiply and multiple accounts are required, the extent of the housing shortage is partially concealed to those most affected by it: those queuing, as we write with Hélène Frichot in an earlier essay, are:

> fed an image of surplus ... Despite the attempt to equitably and anonymously allocate this spatial resource, the interface itself is structured around the illusion of choice. The active waiting that it asks of its waiting subjects speaks less of collective ownership and political claims than of soothing micro-doses of the sensation of abundance and artful selection. In this, it mirrors other proptech interfaces.[43]

Soft tactics can also be used to change the *types of contracts* held by rental tenants without changing ownership or tenure type. Such changes may ease access (making it easier to get a flat) while simultaneously increasing precarity. The soft tactics developed at sites of renoviction (for instance, Husby as mentioned earlier) to circumvent both the use value system and guaranteed security of tenure for renters are, however, likely to continue to be tested and developed, potentially by MHCs as well as private landlords, in the existing rental stock in areas across the outer city. As the plumbing and ventilation systems of modernist blocks continue to approach the end of their lifespan, the piecemeal use of short-term first-hand contracts in (unsupported) anticipation of potentially superfluous concept renovations can be expected to continue, along with the block subletting of business apartments. These measures, which create profit by increasing housing precarity, will continue to be fine-tuned unless the gaping holes in the regulatory framework are closed by municipal and national governments. If renters themselves begin to adopt similar measures in order to ameliorate the effects of higher rents (for instance, through the illegal subletting of non-habitable spaces in apartments), the Stockholm County Administrative Board's warning that "there exists cause for concern" about rising overcrowding seems realistic—and perhaps even overcautious.[44]

In the privately owned tenure categories, it is not lived time (in the form of queue days and labor) that secures access but access to capital. As interest rates rise in Sweden in early 2023, as in many other countries, securing lines of credit in the form of mortgages is becoming increasingly more expensive. Sweden's financial supervisory authority *Finansinspektionen* observe continuing growth in the amount being borrowed by Swedish households for housing, noting that 82% of all household debt takes the form of mortgages, and those mortgages have risen 7.9% per year on average over the last 20 years.[45] The authority also notes growth in the secondary loan market, as loan applicants attempt to meet the 15% deposit (*kontantinsats*) required to secure a mortgage in Sweden. First-time home buyers must engage in the risky business of either taking a secondary loan without security or mobilizing inherited wealth to pay this deposit, reinforcing the class dynamics raised by Listerborn and Molina whereby "good housing" becomes a largely "inherited" good—a development that Lisa Adkins, Melinda Cooper, and Martijn Konings term the rise of the "asset economy."[46] Should mortgage costs or the cooperative association fees rise beyond what is tenable for, for instance, a single-person household, it can be expected that owner-occupiers and tenant-occupiers alike may start to deploy soft tactics learned from the slum landlords themselves. Through the subletting of rooms in already small apartments in the block suburbs, or in 30-square-meter service buildings in the gardens of the villa suburbs, *densification without development* can be expected to proceed and overcrowding increase. Far from public transport and services, a (literally) uncountable number of subletting renters may find themselves renting as lodgers without documentation, without guaranteed security of tenure, and without recourse to basic building maintenance. Worse still, they will likely be subletting from landlord-housemates who have assured their own access to housing through a heady mix of privilege and debt: picture a precarious rentier class of retirees and indebted young adults supporting their own housing arrangements on the backs of a subletting housing precariat. Add the intersectional factors of race and gender to this mix, and the situation begins to look far from "socially sustainable."

A final "modification to access" that can occur without changes to tenure or ownership occurring is the loss of all access to any housing: homelessness. As Baeten et al. observe: "Once evicted, most people move directly into homelessness since it is difficult to find new housing as landlords tend to not rent out to people with a conviction or an eviction."[47] Sweden is at present witnessing rising homelessness nation-wide, particularly amongst families with children, a tragic development addressed in the government inquiry into socially sustainable housing provision, *Sänk tröskeln till en god bostad* (*Lower the Barriers to [Accessing] Decent Housing*), led by former environment minister Karolina Skoog (2016–19) of the Green Party.[48] As that investigation notes,

> Families with particularly weak purchasing power are finding it hard to get their needs met by the housing market. Renting from private individuals involves in many cases an undesirable level of housing insecurity and paying higher rents than those charged on the regular market. Such a solution can work well for many in a period of transition, but for families with children it can lead to overcrowding, financial pressure, and forced relocations, which in turn can affect the opportunities for children to have a good childhood.[49]

Hard Changes: The Material Construction of Living Environments in New Stockholm

Individual moments of change in the built environment (for instance, the construction of a new apartment building or the demolition of an existing one) take on the character of an "event," whereby effects spill over, creating ripples that reveal the mutual dependencies at play in a given territory. Some of these effects are immediate, playing out at the moment that the event occurs; in the case of the construction of a building, they may take years to surface. Nonetheless, *in aggregate* new residential buildings make *hard changes*: they shift statistical norms and modify urban characters, changing tenure compositions, raising property and rent values, and inflating densities, placing the bodies of new and existing residents in closer proximity to each other.

The Future Is Unevenly Distributed

"The outer city," a designation used in this book, maps onto a geographic entity that we have previously named "the middle ring"; this ring does not break the central role played by the City of Stockholm within the region: 33% of all new apartments (4,844 of 14,495 dwellings) approved in the Stockholm region in 2017 were located in the City of Stockholm.[50] The ring starts at the outer edges of the city and excludes the stone city within the tollgates—it was in areas *outside the tollgates* that 75% of those 4,844 apartments were approved, and when these apartments are added to those located in the other municipalities of the outer city, this figure accounts for 79% of the 14,295 apartments. The outer city is thus *in aggregate* a site for the transformation of existing living environments and the creation and destruction of housing arrangements through new development. This is not to say that transformation, in the form of the insertion of new housing, was equally distributed.

Through the atlas *Bygger vi en blandad stad?*, Secretary, together with our collaborators at KTH and the Region Stockholm, mapped the locations of new multi-unit housing (again using planning permit data and taking the boom year of 2017).[51] This earlier study shows clearly that urban changes—in the form of new multi-unit additions to the housing stock through planning approvals in 2017—tend to occur in areas where such changes have *already* or *recently occurred*; other areas seem to be buffered or insulated from transformation of this type.

For instance, of the 337 new multi-unit residential buildings that we mapped, 42% were located in areas where the existing housing stock did not have a dominant age (that is, not more than 60% of housing stock was from a particular 20-year period) and 31% were located in areas that were predominantly "new" (that is, where over 60% of the housing stock was built 2001–17). Numbers of approved new multi-unit housing buildings plummet as the building stock gets older, with less than 8% of new buildings being approved in modernist and late-modernist areas respectively (that is, those built 1941–60 and those built in 1961–80 respectively) and under 3% occurring in areas predominantly built before 1941. (The postmodern era, 1981–2000, showed a low number of new buildings, but this period was characterized by an oversupply of housing and lower construction rates, meaning that it constitutes a proportionately small category.) New development, in other words, becomes less and less likely as one moves inwards in the temporal "year rings" described in Stockholm's *Building Ordinance* (mentioned earlier), from the present backwards towards the past.

Similar dynamics emerge when we examine the tenure status of sites of change. Addressing two tenure forms—rentals and "privately owned" housing (an amalgamation of owner-occupied and tenant-occupied forms)—the *Bygger vi en blandad stad?* atlas shows that 52% of all new multi-unit housing projects were located in areas without an existing dominant tenure type (i.e., where not more than 70% of the housing stock was either rental or privately owned, a condition that applies to 35% of the region)—this was the case for 59% of all new rental projects and 53% of all new privately owned projects. In comparison, only 14% of projects were located in "rental" areas (a condition that in turn only applies to 12% of the region) and 27% of projects were located in "privately owned" areas (a condition that applies to 46% of the region, by virtue of the 32% of areas that are majority owner-occupied and 14% of areas that are majority tenant-occupied).

Finally, this pattern also exists when looking at socioeconomic conditions. Turning to the household structure of sites of change, 57% of new projects (88 of 154) were located in areas without a dominant household structure (that is, areas where no one household type constituted more than 50% of existing households). This can be compared to 27% (41 projects) that were located in areas where single-person households were the norm, 13% (20 projects) in areas where nuclear families comprising of a couple with children were the norm, and 4% in areas where "other" structures (couples without children and single parents) were the norm. The preference of new development for "blended" areas takes on a darker character when new multi-unit housing projects are mapped against median income levels. We note less than 1% of new multi-unit housing projects addressed in our previous study were located in areas in the highest income category (that is, areas defined by a median annual income of over 600,000 SEK) and only 9% of projects were located in areas in the lowest income category (under 200,000 SEK). In contrast, 63% of new projects were located in areas in the lower-middle bracket (200,000–400,000 SEK/year) and 27% in areas in the upper-middle bracket (400,000–600,000 SEK/year).

In the final report released before their closure under budgetary cuts introduced by the (currently ruling, then opposition) conservative (M-L-KD) coalition government, which was and is allied with the far-right Sweden Democrats, the Delegation for Segregation ("Delmos") noted that: "Extensive segregation exists in Sweden's 10 largest municipalities and in 2018 almost 60 percent of the population lived in a municipality that was more segregated than the national average in 1990."[52] Focusing on the residential segregation of populations based on socioeconomic characteristics (income, education level, or employment)—rather than demographic (gender, age, and household type) or ethnic (nationality, migration background, religion, or identifications of ethnicity) factors—Delmos point out that in the City of Stockholm, the most socioeconomically segregated residential areas are by far wealthy areas (those in the top quintile) followed by poor areas (those in the bottom quintile).[53] In our earlier analysis, we concluded that:

> the construction of new housing in the Stockholm region in 2017 did not deal with, or counteract, segregation in 9 of 10 cases. This is a deeply concerning situation that points to serious deficiencies in the planning activities of the 26 municipalities that compose the Stockholm region.[54]

The results reviewed above indicate that areas with a dominant building age, tenure form, household structure, or that are particularly wealthy or particularly poor, *are not preferred sites for contemporary housing development* in the Stockholm region. If the existing city, recalling Karin Grundström and Irene Molina, as well as Christian Björk's accounts of the segregating force of modern planning, is once characterized by *social differentiation* produced through *homogeneous clusters of tenure form related to building type* and tied to *class status*, then these clusters are clearly being maintained—by being avoided—by contemporary urban development strategies. New multi-unit housing is thereby, consciously or not, reinforcing the almost century-old modernist ambition of "producing, through planning, local and class-bound communities."[55]

Concluding Discussion: Blended and Dense Fillers and Implants

Contemporary capitalism, with its complex flows of signs (including capital) and concatenating material effects, presents what Josef Vogl identifies as "a problem of interpretation."[56] Vogl suggests that financial markets do not lend themselves to narrative treatment because capitalism is, at its heart, fundamentally irrational. In making his argument, he refers to the "bubbles, runs, busts, and booms . . . 'financial panic' or 'euphoric escalations'" that are contradictorily seen as both impossible and inherent characteristics of financial markets.[57] Critically interrogating architecture, just like critically interrogating capitalism, demands that we find ways to talk about the seemingly unrelated and desynchronized, the things we idealize and naturalize, and the things we nihilistically accept as fate. Our housing arrangements are one of the architectures that we would do well to understand as intentional, planned (by someone), and amenable to mapping, analysis, and change. As we argued in the opening, the aggregate snapshot offers us a theoretical tool with which to understand connections.

As far as the "boom year" of 2017 can be generalized, in line with the work of a number of prominent gentrification scholars in Sweden, we have suggested that the documented displacements witnessed in low-income areas appear to be the result of *soft tactics* (i.e., tenure transfers, temporary contracts, subletting, densifications of the interior, and renovictions) rather than *hard changes* (i.e., new multi-unit housing development). This is because whilst soft tactics can be deployed anywhere and by anyone at all scales—from the subletting of a closet to the block subletting of a neighborhood—*hard changes* are here shown to strongly target middle-class areas that are already "blended" in tenure, type, and household structure, or to virgin land not already subject to modernist planning norms. By largely avoiding wealthy enclaves *and* low-income areas, today's hard changes effectively reinforce the "social differentiators" that were installed during modernism.

In already-middle-class areas of villa and block suburbia, new housing projects operate as densifying "fillers," expanding the density of the tissue like collagen in a pair of newly re-pouted lips. The injection of small apartments, which are most likely tenant-owned, might in some cases attract further middle-class subjects; in other cases, such areas will be further densified as residents struggling with insecure loans expand the housing precariat by taking in lodgers or compromising their own spatial needs through "interior densification" tactics (overcrowding).

In the case of greenfield and brownfield sites, pre-blended, middle-class "implants" are cooked up, made of tenant-occupied and rental apartments, wherein the rental apartments that are added to the mix introduce residents tied to paying (higher) assumed rents, who are in the same situation as our stressed-out indebted men and women of middle-class suburbia and likely to resort to the same soft tactics of interior densification where possible. Finally, in the dense and small apartments of both infills and implants, block subletting thrives, providing the displaced who are excluded from lodging with a middle-class family by discriminatory selection processes with an exorbitantly expensive short-term fix to immanent homelessness. Whilst soft tactics appear to set up the blended conditions necessary for the arrival of future hard changes, hard changes contain the preconditions for a future exercise of soft tactics.

"Whilst the middle ring offers a diverse range of environments," we once wrote about Stockholm's outer city, "it appears to long for a deeper connection to the center, beyond this rail infrastructure. This may explain the 'urban' qualities of infill projects within this ring, which dreams of nothing more than becoming a city, every day."[58] In light of the schema set out in this article, what we witnessed in our study of 14,495 new flats was less a longing for urbanity than urbanity as a *byproduct* (which we can be taught to desire). The gentrification of gentrified areas in middle-class block suburbs and villa suburbs is, in our reading, far less a matter of constructing "living environments" than constructing "housing arrangements." This poses a question for our own discipline: what new buildings, typologies, morphologies, and visions need to be constructed, if a new set of more just, more meaningful, and more generous housing arrangements are to emerge? What soft tactics in turn might be dreamed up to deal with precarity without multiplying it? Finally, what regulatory measures might need to be invoked in order to deal with the forms of urban change outlined here and the displacement, precarity, and interior densification that they bring into being?

1 Guy Baeton, Sara Westin, Emil Pull, and Irene Molina, "Pressure and Violence: Housing Renovation and Displacement in Sweden," *Environment and Planning A* 49, no. 3 (2016): 632.

2 The term "living environment" draws on the title of the governmental policy addressing architecture and the built environment, *Politik för gestaltad livsmiljö [Policy for a design living environment]*. See: Kulturdepartementet [Department of Culture] *Politik för gestaltad livsmiljö*, Prop. 2017/18:110 (February 22, 2018), https://www.regeringen.se/rattsliga-dokument/proposition/2018/02/prop.-201718110/.

3 In this task, we rely on the results from two recent empirical studies: the book *14,495 Flats: A Metabolist's Guide to New Stockholm*, a self-initiated practice-based research study that Secretary self-published in 2021, and *Bygger vi en blandad stad? [Are We Building a Blended City?]*, a critical cartographic atlas that Secretary produced in collaboration with KTH Royal Institute of Technology in Stockholm with support and data from the Region Stockholm and published in 2022. Helen Runting, Karin Matz, and Rutger Sjögrim, *14,495 Flats: A Metabolist's Guide to New Stockholm* (Stockholm: Secretary, 2021); Helen Runting, Frida Rosenberg, Erik Stenberg, and Gaudy Orejuela, *Bygger vi en blandad stad?* (Stockholm: KTH Royal Institute of Technology and Secretary, 2022).

4 These include Daniel Movilla Vega, ed., *99 Years of the Housing Question In Sweden* (Lund: Studentlitteratur, 2017); Brett Christophers, "A Monstrous Hybrid: The Political Economy of Housing in Early Twenty-first Century Sweden," *New Political Economy* 18, no. 6 (2013): 885–911; and Karin Hedin, Eric Clark, Emma Lundholm, and Gunnar Malmberg, "Neoliberalization of Housing in Sweden: Gentrification, Filtering, and Social Polarization," *Annals of the Association of American Geographers* 102, no. 2 (March 2012): 443–63.

5 "[A]n architectural theory of the twenty-first century must work with excess. Rather than with reductive abstraction—a necessary part of the design process—theory adds layers to a situation, working above and beyond the optimized demands of practice, through techniques of aggregation, exaggeration, and connection." Helen Runting, "Architectures of the Unbuilt Environment" (PhD diss., KTH Royal Institute of Technology, Stockholm, 2018), 45.

6 Statistics Sweden(SCB), "Antal lägenheter efter region, hustyp, upplåtelseform och år, Stockholms län, 2021" [Number of dwellings after region, typology, tenure, and year, Stockholm County, 2021], extract from database, accessed January 5, 2023, https://www.statistikdatabasen.scb.se/pxweb/sv/ssd/START__BO__BO0104__BO0104D/BO0104T04/table/tableViewLayout1/.

7 Ibid.

8 City of Stockholm, *Stockholms Byggnadsordningen [Stockholm's Building Ordinance]* (Stockholm: Stockholms stad, 2020).

9 Karin Grundström and Irene Molina, "From Folkhem to Lifestyle Housing in Sweden: Segregation and Urban Form, 1930s–2010s," *International Journal of Housing Policy* 16, no. 3 (2016): 316–36, DOI: 10.1080/14616718.2015.1122695.

10 For a guide to the Swedish planning system in English see: Mats Johan Lundström, Charlotta Fredriksson, and Jacob Witzell, eds., *Planning and Sustainable Urban Development in Sweden* (Stockholm: Föreningen för samhällsplanering, 2013).

11 Catharina Thörn and Håkan Thörn, "Swedish Cities Now Belong to the Most Segregated in Europe," *Sociologisk Forskning* 54, no. 4, special issue, "Look at What's Happening in Sweden" (2017): 293–96.

12 Christian Björk, "Sambanden mellan funktionalistisk stadsplanering och planerad segregation" ["The Link Between Functionalist Planning and Planned Segregation"], *PLAN* 2–3 (2018): 52.

13 See for instance the recent op-ed Kent Persson, who is the director of social policy for the private developer Heimstaden. Kent Persson, "Dags att tala om social housing" ["It's Time That We Talk About Social Housing"], *Fastighetstidningen*, September 26, 2022, https://fastighetstidningen.se/dags-att-tala-om-social-housing/; Hyresgästförening [The Swedish Tenants' Association], "Därför är social housing en dålig idé" ["Why Social Housing Is a Bad Idea"], accessed February 16, 2023, https://www.hyresgastforeningen.se/var-politik/a-o/bostadspolitiken_a-o/social-housing/.

14 Statistics Sweden, "Antal lägenheter."

15 Stefan Björk, an investigative analyst for the Swedish Union of Tenants, explains "this tenure form premieres housing an object for financial speculation by individuals. These apartments can be rented out to whoever they want, which we are skeptical of, as it introduces a greater number of insecure rental contracts. Another main reason that often is given for building owner-occupied apartments is that they can be block sublet as apartment hotels." See Linda Dahlin, "Stor ökning av ägarlägenheter – har tiodubblats på ett år" ["Large Increase in Owner-Occupied Apartments—Tenfold Increase in One Year"], *Hem och Hyra*, October 16, 2020, https://www.hemhyra.se/nyheter/stor-okning-av-agarlagenheter-har-tiodubblats-pa-ett-ar/. Quote translated by Helen Runting.

16 Brett Christophers, "A Monstrous Hybrid: The Political Economy of Housing in Early Twenty-first Century Sweden," *New Political Economy* 18, no. 6 (2013): 889.

17 Hannu Ruonavaara, "How Divergent Housing Institutions Evolve: A Comparison of Swedish Tenant Co-operatives and Finnish Shareholders' Housing Companies," *Housing, Theory and Society* 22 (2205): 213–36.
18 Carina Listerbon and Irene Molina, "Rätten till bostaden eller kris i bostadsfrågan" [The Right to Housing or a Crisis in the Housing Question?] in *Bortom systemskiftet: mot en ny gemenskap*, eds. Niklas Altermark and Magnus Dahlstedt (Stockholm: Verbal, 2022), 503.
19 Statistics Sweden, "Antal lägenheter."
20 Martin Grander, "For the Benefit of Everyone? Explaining the Significance of Swedish Public Housing for Urban Housing Inequality," (PhD thesis, Malmö University, 2018), viii, ix. We also note that in line with reforms introduced in 2011, Swedish MHCs are required to operate in line with "business principles."
21 Stockholms bostadsförmedlingen, "Bostadsförmedlingen 2021," accessed January 15, 2022, https://bostad.stockholm.se/globalassets/broschyrer/arsberattelsen_ta_2021.pdf.
22 Lisa Svensson, "Josefin tvingades flytta flera gånger med dottern – så breder korttidskontrakten ut sig" ["Josefin Was Forced to Move Many Times With Her Daughter—This Is How Short-Term Contracts Are Spreading"], *Hem och Hyra*, October 26, 2022, https://www.hemhyra.se/nyheter/josefin-tvingades-flytta-flera-ganger-med-dottern-sa-breder-korttidskontrakten-ut-sig/.
23 Statistics Sweden, "Antal lägenheter,"
24 Statistics Sweden (SCB), "Hyra och hyresförändring efter region, 2021 och 2022" ["Rent and Changes in Rent per Region"], accessed February 17, 2023, https://www.scb.se/hitta-statistik/statistik-efter-amne/boende-byggande-och-bebyggelse/bostads-och-hyresuppgifter/hyror-i-bostadslagenheter/pong/tabell-och-diagram/hyra-och-hyresforandring-efter-region/.
25 Blocket estimates that an average rent for a 1-bedroom flat is 13,000 sek. We note that the average size of a 1-bedroom flat in Sweden is 59 square meters. See Blocket, "En halvårsrapport från Blocket Bostad: Januari till juni 2021" (Stockholm: Blocket, 2021).
26 Listerbon and Molina, "Rätten till bostaden."
27 Ibid., 508–9.
28 Länsstyrelsen Stockholm [the Stockholm County Council], "Läget i länet: Bostadsmarknaden i Stockholms län 2022" ["The Lay of the Land: The Housing Market in Stockholm County 2022], 2022:15 (Stockholm: Länsstyrelsen Stockholm, 2022), 68.
29 Baeten et al., "Pressure and Violence."
30 Ibid.
31 Ibid.
32 Filip Magnusson, "Över 1 200 hyresrätter har aombildats i Stockholm" ["Over 1,200 rental dwellings have undergone tenure transfer in Stockholm"], *Mitt i Stockholm*, June 4, 2022, https://www.mitti.se/nyheter/over-1-200-hyresratter-har-ombildats-i-stockholm-6.27.36762.063255850d; Alexander Kuronen, "Stadens nya styre vill bygga fler hyresrätter" ["The City's New Leadership Want to Build More Rental Housing"], *Mitt i Stockholm*, November 4, 2022, https://www.mitti.se/nyheter/stadens-nya-styre-vill-bygga-fler-hyresratter-6.3.41770.797c27768f.
33 Linda Dahlin, "Stopp för ägarlägenheter i Stockholms stad: 'Nu vill vi satsa på allmännyttan'" ["Stop to Owner-Occupied Apartments in the City of Stockholm": 'Now We Want to Invest in Municipal Housing Companies'"], *Hem och Hyra*, November 30, 2022, https://www.hemhyra.se/nyheter/stopp-for-agarlagenheter-i-stockholms-stad-nu-vill-vi-satsa-pa-allmannyttan/.
34 Kristina Wahlgren and Anders Paulsson, "Mångmiljonaffären klar: MKB har tagit över skandalföreningen i Malmö" ["Multimillion Crown Deal Sealed: MKB Has Taken Over the Scandal-Plagued Housing Co-op in Malmö"], *Hem och Hyra*, December 15, 2021, https://www.hemhyra.se/nyheter/mangmiljonaffaren-klar-mkb-har-tagit-over-skandalforeningen-i-malmo/.

35 Ida Karlsson, "Miljonsvindeln i Sollentuna: Inte första gången en bostadsrättsförening plundras" ["Million-Crown Scam in Sollentuna: Not the First Time a Housing Co-op Has Been Plundered"], *Hem och Hyra*, March 19, 2021, https://www.hemhyra.se/nyheter/miljonsvindeln-sollentuna-inte-forsta-gangen-en-bostadsrattsforening-plundras/.

36 Ilhan Kellecioglu, "Rapport inifrån 'Hemblahelvetet': Röster från Hemblas bostäder i Husby, Stockholm" ["Report from Inside 'Hembla Hell': Voices from Hembla's Apartments in Husby, Stockholm"] (Stockholm: Mapius 30, 2021), https://orttillort.org/wp-content/uploads/2021/10/MAPIUS_30_Digitalbok.pdf.

37 Brett Christophers, "Mind the Gap: Blackstone, Housing Investment and the Reordering of Urban Rent Surfaces," *Urban Studies* 59, no. 4 (2022): 698–716.

38 As documented by Ilhan Kellecioglu. See Kellecioglu, "Rapport inifrån 'Hemblahelvetet'."

39 Kellecioglu, "Rapport inifrån 'Hemblahelvetet'"; Dominika V. Polanska, Sara Degerhammar, and Åse Richard, *Renovräkt!: hyresvärdars makt(spel) och hur du tar striden* [*Renovicted: The Power Games that Landlords Play and How You Can Take Up the Fight*](Stockholm: Verbal Förlag, 2019); Dominika V. Polanska and Åse Richard, "Bortträngning pågår: Renovering som kulturellt trauma" ["Expulsion Under Way: Renovation as Cultural Trauma"], *Sociologisk Forskning* 55, nos. 2–3 (2018): 415–39; Guy Baeton, Sara Westin, Emil Pull, and Irene Molina, "Pressure and Violence: Housing Renovation and Displacement in Sweden," *Environment and Planning A* 49, no. 3 (2016): 631–51.

40 Christophers, "Mind the Gap."

41 Eva Jonasson, "Bostadsbolaget köper fastigheter i Hammarkullen" ["Bostadsbolaget Buys Properties in Hammarkullen"], *Sveriges Allmännytta*, November 3, 2015, https://www.sverigesallmannytta.se/bostadsbolaget-koper-fastigheter-i-hammarkullen/; Ort till Ort, "Om kampanjen 'Kommunalisera Hembla!'" ["About the Campaign 'Municipalize Hembla!'"], accessed February 17, 2023, https://orttillort.org/om-kampanjen-kommunalisera-hembla/.

42 Ort till Ort point to the Expropriation Law, chapter 2, paragraph 7, which states that "Expropriation is permitted to occur in order to maintain a property in sufficient condition in situations where gross negligence exists or risks occurring." Ort till Ort, "Om kampanjen 'Kommunalisera Hembla!'"

43 Hélène Frichot and Helen Runting, "The Queue," *e-flux architecture* (September 2019), https://www.e-flux.com/architecture/overgrowth/282654/the-queue/.

44 Länsstyrelsen Stockholm, "Läget i länet ... 2022."

45 Finansinspektionen, "Den svenska bolånemarknaden" ["The Swedish Mortgage Market"], April 20, 2022, https://www.fi.se/contentassets/3b77b17e98524f1f9e026a7ceb4423c7/den-svenska-bolanemarknaden-2022.pdf.

46 Lisa Adkins, Melinda Cooper and Martijn Konings, *The Asset Economy: Property Ownership and the New Logic of Inequality* (Cambridge: Polity Press, 2020).

47 Baeten et al., "Pressure and Violence," 635.

48 Karolina Skoog, "Sänk tröskeln till en god bostad" ["Lower the Barriers to [Accessing] Decent Housing"], SOU 2022:12 (Stockholm: Statens offentliga utredningar, 2022).

49 Ibid., 22. Translation by Helen Runting.

50 Runting, Matz, and Sjögrim, *14,495 Flats*.

51 Runting et al., *Bygger vi ett blandad stad?*

52 See: Delegationen mot segregation, "Segregation i Sverige – Årsrapport 2021 om den socioekonomiska boendesegregationens utveckling" ["Segegation in Sweden: Annual Report 2021 on the Development of Socioeconomic Residential Segregation"] (Stockholm: Delmos, 2021), 5. Translation by Helen Runting.

53 Ibid.

54 Runting et al., *Bygger vi en blandad stad?*, 87.

55 Björk, "Sambanden mellan funktionalistisk stadsplanering och planerad segregation."

56 Joseph Vogl, *The Specter of Capital (Cultural Memory in the Present)* (Redwood City: Stanford University Press, 2014).

57 Ibid.

58 Runting, Matz, and Sjögrim, *14,495 Flats*, 39.

Postage-Stamp Planning

An Interview with Sara Vall

Sara Vall (SV)

Helen Runting (HR)

Sara Vall is an architect and municipal urban planner who lives in Hökarängen with her partner and two children. She has been active in local development politics, contesting a proposal to transform her street.[1] In this interview, she shares both her knowledge of the area's recent transformations as a resident and her critique of the area's planning.

HR When did you move to Hökarängen and why?

SV I moved to Hökarängen in 2016, into a cooperatively owned apartment that was built in the 1960s, and is owned by HSB. My partner and I were living in the inner city, on the island of Södermalm, in a small apartment on the ground floor. We wanted to move to a bigger apartment, but we didn't really know where, so first we looked at Årsta [the closest "suburb" to Södermalm], but when it turned out that we couldn't really afford Årsta, we started looking further out—there weren't that many apartments up for sale at that moment—and then we found this one. My partner fell in love with it, so we bought it before it went to auction, for far too much money—all the money we had.

When we bought our place, that was at the start of the shifts that you see in Hökarängen today. When we moved here in 2016, none of the new developments along our street, Lingvägen, existed. When we first came to look at the apartment, I thought it was in the middle of nowhere, but now I think they've built something like 600 or 700 new apartments over the last 4 to 5 years alone within a radius of 500 meters of the metro station. That's a lot! The building closest to the metro platform is student housing, but many of the other buildings contain larger apartments for families, so a lot of new residents have moved into the area. Hökarängen has grown, but the only thing service-wise that has been added is one new preschool, which replaced an old one that was operating from *barracker* [portable buildings]. The metro station is full with people, and Mat Dax, our local supermarket, is busier. The local healthcare clinic, which is in the center—it's a private one, of course, aren't they all?!—has such a long waiting list. You could wait years and years to register. But when we moved in, there was still time to get on the list. We came before all the new infill projects.

This was also around the time when strategies such as the signage strategy—an initiative of the municipal housing company, Stockholmshem, which owns a large proportion of the rental housing in the area—started to have an effect. You could see the clientele starting to shift a bit in the center. There was a shop called Järnman ["Iron Man"], a hardware store. It was run by a man who had taken it over from his father, and it had been there since Hökarängen was built, basically. It was such a nice shop, quite big. And all of these other random shops. Few of them exist anymore; now, you have the sourdough bakery; Kollektivet, which sells hip tapas; and the toy shop that sells toys made of ecological wood. You could see the changes happening gradually, but I think it would have started to really become clear around 2016, when we moved in.

HR Have these changes affected the tenure structure of the area, either through *ombildningar* [tenure conversions] of rental flats to cooperatively owned or through the sale of publicly owned rental to privately owned rental? You mentioned that you live in a cooperatively owned apartment?

SV Hökarängen has a high proportion of rental apartments, and it has always been like that. Not to give a lecture about the history of Hökarängen—I mean, I'm not an expert—, but in the beginning, Hökarängen was the first metro line to be built from Slussen [one of the central, inner-city nodes in Stockholm's subway network]. Hökarängen was built before Farsta, the current end of the line, which came later.

So Hökarängen comes out of the idea of *Folkhemmet* ["The People's Home," the driving ideology of the modern Swedish welfare state] and a real idealism in city planning terms: someone actually sat down and said, "Let's make a well thought through plan for how we can create a good environment and society here." First came *egnahemsbyggen* [the self-built worker's housing] in the 1920s and 1930s, which you can see in Enskede. Hökarängen came a bit after that—it was built in the 1940s, which is evident in its *grannskapsenheter* [neighborhood units].

A few years ago, the right-wing political block in City Hall wanted to privatize part of the central residential area of Hökarängen—they put forward a proposal to do this, at least. But Hökarängen is generally quite left-wing and there was such a loud discussion, and such a huge self-organized resistance against this proposal; the residents managed to put a stop to it and no tenure conversions took place.

Hökarängen used to be called "Krökarängen" [roughly translated, "Boozetown"] and it has this aura of being an outpost for people who have fallen out of society's safety net. There are lots of rental apartments, and historically there have been a lot of *genomgångsboenden* [temporary housing] and *provboenden* [test housing] that are run by social services—so, you know, if you got out of prison, or came out of rehab, or something else happened and you needed an apartment while you tried to fix things, this would be where you might end up. Hökarängen had a lot of this type of housing, and the nickname Krökarängen stems from that history. There are still traces of this left. There's still a lot of alcoholics and junkies hanging around, and some violence connected to that in the center. I saw the other day that the local newspaper, *Mitt i*, was interviewing all the political parties about what they want to do with Hökarängen's development, and of course the right wing want to have more security cameras, and guards stationed on the square; there have been some problems with drug dealing and violence in the center of Hökarängen, despite the gentrification.

HR There are still a lot of *terrains vague*, in-between spaces, right?

SV When we first moved to Hökarängen, I would hear woodpeckers when I walked to the metro. It was silent enough to hear birdsong. Between the street Lingvägen and the train tracks, there was a strip of land, 10 to 30 meters in width; it was not a "forest" per se, but an *impediment* [a Swedish term for forested land that is not dense enough to be used for timber production, here translated as "forest tract"] that was a corridor for all these birds. That disappeared with all the new infill developments. In 2018, I had my first child and that was a big shift in my life. As a planner and architect, I've always been looking at the city in sort of an efficient way, you know, like "Here's dead space/wasted space, this could be used for something, why isn't there a building here?" When you have a child, you go through so much *VAB* [an acronym for *vård av barn* ("care of children"), widely used as a verb meaning "to take care leave"]. You have all this time to kill, and you go out with a one-year-old and you don't know what to do. So you walk around, not on the formal streets but on the walking and cycling paths. I realized that we can walk pretty far without ever having to cross a road—my son, I mean, he can run freely because of this. For me, this forest tract is just a small gap with some trees, but for him that's a forest to explore. I will always have that filter, I think, when I look at cities—seeing them through the eyes of a child, things become completely different.

Those spaces are becoming increasingly fragmented as they are being developed. The City of Stockholm doesn't have a master plan for Hökarängen. They are just *dabbing* at the land, applying plans as if they were postage stamps [*frimärksplaner*]. There's not one person, or even a few people, that have the full picture. Rather, it's like "Oh, here's a gap, let's do something ... Oh, here's another gap..." Without the full picture, they only end up planning for residential buildings, and they are taking all of these forest tracts, which people actually use, that have a purpose, to do that.

HR The morphology of Hökarängen likens a series of "islands within islands"; in this archipelago of neighborhood units, separated by these forest tracts, do the residents of different parts get to know each other—does this structure affect the social relations of the area?

SV It does a bit. The preschool where my son goes is really big; among the parents of his closest friends, you have a preschool teacher and a supermarket worker; Spotify workers; a subway driver; a nurse and an engineer. But that's in the preschool. After that, you have *det fria skolvalet* [the "free choice of schools" policy] which creates a different situation. I really think Hökarängen still has a good social mix! Affordability is still an issue though. If you look at the new rental blocks on our street, the architects Dinell Johansson and the landlord Primula worked their asses off to make them affordable, but they still cost more than older rental apartments in downtown Hökarängen, perhaps double. And it's impossible to *get* an older rental apartment in Hökarängen, though. The queue [for being allocated a rental apartment through the City of Stockholm's rental brokerage] is so long; I mean, I've been in the queue for 15 years and I would never get an older rental apartment in the center of this area! The old building stock is dominated by smaller 1-bedroom and 2-bedroom apartments. We just had our second kid, and I don't know what we're going to do, because I love Hökarängen, but there are so few 3-bedroom or 4-bedroom apartments.

HR Why do you think that Hökarängen has attracted young families with kids?

SV Hökarängen has so many rental apartments, both new ones and old ones. It has row houses, both tiny, cute ones and bigger expensive ones (the tiny cute ones are also expensive!). You have a small area of self-built workers' housing. And the art space Konsthall C has had a big impact on putting Hökarängen on the map for people, in the shift from "Krökarängen" to "that place where Konsthall C is." When I moved from Barcelona to Stockholm in 2008, it's one of my first memories, being a student at the School of Architecture and going to Konsthall C. This was before I had a smartphone, and I took the wrong exit from the subway; it was snowing and dark—it was in January—and I was asking people "Do you know where Konsthall C is?" They were all like "What is that?!" and it wasn't until I started asking about "the big building with the laundry in it" that people understood what I was talking about. Konsthall C is known for taking over a communal laundry building, and from a normal Hökarängen residents' point of view, it's probably still "the laundry place" and not "the art space," even today.

So, what is it with Hökarängen? I think it's still close to the city center—for people working, it's not far, you don't have to commute a long way. You have two lakes within a 10-minute bike ride, and there's quite a number of really nice playgrounds and *parklekar* [adventure playgrounds]—we have one with horses and goats and hens, just a 5-minute walk away. There is still an infrastructure present that is just . . . *very relaxed*.

HR Given that you live in the southern part of Hökarängen, which is two stops from the end of the subway line at Farsta Strand, which in turn is the municipal boundary of the City of Stockholm, do you perceive yourself as living on the edge of the city?

SV During the pandemic, I was in central Stockholm so few times, I can barely remember going there. Hökarängen was my entire world. But because Farsta is further south, and because I used to work even further south, it didn't feel like I was living at the last outpost. I have to remind myself sometimes that I still live in Stockholm, because I feel a bit disconnected from the city center. From a city planner's perspective, I also feel that we're in the periphery because the city planning department would never plan Östermalm [the richest area in the inner city] the way they are planning Hökarängen! Here, they can rely on nobody noticing, because very few understand the process. When I talked to my neighbors about the new *detaljplan* [detail plan] proposal for our street, they were like, "What's a detail plan?!" You know? You can't expect people to *question* what's going on when they don't understand the basic fundamentals of urban planning. Even I don't understand sometimes.

HR We visited the popular bakery BAK recently for the first time, which has such a classic "urban" aesthetic. In a typical Stockholm suburb, you might find a pizzeria and, if you're lucky, a sushi place. That's it. Why do you think Hökarängen has so many slightly classier restaurants, slightly nicer cafés?

SV Isn't it classic gentrification? A highly educated creative class move to Hökarängen, and they attract businesses like Kollektivet and BAK that benefit from the on-average lower rents than in the city center. They find all this potential that has always been there but simply hadn't been activated. It could easily die, I guess, if the rents went up a lot, for instance. The positive effects of these people being here were also enabled by Stockholmshem, who wanted to facilitate a gentrification process. So, for a short while, I know that their strategy was to have really low rents on the central street of Hökarängen. The signage program was also accompanied by a lot of other measures to enable the situation. Stockholmshem also said "no" to things that they didn't want—they didn't want to have real estate agents, for instance, but they did want a pharmacy, a healthcare center, the toy shop, the tattoo shop . . . They wanted a good mix. Someone sat down and thought this through—like a recipe for gentrification, I guess.

HR It's so striking that it was Stockholmshem—a municipal housing company—and not the City of Stockholm that drove these changes. I mean, the latter is meant to maintain a "planning monopoly" and make planning decisions in a democratically accountable way. The former has a legal responsibility to act like a business and generate profits. They're quite different beasts.

SV Stockholmshem has a board that includes political representation (the major parties are represented with chairs on that board), and they also have their own urban planning department, so they don't answer to the City, they're independent. They have their own urban specialists and city planners doing their own strategy work, and Hökarängen is of high interest to those people. I guess that they highlight some areas, especially areas where they've previously had problems, and in those areas, they actively enable the gentrification process. In my experience, almost nothing that happens in Hökarängen is driven by the City Planning Department at the City of Stockholm. I mean, if they would have wanted to take a direction, on anything, it would have been articulated somewhere. But it's not.

HR It seems, when looking at Hökarängen through an architectural lens, that there is a real desire to reflect the existing typologies in new developments. Would you agree?

SV I think this has been important for the politicians making the decisions, and it's written somewhere in the comprehensive plan that all new buildings should reflect existing conditions. The new tower blocks on the street Lingvägen have sort of the same shape and their façades are at the same scale as the older tower blocks, but the volumes themselves are bigger because apartments today are so much bigger than in the 1960s—the floorplates are getting deeper and the building envelopes are getting *chubbier*.

The City wants this wave of current redevelopment to be *stadsmässig* ["city-like"], whatever that means. It's weird, 'cos they always want ground-floor spaces for shops or commercial or service activity, but there's rarely a market for that. In the Primula tower blocks on Lingvägen, there was supposed to be a kiosk or something at the ground floor. Because there is no customer base for that, Primula made the best out of a bad situation by putting a collective laundry with a large window there, so on a dark winter's evening when you're coming home from work you see that it's lit up and there are people doing their laundry.

If you look at the old housing in the center of Hökarängen, those buildings are all three stories, they are *lameller* [slab blocks], and the apartments are a half-floor up from the entrance. They could never afford that nowadays—now, you have people living on the ground floor, always having their curtains drawn. So, there is this idea of making it "urban," but the city doesn't have the recipe for it. And the building companies don't follow through.

HR The infill projects of the past 5 years seem to have quite respected architecture offices behind them. Instead of standardized, industrial housing units that are just plonked on site, it seems like both up-and-coming and established architects have been used. What's with that?

SV There *is* a really tragic development on the southwest side of the railway that is exactly what you expect when you think about "infill projects in the suburbs." Those buildings were built before we moved to Hökarängen. Everything built after that has been better, design-wise. I don't know why it got better. I don't think that the design ambition is being driven by the municipality. I don't think that they have had a hand in that; it's more likely that when the area became more attractive, it attracted housing companies and architects with higher design ambitions.

When Hökarängen was planned in the mid-twentieth century, it was very cutting edge, everything was very well thought through. There was a high level of experimentation. The metro was new. The pedestrian street was brand new in a Swedish context. I mean, they tried hard, and it worked. Everyone I've talked to who lives in Hökarängen loves it. It's super-sad when the new isn't adding to that—you know, it's like you made this beautiful cake and then you put something horrible on top. I'm not doing the NIMBY thing, I do think that you can add to environments like this, but you need a more elaborated strategy.

What the City of Stockholm has is an Excel sheet. When they sign up for big infrastructural projects, which cost billions and billions of crowns, they commit to building lots of housing in return. The comprehensive plan nominates a series of *tyngdpunkter* [nodes] where the majority of those housing projects should be placed and Farsta is one of them. Hökarängen is in the same *stadsdel* [city district] as Farsta and thus in that cluster. And it has a subway station, which makes it doubly attractive. In the end, for the City, it comes down to filling in that Excel spreadsheet at the end of the year with how many residential buildings were built, so that in the next election the City can say, "Hey, look at us, we built X number of new apartments." I have tried to backtrack in order to find answers to the questions "Why doesn't anyone have *the full picture*?" and "What *is* the plan for Hökarängen as a city district?"

The answer is that it would be horrible for the City if everyone had the full picture: then everyone would understand that this is madness and that no one is in control. That's why it's better for them to do *postage-stamp planning*.

1 See Matias Kamgren, "Arkitekter tar fajten om Lingvägen" [Architects take on the fight regarding Lingvägen], *Mitt i Söderort* (March 30, 2021), https://www.mitti.se/nyheter/arkitekter-tar-fajten-om-lingvagen/repucD!VTDcdffVYwQTxKO7HKllig/.

SIFAV (The Southern Districts' Institute for Other Visions)

Maryam Fanni and Elof Hellström

Everything is being privatized and sold off and in this way, one population is to be replaced by another. During the neighborhood makeovers of neoliberalism, almost anything can be used to produce and market identity. In this essay, Maryam Fanni and Elof Hellström of SIFAV (Söderorts Institut För Andra Visioner, or The Southern Districts' Institute for Other Visions) take a closer look at neon lights, a prominent feature of the neighborhood of Hökärangen.[1]

> The poem stands and shines flashes
> Hovers with its neon medallions
> Anonymous light patterns switch on and off
> Advertisements for the new era[2]

In the flashing lights of a Copenhagen night, "punk poet" Michael Strunge locates a calm of sorts—here, in shadows that are erased at dawn, identities warp and twisted things can happen. Life can happen. Neon light illuminates the things that do not find a place in the strict categories of the day; in the depths of the night, it creates a secret space where bodies intermingle with each other and the city. Strunge's poem also poses a critique: as the patterns of light and darkness flicker, they also constitute a form of advertising, promoting not products but the dawning of a new era.

> *Bageri* [Bakery], *Bankomat* [ATM], *Barnkläder* [Children's Clothing], *Bokförlag* [Publisher], *Brodyr* [Embroidery], *Bryggeri* [Brewery], *Cevicheria* [Ceviche Restaurant], *Cykelverkstad* [Bike Repairs], *Film* [Film], *Frisör* [Hairdresser], *Fritidsgård* [Youth Recreation Center], *Guld* [Gold], *Hudvård* [Skincare], *Hökarängens centrum* [Hökarängen Center], *Järnhandel* [Hardware Store], *Kaffe* [Coffee], *Kontor* [Office], *Leksaker* [Toys], *Lokalrätten* [The Local Dish], *Låssmed* [Locksmith], *Penningöverföring* [Money Transfers], *Pizzabutik* [Pizza Shop], *Ramverkstad* [Framers], *Remake* [Remake], *Restaurang* [Restaurant], *Sushi* [Sushi], *Tatuering* [Tattoos], *Tobak* [Tobacco], *Tvättstuga* [Laundrette], *Yoga* [Yoga], *Zoo* [Petstore].[3]

In 2011, the municipal housing company Stockholmshem initiated the development project Hållbara Hökarängen [Sustainable Hökarängen]. The aims of the project were threefold: development of the center (by “strengthening the ‘50s vibe and creating a sustainable range of services”), investment in the arts (by encouraging artists to move into ground-floor premises, regardless of whether these spaces were already occupied), and instilling “a holistic approach to property maintenance including a commitment to sustainability investments.”[14] One of the changes, and perhaps the most visible, were the new neon signs. In and around the center of Hökarängen, old signs have been taken down, renovated, or replaced. Some of these are from the renovation of the center in 1998, when the idea of renovating in the style of the 1950s was first introduced and the first round of neon signs were installed. But the majority of signs are from 2011 or later. Today, there are 34 neon signs in Hökarängen (although they actually use LEDs, which are more environmentally friendly and brighter than neon, they imitate neon and are referred to as such).

Figure 1: Inventory of neon signage in Hökarängen. SIFAV, 2013.

> Even if these signs have become more common in rural areas, neon light will always be the light of the city, not the countryside. Where neon sign exist in a rural setting, there is always an initiator, a consumer, who has chosen to view the countryside as a city or envisioned the countryside being urbanized. This could also be a dream shared amongst a group of traders, who together have held a collective idea about development, about transforming the desolate countryside into a vibrant city.[5]

The neon signs are part of a so-called "1950s amplification" that is to be performed as part of an investment in the center of Hökarängen by the municipal housing company Stockholmshem. The project Hållbara Hökarängen [Sustainable Hökarängen] has produced a signage policy and manual for local businesses which provides instructions with respect to how they can (and should) achieve a "'50s vibe." The purpose of the signage policy is to create a coordinated image of Hökarängen's commercial center and the suburb as a whole, and to thereby imbue the area with "economic and social sustainability."[6] This goal aligns snuggly with the City of Stockholm's Vision 2030, which aims to "profile" different parts of the city, essentially proposing to market entire areas with the help of simplified images and identities.

Neon is an important element in achieving the "50s vibe" required by the signage policy; the signage strategy is appended to all lease contracts for commercial premises in the center and all commercial tenants are offered a free neon sign when signing their lease. This gift is, however, conditional: if the contract is to be extended, the policy stipulates, further signage and façade rules must be followed.[7] Personal taste is thereby made subordinate to aesthetic regulations, which in turn are based on an imaginary of Sweden in the 1950s.

The signage policy is intended to function as pedagogical inspiration and an instruction manual, showing how the 1950s might be arranged. But who has access to this kind of nostalgia? And what do the 1950s represent? '50s retro can also be described as reflecting nuclear family and whiteness norms, modernist notions of progress as they were inscribed in the concept of *Folkhemmet*

[The People's Home], and a Sweden that had not yet experienced non-European immigration. Who is served by such nostalgia? And what happens to those who cannot relate to, or have no interest in, the Sweden of the 1950s?

While a neon script busily takes over Hökarängen, another investment in another commercial center is underway in the nearby suburb Högdalen. In an inauguration speech for the center, which took place in the fall of 2012, the CEO of Citycon, the company that owns Högdalen's center, shared his views of handwriting:

> Isabelle, the center manager, has run a training program for our tenants, the shopkeepers, regarding how they can be more professional about their signage. By reducing the amount of handwritten signage and the signs that people just put up because they want to sell a particular product that day—by means of more professional signage, things have become much, much better.

Businesses that used a lot of handwritten signs were pushed out of Högdalen, to the advantage of businesses with more organized, planned—and, in this way, more expensive—signage. The spontaneity and flexibility that accompanies writing with a marker pen, a practice which previously allowed traders to make new signs without having to contract a printer, is in this way forcibly removed.

In Hökarängen, handwriting is also being eroded as a practice, albeit in a different way. The signage policy specifies that freestanding street signs should be avoided, and if they are used, they should take the form of chalkboards with wooden frames. Here, handwriting is permitted in cases where it represents exclusivity and nostalgia, but this comes at the expense of expressions of contemporaneity. The formal and mass-produced neon signs constitute a typographic ideal that replaces the existing styles and impressions of a place. Just as the "'50s vibe" borrows welfare-state aesthetics whilst emptying them of content, the cursive script of the neon signs flirts with that of the handwritten communiqué, emptying the latter of defining characteristics like individuality and imperfection.

> Alpha60: "I shall calculate so that failure is impossible."[8]

In this way, anything that is undecidable or multifaceted in the viewer's encounter with place disappears. Any ambiguity that might exist in this uniform signage is hardly of a kind that would invite a collaborative production of meaning—rather, the signs reinforce the existing order and the sharp divisions between inside and outside that are at work in Hökarängen's center. No matter what (neo) liberal politicians and business representatives say, no place can be "for everyone"—every space is suspended between openness and delimitation. What is paradoxical in all of this is that the disciplining kind of space that is brought into being by the neon signs is presented as the result of citizen participation (paraphrasing the welfare state and claiming to act as a model of "sustainability") at the same time that it is in fact the result of a top-down, profit-seeking, consumption-focused strategic intervention.

> Through conscious design efforts, Hökarängen can become a home for many who would otherwise be drawn to inner-city neighborhoods—for example, Södermalm.[9]

Traditionally, business identification signage has advertised opportunities for spontaneous consumption to a broad audience: "cinema," "bar," "café," etc. What is new in Hökarängen is the fact that words like "publisher," "office," "recreation center," and "laundry" appear in neon, and that rather than a general audience these are directed at specific user groups. The neon signs do not show company names but only the kind of business or activity that occurs on the premises, and those who would like to advertise their company can pay for their own signage. The gift of the signs is thus not intended to support individual businesses so much as to create visual uniformity and emphasize the quantity of activities taking place in the area. The number of neon signs can, in this sense, be described as encouraging the consumption of the area itself rather than the consumption of goods or services available in the area.

What we witness in this move is an attempt to strengthen the place's "legibility"—a term that is accorded increasing weight in an urban economy in which consumption has become more important than production. In order to make them "attractive," places are given a history (as if they didn't already have one—as if they didn't have thousands–already!). As urban historian Håkan Forsell writes in the collection of essays *Bebodda platser* [*Inhabited Places*], these top-down narratives act "like real estate agents, selling the built environment" and transforming areas into goods that can be packaged and sold.[10] For housing companies, the potential for successful storytelling is as important as the place itself. The wrapping, it is central to understand, actively changes that which it wraps; in targeting specific groups, these glittering packages not only produce a reality—in so doing, they displace others.

Clearly not everyone is expected to respond to subway ads like visitstockholm.com's[11] story about how the inner-city area of Hornstull, Södermalm, has now "added a fork to its knife" in order to update its old moniker, Knivsöder ["Knife Söder," an ironic reference to how dangerous the area was "back in the day"]. The point of such ads is to create a name that can cut through the white noise, stand out in the constant competition between places, and attract a population with means. This is the same logic that is applied when the suburb of Järva is branded "IT and Science," the infrastructural node of Älvsjö becomes "International Fairs," and Hökarängen becomes "green and comfy retro." All of these parts are integral to the Stockholm that is parceled up and sold under the copyrighted slogan "The Capital of Scandinavia."

To make a place legible is also to make a place saleable, which in Hökarängen can be understood in light of the fact that since the re-regulations of 2010, municipal housing companies are to operate just like any other company. The law on municipal housing companies is clear: "a muncipal housing company shall be run in accordance with commercial principles" and thus seek to generate profit.[12]

Neon lights
Shimmering neon lights
And at the fall of night
This city's made of light.[13]

Neon lights also function as traces in the night, symbols of the kind that we each read differently. For some, they promise the liberating dissolution of the dancefloor, for others they are an impediment to a good night's sleep. For others still, they are a symbol of triumph—like the cover story that ran in the local newspaper *Mitt i Söderort* last spring, "FROM ROTTEN SUBURB TO TRENDY CENTER." The problem with narratives about urban transformation like this is not the neon signs, the organic stores, or the artists, but a disembodied politics that cements spatial injustices through commodification, privatization, and the maintenance of a housing crisis, and does so to the advantage of housing companies and private homeowners. So many other things are connected to these signs: words are twisted to the point that they take on other meanings, images are taken hostage and re-presented in radically altered form. Neon lights flicker, and in the shadows, one population is replaced by another.

1 This text was first published in Swedish as: Maryam Fanni and Elof Hellström, "Neon Lights," *Brand* 4 (2013): 18–21. It is here published for the first time in English translation, a decade later. Translation by Helen Runting.

2 Michael Strunge (pseudonym Simon Lack), "Neonpoemet" [1985], *Verdenssøn* (Oslo: Gyldendal, 2015). English translation by Justina Bartoli.

3 List of text on internally illuminated business signs in Hökarängen in 2013, as recorded by Maryam Fanni and Elof Hellström.

4 Stockholmshem and ÅWL, *Skyltprogram: Hökarängen C* (January 12, 2012) (Stockholm: Stockholmshem and ÅWL, 2012).

5 Thomas Eriksson, *Neon: Eldskrift I natten.* (Stockholm: Rabén Prisma, 1997). Translation by Helen Runting.

6 Stockholmshem and ÅWL, *Skyltprogram.*

7 Ibid., 22.

8 *Alphaville*, directed by Jean-Luc Godard (Warner-Tonefilm, Chaumiane Production, and Filmstudio F.P.A., 1965), 1:33:00.

9 Stockholmshem and ÅWL, *Skyltprogram.* Translation by Helen Runting.

10 Håkan Forsell, *Bebodda platser : studier av vår urbana samtidshistoria* (Stockholm: Arkitektur Förlag; 2014). Quote translated by Helen Runting.

11 City of Stockholm, "Official guide to Stockholm for visitors and talents City of Stockholm," accessed November 4, 2022, https://www.visitstockholm.com/about-visitstockholmcom.

12 Government of Sweden, *Lag (2010:879) om allmännyttiga kommunala bostadsaktiebolag* [Law about municipal housing companies], SFS nr: 2010:879, https://www.riksdagen.se/sv/dokument-lagar/dokument/svensk-forfattningssamling/lag-2010879-om-allmannyttiga-kommunala_sfs-2010-879.

13 Kraftwerk, "Neon Lights," track 5 on *The Man-Machine*, Capitol Records, 1978, vinyl.

South of the South in Venice of the North: Theorizing Change in Hökarängen

Secretary

Helen Runting, Rutger Sjögrim and Karin Matz

Though the mist has cleared, the sun hasn't yet found the horizon and suburbia is bathed in a dark blue light. Patches of ice and moss cling to the exposed rock walls of the subway cutting and the concrete underpasses are full of moving shapes in nose-to-knee down jackets, gloves, and woolen hats. It's one of those Scandinavian winter mornings when all you want to do is stay in bed, but like everyone else—crowds of students and office workers, men in headphones and a lady with camera equipment who probably works in media—you have to get to work. The smaller children and parents take earlier trains, and tradespeople and service personnel left long ago, when it was still pitch-black and foggy. This morning falls in the latter part of the monthly salary cycle (almost everyone in Sweden gets paid on the same day, syncing the population in terms of consumption habits) and buying a take-away coffee is an avoidable excess. As such, when a figure appears at the glass sliding doors outside the ticket hall of the subway station offering free paper cups of steaming hot coffee to morning commuters, you are genuinely, deeply grateful. The man has slicked-back hair, perfect teeth, and a micro-down vest; behind him is an advertising roll-up in tasteful cobalt, its message repeated on the coffee cup: a Nordic-sounding real estate brokerage. He constitutes an odd, almost spectral presence in a modernist suburb dominated by multi-unit rental housing, that guy. When you get to work, the empty cup remains on your desk. An anomaly.

This chapter tells a story about those Stockholm suburbs that lie "south of the South (island)" (*söder om Söder(malm)*), a diffuse and debated geographic zone, where all three authors of this essay live, in apartment buildings in neighborhoods built in the decade following World War II, close to the ends of southbound "green" subway lines. Specifically, the chapter addresses Hökarängen, the third-last stop on the southbound Farsta strand line. Hökarängen is both representative of the *south of the South*, but also special in the way it amplifies particular conditions: it is more valorized, architecturally, for its 1950s' architecture than Hagsätra, Rågsved, or Bagarmossen, where we live. It was built slightly earlier, has been more intensively developed in the past decade, and was not only a blueprint for the construction of suburbs like ours but is also a kind of litmus test when it comes to the future that densification is bringing into being. If angels with slicked-back hair ever handed out free paper cups of coffee in Hökarängen, this probably would have happened a few years back. According to Hökarängen resident, architect, and planner Sara Vall, who is interviewed earlier in this section, it probably would have happened around 2013. Or perhaps, if we listen to the account offered by SIFAV, which follows the interview with Sara, real estate agents (or promo boys dressed as real estate agents) were never needed here: through the Hållbar Hökarängen ("Sustainable Hökarängen") policy of the municipal housing company (MHC) Stockholmshem, the built environment itself could be dressed up and packaged in such a way as to communicate the message of marketization all on its own.

In this chapter, which functions as a concretization and expansion of the introductory chapter and as a contextualization of the earlier essay and interview, we provide an account of urban transformation in the southern suburb of Hökarängen in Stockholm. In this, we first aim to situate the theoretical framework and vocabulary sketched in the opening chapter of this section—showing how the "soft tactics" and "hard changes" identified there play out in material terms. Secondly, using the shift in scale from region to suburb, we seek to bring other concepts into play, revealing a financialization of spatial resources and mindsets which we discuss under the auspices of Sara Westin's term "gentrification of the mind."[1]

A Decade of Infill: Hard Change in Hökarängen

Hökarängen lies *outside the toll gates* but within the City of Stockholm, 18 minutes by bike from Trångsund in the neighboring *wreath municipality* of Haninge, 25 minutes by bike from Huddinge Centrum in Huddinge, and 41 minutes by bike (or 29 minutes by subway) from Stockholm's Central Station (see Figure 3, page 330). This location places it in the inner part of *the middle ring* of the Stockholm region, and thus on the interior edge of *the outer city*. In administrative terms, it is also part of Söderort, a municipal district (*kommundel*) that takes in 52 city districts (*stadsdelar*), which are grouped in five administrative city district areas (*stadsdelsområden*): Enskede-Årsta-Vantör, Hägersten-Älvsjö, Skarpnäck, Skärholmen, and, finally, Farsta, where Hökarängen is situated. In Stockholm slang, Söderort is referred to as "south of the South."

Purchased by the City of Stockholm in 1908, the land that Hökarängen sits on was first developed for the purposes of a residential suburb through, first, the construction of Tobaksområdet, one of the many neighborhood units that make up the suburb (finished 1949); then the opening of the green subway line, which terminated at Hökarängen (finished 1950); and finally the construction of the center, including its pedestrian street in 1952, in line with a plan drawn by architect David Helldén in line with a commission from planner and architect Sven Markelius.[2] This historical development placed Hökarängen at the heart of *Folkhemmet* ("The People's Home"), a figure of thought associated with the development of Swedish modernism and the social-democratic project of the twentieth century. It also bequeathed the area with a considerable stock of rental apartments, the majority of which were, and continue to be, managed by the municipal housing company Stockholmshem. Preceding the Million Program of 1965–74 by more than a decade, Hökarängen—like several other green line suburbs, including Bagarmossen, Björkhagen, Kärrtorp, and Bandhagen-Högdalen—has been spared much of the stigmatization suffered by other modern suburbs built during, just before (for instance, Rågsved and Bredäng) or just after the program (for instance, Dalen and Skarpnäck). As Jennifer Mack (whose thoughts on suburbia, disturbia, futurbia form the second chapter of this book) writes, with reference to the earlier work of Urban Ericsson, Irene Molina, and Per-Markku Ristilammi on the Million Program and media, "late modernist neighbourhoods have often been treated as untouchable spaces, shown in aerial views as regular arrangements of identical housing blocks with wide lawns, in close-ups of modernist façade treatments out of context, or in salacious pictures of burning cars, graffiti, police in riot gear, or tell-tale crime scene plastic tape."[3] While, as Sara Vall explains in her interview, Hökarängen has been associated with vulnerable groups and been labelled with derogatory nicknames of its own, the area is not subject to the generalizing, often racializing critique levelled at "the" Million Program.

As shown in the maps presented on pages 332 and 333, Hökarängen's bones are modernist, rental-tenure apartment blocks in landscape settings. In 2021, the suburb's housing stock comprised of 5,347 apartments and 304 single-unit dwellings (villas and row houses); of these, 79% were rental tenure, 20% were owned by individuals via cooperative housing associations, and 0.02% (only 89 dwellings) were owner-occupied.[4] Compared to the Stockholm region, this constitutes an extremely high percentage of rentals—in 2021, 43% of multi-unit dwellings in the region were rental, 57% were cooperatively owned, and 0.1% were owner-occupied.[5] Further, of Hökarängen's 4,459 rental dwellings (all of which were in multi-unit housing), 3,398 (76%) were owned by MHCs and 1,061 (24%) were owned by private landlords.[6] Again, this indicates a significantly higher proportion of MHC-owned housing than the regional average—in the Stockholm region in 2021, 35% (140,653) of the region's 400,151 rental dwellings were owned by MHCs.[7] Of the area's 5,347 apartments in 2021, a little over 19% (1,010) were built in the period 2010–20 (a figure we trace to just 10 development projects).[8] This is slightly higher than in the proportion of new build in the Stockholm region, where 119,143 new apartments were built 2010–20, accounting for just over 15% of the existing stock of apartments at 2021 (770,275).[9] The regional average includes the inner city and central development nodes of the period like Hammarby Sjöstad, Liljeholmskajen, etc., indicating that Hökarängen punches well above its weight as a relatively peripheral suburb.

The morphology of Hökarängen is, like Stockholm itself, archipelagic: buildings are clustered around streets and courtyards in order to form islands called "neighborhood units." The subway cuts the area in two, dividing the east from west, and it is not until you glance at the topographic map (Figure 10 on page 333) that it becomes apparent that the units in fact crown hills, with the forested tracts that separate the units, absorbing the steeper terrain. Looking to the location of new housing in the period 2011–20, it is clear that these forested slopes have formed the preferred sites for new development, alongside exposed strips of land adjacent to the subway, where noise regulations have been met through the use of access balconies on the "quiet side" of the building and a relatively closed facade to the tracks. If the suburb's housing stock continues to grow by 20% every 10 years, it is not hard to imagine that these patterns will continue, as flat sites are carved out or built up on the remaining forested ridgelines and the subway is slowly built in, in its valley.

New build introduces new housing arrangements through shifts in tenure, rent levels, housing prices, and densities. Of the 1,000-odd apartments built 2010–20 in Hökarängen, 43% were privately owned, in the form of tenant-occupied housing, 48% were rentals owned by private landlords, and 9% were rentals owned by MHCs. This clearly indicates an adjustment of the existing tenure and ownership structures, reducing the *proportion* of rental apartments, reducing the *presence* of MHCs (in Hökarängen, Stockholmshem, and Familjbostäder), and introducing a plethora of new, private rental actors (in Hökarängen, the large actors Primula and Besqab, but also smaller actors like Bergsundet, Nordfeldt, Heba, and Gimle). This adjustment confirms some of the main tenets of the "blended city" discourse, which was in particular advanced in a series of reports on "social sustainability" commissioned for the City of Stockholm between 2015 and 2017, when the City was led by a coalition government formed by the Social Democrats (S), the Greens Party (MP), the Left Party (V), and the Feminist Initiative (FI).[10] Åsa Dahlin and Christoffer Carlander, authors of the report *Vägen hem: Socialt hållbar bostadsförsörjning i Stockholms stad* ("The Way Home: Socially Sustainable Housing Provision in the City of Stockholm"), for instance, describe the advantages of "social blending," which they see as combatting not only segregation but the mounting housing crisis.[11] What is interesting, though, is that the "blending" that they suggest is bi-directional: as they write, "the housing stock of a city can be blended by the complementary addition of that which is limited or completely lacking," going on to add that, "another possibility for which international examples exist is that each new project be built in a blended manner."[12] Whilst this sounds like a welcome panacea to earlier modernist policies of "social differentiation" (discussed in the introduction to this section) and thus an important strategy in combatting segregation, in reality these policies resulted in infilled insertions (what we call "fillers") of privately owned flats (both owner-occupied and cooperatively owned) in rental areas, while new rental (which proportionally flags behind the former category in the region) is used as a "mixer" to "pre-blend" new neighborhoods (what we call "implants") in the outer city. Nowhere is it articulated why a lack of commodified housing constitutes a "problem" that would require policy attention; nor is it clear how the addition of new cooperatively owned flats might ameliorate a housing shortage and affordability crisis. What we can say is that in the case of Hökarängen, ten years of "hard changes" have left the area with somewhat fewer forested tracts, proportionally fewer rental flats, a new generation of renters who rent from a range of private landlords at assumed rents (and a handful of new renters who pay assumed rents to MHCs), as well as an influx of individuals who own their flats through cooperative associations.

Gentrifying with Words: Soft Tactics in Hökarängen

As we suggest in the introduction to this section, not all change comes packaged in concrete (or massive timber): many of the urban transformations witnessed in the living environments of contemporary Stockholm take the form of soft tactics, deployed by individuals and property owners in ways that alter "housing arrangements." These tactics alter tenure, ownership, values, or access, without considerable changes being made to the material form of a city.

Hökarängen is a site of surprising resilience when it comes to many of the soft tactics that have been deployed specifically to erode rental rights in other parts of Stockholm (many of these are discussed in the introduction to this section). The suburb is a, if not *unique*, then at least *prime example* of the power of residents to resist tactical pushes for the "tenure transfer" of rental housing stock to individual ownership through housing associations. In the previous mandate period, a conservative coalition government entered power in the City of Stockholm (2018–22), determined to activate a dormant regulatory mechanism to sell off rental housing to tenants (similar to a British Right to Buy scheme). Accompanying this move, the tenure transfer process was rapidly professionalized, forming a lucrative business for specialized consultants. 1,000 apartments were slated for transfer in Hökarängen; because residents voted against these privatizations—and thus against the allure of short-term financial gains and entry into the property market—none of these privatizations went ahead. Speaking to the large daily newspaper *Dagens Nyheter*, resident Fredrik Cerha described his entry into housing activism following the announcement of the plans, explaining, "I could have earned a pile of money if my flat was privatized. But I like Hökarängen how it is. All kinds of people live here. I don't want more gentrification and I like the idea of municipal housing companies."[13] By virtue of the strong presence of the municipal housing company, Hökarängen similarly side-stepped the "renoviction" strategies witnessed in late-modernist areas like Husby in Stockholm's north in recent years, and even the piecemeal "concept renovations" that have led to shock increases in rent and the instigation of short-term contracts in many areas. Hökarängen is thus not an area associated with displacement—at least not of the traditional kind.

Following the work of Rowland Atkinson, Swedish human geographer and housing researcher Sara Westin argues that "an individual can be displaced without having moved a meter."[14] Addressing the effects of the language used by Swedish economists when they advocate for the introduction of market rents (and the deregulation of the non-means tested, rent-negotiated rental system), Westin locates a form of psychic displacement whereby tenants are "alienated" from "feeling at home." It is worth quoting her at length here:

> Being at the center of the economists' rhetoric on Sweden's need for market rents – a rhetoric, which tenants today are exposed to either through the radio, the newspapers, or public meetings where experts are invited to discuss the topic of housing and rent – the individual tenant may (involuntarily) start to introject their words and view herself as a stumbling block, not only to the market, but to the welfare of society as a whole. She may start to doubt if she really has the right to live where she lives. And given what dwelling means, doubting one's right to dwell is closely related to doubting one's right to exist.[15]

Westin's point is a strong one, even if we prefer to read this process through an epistemological lens of the performative utterance—the statement that does what it says, and words that constitute subjects as bearing particular traits—as laid out by Judith Butler rather than the phenomenological, Heideggerian framework relied on by Westin.[16] "This distinction means that we are less interested in respecting a pre-existing and potentially essentialized relationship to "dwelling" and rather see an urgent need to reimagine housing arrangements that see subjects participate in the performance of an ongoing, affirmative construction of themselves as being "at home." That said, the notion of "gentrifying with words" that is introduced and developed by Westin is helpful in identifying and understanding the effects of two very specific types of "soft changes" that emerge in our case study of Hökarängen.

Predatory Subletting

It is mid-morning when we log in to Blocket, Sweden's largest marketplace website.[17] While there are many places that one might look through to find a sublet in this city, Blocket is one of the more well-known interfaces, which has struggled to professionalize its interface, now baking in digital ID and insurance plans in order to "protect" the parties that seek to buy and sell through its diffuse platform. There are seven apartments available to sublet in Hökarängen, one of which is missing an accurate address. Of the remaining six, five are rental flats and one is cooperatively owned. Having realized that this is hardly a statistically secure sample, we are about to log out, but notice an odd ad. A user who we have renamed Jonas is seeking a lodger to sublet a room in his flat. The room is 3 square meters and costs 3,700 SEK per month. Assuming this is a mistake, I expand the comment field to read his ad: "The room is small and furnished. Included in the rent is electricity, a shower, a kitchen with a microwave and cooking equipment, access to the communal laundry, internet." I skip through the description of the area to the details about the room:

> You may rent the room if you are neat and have a secure daily business/job (and are often out during the days). The kitchen can only be used minimally. No smoking. Notice 1 month. Deposit 3,700 SEK, rent 3,700 SEK. I am a 35 year old guy, and I have a pet. I don't want you to be registered to my address, you have to have your own address... The rental period can be up to 8 months or longer if you take care/behave yourself.[18]

Jonas has attached two images. The "room" is a closet that has been furnished with a bunk bed. It does not have a window. It doesn't say how big Jonas' apartment is, but according to the Stockholm Housing Agency, rent for a one-bedroom flat in his building costs 5,448 SEK per month. The lodger will likely pay 68% percent of Johan and his pet's rent. I scroll further. A woman who we will call Barbara is also looking for a lodger. Barbara writes:

> Hello! I am looking for someone to share my spacious three roomed flat with in Hökarängen. The rent is 6,550 SEK per calendar month with a security deposit of 6,550 SEK which is to be paid at the time of contracts being signed... Your own private room is around 16 square metres with a 140 cm bed, writing table, etc. As I commute weekly ... you will often be alone in the flat for 2-3 nights a week. When I am at the flat I expect calm and quiet. I am ... in my fifties and I have a little dog who is not very friendly. He sometimes accompanies me when I come to the flat. While I am at work he is in my room or in the kitchen.[19]

Again, I check a similar flat in her building. Rent for a two-bedroom flat (known as a "three room") is 7,212 SEK per month, according to the website of the company Lägenhetsbyte ("Apartment Swap"). Any future lodger will thus likely be paying 90% of Barbara's rent in addition to coinhabiting with her unfriendly dog. Her building, I find out through some digging, will be renovated in the autumn, which is not mentioned in the ad. The other four ads for sublets on Blocket seem reasonable, but I get stuck on Jonas and Barbara. Rather than asking *why* they are engaging such tactics, the performative frame raises a different question, leading us to ask: *What* are they performing? *What new housing arrangements* are these tactics bringing into being? There is a violence and a precarity in their words: these are words that not so much "gentrify" as subjugate—if they come from a place of need, they amplify that need, they reproduce it. Sara Westin writes:

> when your home is reified, you too become reified, and being told the reason you want to stay put is because you want to continue to enjoy a 'rent subsidy', you may introject a view of yourself as someone instrumentally occupying your apartment for the sake of money. A facsimile of yourself, a greedy one, has entered the scene, which may cause self-alienation.[20]

Jonas and Barbara indeed seem to be acting as "copies," imitating profit-maximization strategies that reframe them as rentiers rather than renters. This is of course illegal, and will lose them their "first-hand" contracts if their landlords—Familjbostäder and Stockholmshem—find out. They risk their own displacement through the displacement of others. Both are "alienated" in Westin's terms: both parties are "displaced while staying put." Thus while Fredrik Cerha and the other residents won the battle against the sale of their homes, the psychological effects of such destabilizations linger well after the performance. The letter of offer lies in a drawer, an unactualized possibility.

Virtue Signaling

In 2013, the same year that Sara Vall moved to Hökarängen, and around the time that, in her account, "things started to change," Maryam Fanni (co-author of the essay "Neon Lights," the preceding chapter in this book) wrote in a debate article in the daily newspaper *Dagens Nyheter*:

> nostalgia and retro function today to duplicitously cushion critics of privatization [from its effects], but the question is how far get by shaming the middle class. We could instead look to the bigger picture and ask for whom or what the hipster acts as a faithful instrument.[21]

The project of *shaming the middle classes*, or at least incriminating them, has a long history in Hökarängen. In early 2012, a small consultancy called Sustainable Innovation i Sverige AB was awarded

9.6 million SEK in funding from the Swedish Department of Energy, a sum matched by 29.1 million SEK in funding provided by the MHC Stockholmshem, to undertake a research project called at the time "A Resource Efficient Hökarängen – Energy efficiency of an urban area through behavioral impact and collaboration."[22] According to the final evaluation report, the project Hållbara Hökarängen ran for 4 years, aiming to improve the status of the area and motivate residents not to move, through renewal of the center, cheap artist's workshops, and a comprehensive environmental investment ("A Resource-Efficient Hökarängen") with a series of activities including cooking courses, film nights, and gardening. Seminars with names like "Urban Gardening," "The Car, the Steak, and the Home," "Everyday Chemicals," "Energy Tips for the Home," "Climate-Smart Cooking," "Build an Insect Hotel or Beehive," and "Make Your Own Cleaning and Skincare Products" and a range of different walks and workshops feature heavily in the program, with a clear focus on consumption, moral standpoints, and behavior, rather than material changes or renovations. It was in the context of Hållbara Hökarängen that in early 2012, just a month before the research application was submitted, the architecture office ÅWL developed *Skyltprogram: Hökarängen C* for Stockholmshem. As SIFAV explain in "Neon Lights," it is this document that becomes the guiding "style sheet" for the look and feel of the central pedestrian street in Hökarängen; it is here that the "'50s vibe" of the area is first valorized through terms like "close and cosy," "a pearl," and "modern retro design," while the goal of "becoming a home for people who would otherwise go to Södermalm" cements the class ambitions of the project, which is reinforced by a "dos and don'ts" list which is highly adverse to "cheap and rubbishy signs," "plastic furniture," and "un-aesthetically pleasing lightboxes."[23]

Economic growth and social development become dependent, Jamie Peck argues, under regimes of "urban austerity" on "symbolically resonant, market-oriented and low-cost initiatives," which "marry aspirational goals (creativity, sustainability, livability, etc.) with projects that work with localized incentives and business-as-usual interests."[24] In channeling funding, co-matched by the State through research funding structures, into resident behavior rather than "hard changes," Stockholmshem to some extent spared their tenants the horrendous experience of renoviction, short-term contracts, and rent hikes that have followed renovation programs by MHCs throughout Stockholm's suburbs. This is not to say that another form of displacement did not take place—one that produced symbolic resonances in order to embed a class-biased, *petit bourgeois* ideal of the 1950s shopkeeper into the built environment of the area. What was displaced in this process was not bodies but working-class identities, as SIFAV warn us, and Sara Vall recounts; what must be asked is how deep market logics run, and how much of the general restlessness seen in Hökarängen's digital footprint—its sublets, its apartment swaps, its real estate sales—builds on aspirational performances and psychic displacements.

Conclusion

It's not the sourdough bakery BAK, where you can buy a hard-boiled egg with a tiny individual tube of Kalle's Kaviar and a salad to have with a strong espresso (Figure 19, page 334), or the presence of the art space Konsthall C, with its clean concrete spaces and public program, that are at issue. It's not even, really, those damn neon signs, per se. What we must be alert to in learning from Hökarängen is the way in which financialization doesn't always look like Blackstone; that it can also operate as a mindset, a "machinic enslavement" in Maurizio Lazzarato's terms, that can creep under our skins, and into our homes, seeping from the outside in and from the inside out.[25] When this spirit meets the increasing desperation of a housing precariat, a potent and potentially rather violent mix is created. Real estate becomes a mentality that destabilizes those who enjoy the securities of a non-commodified housing sector, motivating them to become "greedy copies of themselves."

This mentality is right in front of us, and many of us bear it with us: it is in the 128 active ads for "apartment swaps" that currently light up the map of Hökarängen, promising people the possibility of spatial upgrades at the cost of never-settling, of constant restlessness; it is in the tactical decision by Konsthall C to build an "Attefalls hus," the ancillary building that you can build without planning permission, which materializes the precarity of subletting in a villa-friendly micro-home package. It is the total lack of planning documents that leave Hökarängen's development up to plot-by-plot decisions that fracture the possibility to distribute resources in space and in time. At its worst, this is the kind of restlessness that can start to turn in on itself, taking on the cast of an auto-immune response: to protect the body from being deprived of its right to housing, the subject cannibalizes the rights of others. It is not important whether Jonas eats sourdough bread or has tattoos or "loves Hökarängen"; what matters is his performance in a deeper "gentrification of the mind." A free cup of coffee is far from an anomaly. It means something. It is a sign.

1 Sara Westin, "Un-homing with Words: Economic Discourse and Displacement as Alienation," *cultural geographies* 28, no. 2 (2021): 239–54.

2 This history has been addressed in depth by, amongst others, architectural historian Martin Rörby. See Martin Rörby, "David Helldén: modernistisk visionär på traditionens grund" [roughly translated, "David Helldén: Modernist Visionary With Tradition As Foundation"], PhD diss. (Stockholm University, 2003).

3 Jennifer Mack, "Impossible Nostalgia: Green Affect in the Landscapes of the Swedish Million Programme," *Landscape Research* 45, no. 4 (2021): 558; Urban Ericsson, Irene Molina, and Per-Markku Ristilammi, *Miljonprogram och media: Föreställningar om människor och förorter [The Million Program and Media: Notions About People and the Suburbs]* (Stockholm: Riksantikvarieämbetet and Integrationsverket, 2002).

4 City of Stockholm, "Områdesfakta: Hökarängen Stadsdel" ["Factsheet: Hökarängen City District"], factsheet, accessed February 17, 2023, https://start.stockholm/globalassets/start/om-stockholms-stad/utredningar-statistik-och-fakta/statistik/omradesfakta/soderort/farsta/hokarangen.pdf.

5 Statistics Sweden (SCB), "Antal lägenheter efter region, hustyp, upplåtelseform och år, Stockholms län, 2021" [Number of dwellings after region, typology, tenure, and year, Stockholm County, 2021], extract from database, accessed January 5, 2023, https://www.statistikdatabasen.scb.se/pxweb/sv/ssd/START__BO__BO0104__BO0104D/BO0104T03/table/tableViewLayout1/.

6 City of Stockholm, "Områdesfakta."

7 Statistics Sweden (SCB), "Antal lägenheter efter region, hustyp, ägarkategori och år, Stockholms län, 2021" [Number of dwellings after region, typology, ownership category, and year, Stockholm County, 2021], extract from database, accessed February 17, 2023, https://www.statistikdatabasen.scb.se/pxweb/sv/ssd/START__BO__BO0104__BO0104D/BO0104T04/table/tableViewLayout1/.

8 See City of Stockholm, "Hökarängen," accessed February 18, 2023, https://vaxer.stockholm/omraden/hokarangen/.

9 Statistics Sweden (SCB), "Påbörjade lägenheter i nybyggda hus efter hustyp, kvartal och region, Stockholms län 2010-2022" ["Construction Initiated on New Builds by Typology, Quarter, and Region, Stockholm County, 2010-2022"], accessed February 18, 2023, https://www.statistikdatabasen.scb.se/pxweb/sv/ssd/START__BO__BO0101__BO0101C/LagenhetNyKv16/table/tableViewLayout1/.

10 See Helen Runting, Frida Rosenberg, Erik Stenberg, and Gaudy Orejuela, *Bygger vi en blandad stad?* (Stockholm: KTH Royal Institute of Technology and Secretary, 2022).
11 Åsa Dahlin and Christoffer Carlander, *Vägen hem: Socialt hållbar bostadsförsörjning i Stockholms stad, interim report for the Commission for a Socially Sustainable Stockholm* ("The Way Home: Socially Sustainable Housing Provision in the City of Stockholm")(Stockholm: City of Stockholm, 2018).
12 Ibid., 28.
13 Fredrik Thambert, "Fredrik var med och stoppade 1 000 ombildningar i Hökarängen" ["Fredrik Took Part in Stopping the Tenure Transfer of 1,000 Flats in Hökarängen"], *Dagens Nyheter*, April 20, 2022, https://www.dn.se/sverige/fredrik-var-med-och-stoppade-1-000-ombildningar-i-hokarangen/. Translation by Helen Runting.
14 Sara Westin, "Un-Homing,": 239–54.
15 Ibid., 246.
16 Judith Butler, *Gender Trouble: Feminism and the Subversion of Identity* (New York: Routledge, 2006 [1999]); Judith Butler, *Excitable Speech: A Politics of the Performative* (New York: Routledge, 1997).
17 www.blocket.se.
18 This quote is taken from a Blocket announcement that was placed on the "Sublet" section of the "Housing" page and read on February 1, 2023. The name of the user has been changed and the quote translated to English from Swedish. Translated by Helen Runting.
19 This quote is taken from a Blocket announcement that was placed on the "Sublet" section of the "Housing" page and read on February 1, 2023. The name of the user has been changed.
20 Westin, "Un-Homing": 246.
21 Maryam Fanni, "Hipsterismen. Gentrifiering är ingen ofrånkomlig process" ["Hipsterism. Gentrification Isn't An Unavoidable Process"], *Dagens Nyheter*, August 5, 2013, https://www.dn.se/kultur-noje/kulturdebatt/hipsterismen-gentrifiering-ar-ingen-ofrankomlig-process/.
22 This information is taken from the research funding application, which was obtained from Energimyndigheten (Ministry for Energy) under public information laws. The application is stamped March 14, 2012 and the project was to start April 1, 2012.
23 ÅWL and Stockholmshem, *Skyltprogram: Hökarängen C* ["Signage Program: Hökarängen Center"], January 1, 2012.
24 Jamie Peck, "Austerity Urbanism," *City* 16, no. 6 (2012): 626–55. See also Ståle Holgersen, "Searching for "Solutions" to Crisis: A Critique of Urban Austerity and Keynesianism," *Human Geography* 11, no. 2 (2018): 47.
25 Maurizio Lazzarato, *Signs and Machines: Capitalism and the Production of Subjectivity* (Los Angeles, Semiotext(e): 2014).

MAPPINGS

Integrating Amsterdam Noord

Edited by Tahl Kaminer

[1]

The photographs in this chapter, with the exception of Figure 11, were taken in summer 2022. They document a later phase of the regeneration of Noord, once key projects of the earlier phases had been completed, and demonstrate the scale of the upheaval. Photographs and maps by Tahl Kaminer (except when stated otherwise).

[1] Overhoeks, Amsterdam Noord. From the right, the Tolhuistuin, the A'dam Tower (formally the Shell Overhoeks Tower), and the Eye Filmmuseum in the foreground. In the background, new towers.

[2]

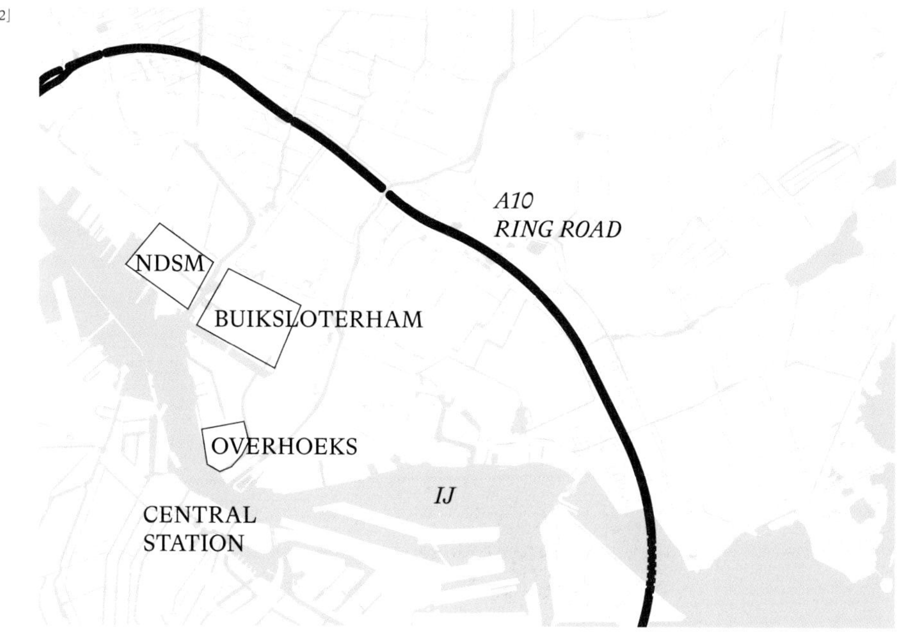

[3]

[2] The location of the NDSM, Buiksloterham, and Overhoeks in Amsterdam Noord.
[3] New housing in Overhoeks.

[4]

[5]

[6]

[4] Long-standing second hand and antique dealer on edge of NDSM and Buiksloterham.
[5,6] "Squatters' chic" at Café de Ceuvel.

[7]

[8]

[7] Schoonschip "floating neighborhood" in Buiksloterham.
[8] New housing at the NDSM.

[9]

[10]

[9,10] “Self-build” CPO housing in Buiksloterham.

[11]

[12]

[11] Swings at the top of the A'dam Tower. Photograph by Martijn Kort, courtesy of A'dam Lookout.
[12] New housing, a school, and an office tower in Overhoeks.

[13]

[13] CPO housing in Buiksloterham.

Cultural Assets in Schöneweide

Edited by Maroš Krivý and Leonard Ma

[1]

This chapter was developed from the work of the 2018 and 2019 studios in the urban studies program at the Estonian Academy of Arts tutored by Maroš Krivý and Leonard Ma, and included Hoi Yee Cheung, Larissa Franz, Jennifer Jackson, Anna Lihodedova, Oskar Brohager Öhrling, Artun Gürkan, Jannat Sohail, Kseniia Taigacheva, and Sean Tyler. Photographs and maps by Larissa Franz, Maroš Krivý and Leonard Ma.

[1] Entrance to RSO along *Bundesstraße 96* (Federal Highway 96).

[2]

Date of Construction

Before 1990

1951–1960

2011–2015

S-Bahn ring

Schöneweide

[3]

[4]

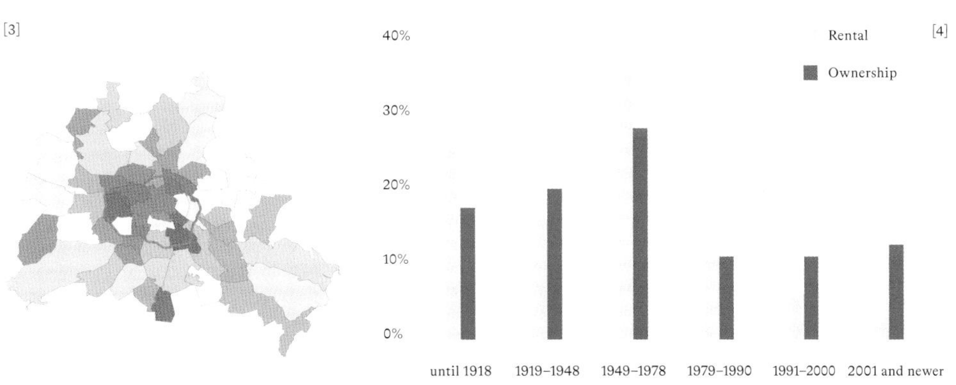

[2] Map of Berlin by building age.
[3] Concentration of rental unit conversions into condominiums 2015–2020.
[4] Proportion of rental and ownership by age of construction.

[5]

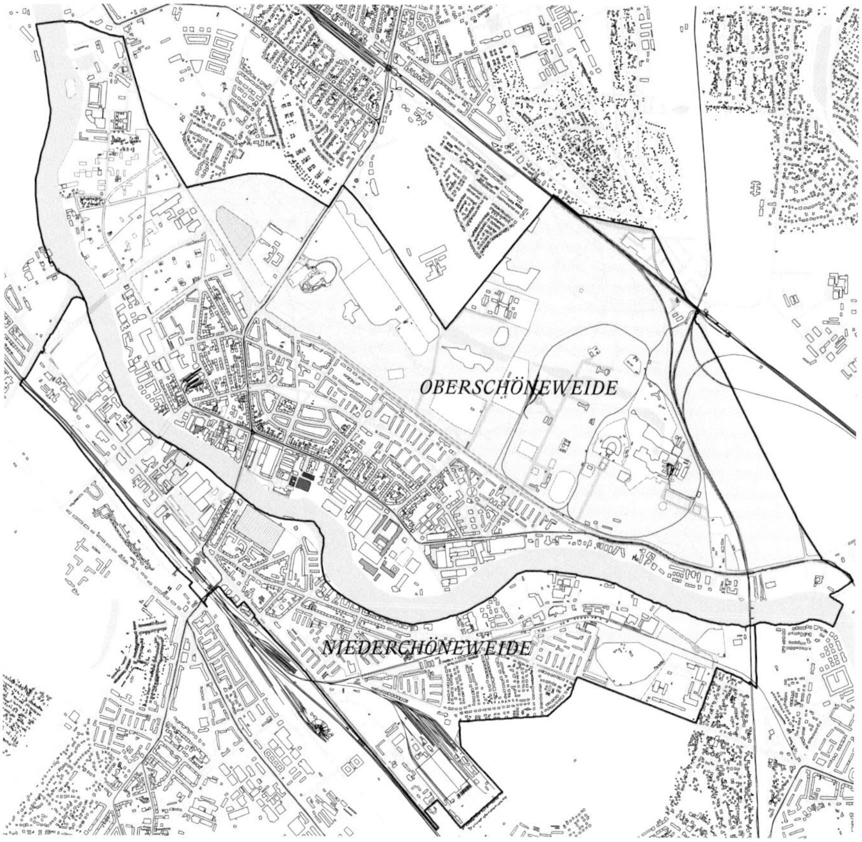

OBERSCHÖNEWEIDE

NIEDERCHÖNEWEIDE

[6]

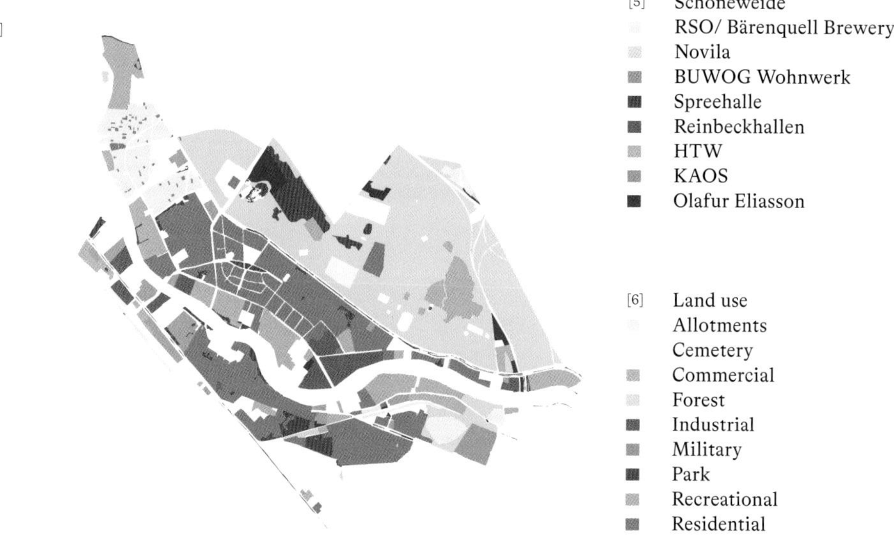

[5] Schöneweide
- RSO/ Bärenquell Brewery
- Novila
- BUWOG Wohnwerk
- Spreehalle
- Reinbeckhallen
- HTW
- KAOS
- Olafur Eliasson

[6] Land use
- Allotments
- Cemetery
- Commercial
- Forest
- Industrial
- Military
- Park
- Recreational
- Residential

[5] Detail of Oberschöneweide and Niederschöneweide.
[6] Actual land use Berlin-Schöneweide.

[7]

[7] Residential construction by age
- Until 1918
- 1918–1933
- 1945–1989
- 1991–Present

[8]

[8] Schöneweide development areas

- Redevelopment Area 1995–2001
Financial subsidies for modernization (rent-regulated)

- Development Area 1999–2009
Financial subsidies for modernization (unregulated)

- Milieu Protection Area 2017–2020
Restrictions on luxury modernization and conversion to owner-occupied apartments

[9]

[10]

[9] ICH LIEBE DICH—South Bank of the Spree adjacent to the new BUWOG development.
[10] I LOVE YOU TOO—North Bank of the Spree with Spreehalle and Alicia Kwadje's studio in grey concrete.

[11]

[12]

[11] Approaching RSO and the Bärenquell Brewery development from the S-Bahn.
[12] Bryan Adams' Spreehalle development on the left, with Reinbeckhallen to the right.

[13]

[14]

[13] View of HTW featuring public artwork symbolizing the former power cable industry weaving through the campus.

[14] The waterfront BUWOG site in Niederschöneweide being prepared for construction.

[15]

[16]

[15] The plaza between Industriesalon and Olafur Eliasson's warehouse.
[16] EMBRACE OUR CULTURE—Entrance to RSO in the refurbished Bärenquell Brewery.

The Normalization of Thamesmead: Part B

Edited by Tahl Kaminer

[1]

This chapter was developed from the work of the ESALA Thamesmead Group 2018–19, which was led by Tahl Kaminer and Alex MacLaren, and included Anna Bateson, Zhiwen Chen, Camille Davison, Lukas Drotar, Jane Gill, Katie-Rose Hay, Laura Haylock, Manbir Kaur, Juliya Lebedinec, Alice Lodge, Catriona Lygate, Ruaridh Maxwell, Lucy Mein, Euan Miller, Ariana Monioudis, Nicola Murphy, Calum Rennie, Yannick Scott, Rahcel Smillie, Benjamin Smith, Yixuan Song, Damien Theron, Linda Veilka, Jamie Wilson, Amy Wooton, Catriona Wright, Jeremy Yen, Yunzhou Fan, and Cho Woon Lau.

[1] An elevated walkway in Thamesmead. Photograph by Anna Bateson, 2018.

[2]

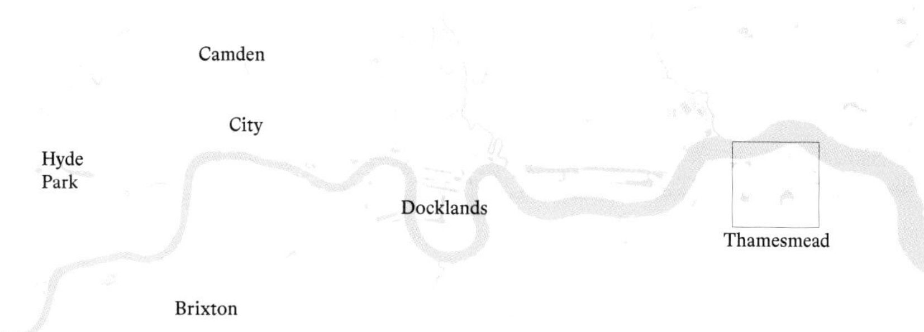

[3]

[2] The location of Thamesmead in London.

[3] A map of Thamesmead. In red, the brutalist development. A. Southmere Lake; B. The later phase of the brutalist development; C. Culture center; D. The elevated sewage pipe runs parallel to the motorway and dissects the area; E. The Traveller settlement; F. Belmarsh Prison; G. The waste treatment plant. Maps by Tahl Kaminer, based on Open Street Map.

[4]

[4] Thamesmead in its early days circa 1970. Photograph courtesy of the JR James Archive and the Department of Urban Studies and Planning, the University of Sheffield. See https://www.flickr.com/photos/jrjamesarchive/

[5]

[6]

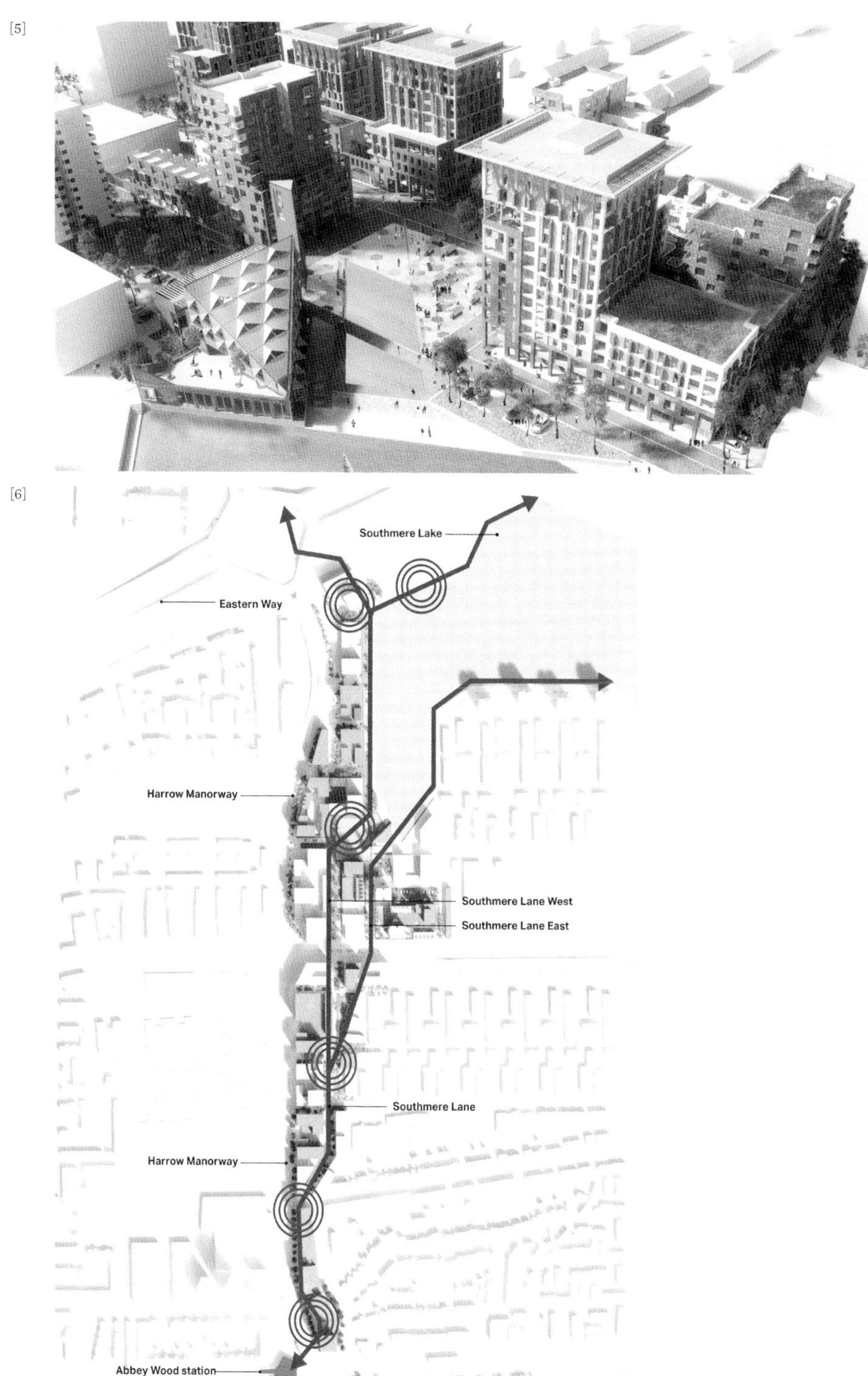

[5, 6] The Southmere master plan commissioned by Peabody. It was developed by Proctor and Matthews Architects alongside Mecanoo Architecten and landscape architects Turkington Martin. Images courtesy of Proctor and Matthews.

[7]

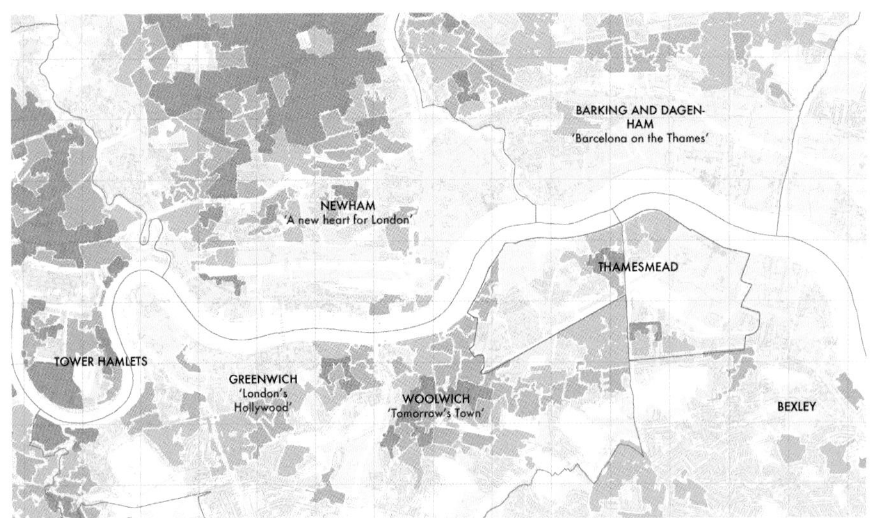

Yellow/green: 1–47
Orange: 48–71
Light brown: 72–102
Magenta: 100–46
Dark brown: 147–303

[8]

[7] Population density, persons per hectare, in East London. Map by Catriona Lygate, Ruairidh Maxwell, and Jeremy Yen, 2018.

[8] A brutalist linear housing complex to the west of the lake, now demolished. Photograph by Anna Bateson, 2018.

[9]

Green: owner-occupied
Orange: social and affordable tenures
Magenta: private rental

[10]

[9] Housing tenure in East London. Map by Catriona Lygate, Ruairidh Maxwell, and Jeremy Yen, 2018.
[10] Thamesmead includes not only the brutalist core but also more familiar suburban forms. Photograph by Anna Bateson, 2018.

[11]

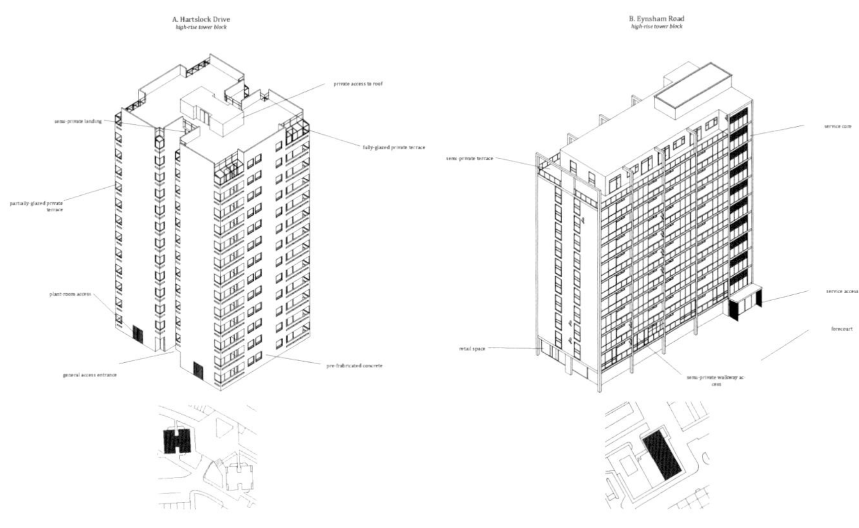

[12]

[13]

[14]

[15]

[11] High-rise typologies in Thamesmead. Drawings by Yannick Scott.
[12] The motorway roundabout and below it, on the sewage pipe, the Ridgeway. Photograph by Anna Bateson, 2018.
[13] The Ridgeway. Photograph by Anna Bateson, 2018.
[14] Maisonettes. Photograph by Anna Bateson, 2018.
[15] Personalized maisonettes. Photograph by Benjamin Smith, 2018.

[16]

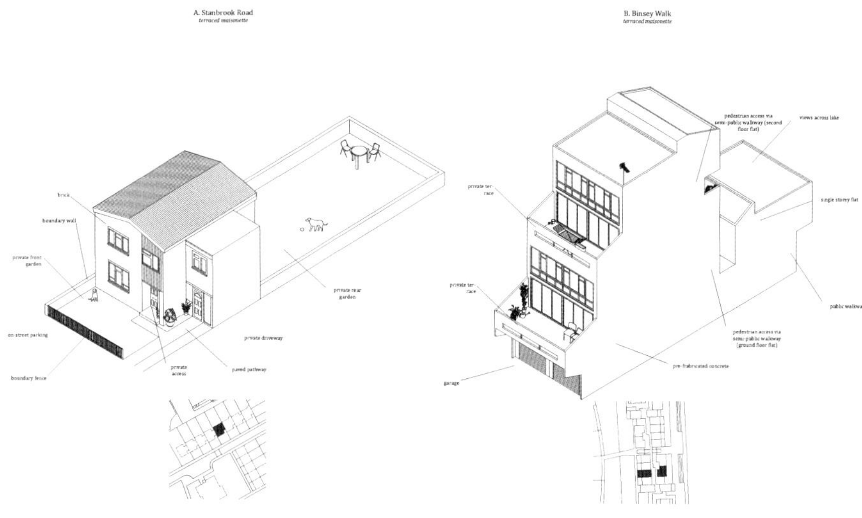

[17]

[16] A “suburban” detached house and a flat in a linear housing complex in Thamesmead. Drawings by Yannick Scott.

[17] An image that confirms stereotypes of such areas, yet the two ominous figures were merely kids fooling around. Photograph by Anna Bateson, 2018.

South of the South in Venice of the North: Mapping Change in Hökarängen

Edited by Helen Runting

[1]

In 2022, the Stockholm-based architecture office Secretary (led by architects Karin Matz and Rutger Sjögrim, and theorist Helen Runting), together with architect Gaudy Orejuela, began a case study of the neighborhood of Hökarängen, using existing data from two earlier studies. The maps and drawings were prepared by Gaudy Orejuela. Photographs by Rutger Sjögrim.

[1] The central pedestrian street in Hökarängen.

[2]

[2] County/region of Stockholm
- City of Stockholm
- Region boundary
- Other city boundaries
- Existing urban footprint
- New multi-unit housing projects approved in 2017
- Regional trains
- Subway lines

[2] All new multi-unit housing projects approved in 2017 in the 26 municipalities of the Stockholm region. The map also shows the existing built-up area and rail lines.

[3]

[3] Stockholm
☐ Case study: Hökarängen
■ Multi-unit housing
■ Single-unit housing
■ Other built form
— City of Stockholm boundary

— Regional trains
Subway lines
-- Blue line
-- Red line
-- Green line

[3] Hökarängen is located in the southern suburbs, on the green subway line, in the City of Stockholm. The majority of its housing takes the form of multi-unit apartment buildings.

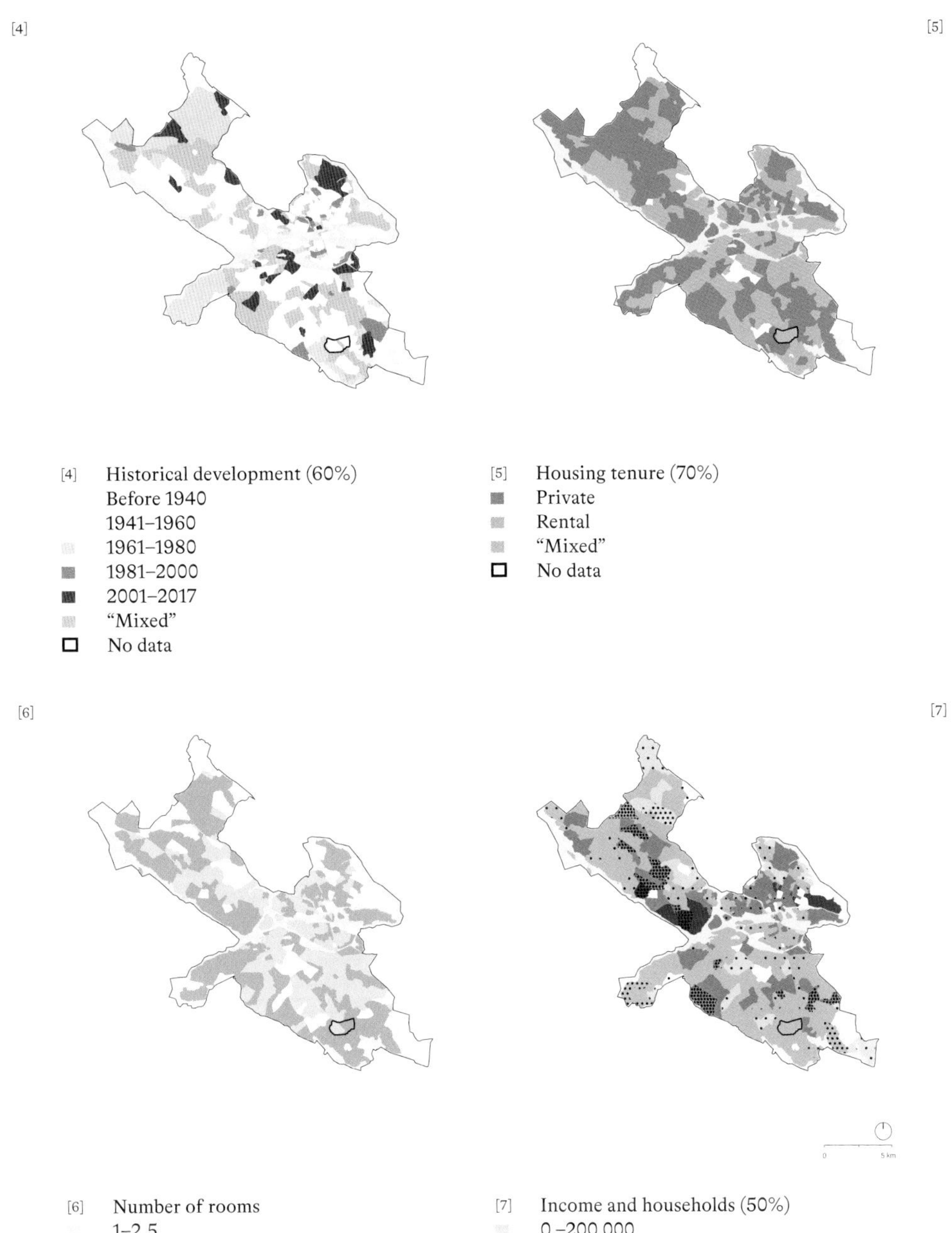

[4–7] Hökarängen was primarily built in the period 1941–1960 and maintains a mix of larger and smaller flats. Average income is in the lower-middle band, and the area is characterized by a high proportion of rental tenure. Data is for 2017 and is aggregated at the "base area" level. Base areas are categorized in relation to a percentage "break value" (i.e., when over 70% of dwellings in a base area are rental, that area is colored orange). Number of rooms was calculated as an average.

[8]

[8] Hökarängen: historical development

1941–1960
1961–1980
1981–2000
2001–2010
2011–2020
2021+

[9]

[9] Hökarängen: housing tenure

Rental (public company)
Rental (private company)
Cooperatively-owned (*bostadsrätt*)
Owner-occupied (*äganderätt*)
Tenure transfer
No data available

1 Stockholmshem
2 Familjebostäder
3 Svenska Bostäder
4 Heba Fastighets AB
5 Bergsundet och Nordfeldt
6 Primula Byggnads AB
7 Gimle Bostad AB
8 Vardaga
9 BRF Skönstaholm

[8] Whilst the majority of buildings were built in the period 1941–60, many infill projects have occurred in the last 15 years.

[9] The area continues to be dominated by rental housing owned by municipal housing companies, but newer developments have introduced private rental and cooperatively owned flats, changing this mix.

[10]

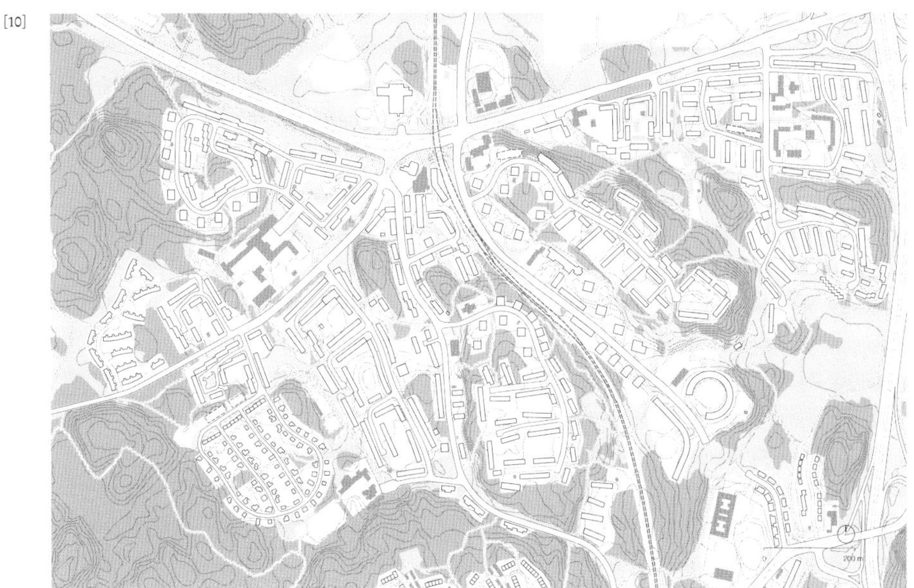

[10] Hökarängen: landscape
Green areas
Forest

[11]

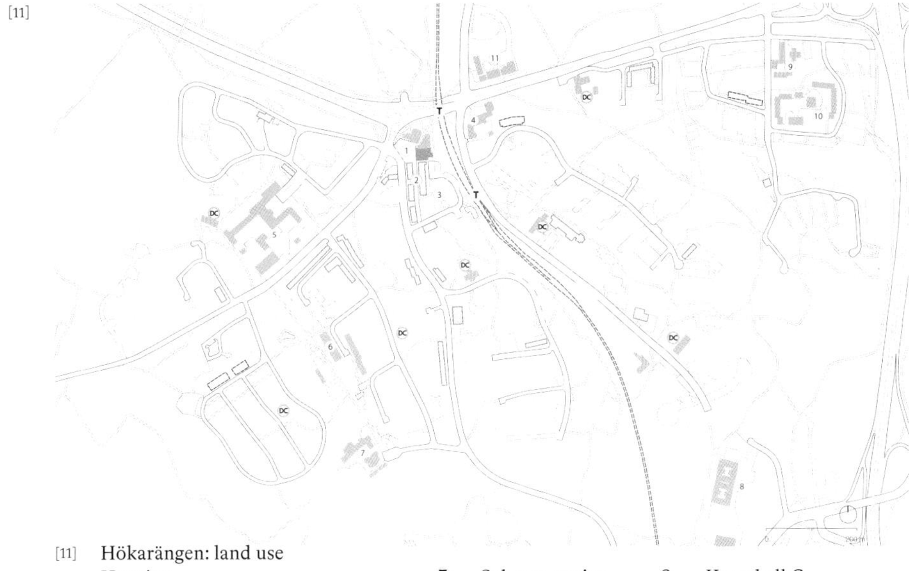

[11] Hökarängen: land use
Housing
Mixed (commercial, active ground floors)
Commercial
Public buildings (schools, fire station)
Offices
Cultural
Institutions

T Subway station
DC Daycare centers
1 David Helldéns square
2 Hökarängen center
3 Nisses park
4 Farsta fire station
5 Hökarängens school
6 Konsthall C
7 Martin school
8 Kvickenstorps school
9 BAK bakery
10 Skönstalholm school
11 Farsta congregation center

[10] The area's neighborhood units form clear "islands" within the suburb, defined by topography and separated by forested tracts. New infill (see [8]) has often been placed on these hilly, forested sites.

[11] The area supports a range of uses with a clear "center" (see [1]), which is structured around Stockholm's first modern pedestrian street.

[12] Hökarängen, 1960 (Lantmäteriet).
[13] Hökarängen, 1975 (Lantmäteriet).
[14] Hökarängen, 1995 (Stockholms stad).
[15] Hökarängen, 2020 (Stockholms stad).
[16] Hökarängen Centrum, 2022.
[17] New private rental for young people on Sirapsvägen.
[18] New cooperatively owned apartment buildings on Tisdagsvägen.
[19] Boiled egg with caviar and side salad at sourdough bakery on Söndagsvägen.

[20] 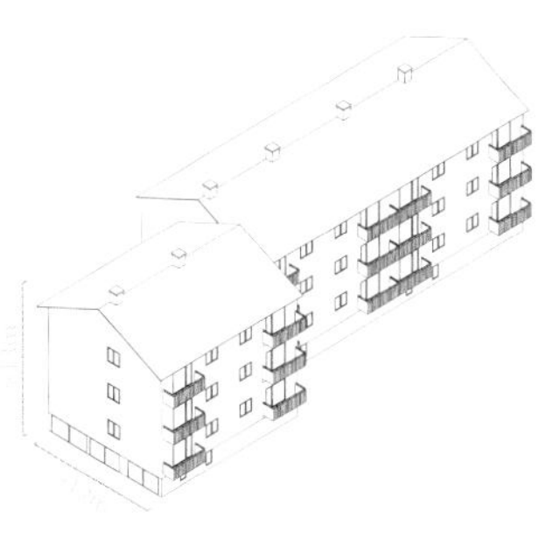

[21] 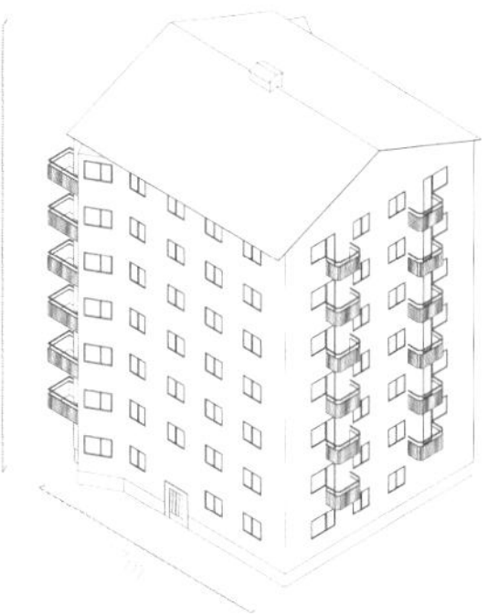

[22] 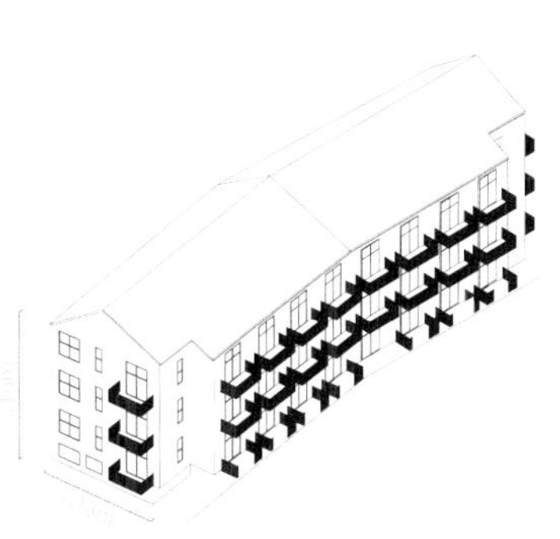

[23] 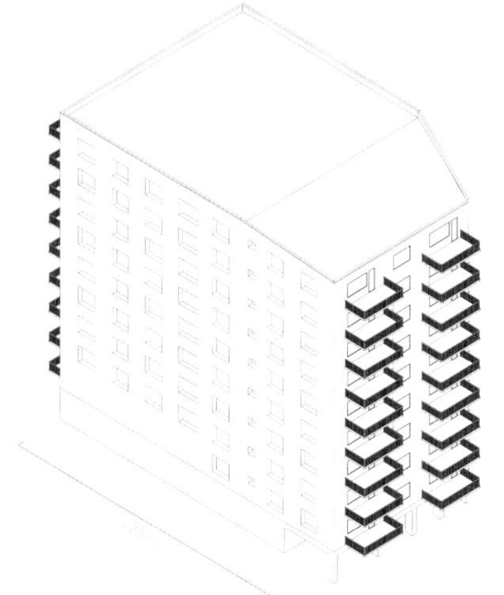

[24] 

[25] 

[20] Original slab block (lammellhus) from 1948, Russinvägen.
[21] Original tower block (punkthus) from 1963, Lingvägen.
[22] New slab block from 2021 on Russinvägen. Architects Andrén Fogelström.
[23] New tower block from 2018 on Russinvägen. Architects Dinell Johansson.
[23] New slab block on Lingvägen.
[23] Old and new tower blocks on Lingvägen.

Other Narratives: Reading Sub/Urban Theory Differently

Ross Exo Adams

Postscript

What might it mean to relinquish the suburb from urban theory altogether? Do we really need to clear more theoretical terrain to describe yet another meta-condition of urban life? Another (sub) site for theorists to claim, describe, universalize, backtrack, or celebrate the profound global diversity thereof, and once again universalize? Don't get me wrong: this is certainly not to dismiss suburbia as a site of inquiry or to say that *the suburb* is somehow an irrelevant or unimportant category of study in the modern world. Quite the opposite. Suburban space—despite its infinitely variegated expressions—names a site that is central to so much of contemporary life on this urbanizing planet. Nor am I intimating that the recent growth in suburban theory is somehow misguided. Its urgency locates real phenomena that are displaying certain burgeoning global tendencies that rightly deserve critical attention, much like the incredible research the authors of this book have brought into the world. Indeed, my gripe is not even with those theorists who have taken the figure of the suburb as a central object of study. What I'm concerned with are the larger forms of inquiry that precede and shape this work, the intellectual contours that have guided a certain body of theoretical inquiry, which has developed over the past century around the conceptual root of suburban space, namely *the urban*. Like every region of scholarship, urban theory institutes certain modes of inquiry and habits of thought that, despite its internal debates, ruptures, or divergences, allow it to maintain a certain consistency in the ways it asks questions and in how others remain well outside its scope of interest.

The Shape of Urban Theory

My contention is that, in all the groundbreaking and important work that has appeared in and around urban theory writ large (urban sociology, urban geography, urban history, etc.) since the early twentieth century, we have nevertheless created a discipline that is paradoxically incapable of grasping the urban *itself* as an object of inquiry. Taken instead as a preexisting, transhistorical site of inquiry, we encounter the urban through its effects, its changes. Ever evolving in the vast diversity of spaces around the world, what urban theorists have long trained their eyes on are the spectacularly unfolding conditions that the urban provides or the processes it hosts. As such, the modes of inquiry that the field has instituted tend to focus attention on discovering, qualifying, and describing various emergent phenomena of urban space.

The epistemological template for the discipline was largely set in place by the Chicago School of Urban Sociology, and this template yielded both a normative output as well as the critical retort to it. Inaugurating what became known as the "Metropolis Era," Burgess's establishment of the "Central Zone Model" set the initial, normative framework for understanding urbanization more generally.[1] From this point, it was a matter for the field to attend to divergences from it. From the metropolis, we are witness to the *megalopolis*, a morphology which issues not from urban centers, but exists in expansive spaces in between them.[2] Like its predecessor, it too points to a global tendency.[3] A generation later, the megalopolis was displaced by the *exopolis*, an urban morphology that turns Burgess's model inside out and marks the beginning of the post-metropolitan era.[4] A predecessor of the planetary suburb,[5] it shows itself to be a global condition. *Planetary Urbanization*, to a certain extent, takes this mode of observation to its logical conclusion: in part responding critically to the Urban Age's populationist and reductive intervention, Brenner and Schmid, along with their collaborators, called for new urban epistemologies to take account of the vast, unfolding spatial assemblies, infrastructures, and sites of extraction that exploded outward from cities and were now spanning the globe.[6]

As a staunch rejection of the Urban Age thesis and the tradition it builds on, Planetary Urbanization bases its scholarship unapologetically in a critical departure that took root in the field some four and a half decades after Burgess's influential model, in Lefebvre's radical Marxist urban sociology.[7] At its core, the application of a Marxian lens to urban theory threw the existing analysis on its head: sociological effects are not simply the outcome of a certain set of spatial conditions; rather, space is first and foremost the product of social relations, principally those of capital, and the two exist in a dialectical relation. The shift that Lefebvre's work introduced allowed urban theory to attend not only to newly observed conditions of urban space and life, but to the processes that structure them in the first place. From David Harvey to Neil Smith to Ananya Roy, to Brenner and Schmid, to Mike Davis, to Rachel Rolniq, to the scholars in this volume, a formidable vector of scholarship continues to insist on the centrality of capitalism to the analysis of urbanization processes worldwide.

Nevertheless, these two disciplinary strands have in a sense become intimately (dialectically!) braided together. Thus, despite the fact that we may now privilege the sociological, political, economic, material, and environmental processes that produce certain conditions in urban space, and although the field has been inflected by every contemporary mode of thought since, there remains a certain commitment to a way of seeing the urban that extends from its origins in Chicago (or Paris, for that matter) to the present. That is to say, urban theory knows its object of study (the urban) as a realm in which a series of novel conditions emerge in an unfolding present. It is a field captivated entirely by the present. Every decade or so, urban theorists invite us to gaze bewilderedly at the strange new spaces and processes that they uncover. We know they're strange because they're different from what we've seen before; they beg descriptions because they do not fit into the names and descriptions that previous generations of urban theory have given us.

To build a discipline around a focus on the present inevitably shapes a specific way of seeing the world, layering its knowledge around lacunae of assumed truths and presuppositions. Taking urban theory as a body of knowledge, we can discern certain unacknowledged aspects of its production. For one, we can see that the urban, as a category, has no particular history. Its longstanding conceptual interchangeability with "the city" has allowed theorists to at once ignore questions of its historical emergence (as well as possible differences between the two terms) while also, more recently, providing a rhetorical prop to open new terrain of study outside of the city. This ahistorical assumption is partially a legacy of Chicago School sociologists, who employed Darwinian-adjacent assumptions in their somewhat positivist understandings of urban space and its relation to society. Yet, even in Lefebvre's groundbreaking *Urban Revolution* of

1970, which comes closest to historicizing the urban as a distinct kind of space, he too falls into traps of ahistoricism and conceptual imprecision.[8]

Second, if we take the urban to be a product of human ingenuity and civilization, it stands to reason that its history is rooted in, and is as old as, humanity itself. It follows, then, that the urban is a historically passive kind of space. Like nature, its diverse changes and expressions are thus understood as being shaped by collective human activities, which in turn are undertaken in order to reflect human values, needs, or modes of organization at any given time and place. Oddly, this seems to hold even for those using materialist or post-structuralist approaches: while histories of urban space may serve as ledgers of the effects of capitalism, sociopolitical regimes, or shifting economic policies, the urban in itself is historically inert, mutating across history as a result of larger, extra-urban logics and processes that shape space to their needs. This basic assumption ingrains itself in the production of knowledge: if the urban is a reliable "screen," when read properly it can project back to its theorists the ways in which sociospatial relations may cohere in larger tendencies that can in turn be made into theory. All of this doubles back to reinforce its initial assumption: if the urban is a carrier of other forces, social transformations, readings, tendencies—if it is a translation of concerted human agency—it has no historical agency in itself. Thus, to ask "What is the urban?" appears at once ridiculous and perplexing. The urban continues to surprise us.

(Post-)Sub/Urban(ism)ization Theory

Yet one cannot help but entertain questions like this when reading much of the new literature on suburban theory. If urban theorists seem unbothered by the constant slippages between terms,[9] suburban theorists seem almost to revel in it. Distinctions between various kinds of suburban spaces are often blurry ("we know one when you see one," as Phelps assures), they nevertheless seem to deserve their own special names.[10] Exurbs, ethnoburbs, peri-urban spaces, edge-cities, globurbs, technoburbs, and boomburbs all echo a similar parade of terms that seemed useful to Taylor and Lang in their account of urban change.[11] Contradiction is never far from the world of suburban theory, either. If notions like "suburban cityscapes" feel rather vague, navigating claims that "post-suburban spaces" are "suburban spaces carried to the extreme," or that "processes of suburbanization contribute to the overall push towards an urbanized world" tells me that you may need to use your gut at times.[12]

After all, suburban theory occupies a somewhat contradictory position. It is at once a theory dependent on a category almost entirely taken for granted, universalized, and made ahistorical, while at the same time claiming to be the actual core of this same category. Just as Brenner and Schmid impel us to look outside of cities for urbanization processes, Roger Keil urges us to see the suburb as the site from which to rethink the entire discipline of urban theory. And like so many others, it is by dint of the sheer and sudden ubiquity of the suburb that we must do so. When we unsettle our city-centric inclinations, we suddenly discover that "At the margins of the metropolis, more than in the increasingly uniform and normed inner cities, new urban forms and ways of life emerge."[13] He goes further: we must "abolish the centralist bias in urban theory and introduce a new way of looking at what we call 'suburban' in the context of urbanization processes overall."[14]

Fair enough. But if the conceit of contemporary suburban theory is to "displace the center" of urban theory (both the old guard and "the city"), the proliferation of conditions it discovers, and the subsequent terms it uses to name them, seem only to reproduce the same basic epistemological maneuvers of urban theory in other sites. Not only does this further entrench the ahistorical, supposedly neutral, nature of the category at its heart, it also further distances the urban (whether sub- or not) from any conceptual clarity or consistency. After all, what is the infinitely diverse global suburb if its definitional qualities seem ultimately to rest on its difference from the cursed city center?

The Urban is a Social Technology

What if we approach the urban from a different angle? Can it be possible that the collective body of urban theory tells another narrative? If the urban languishes in ahistorical and conceptual vagueness, it seems to me that approaching it historically can lend it conceptual clarity. Indeed, as much as we focus on the new, our tethering of novelty to discoveries in the present may indeed preclude us from grasping a larger, more significant emergence—a historical rupture that has gone unacknowledged. And if we challenge the historically passive sense that the urban has assumed in our literature and research, it would no longer stand that such a rupture could be explained away by something like the rise of capitalism or industrialization alone. By focusing less on indicators like changes in population or policy, growth of infrastructural networks, new spatial morphologies or density, do our theories not collectively speak to a certain overarching logic that cohered not so long ago? One that could order space, bodies, property, infrastructure, nature, and territory in a completely new way?

For me, the writings of the nineteenth-century Spanish engineer Ildefonso Cerdá offer an incredible, if not accidental, insight into such a reading.[15] Cerdá is widely known for his plan of the *Eixample* of Barcelona—the iconic grid of chamfered square blocks that extend from its medieval core. Yet, the majority of his work remains in written form, as exhaustive, speculative theories of what he called *urbanización*—a neologism he coined in the early 1860s. Cerdá's writings sought to persuade his peers that he had discovered not a new type of city but a new system for the co-organization of life and infrastructure that would do away with the city altogether. In its place, an edgeless, centerless grid of fluid circulation and low-density domesticity was meant to extend across the surface of the earth, accommodating a systematized distribution of population and services. The *urbe*, as he named this space, was indeed not a city at all but a spatial template that would mediate new relations between society and technology, nature and capital, justice and subjectivity, territory and private property, movement and security, life and labor. Not only would the *urbe* displace the city: it was the medium that would, by its very spatiotechnical disposition alone, render the state and its oppressive politics redundant. In turn, a governance would emerge in its place, as a sociotechnical feature of the *urbe*, that would regulate its fluid, machinic spaces. While Cerdá's purported discovery of *urbanización* is easily dismissible, the abundant pages and volumes in which he described this space-process deserve a closer, more interpretive attention (Cerdá described the *urbe* as both a space and a process of its perpetual expansion: *urbanización*). What I believe his writings capture is less the proposition he took them to be than a careful documentation and description, undertaken with diagrammatic clarity, of an ambient, emergent spatial order that he observed unfolding across the cities and spaces of Europe and the Americas.

My work has long argued that the urban (or urbanization, which, for reasons above, I use interchangeably) has a distinct history that situates it not in a lineage of Mesopotamian settlements, or any ancient city. It has no relationship to the "civilization" that is typically narrated around the earliest human settlements, nor is it some artifact of human ingenuity. Rather, I trace its roots across a different archaeology, one that moves from the spaces, experiences, and relations to land instituted in European colonial settlements, to the technologies of territory developed across early modern European states, to even maritime understandings of space that emerged in this same period. Its appearance in the world, as a coherent, recognizable, and reproducible spatial form—a technology—comes only in the nineteenth century. I like to think of the urban as an invented, yet authorless, social technology introduced to the world in the ascendency to global dominance of European powers, buoyed by the becoming-global of capitalism. In this sense, the urban is intimately structured around the logics of capital and the systems it institutes, while remaining nevertheless adjacent to it. It is also a political technology of governance that nevertheless remains parallel to liberalism and the early nation-state in whose territories it first emerges.

As a social technology, we could say that the urban de-scaled (made scaleless) and interwove territorial logics and technologies of control into a matrix of private property and infrastructures of circulation, building its space around an understanding of the human as the self-possessed individual that in turn inscribed relations of class, gender, and race into space.[16] As it assumes an expansive, edgeless capacity, it achieves spatially what the colonial settlement and plantation complex only partially managed as a technology of appropriation, extraction, and production. All of which foregrounds the violent and racialized dynamics of gentrification, displacement and capital extraction captured in this volume.

Narrating a Different Urban Theory

While urban theory began from the center of the city and moved outward, its many corrective iterations since have brought its focus to the opposite—the far-flung, often uninhabitable spaces outside any metropolitan center. While Keil and others argue for a middle ground in the "suburb" as the site of contemporary urbanization tendencies, Cerdá's invitation for us to comprehend a different kind of space altogether seems to effortlessly encompass both. Indeed, this template goes further to include (and unsettle) what we call "cities" as well—to, as we might say, "suburbanize urban space." Ironically, the morphology, character, and the systems of ownership and governance that Cerdá's *urbe* prescribed yielded an unmistakably "suburban" space. And if, in the wake of Lefebvre, what we observe today as an explosion of planetary urbanization or global suburbanisms,[17] we can again find Cerdá's theoretical project to have anticipated all this as captured in utopian glory on the frontispiece of his 1867 *Teoría general de la urbanización*: "Urbanize the rural, ruralize the urban: Fill the Earth."[18]

Although the presentism of urban theory today somehow allows its analyses of conditions and processes to casually fold into teleological statements or suggestions of inevitability, by understanding the urban as a historically produced social technology, its apparent generalization is at once more historically grounded at the same time that its existence in the world can be seen as less inevitable: just as capital engulfed the vast majority of modern society in a new social relation in the span of a few centuries, the urban as a social technology became planetary and hegemonic in roughly the same time. Yet, because we can historically locate the emergence of each, we are suddenly free from extruding our observations of the present into one-way, fated teleologies. Instead, recognizing the urban as a recent figure—despite its ubiquity and seemingly ineffable growth today—immediately invites us to imagine its disappearance, its replacement with other ways of relating space, bodies, infrastructures, energy, and nature with one another. All of which underscores the need today to develop spatiosocial imaginaries that can supplant the necropolitics and planet-destroying path that liberal capitalism and planetary urbanization have us on.

Suburbia as a Cultural Figure?

Approaching the urban as a social technology may also relieve us of having to construct urban theory around the unstable figure we call "suburbia," and instead allow us to understand it as a cultural figure. This book has organized its material and structured its collective analyses to position the conditions it examines as the outcome of a set of processes endemic to each case study, each of which are interconnected with the larger financialized real estate market and its new forms of gentrification. The site of which happens, in these cases, to be suburbs of major European cities. As such, its outcome stops short of inviting yet another theory of the suburb. Instead, it hints to repositioning it as a situated cultural figure of European life.

If we can talk about suburbia as a cultural figure, it is because it is a term that at once tends to conjure very clear, culturally and historically specific imaginaries, while at the same time disappearing into a thousand fragments the moment we attempt to describe it as a stable, generalizable, sociologically and geographically cohesive figure. What is suburbia one day is another kind of space the next. Even equating suburbia with urban peripheries, peri-urban spaces, or other border conditions seems to always invite examples where the coherence that such descriptions of space may seem to have in one site disappears in another.

Taking suburbia as a cultural figure, we may come to understand more about how capitalist urbanization relies just as much on exploiting rent gaps, land value, fixing capital, or governmental mechanisms of de-risking development, as it does on the production and reproduction of cultural signifiers (like "suburbia") and their respective culturally-situated spaces. Indeed, gentrification is nothing without the production of recognizable, class-specific narratives made spatial to produce a certain world that development regimes can use to continue amassing capital in space.

1 Ernest Burgess, "The Growth of the City," in *The City*, eds. Robert E. Park, Ernest W. Burgess, and Roderick D. MacKenzie (Chicago: University of Chicago Press, 1925), 47–62.
2 Jean Gottmann, *Megalopolis: The Urbanized Northeastern Seaboard of the United States* (Norwood, MA: Plimpton Press, 1961).
3 *Since Megalopolis: The Urban Writings of Jean Gottmann*, eds. Jean Gottmann and Robert A. Harper (Baltimore: The Johns Hopkins Press, 1990).
4 See for example chapter 3 of Edward Soja, *My Los Angeles: From Urban Restructuring to Regional Urbanization* (University of California Press, 2014).
5 A reference to Roger Keil's book of the same title. See below.
6 See https://urbanage.lsecities.net/. For a critique of the Urban Age, see Neil Brenner, "The 'Urban Age' in Question," *International Journal of Urban and Regional Research* 38, no. 3 (May 2014): 731–55.
7 See Henri Lefebvre, *The Urban Revolution*, trans. Robert Bonono (Minneapolis: University of Minnesota Press, 2003), and Henri Lefebvre, *The Production of Space*, trans. Donald Nicholson-Smith (Malden, MA: Blackwell, 1991).
8 Ross Exo Adams, "Lefebvre and Urbanization," *Society and Space* (digital magazine), last modified April 24, 2014, https://www.societyandspace.org/articles/lefebvre-and-urbanization.
9 See the introduction ('What Is Urbanization?') in Ross Exo Adams, *Circulation and Urbanization* (London: Sage), 1–6.
10 Nicholas A. Phelps, "In What Sense a Post-Suburban Era?," *The Routledge Companion to the Suburbs*, eds. Bernadette Hanlon and Thomas J. Vicino (London: Routledge, 2018), 40.
11 Robert E Lang and Peter J Taylor, "The Shock of the New: 100 Concepts Describing Recent Urban Change," *Environment and Planning A* 36, no. 6 (2004): 951–58.
12 Roger Keil, *Suburban Planet: Making the World Urban from the Outside In* (London: Polity Press, 2018); Chapter 3 "Suburban Theory," e-book, (Apple Books).
13 Keil, *Suburban Planet*, Chapter 2 "Suburbanization Explained."
14 Keil, *Suburban Planet*, Chapter 3 "Suburban Theory."
15 See Adams, *Circulation and Urbanization*.
16 Ross Exo Adams, "Enclosed Bodies: Locating Cerdá's Urbanización within Federici's History of Capitalism," *Aggregate* 10 (November 2022), DOI: 10.53965/BLVM4342.
17 A reference to the title of an SSHRC Major Collaborative Research Initiative launched by Roger Keil and his collaborators at York University in 2011.
18 Ildefonso Cerdá, *Teoría general de la urbanización, y aplicación de sus principios y doctrinas a la reforma y ensanche de Barcelona* (Madrid: Imprenta Española, 1867), frontispiece.

Contributing Authors

Ross Exo Adams is assistant professor and co-director of architecture at Bard College. He is the author of the book *Circulation and Urbanization* (Sage, 2019). Working at the intersections of architectural and urban histories with political geography and environmental humanities, his research poses questions about how practices of design produce and reproduce relations of power in space.

Penny Bernstock is a senior research fellow (visiting) at UCL. She has been undertaking research on housing and urban regeneration in East London for more than thirty years. She previously directed the Centre of East London Studies at UEL and is co-chair of TELCO's (Branch of Citizens UK) Olympic Strategy Group.

Juliet Davis is professor of architecture and urbanism and head of school at the Welsh School of Architecture, Cardiff University. Her teaching and research span the fields of architecture, urban design, and city planning history/theory, reflecting interests in regeneration, the making of post-industrial cities, and the politics and ethics of design practice.

Tahl Kaminer is reader in architectural history and theory at Cardiff University. He is the author of *The Efficacy of Architecture* (Routledge, 2017) and *Architecture, Crisis and Resuscitation* (Routledge, 2011), and co-editor of the anthologies *Urban Asymmetries* (010, 2011), *Critical Tools* (LLV, 2011) and *Houses in Transformation* (NAi, 2008).

Anne Kockelkorn is assistant professor of history and theory of the city and the architecture of urban housing at the University of Gent. Her forthcoming monograph *The Social Condenser II* investigates the transformation of housing production in France before and after the neoliberal reforms of 1977. Together with Susanne Schindler and Rebekka Hirschberg, she is currently preparing the book *Cooperative Conditions: A Primer on Architecture, Finance and Regulation in Zurich* (Zurich: gta Verlag).

Maroš Krivý is an urbanist and historian. He is Marie Skłodowska-Curie fellow at the Canadian Centre for Architecture and associate professor of urban studies at the Estonian Academy of Arts.

Leonard Ma is a Canadian architect based in Helsinki. He is a member of New Academy, and teaches urban studies and architecture at the Estonian Academy of Art. His research focuses on neoliberalism, financialization, and the legacy of the welfare state, and has been published in *e-flux*, *The Avery Review*, *Drawing Matter* and *AA Files*. Leonard is a practicing architect and founding member of PUBLIC OFFICE.

Jennifer Mack is associate professor and docent at KTH School of Architecture and a Pro Futura Scientia Fellow of the Swedish Collegium for Advanced Study. Mack's monograph, *The Construction of Equality: Syriac Immigration and the Swedish City* (University of Minnesota Press, 2017), received the Margaret Mead Award from SfAA/AAA in 2018. She has co-edited the anthologies *Rethinking the Social in Architecture* (Actar, 2019) and *Life Among Urban Planners* (University of Pennsylvania Press, 2020) and is a member of the editorial board of *Thresholds*.

Timothy Moore is a founder of Sibling Architecture, senior lecturer at Monash University, and the curator of contemporary design and architecture at the National Gallery of Victoria in Melbourne, Australia. From 2010–11, he worked as managing editor of *Volume* magazine based in Tolhuistuin, Amsterdam.

Helen Runting is a planner and architectural theorist. She holds a PhD in critical studies in architecture (KTH) and regularly publishes essays on the politics of design. Helen is a co-author of the prize-winning *14,495 Flats: A Metabolist's Guide to New Stockholm* (2021) and a co-editor of the anthology *Architecture and Feminisms: Ecologies, Economies, Technologies* (2018).

Secretary is a Stockholm-based architecture office founded by architects Karin Matz and Rutger Sjögrim and planner/theorist Helen Runting. The practice is built on a shared interest in the capacity of architecture to facilitate a dignified life at the scale of the population. Secretary produces buildings, artworks, and publications that give form to the late welfare state in the twenty-first century. Secretary regularly collaborates with architect Gaudy Orejuela, who assisted in compiling the Mappings section of this book.

Söderorts Institut För Andra Visioner (SIFAV) [The Southern Districts' Institute for Other Visions] was an interdisciplinary group based in Stockholm (2012–18), which investigated the city, its commons, and its privatization through collective writing, radio, city walks, ready-mades, reading groups, and other artistic methods. The group consisted of Elof Hellström, Maryam Fanni, Sarah Degerhammar, and Klara Meijer; "Neon Lights" was authored by Maryam Fanni and Elof Hellström.

Paul Watt is professor of urban studies in the Department of Geography, Birkbeck, University of London. He has published widely on social housing, urban regeneration, homelessness, gentrification, and suburbanization. His most recent book is *Estate Regeneration and Its Discontents: Public Housing, Place and Inequality in London* (Policy Press, 2021).

Acknowledgements

We would like to thank Lorens Holms and Penny Lewis for allowing us to test our ideas at the AHRA *Architecture and Collective Life* conference in 2019, and the many contributors to this project at diverse stages, including students, colleagues, and friends.

Travel to Berlin was supported by the Cultural Endowment of Estonia. Helen Runting's work was supported by an architecture stipendium from the Royal Swedish Academy of Fine Arts in Stockholm, through the Ivar och Anders Tengbom Foundation. Tahl Kaminer's Leverhulme Research Fellowship (The Leverhulme Trust) supported the London research. The book itself was kindly supported by the Estonian Academy of Arts and the Welsh School of Architecture.

Project management jovis Verlag: Franziska Schüffler
Copy editing: Helen Runting
Proofreading: Bianca Murphy
Cover image: Lucy Mein
Cover and design concept: jovis Verlag
Printed in the European Union.

Bibliographic information published by the
Deutsche Nationalbibliothek
The Deutsche Nationalbibliothek lists this publication in the
Deutsche Nationalbibliografie; detailed bibliographic data are
available on the Internet at http://dnb.d-nb.de

jovis Verlag GmbH
Lützowstraße 33
10785 Berlin
www.jovis.de

jovis books are available worldwide in select bookstores.
Please contact your nearest bookseller or visit www.jovis.de
for information concerning your local distribution.

ISBN 978-3-86859-762-2 (softcover)
ISBN 978-3-86859-873-5 (e-book)

This book was made possible by the kind support of
The Estonian Academy of Arts (EKA), the Welsh School of
Architecture (Cardiff University), and The Leverhulme Trust.

LEVERHULME
TRUST